An Introduction to Western Sidereal Astrology

Third Edition

Kenneth Bowser

Third Edition

ISBN-13: 978-0-86690-677-7

Published by:
American Federation of Astrologers, Inc.
6535 S. Rural Road
Tempe, AZ 85283

www.astrologers.com

For my pretty Colleen

I wish to thank Ronnie Gale Dreyer and Kenneth Irving for their encouragement and advice that steered me to the American Federation of Astrologers. Ken Irving's offer of a position as a personal service astrologer for American Astrology magazine in 1979 was the critical event that initiated my long metamorphosis from avid enthusiast to professional astrologer.

I wish also to acknowledge the tremendous impact on me of the two individuals whom I consider the greatest of all twentieth century astrologers: Cyril Fagan and Charles Edwin Owen Carter.

Most important, my long-time partner Colleen Mauro, was my constant support throughout the writing of this work.

Contents

Introduction

In January 2011 Parke Kunkle, a Minnesota community college instructor ignited a national firestorm of controversy in the astrological community when he pointed out that the signs of the zodiac no longer correspond to the constellations of the same name. This issue has been vigorously debated by astrologers for the last 65 years.

People new to astrology are often confounded by the two main schools of thought within it: tropical and sidereal. Tropical astrology reckons positions of bodies from the northern hemisphere vernal equinox. The term tropical, from the Greek τροπικοσ (tropikos, a turn or turning), refers to the Tropics of Cancer and Capricorn that describe the limits of the tropics. In this system, the zodiac is defined by the seasons and is disconnected from the stars as a frame of reference. It gained currency late in the first millennium BC in the Greek world and is practiced today primarily in the West.

Sidereal astrology from the Latin sidus (star) reckons positions of bodies from the fixed stars. In this system the zodiac is defined by the stars themselves and is disconnected from the seasons as a frame of reference. Sidereal astrology is the original form of the art. Its antecedents date from mid second millennium BC; it gained currency in the Near and Middle East in the first millennium BC. Sidereal astrology is practiced today primarily in India and among some Westerners, mostly British and American.

There are two schools of sidereal astrology: Eastern, also known as Indian, Vedic or Hindu astrology; and Babylonian, also known as Western sidereal astrology. Babylonian astrology is a familiar quantity in academia because it is very well documented. Western sidereal astrology is built around the re-discovery in the nineteenth century of the sidereal zodiac employed in Assyria and Babylonia (modern Iraq) that spread throughout the Near and Middle East and the Mediterranean world.

Eastern and western methodologies are similar in some respects, but the differences are great enough that the two schools can only be considered cousins, rather than brothers, joined mainly by their use of the sidereal zodiac. Western sidereal methodology is closer to tropical astrology with the sidereal zodiac substituted for the tropical.

The difference between tropical and sidereal reckoning is due to the phenomenon of precession of the equinoxes which is explained in detail in appendix two. The word "precession" derives from the Latin verb praecedere, to precede. Precession, as used here, refers to the gyration of the rotation axis of a spinning object like a child's spinning top. The Earth's spin axis precesses in the same way. Precession of the equinoxes refers to the slow westward motion of the solstitial and equinoctial points along the ecliptic. The term "precession of the equinoxes" was first used by Copernicus (1473-1543).

The Greek genius and best-known astronomer of his day, Hipparchus of Rhodes (flourished 146-127 BC), is credited with the discovery of precession. His work on precession is lost except for the title, "On the Displacement of the Solstitial and Equinoctial Points," details of which are mentioned in Claudius Ptolemy's Almagest, the most important astrological and astronomical work of Late Antiquity. Hipparchus' only work that has survived intact is the "Commentary on the Phaenomena of Eudoxus and Aratus." Ptolemy (. AD 100-175) is the main source of other works by Hipparchus.

By comparing his own contemporary observations of stars with older positions of the same stars, Hipparchus noted a difference in their distances from the equinoxes. Specifically he noted that Spica, the brightest star in Virgo, was observed eight degrees east of the autumnal equinox 150 years before his time, but only six degrees east of the autumnal equinox in his own time (which is a westward motion of the equinoxes).

The case has been made by G. J. Toomer[1] that Hipparchus concluded, at least at one point in his reasoning, that the equinox had moved (which is actually what had happened), and thus that it cannot be regarded as a fixed point on the ecliptic into perpetuity. However, this position (that the equinox had moved) was the end result of a long process that was intimately bound up in Hipparchus's determination of the difference between the tropical year and the sidereal year. It is therefore not completely clear from the modest remnants of his work that he was confident of which frame of reference—the stars or the equinoctial points—was moving in relation to the other until probably, Professor Toomer thinks, the very end of Hipparchus's career. The false speculation of a regular eight-degree oscillation of the equinoctial points called trepidation, sometimes attributed to Hipparchus, is actually from the fourth century A.D. Another modern authority with impressive astronomical and academic credentials also maintained that Hipparchus did adopt the hypothesis that the equinox had to be moving. The rationale behind that assertion, explained by Professor W.

M. Smart, is that it is unreasonable to assume that every star Hipparchus compared from one era to the next had exactly the same proper motion, which is a requirement if the star field were moving against a fixed equinox.[2]

There is no solid evidence that Hipparchus invoked the tropical zodiac, but it is attributed to him primarily because of what Ptolemy wrote (three hundred years later) about the matter in the Almagest. Regardless of Hipparchus's positions which were various at different times in his career, the conclusion that eventually won out—one of several solutions proposed to explain precession—was that the entire sky was moving as a unit against the Earth fixed in space. This was arrived at in part because Hipparchus (and later Ptolemy) couldn't detect any motion between stars, rather only between the stars and the equinoxes. Hipparchus' probable final conclusion that the equinox had moved was not, however, the position that was adopted in the ancient world. Rather, the hypothesis adopted by Ptolemy that the stars had moved was based on the fundamental assumption of his day that the Earth was motionless in space and the center of the universe. That is the basic tenet of geocentrism: the idea that all bodies orbit a fixed Earth. If one sees motion between oneself and another object and one cannot detect oneself in motion, the conclusion is ineluctable: the other thing must be moving. That is the ultimate result of the geocentric concept of solar system geometry embraced by the Greeks. There was no experiment devised in Hipparchus's or Ptolemy's time that could demonstrate the motion of the Earth. Their geocentric assumptions were reasonable for their time.

If one views precession from the perspective of a motionless Earth, absolutely fixed in space forever, the celestial longitude of the stars increases by slightly more than 50 seconds of arc per year, a degree of arc in almost 72 years and an entire thirty-degree sign in approximately 2150 years. (Hipparchus had it nearly right; he proposed an increase of almost 46 seconds of arc per year, Ptolemy proposed 36 seconds of arc per year.) Seen from the deeper and true perspective of the Earth in motion in several modes revolving around the Sun, the Earth's celestial pole precesses and the equinoxes retrograde past the fixed stars with a period of 25,800 years. This true perspective also accounts for the astrological "ages" (the Age of Aries, Age of Pisces, Age of Aquarius etc.) that are entirely sidereal phenomena and have nothing to do with tropical zodiac reckoning.

The displacement between tropical reckoning that appears to be fixed in space but is actually moving, and sidereal reckoning that appears to be moving in space but is actually fixed, is presently almost 25 degrees. Since the Northern Hemisphere spring equinox moves to the West with respect to the stars, the sidereal signs are 25 degrees to the east of where they were described at the beginning of the Age of Pisces in AD 221. That apparent movement, however, is an illusion, not something real, as the stars have not moved in eighteen centuries except for a tiny handful of seconds of arc. Within the framework of tropical reckoning the sky moves with respect to fixed civil dates; within the framework of sidereal reckoning, civil dates move with respect to the fixed stars. Since the Gregorian Reform of the Julian calendar in 1582, the northern hemisphere vernal equinox usually occurs on March 21 that marks the entry of the Sun into the tropical sign Aries. That date however has nothing to do with the stars in Aries during the present era. If one could look at the stars behind the Sun on March 21, 2011 one would see the stars in the western fish of Pisces with the Great square of Pegasus above the zodiac and Cetus the whale below the zodiac. The constellation Aries is far to the east of the northern hemisphere vernal equinox. Twenty-five degrees is a massive expanse of sky. People who actually look at the sky are astonished at the discrepancy between tropical and sidereal reckoning. In 2011, in terms of the 12-fold equal division zodiac employed by the Babylonians, the Sun reaches Aries in most years on April 15. That means that at any location in either hemisphere where the Sun is visible on that date, if one could block out the Sun and look at the stars behind it one would see the stars in Aries with Triangulum and a corner of Perseus above the zodiac and Hydra and Eridanus below the zodiac.

It wasn't always like this. Tropical and sidereal reckoning were exactly coincident—completely identical—at the end of the Age of Aries in AD 221. They were so close to being identical for so long that throughout the second and third centuries of the Christian Era nobody could tell the difference between tropical and sidereal reckoning without instruments and or a marking star.

Claudius Ptolemy wrote about what anybody would have seen in his day if they had gone outside at night with horoscope in hand and looked from the horoscope to the sky. The symbolic rendering of the zodiac on the horoscope would roughly duplicate the evidence of one's eyes. Yet Roman astrologers in Late Antiquity, and certainly during Ptolemy's day, were clearly using a combination of outdated sidereal and inaccurate tropical standards that were merely approximate even by the standard of the day, much less modern standards. The great majority of the positions of the horoscopes from the Roman world of Late Antiquity are sidereal from an earlier period and the tropical ones reckoned from an Hipparchan equinox (0 Aries = vernal equinox) are adjusted for precession (using Ptolemy's grossly inaccurate value for precession) which betrays a lack of understanding of tropical reckoning. A large proportion of Roman horoscopes from Late Antiquity also include the distance of a planet from a star that shows further sidereal influence and lack of confidence in an equinox unmarked by a star. Tropical reckoning was much better established as a medieval standard than an ancient one. Ptolemy's account of the sky circa AD 140 when the Almagest was being written is not what one sees today. The Sun rose with the first degree of Aries in Ptolemy's lifetime as an astronomical fact. Now (2011) the Sun rises with five degrees of Pisces in an equally undeniable fashion. The Age of Aquarius will begin in AD 2376 when the Sun rises with 29 Aquarius 59 at the Northern Hemisphere vernal equinox.

The discrepancy of 25 degrees leads directly to a bigger issue—the ultimate issue actually—for an astrologer to consider: tropical reckoning un-couples the zodiac from the stars. If the sky is defined by one set of criteria (the fixed stars) at one period and a different set at a later period (the equinoctial points), then identical calendar dates will not describe the same parts of the sky though both sets of criteria have the same name. The issue is whether trait characteristics derive from the tropical signs or the sidereal signs. A related matter, the question of how and why the tropical zodiac displaced the sidereal zodiac in the West is also explained in appendix two.

That these issues are debated at all among Western astrologers is due primarily to the work of Cyril Fagan (1896-1970) whose life from 1916 until his death was devoted to astrology. He realized in 1944 after many years of study that the zodiac employed in the ancient world, before Greek influence was felt, was sidereal. Fagan was originally a tropical astrologer who encountered intense resistance from British and American astrologers when he substituted sidereal zodiac parameters used in Babylon for a tropical zodiac format. All subsequent siderealists in the United States and Europe cut their teeth on Fagan's books, magazine columns and his open-ended debates with the leading tropical figures of the 1940s, 1950s and 1960s. A more detailed explanation of Fagan and his work are in appendix one.

I am one of those deeply influenced by Fagan's work. I became a student of astrology in 1970 as a tropicalist. I met Jim Lewis (1941-1995) in 1972; he was just then getting his business, Astro*carto*graphy, off the ground. His very interesting lectures to a dozen rookies seated on the floor of his spartan apartment were a tremendous stimulus to young enthusiasts hungry for information. He was a lifelong tropicalist but he many times spoke of his respect for the siderealists for their technical skill. In consequence of Lewis' fair-minded attitude and ever curious myself, I attended a lecture given by a San Francisco siderealist, John Mazurek (1919-2003) also beginning in 1972. I attended Mazurek's lectures for three years and by the end of that time had defected from the tropical ranks.

Sidereal astrology attracted me for four basic reasons: first, I had problems reconciling what I had learned about the signs with what I observed in people like President Ronald Reagan who was a tropical Aquarius but a sidereal Capricorn. As a long-time California resident I had observed Reagan since his rise to power in the mid 1960s as governor of California. He didn't appear to me to display Aquarian traits but the Capricorn qualities were quite marked. There were a lot of people like Reagan in my experience who were spectacularly bad tropical fits but easy to see in a sidereal context. Second, the tropical signs don't even remotely correspond to the constellations that are their namesakes. That fact spurred me to understand the facts behind the tropical-sidereal disconnect. Third, sidereal solar and lunar returns were the best predictive technique I had encountered as an astrologer. Fourth, I was fortunate to become acquainted with several outstanding members of the second generation of modern siderealists, most notably Arthur Blackwell (1942-1992) and Paul Schure (1948-2007). They were by far the best interpreters I had met of any stripe and I wanted to understand their reasoning.

I set up and studied the horoscopes of everyone around me, attended lectures by renowned astrologers whenever possible and read the works of master astrologers, mainly Ptolemy, Abu Ma'sar, Guido Bonatti, William Lilly, John Worsdale, A.J. Pearce, Walter R. Old, W.J. Simmonite, Charles E.O. Carter, B.V. Raman and, of course, Fagan. In college I took every class that was directly or indirectly related to astrology from celestial navigation, astronomy, the histories of Egypt, India, Assyria, Babylonia, Greece and Rome to the Akkadian, Greek and Latin. languages.

This book is not directed at any particular level of experience. It will be of value to novices, intermediate and advanced students. The first six chapters cover the astrological basics: planets, signs, aspects and houses. The second section, which is the biggest section of the book, covers the 45 planet combinations. The third section deals with interpretation with specific illustrations of the horoscopes of well-known geniuses, politicians and notorious figures. There are three appendices. Appendix one is a brief history of the sidereal zodiac. Appendix two addresses the tropical-sidereal question. Appendix Three addresses the exaltations.

Kenneth Bowser
2015
Minneapolis, Minnesota

Chapter One

Nomenclature and Categories

The main tools of astrology are the constellations of the zodiac and the planets. While the determination of some star patterns was undeniably a prehistoric activity, the evidence available to date suggests that the antecedents of the modern night sky were organized into constellations beginning in the third millennium BC. Modern research suggests that the peoples who made the greatest contributions were the Egyptians, the Babylonians, particularly from the period around 2300 BC, as well as the Minoans (on Crete) and the Phoenicians.[3] The constellations behind the Sun as seen from the Earth comprise the zodiac. The boundaries of the astronomical zodiacal constellations conform approximately with 30-degree segments of the sky, although the sidereal signs conform to exact 30-degree sections of space that overlay the constellations.

The constellations of the zodiac with their symbols are:

♈ Aries	♎ Libra
♉ Taurus	♏ Scorpio
♊ Gemini	♐ Sagittarius
♋ Cancer	♑ Capricorn
♌ Leo	♒ Aquarius
♍ Virgo	♓ Pisces

Each constellation has two categories that broadly describe its nature: its element and its quality, known collectively as the quadruplicities and the triplicities respectively. The elements are fire, earth, air and water; the qualities are cardinal, mutable and fixed.

The fire group is characterized by aggressiveness, the desire for high status, the desire to lead and control, the desire to surround oneself with quality and to excel in knowledge and achievements that command respect. The fire constellations are:

Aries, Leo and Sagittarius

The earth group is characterized by the desire for tranquility, stability, safety and good health. They are practical, conscientious, hard working and interested in the structures and the logic of the world. The earth constellations are:

Taurus, Virgo and Capricorn

The air group is characterized by intellectual, casual, progressive and tolerant propensities that make them amenable to change. They are open-minded, pleasant and often detached. They may appear superficial but their interests are limitless. The air constellations are:

Gemini, Libra, and Aquarius

The water group is characterized by a nurturing, emotional, sensuous and intuitive orientation to life. They are the deepest of the four groups and are swayed by issues that relate to morality, religion, patriotism and the virtues. The water constellations are:

Cancer, Scorpio and Pisces

The cardinal constellations are enterprising, active, industrious and initiate activity. They like to manage others. They strive for improvement of conditions and to implement ideas that bring plans into manifestation. The constellations of the cardinal quality are:

Aries, Cancer, Libra and Capricorn

The fixed constellations display implacable resolve, strength of will, consistency and stubborness. They are the strongest of the zodiacal types and often display remarkable executive ability that cause others to rally around them. The constellations of the fixed quality are:

Taurus, Leo, Scorpio and Aquarius

The mutable constellations do the work of the world. They are the most talented, adaptable, cerebral and sensitive of the three qualities but lack the power and ambition of the other two. Their main virtues are ideas and inspiration that are often seized upon and exploited by the other two qualities, or the talents of the mutables are given over to the service of others. The constellations of the mutable quality are:

Gemini, Virgo, Sagittarius and Pisces

The planets and their symbols are as follows (note that the Sun and the Moon are grouped with the planets):

☉ Sun	♀ Venus	♄ Saturn	♇ Pluto
☽ Moon	♂ Mars	♅ Uranus	
☿ Mercury	♃ Jupiter	♆ Neptune	

Most zodiacal placements are either beneficial or neutral to the planets. Each planet has special associations with constellations with which it is similar in nature. The planets are said to "rule" or "own" such constellations. A planet in its own sign functions extremely well. If a planet is in a sign directly opposite the one it rules, the planet's function is impaired. The constellation opposite the rulership placement is its "detriment." Remember that,

Mars rules Aries	Mars's detriment is Libra
Venus rules Taurus	Venus's detriment is Scorpio
Mercury rules Gemini	Mercury's detriment is Sagittarius
The Moon rules Cancer	The Moon's detriment is Capricorn
The Sun rules Leo	The Sun's detriment is Aquarius
Mercury rules Virgo	Mercury's detriment is Sagittarius
Venus rules Libra	Venus's detriment is Aries
Mars and Pluto† rule Scorpio	Mars's detriment is Taurus
Jupiter rules Sagittarius	Jupiter's detriment is Gemini
Saturn rules Capricorn	Saturn's detriment is Cancer
Uranus rules Aquarius	Uranus's detriment is Leo
Neptune rules Pisces	Neptune's detriment is Virgo

The intrinsic natures of the planets are explained in chapter two, but their tendencies to work positively or negatively should be recognized from the beginning. The planets primarily associated with success, happiness, good fortune, recognition and good health are Jupiter and Venus, called the greater and lesser benefics respectively. Uranus also acts in a distinctly positive manner unless it is configured with a malefic.

The planets primarily associated with difficulty, hardship, strife, failure, delay and poor health are the greater and lesser malefics, Saturn and Mars, respectively. Neptune also acts in a distinctly negative manner unless it is configured with a benefic.

In addition to rulership and detriment, the sign of a planet's exaltation is the best place for it to reside, and the opposite position is where a planet is in its fall, which is the worst place for it to

†Pluto's detriment is not yet established as it was only discovered in 1930.

reside. Taken together, the most fortunate placements for planets are the signs of their rulership and the signs of their exaltation. Planets so placed are termed "dignified." Planets in the signs of their detriment or fall are termed "debilitated." Dignities and debilities are a matter of great importance in sidereal astrology. New converts to the sidereal camp from the ranks of tropical astrologers often remark that the dignities and debilities come alive in the sidereal framework, since they have no relevance whatever in a tropical format.

The exaltations and falls are:

Sun is exalted in Aries	Sun is in its fall in Libra
Moon is exalted in Taurus	Moon is in its fall in Scorpio
Mercury is exalted in Virg	Mercury is in its fall in Pisces
Venus is exalted in Pisces	Venus is in its fall in Virgo
Mars is exalted in Capricorn	Mars is in its fall in Cancer
Jupiter is exalted in Cancer	Jupiter is in its fall in Capricorn
Saturn is exalted in Libra	Saturn is in its fall in Aries
Uranus is exalted in Sagittarius*	Uranus is in its fall in Gemini*
Neptune is exalted in Aquarius*	Neptune is in its fall in Leo*
Pluto is exalted in Cancer*	Pluto is in its fall in Capricorn*

*The exaltation placements of the outer plants are their positions in the sidereal zodiac for the Babylonian civil year that corresponds to the heliacal phenomena for the visible planets: 786-785 BC (see appendix three). Heliacal phenomena are the positions in the zodiac and dates in time when the planets are last seen before a period of invisibility that may last for weeks or months or first seen after a period of invisibility that may have lasted for weeks or months. Neptune and Pluto are invisible without telescopic aid and thus cannot have heliacal phenomena. Uranus is at the very limit of human vision but was mistaken for a faint star until recognized as a planet in 1781. As a practical matter Uranus does not have heliacal phenomena either.

Planetary Rulers and Exaltations of the Signs

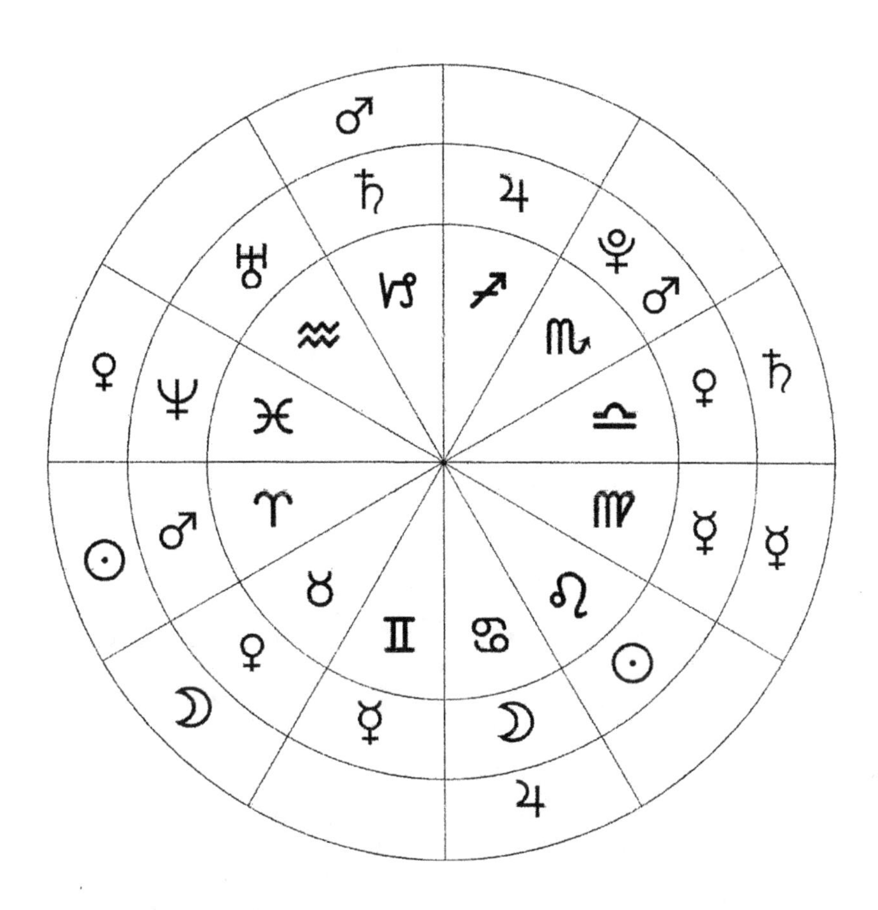

Diagram Key

Inner circle : Signs
Middle circle : Planet rulerships
Outer circle : Planet exaltations

Chapter Two

The Planets

The planets are the most important part of astrology. The constellations and the houses (discussed in chapters three and four) set the scene but the planets are the actors. There are three ways to evaluate planets: their inter-relations in the natus, which is a big part of what constitutes the interpretation of the horoscope, their inter-relations in transit (the current positions of the planets) and transits to natal positions.

Sun ☉ and Moon ☽

The Sun and the Moon are the most important bodies in a horoscope. The Sun represents one's deepest most fundamental character, which may not be apparent until adulthood. The Moon has more to do with one's early life and the family and circumstances into which one was born. The Sun usually represents the father but occasionally the mother is the solar figure, especially if her influence is more telling than the father's. This has always been so and is no concession to the modern world. The Sun is consciousness and character in action. It is the spirit that animates the flesh or physical vehicle that is the province of the Moon. Ninety-nine percent of the mass of our solar system is in the Sun. All other bodies are satellites of the Sun, held captive in their orbits by the Sun's immense gravity, and shine by reflected sunlight. The Moon represents one's emotional component in contrast to the will, which is solar; the Moon is also symbolic of ordinary, everyday life: the prevailing condition, what is happening now. The Moon usually represents the mother but as with the Sun, that rule is not invariably true. This has also always been true and constitutes no concession to modern permutations of family dynamics. This writer espouses no polemic with regard to contemporary gender, sociological, cultural, psychological, religious or political views, except to resist their insertion into an already old body of astrological lore that has seen many passing fashions come and go.

The Sun represents will and intention. It is forceful, dynamic, clear, virtuous and the seat of the life force. The Sun is chiefly concerned with self-satisfaction through self-expression. It represents the "I am," one's unique nature that is perfect and complete. The qualities that are particularly solar are the reputation and self-esteem, the abilities, courage, strength, resolve, achievements and wisdom of the native. The constellation that holds the Sun, the planets and stars configured with it, and its location in the horoscope, indicate the primary orientation of the life. The strongest placement for the Sun is the noon position. Someone with the Sun here, or to a lesser degree on the horizon, especially sunrise, would have authority, responsibility and power in life to a degree that would command respect, admiration, envy and awe, other things not considered.

The Moon represents one's home, physical person, family, usually the mother and the important women in the life. Often the public face that others see is lunar, in particular if the Moon is more powerfully placed in the horoscope than the Sun. The deepest level of one's true character is not always on display. Lunar qualities are not as big or strong as solar qualities but they are deeper. Personal idiosyncrasies and inclinations are lunar. These personal habits and mannerisms are generally known only to family and friends, again, unless the Moon is more prominently placed than the Sun. The Moon is more automatic and less deliberate than the Sun. Sexuality is particularly lunar because the Moon is directly related to one's animal nature. Sexuality, strictly speaking, is really an interplay between the Sun, Moon, Venus and Mars, but the Moon has as much to do with whom is liked and desired as Venus, but the Moon is the more carnal of the two. One may not know why one likes or dislikes someone else but there is no denying the fact of it. Lunar qualities tend to be unconscious, automatic and are associated with an older part of the brain than the Sun, whereas the Sun is the essence of consciousness and self-awareness. People with the Moon prominently placed are particularly sensual and tender, and if the Moon is unafflicted, they are quite engaging, agreeable and warm. The Sun more strongly placed in the horoscope than the Moon makes the native self-centered, ambitious and desirous of fame.

Mercury ☿

Mercury represents ideas and information, their conception, manipulation and transmission. Along with the Sun and the Moon position, Mercury has most to do with one's occupation. The condition of natal Mercury says a lot about the quality of the intellect, one's education, oratorical, literary, mathematical and technical capacities. Transport, communication, languages, conveyances, engineering and their research and development are areas often emphasized when Mercury is strong in the horoscope. When Mercury is prominently placed, the native is commonly an intellectual, a teacher or an artisan whose superior ability lifts him above his fellows. There is also a proclivity toward politics, debate, sales, office work and civil administration when Mercury is strong.

Venus ♀

Venus represents the sense of beauty of the native and all things and people that please and attract him. It relates to the aesthetic sense and internal evaluations and comparisons that manifest as taste. The spouse and the persons, things and pursuits with which one becomes engaged, when choices can be made, are Venusian. Venus is known as the lesser benefic because she relates to those things in life that evoke a positive response on a personal level, in particular the pleasure that attends personal relations, social and sexual. Venus prominently placed in the horoscope, in the horizon or meridian, usually symbolizes physical beauty, and a warm, friendly, fun-loving disposition unless the planet is badly afflicted.

Mars ♂

Mars is an active, competitive, externally directed quality somewhat like the Sun, but it is so aggressive that its action is often hurtful and harmful; for that reason, Mars is known as the lesser malefic. The ancient Egyptian pictogram for Mars is a knife. While Mars easily equates to discord and actual fighting, most often it manifests as irascibility, strong effort, contentiousness and the desire to dominate others. Its most accepted manifestation is sport where speed, strength, coordination and mastery of technique usually don't kill people, although injury is rampant. People with Mars prominently placed in the horoscope often excel in athletics or are the victors in combat. They display recklessness, fearlessness, daring, willfulness, strong competitiveness and like to celebrate their physical prowess.

Jupiter ♃

Jupiter is known as the greater benefic because the success it symbolizes is experienced in the world, beyond the arena of the merely personal. Jupiter represents quality and all the elements in life that bring, status, renown, respect and happiness. It symbolizes wealth and the professions that supply it, in particular the law. It also symbolizes commerce and manufacturing on a big scale, transoceanic shipping, finance and banking, publishing, career government officials and diplomats. Jupiter is somewhat less prominent in the rough and tumble of politics unless the political figure is widely regarded as a statesman. Many of these examples carry negative connotations, but it should be understood that in its pure form, Jupiter strongly placed is symbolic of one who takes the long view of things, who provides employment for others and who creates conditions or an enterprise that can expand and be of enduring value to people at large. Jupiter is not merely enterprising but also philanthropic. It represents good fortune legitimately gained. Jupiter shares with the Sun the quality of one's reputation. Someone with Jupiter prominent in the horoscope is often apparently lucky or one in authority as an editor, executive, administrator, judge, manager, boss or foreman. Such a person has to make judgments and decisions that affect many others. People with Jupiter to the fore are honorable, ambitious, careful, constructive and often conspicuously academic.

Saturn ♄

Saturn is known as the greater malefic because the difficulties and limits it symbolizes are more far-reaching in scope and longer lasting in effect than the action of Mars. The action of Saturn is to confound, slow, or end something, to make it stable and unchanging. It is the opposite of Jupiter in that it frequently represents failure, contraction, disappointment and dismay. Jupiter is liberal, outgoing and generous. Saturn is conservative, insular, and poor. It represents time, structure, rules, cosmic order and the harsh realities of life. Saturn is often called "the teacher," not because it is didactic but because its lessons cannot be circumvented, despite continuous effort by almost everyone to contravene or supercede them. Those efforts end if and when the native reaches maturity. Saturn is particularly hard in youth unless one rejoices in the order of mathematics, physics and the bounds and limits of life. The only freedom it confers is the freedom gained through discipline; until then one is subject to those elements in life that require slow, steady, persistent and often great effort to master. In the short run, Saturn represents loss, anguish, lack of freedom, austerity, thwarting of initiative and an endless work regimen. In the long term the person who has properly integrated Saturn is profound, without illusion, dependable, responsible, prudent, serious, has an appreciation for order and is a glutton for work. The person with Saturn configured with the lights, especially the Sun, or prominently placed in the horoscope, is often lonely no matter how capable, shy in public no matter how affable in private, and may single-handedly control great enterprises as a bulwark against deep insecurity; or the person with a badly placed and debilitated Saturn may languish in prison for his difficulties in learning Saturn's hard lessons.

Uranus ♅

Uranus is excellent, outstanding, avant-garde and represents all things classically good. For example, persons little exposed to music, upon hearing Beethoven's fifth symphony or Miles Davis's Kind of Blue, generally appreciate those works because they are beyond mere style. The action of Uranus is surprising, even shocking; but it always is about the truth of a matter—there is no pretense or caprice in Uranus. Uranus consistently relates to the unexpected, the innovative and the unconventional. Unless configured with a malefic, it is benefic in action and even configured with a malefic one should not be rigidly judgmental about the quality of its effect, depending upon the rest of the horoscope. For example, Pope John Paul II (born May 18, 1920) had Saturn closely opposed Uranus. It made him a reformer within the ultra-conservative milieu of the church as opposed to a rebel. Uranus is concerned with all things new, the excitement of discovery and things that happen to the native for the first time. It is quite unpredictable and literally relates to foreign people, places and languages. It is an extremely headstrong influence, but cool and detached. The people who have it prominently placed in the horoscope are often wild and ungovernable; but Uranus so placed is frequently the sign of original talent. In any case, Uranus is the ultimate free spirit. One who has it as the dominant planet cannot be expected to live a conventional life.

Neptune ♆

Neptune is a nebulous, mystical quality intimately connected to the spirit world. It is also as deeply connected to addiction, misrepresentation, and all things bogus or insubstantial, glamorous, fashionable and dramatic. Neptune is an insidious malefic. The genuinely spiritual and inspirational element is usually not its first manifestation, especially in transit, but that certainly is its best manifestation. Neptune is expansive, given to flights of fancy and is therefore good for people whose stock in trade is fiction or elements of the imagination. It is strongly inclined toward the more rarified and transcendent forces in life but its negative side often gets mixed up with its good side. For example, one with Neptune in the meridian or on the horizon is occasionally aware of what is going to happen before it does or knows what other people are thinking; but the Neptunian people usually can't tell the difference between what they've tuned into and their own mental chatter. They frequently mistake one for the other. Neptune tends to weaken the planets it touches and to make people who have it strongly placed inclined toward the theatre and the occult. In many respects it is the opposite of Uranus. Where Uranus relates to the excitement of discovery and the possibilities inherent in the future, Neptune gets agitated about loss, scandal, entrapment and jeopardy from dishonorable parts of one's past. Where Uranus is independent, Neptune is dependent; where Uranus is symbolic of those things which are so compelling that they transcend eras, Neptune is caught up in fashion, trends and contemporary attitudes that are as ephemeral as the weather. The Neptunians are nevertheless kind, idealistic and generous, often to the undeserving. This planet plays a prominent role in the horoscopes of people who, if they are not dramatists, occultists, or musicians, are deeply religious. Neptune relates both to inspiration and delusion. It is the most sensitive planet and the most tantalizing but also the most unreliable and the most confusing.

Pluto ⯓

Pluto makes extreme whatever it touches. It acts in an all or nothing manner. Its action is divisive and makes people feel isolated, disconnected, or cut off from others. There are two types: many Plutonians are distinctly gentle, unassuming and barely noticed due to a powerful desire for privacy and seclusion. Configured with the lights, especially the Sun, the native may even be anti-social, sometimes a complete misfit, and one who finds fault with the habits and predilections of society. The action of the planet is convertible, that is, configured with a benefic its effect can be miraculous but with a malefic, it can be quite difficult.

The other side of Pluto prominently placed in the horoscope gives remarkable ambition that can make the native appear power hungry. The person with Pluto so placed will also very likely be irascible, driven and unwilling to share power. The Plutonian may have power over the masses or retreat utterly from them as a recluse; sometimes both conditions apply since Plutonians often like to rule behind the scenes and find great satisfaction in wielding power in secret or under the noses of others incognito. Many people with Pluto as the dominant planet in the horoscope work alone or at night so as to have as little contact with others as possible. Conversely, people who make it their business to be in the middle of contentious or crisis issues like police, trial lawyers, politicians or medical doctors frequently have this planet powerfully placed in their horoscopes. It is also prominent in the horoscopes of psychiatrists and psychologists whose stock in trade is the unconscious, or the issues in life that are ostensibly beyond reach. Pluto in its highest manifestation represents the luminous, the supernatural and the collective unconscious that people feel is real but can't readily apprehend. At its worst Pluto is pure unadulterated catastrophe, and either way, one doesn't so much "handle" Pluto as one is handled by it. There is a transcendent quality about this planet that is blithely bandied about in some circles as though it could be served up on a platter. But if the transcendence of Pluto is ever experienced, it usually entails psychological pain as a consequence of initiation into higher levels of consciousness.

The Moon's Nodes ☊ and ☋

The plane of the Moon's orbit is inclined five degrees to the ecliptic, and the intersections of the Moon's orbit with the ecliptic are the Moon's Nodes. The Moon reaches its North Node (☊) when it crosses the ecliptic moving from south to north; it reaches its South Node (☋) when it crosses the ecliptic moving from north to south. The Nodes of the Moon relate to the public impact of the character or works of the native. A planet conjunct the Nodes becomes more important than it would be alone. Indian astrologers attribute great power to them. The Indians even go so far as to give the Nodes the power of a planet even though they are merely places, not bodies. Eclipses can only occur if the lights are near the Moon's Nodes. The North Node is considered somewhat fortunate but often confounding, and the South Node is considered generally unfortunate and usually confounding. The North Node is also related to material things that are much desired and the South Node to spirituality, mysticism and the parts of life where one can be at a disadvantage. Fagan didn't use the Nodes of the Moon but many modern Western siderealists do use them, although Westerners do not confer on the Nodes the enormous significance they enjoy in India. Some astrologers confidently proclaim that the Nodes relate to one's past life or karmic status, although how they could know that is unclear if indeed it is true; thus no assertion about prior incarnation with regard to the Moon's Nodes is advanced in this work.

Chapter Three

The Sidereal Signs

The region of the zodiac called Aries has nothing to do with the vernal equinox, that is, spring in the Northern Hemisphere. Aries was the constellation that rose at the time of the vernal equinox during the Hellenistic Period and the Roman Imperial Era when astrology was gaining currency in the West. That is why the tropical zodiac is reckoned from Aries. If tropical astrology had gained currency in the West during the Age of Taurus, that is, when the constellation Taurus rose at the time of the vernal equinox (which was the case during the third and fourth millennia BC), tropical zodiac reckoning would begin with Taurus. Aries had been rising at the time of Northern Hemisphere spring since the opening of the second millennium before the Christian Era. The sidereal sign Pisces has appeared on the horizon at the time of the vernal equinox since the third century AD but that constellation is not associated with spring either. It is a mistake to attribute the characteristics of the seasons to the constellations because the seasons rotate through all of the constellations on the ecliptic over a period of 25,800 years. Moreover, since the Northern Hemisphere spring is the Southern Hemisphere fall, it is evident that seasonal associations could never have been correctly characteristic of any of the constellations; thus when the zodiac came to be mistakenly associated with the seasons, it only appeared to be approximately true for a century or two (and only precisely true for a single moment) during Late Antiquity, and for the Northern Hemisphere only. Yet the level of knowledge about geodesy in general circulation in the West was too low before and after the fall of Rome to understand some of the basic problems associated with civil and astronomical reckoning. Additionally, due to ignorance of the geometry of the solar system, there was no way to resolve the issue of seasonal versus stellar orientation until the geocentric universe was replaced by the heliocentric universe.[4] The tropical zodiac was a fixture in the West long before heliocentrism finally won out. In the ancient world the Greeks assumed a geocentric universe, which the Romans, much inferior to the Greeks in science, never contested. The heliocentric universe was not conclusively proved until the work of Copernicus, Kepler, Galileo and Newton showed the way in the sixteenth and seventeenth centuries.

Astrology probably evolved as a topic of discussion among women at washing sites at river's edge and campsites while preparing food, talking among themselves about their children and their husbands. In an age before illumination beyond the light of a hearth was the norm, there were few things to do at night as a commonplace activity. One of them was to view the heavens daily, in detail with great interest, such that knowledge of the sky became part of the natural education of every person. People who displayed similar behaviors who were born with planets in common in the zodiacal framework—and duly noted by women who have been better students of character than men—slowly added to the body of lore that became increasingly invested with meaning over time. That is not to say that the zodiac is an anthropomorphic projection onto the sky; rather, the immutable qualities associated with certain parts of the sky came slowly to be recognized, which recognition manifested as meaning. The constellations of the zodiac—the sidereal signs—were recognized as meaningful because of their consistency.

Aries ♈

Planets in Aries or Aries on the Ascendant coincide with very marked traits. Mars rules Aries. Aries is the exaltation of the Sun, the fall of Saturn and the detriment of Venus. Aries people, like the other fire signs, Leo and Sagittarius, also called the royal signs, think that their intrinsic worth is greater than the people around them. Aries people are directive, assertive and yearn to be in positions of authority. They are self-assured and confident that they know how to perform any task better than anyone else. They do, in fact, have a great deal of executive ability, enjoy giving orders immensely and in getting others to do their bidding.

Emphasis in this constellation gives a distinctly aggressive, willful, selfish personality especially if it contains the Sun or Moon. Aries is decidedly masculine. Women with either of the lights (Sun and Moon) in Aries, though they may appear feminine, have the temperament of a man. The Aries people want to lead whether they have the ability to manage a task or not. Naturally then, their ambition frequently outruns their ability, though as many geniuses have placements here as elsewhere. They can start enterprises and overcome obstacles that would be too daunting for other types. People with the Sun in Aries cannot take criticism and become incensed when it is directed at them. The Aries people are generally formidable personalities who frequently overpower others who may see them as mean, egotistical, overbearing and presumptuous. Their confidence and progress in life may appear compromised if Saturn configures the Sun, in particular if Saturn is higher in the sky than the Sun, or if a constellation like Pisces rises; but the strength and ambition of the Sun in Aries to control events will tell in the end.

If Mars is placed in Aries in the horoscope, the planet is particularly unrestrained in its expression which manifests often as a celebration of aggression. A good example is the great boxer, Muhammad Ali. Even when not inclined toward violence or athleticism, the native with Mars so placed would be conspicuously daring and more forceful than people with Mars in a less auspicious placement. In the same way, the Sun, because it is exalted in Aries, functions marvelously well there; like Mars, the solar qualities and the Arian qualities are similar. People with the Sun in its exaltation are able to get what they want and sway others through the sheer force of their personalities. Jack Nicholson (April 22) one of the kings of Hollywood and one of the premier actors of his time, displays the essence of this solar placement and the sense of superiority that goes with it, because his Aries Sun is near the Midheaven (the strongest spatial placement in a horoscope at the top of the chart). Nicholson's Venus is also in Aries where that planet is in her detriment and functions particularly badly. A gentle planet like Venus often suffers in Aries unless Jupiter is also present. Often one's love life is a series of train wrecks, and only really works when the mate wholly acquiesces to the native; or if the Sun is in a retiring constellation like Pisces, Venus in Aries suggests that the mate has a fiery temperament. Venus in Aries is often symbolic of someone who has experienced harshness and occasionally emotional damage at the hands of people from whom comfort, solace, pleasure and support usually come.

Notable personalities with bodies in Aries are, Charlemagne (Sun, Venus and Jupiter), Catherine de Medici (Sun, Mercury and Uranus), Queen Elizabeth I (Moon), Catherine the Great of Russia (Sun and Mars), Queen Elizabeth II (Sun), Jacqueline Kennedy Onassis (Moon) and Bill Clinton (Moon). The Sun enters Aries during the current era on April 14 or 15 depending on leap year and time zone, although that date will advance by one day in approximately 72 years due to precession.

Taurus ♉

Planets in Taurus or Taurus on the Ascendant coincides with a gentle and even-tempered quality unless Mars is in the Ascendant or conjoined to one of the lights. Venus rules Taurus and the Moon is exalted in this sign. Emphasis in this constellation gives a sweet natured, friendly, social personality, especially if it contains the Sun or Moon. Taurus is decidedly feminine. Men with emphasis in this constellation, though they may appear distinctly masculine, will be soft and engaging in temperament and disinclined toward harsh words or unkind behavior. The Taureans are nevertheless direct, without pretense, speak the truth and generally evoke the admiration of their fellows for their unflagging loyalty and unassuming modesty. Taureans stand for something solid, but usually don't inflict their views on others unsolicited. They are not confrontational but are courageous if pushed to the limit. Emphasis in Taurus produces a passionate nature; in fact if this wonderful constellation can be faulted at all, its sensuous disposition would be the culprit, inasmuch as erotic caprice tests their steady natures. Taurus is especially fond of nature, and is tender, generous and gracious to everyone. Sometimes they may appear too nice, or too much swayed by the pleasures of the flesh, but their generosity of spirit, perseverance and steadfast application to a task stand them in good stead. Their resolve and application in matters that engage their interest is amazing and they may found movements or traditions that continue long past their deaths. William Lilly, Jim Lewis and Cyril Fagan are well known astrologers with the Sun in Taurus.

It is fitting that the two most feminine bodies, Venus and the Moon would find themselves well positioned there. The Moon exalted in Taurus on the horizon or the meridian (the strong places in a horoscope) can make one the object of adulation or a person with so much sexuality that it overflows into the public awareness. Good examples of the Moon so placed are Edith Piaf, a national institution in France and the actress, Brigitte Bardot. Claudia Schiffer, with the Moon in Taurus but not angular (i.e., not near the horizon or meridian), shows how a somewhat lesser degree of fame and attention attends this most feminine placement when it doesn't get the strength of angularity. People who are monuments to sensuality like Marilyn Monroe very often have the Sun in Taurus, and likewise, a great beauty like Elizabeth Hurley, is a fine example of Taurus at its most exquisite. Bob Hope is an example of Taurus at its most affable and entertaining. The point is that Taurus evokes pleasure, desire, admiration and popularity in both sexes. The Taureans are inordinately fond of their comforts and the money to buy them. They take pains to ensure that their money is well managed. That is why Mars, the polar opposite of Venus, is hurtful and disruptive in Taurus. Mars, itself full of desire, is sometimes symbolic of sexual excess or aberration in Taurus. Persons subject to vices of various kinds often have an afflicted Venus or Venus's constellations, Taurus and Libra, contain malefics, which are themselves afflicted by other malefics.

Taurus is well represented by John F. Kennedy (Sun and Venus), the Marquis de Sade (Sun and Jupiter), Clint Eastwood (Sun), Queen Victoria (Sun and Moon) and Pope John Paul II (Sun, Mercury and Venus). The Sun enters Taurus on May 15 or 16 depending on leap year and time zone during the current era, although those dates will increase by one day in approximately 72 years.

Gemini ♊

Planets in Gemini or Gemini rising confer on its natives a juvenile quality that is quite marked, especially when the Sun or Moon is in this constellation. Mercury rules Gemini and Jupiter is in its detriment there. Gemini is nearly gender neutral, although it tilts slightly toward boys, but like Mercury's other constellation, Virgo, it relates to children of both sexes before they have reached the age of puberty. Women with many planets in Gemini typically appear far younger than their years, and usually no matter how grave and weighty their endeavors, both sexes manage to bring levity, mischief and play into their relations with others. Gemini is intellectual, curious, a quick study and a natural student. They write and speak well, but are often superficial, irreverent and live off their quick wits. Many of them have no problem walking the fine line between legitimate, if brutal, competition and scandalously unscrupulous behavior. It should be no surprise then, that Mercury in the ancient world was considered the patron of thieves as well as merchants. Commerce and sales call to the Gemini people. They have a head for business and white-collar work, things literary, intellectual, and very often medical, from technicians to doctors. They are the least religious, in the formal sense, of all the zodiacal types, but probably the most fun. The rest of the horoscope will show if the native is brilliant or shallow. In either case, he will be mentally adroit to a noteworthy degree. Gemini people are also drawn to the field of communications as much as to business per se. They find their way into radio, television, magazines, newspapers and advertising in large numbers as those areas are foils for their nervous energy and non-stop stream of articulate and clever ideas, schemes and theories.

They are usually not markedly introspective unless the influence of Saturn or Neptune is prominent; they have short attention spans and are much attuned to the moment at hand. They are also particularly fond of travel, athletics and speed, whether on foot, horseback, by car, racing yacht or any other means. The sense of having a new scene appear before their eyes every second, as in transit, is satisfying to their childlike curiosity and wanderlust. No planet is exalted in Gemini; like Virgo, it is purely Mercury's house.

Good examples are Princess Diana (Sun and Mercury), Jean-Paul Sartre (Sun, Mercury and Neptune), George Sand (Sun) and John D. Rockefeller (Sun and Moon). The Sun enters Gemini on June 15 or 16 depending on leap year and time zone during the current era, although those dates will increase by one day in approximately 72 years.

Cancer ♋

Planets in Cancer or Cancer rising confer on its natives a nurturing and family oriented quality that is typically the salient feature of this constellation, especially if it contains the Sun or Moon. The Moon rules Cancer. Jupiter, the greater benefic, is exalted in Cancer because this constellation is the best Petrie dish in the zodiac; that is, Cancer provides the environment most conducive to healthy, robust and fast growth. The lesser malefic, Mars, is in its fall in Cancer and the greater malefic, Saturn, is in its detriment in this sign. The two traditional malefics function badly in Cancer because its domain is typically tender, soft and young and therefore unable to handle the harshness of Saturn and Mars. Dysfunctional families are very often attended by Mars and Saturn in Cancer. The Moon is pre-eminently concerned with women, domesticity and interpersonal relations. Someone with the Moon in Cancer has a charming and disarming nature which retreats from confrontation but makes everyone feel at ease, welcomed and protected as if in the bosom of their own families. Unless there are afflictions to the Moon, someone with the Moon in Cancer will be effortlessly popular. Men with either of the lights in Cancer generally feel most comfortable at home, and are likely to put much time and effort into improving and maintaining it. The desire to own land is also common with this placement. The desire to have children and to enjoy the pleasures of family life is stronger still. Even without children, the Cancer people typically look out for others or try to foster conditions that supply the requirements of people in need. It makes them feel like they are acting in accordance with their natures to be a wellspring to others. Food preparation is the standard manner of manifestation of this nature, which commonly produces culinary excellence among Cancer natives.

This placement is very sensitive to subtleties of feeling and mood to which other constellations, except Pisces, are oblivious. This group rarely dismisses the occult, although due to their pronounced conventional tendencies (unless Uranus is prominent in the horoscope), they may not admit it openly. It follows too that they find it easy to go overboard with regard to the feeling side of life and thus walk a fine line between a rich imagination and exaggeration. In a similar vein, the Cancers frequently drift over the line from generous accommodation to compliancy, unless the Sun in particular, is strengthened by contacts with more stern planets. When it is so strengthened, Cancer can be a shrewd businessman always looking to expand. They are also generally inordinately supportive of not merely their families, but their churches, country and cultural traditions: all the "home teams."

Good examples of Cancer are Mohandas Gandhi (Moon), Elizabeth II (Moon), Carl Jung (Sun), the emperor Augustus (Jupiter), William Shakespeare (Jupiter) and Percy Bysshe Shelley (Sun, Venus and Uranus). The Sun enters Cancer on July 17 or 18 depending on leap year and time zone during the current era, although those dates will increase by one day in approximately seventy-two years.

Leo ♌

Planets in Leo or Leo rising confer on its natives indomitable will and the attitude that they were born to the purple. Leo is ruled by the Sun. It is distinctly masculine, egotistical, proud and magnanimous. Uranus is in its detriment in Leo and no planet is exalted there; no other body is on equal footing with the Sun. Leo is pre-eminently *the* royal constellation, and like the other two fire constellations, Aries and Sagittarius, Leo is upwardly mobile, ambitious and aristocratic but it is the strongest of the three. Leo is concerned first and foremost with power: getting it, wielding it and maintaining it. In the ancient world Leo was considered the most fortunate constellation because it was associated with political clout. The glyph is a symbol of pharaoh's double crown uniting Upper and Lower Egypt. Among the most noteworthy qualities of Leo are their imposing presence, unshakable resolve, courage and will to lead. Those who are confounded by them complain of their insufferable arrogance, measureless conceit and overbearing behavior. Women with the lights in Leo are not necessarily masculine in appearance although they will appear grand, elegant and magnificent to a degree that is unnerving to women with less ego strength. All the other bodies in the solar system are satellites of the Sun and Leo people often let others know that they see themselves as the center of the universe and everyone else as lesser beings. The attitude is exemplified perfectly by Louis XIV, king of France (1638-1715), the "Sun King," who had the Sun in Leo and the Moon in Cancer, whose statement, "L'état, c'est moi." ("I am the state"), could be the motto for most Leos. In contrast to such haughty behavior, well-developed Leos take care to dispense favor and advantage to those whom they consider deserving wherever possible. If not in a position to act in such a grandly liberal manner, they dream of it and take action to become so; but in contrast to Aries which will walk on and over people to get to the top, Leo usually acts in an honorable way, though relentlessly, to get to what he sees as his proper station in life.

Leo commands respect due to its strength, virtue and regal bearing which outshine people who are often more capable but whose ambition cannot match the dynamic Leo personality. They sometimes become deeply religious when they internalize that God is the ultimate source of power. Until such a time they are their own favorite subject. Their faith in themselves is astounding; their interests are paramount in contrast to the Cancer personality who makes the interests of others the focus of their lives. It should be no surprise then that the life force is particularly strong in Leo. These people can recover from injury and illness that would kill most others. Leo people will usually respond in an exemplary manner to opportunities that afford them glory, as the examples show.

Alexander and Napoleon were drawn to combat like moths to flame, but it is less well known that Lyndon Johnson was decorated for gallantry under fire in World War II. Leo steps up when it looks like all is lost to show their mettle when all about them are beaten. Leo is naturally the province of big personalities like Alexander the Great (Sun and Venus), Napoleon Bonaparte (Sun, Mars and Neptune), Lyndon Baines Johnson (Sun, Moon, Mercury, Mars and Jupiter), Bill Clinton (Sun) and Steve Jobs (Ascendant). Alexander was born to royalty but Napoleon and Clinton rose from poverty and obscurity on sheer will and talent to become heads of state. Steve Jobs was not impoverished but he certainly rose from obscurity on will and talent to become a dynamic chief executive officer and billionaire. The Sun enters Leo on August 17 or 18 depending on leap year and time zone during the current era, although that date will increase by one day in approximately 72 years.

Virgo ♍

Planets in Virgo or Virgo rising confer on its natives a powerful mental orientation to life. Virgo is ruled by Mercury, which is also exalted in this constellation. Virgo is the sign of the engineer, the academic, the technical virtuoso who is in his element in the classroom, the laboratory, and associated with research and development. While they are renowned for their steely nerves and courage under fire, that quality relates in large part to the major deficiency of this constellation: Venus is in her fall in Virgo. Virgo people are often criticized as cold; and in fact they are somewhat less developed in terms of feeling tone than the other constellations. They are not without feeling but they tend to analyze their feelings in a detached manner and not to feel love, fear and the standard array of emotional components with the same depth as the other constellations. The mind is emphasized with Virgo at the expense of the heart, yet Virgo is kind, gentle and unassuming. It tends to be gender neutral but tilts slightly toward girls. Men with this placement are not generally feminine but so cerebral that unless Mars is prominent in the horoscope, they are not likely to take a great interest in sports, hunting, competition or the traditionally masculine pursuits; yet they make superb military strategists and commanders if the rest of the horoscope supports that endeavor. There is a love of order, analysis and all manner of rational discourse. Virgo people are natural students and tend toward the technical subjects whereas Gemini, Mercury's other constellation, tends toward things literary, although this is by no means a rigid rule. Bear in mind that Isaac Newton had the Moon in Gemini, Albert Einstein had Gemini rising and Nikola Tesla had the Sun in Gemini and the Moon in Virgo.

Virgo, like the other earth constellations, Taurus and Capricorn, has a strong practical bent. Virgo wants to apply its knowledge here and now in the world. Virgo finds enormous satisfaction in understanding natural physical laws and seeing the principles of those laws expressed in form, particularly in machines and devices that are the offspring of the mind. Virgo people make excellent teachers and typically appear at their best dispensing information to the rest of us who lack their sheer intellectual horsepower. They are also consistently interested in matters of health, diet and hygiene to such a degree that if Virgo rises and its ruler Mercury is afflicted by the malefics, the native may be a hypochondriac. Virgo's opposite number, Pisces may well find its perfect mode of expression composing a symphony; Virgo finds the same satisfaction and sense of beauty looking at a blueprint or mathematical equations.

Margaret Thatcher, Britain's first female prime minister, is a fine example of the Sun (and Mars) in Virgo. She earned a graduate degree in chemistry before taking up the law. Dwight Eisenhower, with the Sun (and Mercury) in Virgo, rose from Kansas farm boy to supreme commander of the Allies in World War II and finally to president of the United States with no other advantage than his brain. Bill Gates, the wealthiest man on the planet, has Mercury exalted in Virgo (and Gemini rising). The total mix of the horoscope tells the whole story, but someone with exalted Mercury is likely to see potential earlier than their fellows and exploit it to the hilt. Gates parlayed his ideas (and the ideas of others) on how to organize, manage and dispense information into an empire. The Sun enters Virgo on September 17 or 18 depending on leap year and time zone during the current era although that date will advance by one day in approximately 72 years.

Libra ♎

Planets in Libra or Libra rising confer on its natives a friendly, introspective, gentle and peace-loving disposition, but Libra is first and foremost concerned with beauty and art. Librans are able to see the artistic component in ordinary life that others miss altogether or can't appreciate until the Librans show them with their own illustrations, designs or criticism. Libra is distinctly feminine, befitting its association with Venus, the lesser benefic. Venus also holds dominion over Taurus but Libra has an even better aesthetic sense than Taurus. Libra's ability and excellent taste in the fine arts are essentially its signature. Libra is the fall of the Sun and the detriment of Mars. That is, the Sun exalted in Aries, the constellation opposite Libra, functions least well in Libra. Libra is nothing like the Sun; and likewise Mars, which is most closely associated with Aries, is also quite unlike

Libra. Where Aries forces its way, Libra gives way; where Aries asserts, Libra reflects; where Aries is loud, impatient and precipitate in action, Libra is beautiful, smooth and cultivated; where Aries is daring, Libra considers such action ill-advised. Part of that sentiment (caution) derives from the exaltation of Saturn in Libra. The only negative feature of Saturn's exaltation in Libra is the extremely poor memory that is commonly the lot of this group when the lights, particularly the Sun, are placed in it.

Librans often don't do as well in school as might reasonably be expected because of this factor. Saturn maintains things as they are and resists change. It functions well in Libra because the orientation of that constellation is to freeze all good things and conditions in time so that they would forever remain undisturbed. In the same way, when an artist renders his subject just as he wants it to capture or evoke an effect, he stops; the effect he sought having been achieved. Libra wants to get to the state of mind or place wherein conditions and objects, especially objets d'art, convey precisely an emotional tone consistent with harmony, grace, artistry and peace. Libra is sensuous, strongly inclined toward pleasure, accommodation, consideration for others, and shrinks from strife, dissension and all things coarse or vulgar.

Men with the Sun in Libra may appear effeminate unless Mars is strongly placed in the horoscope, in particular with the lights or in the angles, or they may be so good looking that they could be called "pretty boys" like some movie stars or male models. With few exceptions, Libra is the antithesis of the rugged outdoors type of man and the epitome of such consummate beauties as Catherine Deneuve. Librans are also frequently hedonists and easily spoiled by a life of ease, but their artistic sophistication is superb; their diplomacy both personally and politically admirable, and their ability to provide leisure and pleasure for others, distinctly remarkable. Good examples of Libra are Marie-Antoinette (Sun and Venus), Edward VII (Sun), Charles, Prince of Wales (Sun) and Johnny Carson (Sun). The Sun enters Libra on October 17 or 18 depending on leap year and time zone during the current era, although that date will advance by one day in approximately 72 years.

Scorpio ♏

Planets in Scorpio or Scorpio rising confer on its natives a confrontational, powerful and courageous temperament. Scorpio is aggressive, insistent, penetrating and intense. It likes to fight and is deterred by nothing. Even women, tiny in stature, with the Sun or Ascendant here, will stand up to cruel or overbearing bosses who have everyone else cowed. Like all the fixed signs, Scorpio is imbued with unshakable resolve. They stand for something solid and are at their best in emergencies or when stakes are high. Scorpio has a soldier-like quality and will step up to protect or defend anything important, at risk of life and limb. The less well developed among them may find it easy to abuse their natural aggressiveness to become bullies, and even the best of them have a mean streak that can get them into trouble if it escapes containment.

Scorpio in the ancient world was associated with Mars, the god of war and while Mars still rules Scorpio, since the discovery of Pluto in 1930, many astrologers have come to feel that Pluto has as much affinity with Scorpio as does Mars. Scorpio has a dual quality and therefore co-rulers, Mars and Pluto. In its lower manifestation, Scorpio is indeed the soldier but there is a mysterious quality about this constellation that relates to levels of awareness that few people attain. All of the water constellations, Cancer, Scorpio and Pisces are privy to the irrational, the intuitive and the occult without having to work for those gifts. Scorpio feels in its bones that life is much bigger than what can be apprehended through only five senses, that some things, dismissed by most people as fanciful legends or outright fraud, are actually grounded in a deeper reality. The kundalini or serpent power is associated with this sign.

Winston Churchill is a superb example of one who spoke of his destiny as though he knew what it was. His prescience in the 1930s regarding German intentions made him the right man to deal with them when he was proven correct. In May 1940, when Western Europe was reeling under the German blitzkrieg and Great Britain was facing the Nazi juggernaut alone, Winston Churchill became prime minister. His maiden speech as prime minister before the House of Commons contains statements which are the essence of what Scorpio is about:

> "You ask what is our policy? I say it is to wage war by land, sea and air—war with all our might and with all the strength God has given us—and to wage war against a monstrous tyranny never surpassed in the dark lamentable catalogue of human crime. That is our policy . . . I have nothing to offer but blood, toil, tears and sweat . . . we shall never surrender. . . . ".[5]

Scorpio is decidedly masculine, distinctly unrefined (Churchill's Moon in Leo is what saved him from boorishness) and the constellation of the Moon's fall and Venus' detriment. No planet is exalted here. The tender Moon is battered in Scorpio which placement suggests that the native's mother is hell-on-wheels and/or that one's early environment was characterized by serious family dysfunction, poverty, ill health or all of these things. Venus in Scorpio, much like Venus in Aries is a placement where one finds harshness, trouble and difficulty where tenderness, solace and comfort normally reside. The love life is often a rocky road with this Venus placement. Scorpio has long been considered one of the "bad" signs (the other is Capricorn) because its natives often suffer violence or injury or they choose to deal with trauma, frequently in a medical or rehabilitative capacity. Since astrology fell under the influence of psychology, particularly in the 1970s, attempts have been made to soften this view (which was reasonable since most tropical Scorpios are sweet and sensuous sidereal Librans). But in the fixed zodiac of the ancient world, Scorpio is a formidable character who is strongly inclined to crush his opposition if provoked.

Scorpio people are often literally concerned with matters of life and death either from the perspective of a hired gun who takes life, or a surgeon who snatches it from the jaws of death. An undertaker whose business is the care of the dead, or a nurse in a new-born nursery whose business is that polar opposite, further illustrate the odd dichotomy Scorpio embraces. Scorpio is like Pluto, lord of the underworld from Greek myth who, during part of the year, would return to the surface of the Earth from the infernal regions. One should think twice before toying with a Scorpion. They are powerful people, often have hard lives, short fuses and do not suffer fools gladly. They may also reach high levels of awareness, even the supernatural, which others may find intimidating and awe-inspiring.

Good examples of Scorpio are Martin Luther (Sun, Mercury and Neptune), Frank Sinatra (Sun and Mercury), Sri Sathya Sai Baba (Sun, Saturn, Venus and Mercury) and Ted Turner (Sun and Venus). The Sun enters Scorpio on November 16 or 17 depending on leap year and time zone during the current era, although that date will advance by one day in approximately seventy-two years.

Sagittarius ♐

Planets in Sagittarius or Sagittarius rising confer on its natives a sense of superiority that is akin to the other fire constellations Aries and Leo, except that this constellation is inclined to be discrete about it. The symbol for Sagittarius is the archer whose arrow flies high and far. In the ancient world Sagittarius was considered the sign of the prophet. Even now these people tend to be philosophical and to take the long view. Jupiter, the greater benefic, rules Sagittarius and Mercury is in its detriment here. Sagittarius is distinctly kind and benevolent. It is likely to be interested in religious questions and a to be church regular or at least someone with a strong faith. Sagittarius is masculine but ever the gentleman, considerate and a generous host. These people are concerned about social class and respectability to a marked degree unless the influence of Saturn is very strong. Since they are inordinately concerned with what other people think, they tend not to stand out due to an outrageous wardrobe or behavior designed to get attention. But upon close inspection, their clothes are likely to be tailored instead of off the rack, and while they abhor ostentatious display, they will drive the best car possible that doesn't make them appear conspicuous. To be conspicuous for the wrong reasons is a great sin to them as it is a sign of bad breeding and bad taste—what the French call (someone who is) mal élevé. In contrast to the other two fire signs, who reign by the force of their personalities, Sagittarius judges value according to what one knows and what one can do. They work hard to get honorable professions for themselves and their children and naturally put a great premium on education. They are nevertheless often criticized for being snobs, not because they are arrogant in the manner of Aries and Leo, but because they are naturally more refined and intellectual than those latter two constellations. Those who lack quality of character often recognize their shortcomings in contrast to Sagittarius. As one of the mutable constellations, Sagittarius lacks the sheer strength of Leo or Aries and sometimes becomes a target for those who feel slighted by the refinement of people with important bodies in this sign. Sagittarius is at home in academia, the law, medicine, the sciences, philosophy and executive or at least management positions.

Although less gifted in the arts than other placements, the finer things in life consistently engage their interest and their homes are often monuments to superlative design and execution. Their enthusiasm for sport from football to Formula One is usually quite marked, but not in the rabid sense that often attends popular events today. Sagittarians are more attracted to it as owners and gamblers, particularly the more expensive sports such as polo, yacht, horse and car racing, than as enthusiasts and participants. They appreciate sport for its evidence of speed, strength, grace and mastery of technique. Unless there are severe afflictions to the lights in Sagittarius, it is one of the most fortunate placements in the zodiac. It is characterized by a noble character, regardless of one's station in life, generosity of spirit, ambition to excel in a career, the avoidance of the sordid and the embrace of virtue. Sagittarius has not been established beyond doubt as the exaltation of any planet, although Uranus was in this constellation during the exaltation year, 786-85 BC. Uranus is a sixth magnitude object, at the very limit of human vision. Uranus and Sagittarius have a lot in common though, especially their association with freedom and excellent works. Mercury, in its detriment in Sagittary, is concerned with objects and principles at hand: rules, axioms, formulae and techniques; but as a hands-on, here-and-now principle Mercury gets diffused in an expansive constellation like Sagittarius. Those with Mercury here are generally not merely glib or simply loquacious; they are often verbose and can go on endlessly about minutiae, rhetorical questions, theoretical , philosophical, occult or spiritual matters.

Good illustrations of Sagittarius are Johannes Kepler (Sun, Mercury, Venus and Uranus), Louis Pasteur (Sun, Mercury, Venus, Uranus and Neptune), Paramhansa Yogananda (Sun and Mercury), Denzel Washington (Sun and Mercury), William Lilly (Moon) and George Washington (Moon). The Sun enters Sagittarius on December 16 or 17 depending on leap year and time zone during the current era, although that date will advance by one day in approximately 72 years.

Capricorn ♑

Planets in Capricorn or Capricorn rising confer on its natives a strong desire for security, borne of a strong sense of insecurity. There is the desire for surety, an appreciation for things that have practical value, the tendency to embrace logic, all things old and traditional and to be suspicious of the new and unfamiliar. Yet this frequently hidebound attitude is occasionally superceded in the higher types of this constellation who rejoice in the natural order of things, especially in science. The Capricorn's profound love of order is perfectly exemplified by the Russian genius Dmitri Mendeleyev, who fleshed out the periodic table of chemical elements according to their atomic weights and established the table as a law of nature. More commonly, Capricorn is considered the most unfortunate, the least desired, the most dull and the hardest sign in the zodiac. Saturn, the greater malefic, rules Capricorn; Mars is exalted here; Jupiter is in his fall and the Moon is in her detriment in Capricorn. Natives of this constellation are usually hard working, but reserved, abstemious, unless the lights are with Neptune, and parsimonious. Often they are attracted to the bizarre and the macabre and find difficulty enjoying themselves at parties and other social functions.

The virtues of Capricorn are the virtues of Saturn: conscientiousness, frugality, organization, discipline, perseverance and stability. But to the same degree they are reclusive, doubters, pessimists, austere and often hamstrung by low self-esteem. Ambition is the province of Sagittarius with which this constellation has become confused by advocates of the tropical zodiac due to the overlap of the tropical signs as they slide through the zodiac. Capricorn is more concerned with being able to survive in security with the least bother. Astrologers often speak euphemistically about Capricorn so as not to put off those with placements here, especially the lights; but when the old guard spoke of being born under a bad sign, they meant this one and Scorpio. Poverty, chronic illness, paralyzing injury, limited or lack of sufficient opportunity when there is powerful talent, unremarkable or unsung talents and undue misfortune of a general nature frequently dog this sign unless it is powerfully configured with Jupiter. If success is attained, it is rarely unqualified. Mozart is a classic example. When none of these conditions obtain, the Capricorn personality may be martyred in some larger cause. Someone who sacrifices the comfortable life he could have to do service for others, like Albert Schweitzer (German medical missionary in Africa) may take on the imposing, often daunting, tasks that Capricorn represents. This sign has perseverance and courage due to the influence of Saturn and the exaltation of Mars; yet the orientation is usually conservative, often depressing or boring in outlook, dour, serious and suspicious. When this is not the case, a well-placed Moon and benefic contacts with the lights come to the rescue. An unhappy early environment and sometimes exploitation are both common.

Capricorn tends to do better in the second half of life. Capricorn is very much associated with farming and rural life. Even a Venus-Jupiter conjunction in Capricorn inclines one toward the cultivation of spectacular gardens, parks, conservatories and landscape design. They often seek refuge in the country. As the Moon is in her detriment in Capricorn; only Scorpio is a worse venue for the Moon. The mother is often cold, remote or unfortunate in her affairs with this placement; indeed, the entire family is often a disagreeable experience for the person with the Moon placed here, or there may be no family at all as with orphans. As Jupiter is in its fall in Capricorn, this constellation is the least profitable locus in the zodiac unless other factors come to the aid of Jupiter. Mars's exaltation in Capricorn gives that planet what it needs to be most effective: bounds, limits and restriction. Just as a bullet in a gun can be discharged in only one direction: through the barrel; likewise, Mars is most effective when limits are imposed upon it so that all its otherwise wild and undifferentiated energy can be concentrated in one direction. Exceptional athletic and martial arts ability often attends this Mars placement.

Capricorn is well represented by Joan of Arc (Sun, Venus and Uranus), Wolfgang Amadeus Mozart (Sun, Mercury and Saturn), Edgar Allen Poe (Sun and Mercury), Martin Luther King (Sun and Mercury), Ronald Reagan (Sun and Uranus), and former Vice President Richard Cheney (Sun); the first Roman emperor, Augustus, had the Moon in Capricorn. The Sun enters Capricorn on January 14 and 15 depending on leap year and time zone in the current era, although that date will advance by one day in approximately 72 years.

Aquarius ♒

Planets in Aquarius and Aquarius rising confer on its natives a liberal, tolerant, progressive orientation, and fairly often a distinctly bohemian temperament. When this is not so, the influence of Saturn and/or Capricorn is generally to the fore, as when the Sun in Aquarius is square Saturn with the Moon in Capricorn. But without extenuating circumstances, Aquarius is the most egalitarian, humanitarian, and freedom-loving member of the zodiac. It is gender neutral like Mercury's constellations Gemini and Virgo. In the current era, it has the most cachet of all the signs although that has not always been so. Uranus rules Aquarius. It is cool, detached, innovative, future-oriented and doesn't run with the herd. Aquarius is the detriment of the Sun, which tends to diminish the stature of the father of the native (even to the extent of calling into question the legitimacy of the patrimony) who may be erratic, irresponsible, weak, a ne'er-do-well, or a talented but unconventional person who may cause conservative members of the family to squirm.

Neptune was in Aquarius during the exaltation year 786-785 BC and even though Neptune is not visible to the naked eye, and therefore cannot have heliacal phenomena, most siderealists feel that Neptune's exaltation in Aquarius is even more fitting than Uranus in Sagittarius. Aquarius gives Neptune what it needs: structure without confinement. Neptune is an amorphous, nebulous, direction-less quality that is extraordinarily receptive but deficient with regard to proper external expression. Aquarius as a fixed constellation imparts a sense of stability to Neptune without impairing its function. Fine examples of Neptune exalted in Aquarius are Johan Sebastian Bach and Alexander Graham Bell. Aquarius is related to a counter-culture orientation: new ways of doing things that break with tradition in order to ensure justice and fair play. It is without prejudice, sees no social or circumstantial barriers, is the least concerned with appearances and calls itself a man of the people. It is the most deviant in general of all the zodiacal types from politics to sex. Those with the Moon here in particular are inclined to indulge tastes that are still widely viewed as taboo, even if more accepted than in earlier eras. Those with Venus here think nothing about becoming involved with someone of a different race, religion or national origin than their own. They are also likely to have unconventional ideas about personal independence in relationship and, as one might guess, they are generally without jealousy. Wanderlust and the ever-present desire for independence cause Aquarians to make their own rules and to be quite intransigent (like all the fixed constellations) about modifying them, accommodating to others or explaining their rationale. They often make good behind-the-scenes managers, if they cannot be independent agents in their careers, so as to avoid the glare of publicity and the unwanted attention that might circumscribe their freedom of action. The Aquarians are also quite disdainful of the posturing and glamour that Leo craves.

Before the discoveries of Uranus and Neptune, Jupiter and Saturn were given rulership over Sagittarius and Pisces and Capricorn and Aquarius, respectively. There are similarities between Capricorn and Aquarius but the differences are greater still. They are both serious and unsentimental but Aquarius is endowed with a sober idealism while Capricorn is inclined to expect the worst;

Aquarius is the quintessential free spirit while Capricorn feels chained to duty and obligation; Aquarius sees possibilitites heretofore unseen while Capricorn's orientation is toward the past and the stark reality of what cannot be changed.

Superb examples of Aquarius are the two greatest of the U.S. presidents to date, George Washington (Sun) and Abraham Lincoln (Sun, Mercury and Pluto), Nicholas Copernicus (Sun and Mars), Jack Kerouac (Sun, Mercury and Uranus), Elizabeth Taylor (Sun, Mercury and Mars), Goethe (Moon) and Michael Jackson (Moon) show the wide range of this placement. The Sun enters Aquarius on February 13 or 14 depending on leap year and time zone in the current era, although that date will increase by one day in approximately 72 years.

Pisces ♓

Planets in Pisces or Pisces rising confer on its natives a degree of sensitivity so great as to be sometimes unwelcome. People with Pisces rising in particular often, without effort, can accurately feel the particulars of the mood and conditions of strangers who walk past them in the street. They can't turn it off. Neptune rules Pisces which is why this constellation is the most psychic, profoundly idealistic and sensitive—indeed oversensitive—of all the constellations. It is a sweet and gentle constellation as befits Venus' exaltation in this sign. Mercury is in its fall in Pisces. People lucky enough to have Venus in Pisces are usually outstanding as spouses. Pisces is feminine. Men with emphasis in this sign, especially the lights, while they may be undeniably masculine in appearance and general orientation, tend to have the temperament of a woman. Often the Pisces people are more concerned with the welfare of others than themselves, and as a result they are often sorely used and abused by people who see them as an easy mark, or are unappreciative of their generous and considerate ministrations. Victimization, both the attitude that invites it and the actual circumstance of it, are frequently visited upon this placement. Often people with Pisces emphasis will create their own little drama in this regard due to their decided tendency toward self-delusion and unconscious manipulation—both the result of the planet Neptune. The propensity to experience problems with drugs, alcohol, gambling and other vices of excess, as well as the scandals that attend them, is very common with Pisces. It is the best constellation for one who aspires to a career in entertainment and the dramatic arts (and all its related fields from set design to make-up) because these people can effortlessly put themselves into someone else's shoes. They tend to drift away from themselves and the present automatically, to the extent that they may feel uncomfortable when they cannot get into character or are forced to stay on point in the present. The unfortunate consequence of that tendency is that they tend not to see themselves clearly. The muses of music and dance, Euterpe and Terpsichore respectively, are at home in this constellation. The worlds of spirituality, religious fervor, the occult, fantasy and glamour are the arena of Pisces; but also instability, neurosis and various manifestations of confusion.

It follows then that Mercury is in its fall in Pisces since facts and the practical manipulation of data are the antipathy of the nebulous world of this constellation. Typically those with Mercury in Pisces have difficulty in the classroom, especially in mathematics. Their academic advance is usually slow or unremarkable and school is merely endured. Learning disabilities, reading and pronunciation problems and a general lack of mental dexterity plague these people unless Saturn and Mars come to the aid of this debilitated Mercury. Mercury in Pisces is not symbolic of stupidity but rather of one who is hard-wired differently than the rest of us. Albert Einstein had Mercury in its fall in Pisces closely conjoined to Saturn also in Pisces, and both very closely mundane square Mars exalted in Capricorn (see chapter six for mundo squares). That planet combination, Saturn-Mercury-Mars, is typical of those with prodigious mental power. Mercury conjoined to Saturn in Pisces was symbolic of one who could find the order in abstraction, made extreme by the mundo square (Mercury and Saturn culminated as Mars set) to Mars, which powered him deeper into the nature of reality than most people can understand. But he didn't speak a word until the age of three and didn't stand out to an extraordinary degree at school until the age of eleven. As an adult he was critical of learning by rote and felt that broad principles in education were sacrificed to lesser rules. Pisces, like Sagittarius, sees the big picture, but since the Piscean apprehends it generally by intuitive means, which leap-frog over logic, the world that worships logic often disparages what Pisces has to offer, except in the arts. This writer knows of a magazine editor with Mercury in Pisces. She has the standard deficiencies of Mercury in Pisces but is an excellent editor due to Jupiter exactly semi-square the debilitated Mercury. One of the arenas of Jupiter is publishing. Without such extenuating circumstances, Mercury in Pisces can be a serious limitation in a technical and literary world. In the main, Pisces is a kind, generous, deeply intuitive and sympathetic placement, but it is also sneaky and inclined constantly to disassociate (which often manifests merely as day-dreaming).

Good examples of Pisces are Johann Sebastian Bach (Sun), Edgar Cayce (Sun), Albert Einstein (Sun, Mercury and Saturn), Tennessee Williams (Sun and Mercury), Billie Holiday (Sun and Mercury) and Robert Downey Jr. (Sun, Mercury and Venus). The Sun enters Pisces on March 15 or 16 depending on leap year and time zone in the current era, although that date will advance by one day in approximately 72 years.

Chapter Four

The Houses

The Babylonians considered the houses to be the sidereal signs themselves but since the advent of the horoscopus or Ascendant, a Greek invention, many ways of dividing up the sky into spheres of astrological influence have come into vogue and out again. The houses are like sections of an orange that divide the celestial sphere into compartments that deal with basic life activities. The planets are the actors but the houses set the scene. The houses are supposed to provide a level of specificity that is a supplement to the planets in the various constellations and their aspects.

The houses in astrology constitute a battleground because of the lack of agreement among professionals over which house system, if indeed any, is best. Western siderealists maintain that all the house systems are over-rated and that the houses are the least important and least consistent astrological index. In stark contrast to this view, most tropical astrologers consider houses and house rulers in the first rank of importance. The sidereal position is to accord the houses secondary importance and to emphasize the very old doctrines of angularity and dispositors.

Dispositors are the rulers of the signs that planets occupy. For example, if the Moon is in Virgo, Mercury disposes the Moon. The angles are the horizon and the meridian. Medieval astrologers, in particular, consistently emphasized the angles and angular houses. The angles, most of all, and the angular houses (sometimes called the foreground) are the main arenas in the horoscope. The angular houses—one, four, seven and ten—have tremendous power. A planet in any of these houses is more important than those remote from the angles. Siderealists also look to the dispositors of the angular houses, especially the Ascendant. A planet near the angles is also very strong if the planet is near the horizon or meridian but not actually in an angular house. For example, if Mercury is just below the horizon in the sixth house, but is still close to the horizon, especially within five degrees, it has more power by virtue of propinquity to the angles than other sixth house planets would have further below the horizon. Likewise a planet near the Midheaven, whether in the ninth or tenth house, has great power both because of its elevation and proximity to the Midheaven.

Often the sixth or twelfth house contains the square to the meridian. If a person has 12° Aquarius in the Midheaven, for example, the squares to that position, 12° Taurus and 12° Scorpio, will often be in the twelfth and sixth houses. Planets that are closely square the upper meridian (cusp of the tenth house) and lower meridian (cusp of the fourth house) are powerful and cannot be relegated to secondary status; likewise, planets that are closely trine or sextile the horizon or meridian have more importance than planets without such a connection. The orbs have to be close—not more than a degree and a half—for obvious effects.

The houses that come after the angular houses are called the succedent houses. These are houses two, five, eight and eleven, of which the fifth is the most fortunate and the eighth the most unfortunate. Planets transiting through succedent houses don't usually pack the same punch as planets that are in or near the angles or in the angular houses. The houses that come after the succedent houses are called the cadent houses. These are houses three, six, nine and twelve, of which the ninth is the most fortunate and the twelfth the most unfortunate. As with the succedent houses, planets in cadent houses are far from the main arena of the horoscope unless they are near the cadent-angular border, where they begin to take on the power of the angles.

Western astrology, both tropical and sidereal, puts south at the top, unlike the standard convention in modern cartography, according to which north is "up." In the temperate latitudes of the Northern Hemisphere the Sun never gets directly overhead. The Sun can be in the zenith—that is, directly overhead—only in the tropics. Ancient Babylon was at latitude 32N33, where the Sun was always to the south of an observer on any date. All of Egypt, from the first cataract on the Nile at Aswan to the Nile delta, is also north of the tropic of Cancer; thus the Sun is always to the south of any Egyptian observer on any date. In order to avoid turning one's back on the Sun, even symbolically, and thereby to dishonor the Egyptian Sun god Ra or the Babylonian Sun god Shamash, the southern meridian was placed at the top of the horoscope. Facing south, east is to one's left and west to the right, which explains the rationale of the orientation of a Western horoscope that places the Ascendant at the 9 o'clock position.

First House

The first house, one of the angular houses and quite powerful, is reckoned from the eastern horizon in a counterclockwise motion down to the cusp of the second house. All of the first house is below the horizon except the initial point of it that coincides with the eastern horizon itself; this is the place just coming into manifestation or view. The first house relates to the self in a broad sense. For example, someone born at sunrise or with the Sun just about to rise will be more egotistical, selfish and ambitious than one with Saturn in the same position. The Saturnian person may be filled with self-doubt, caution and reserve and take a long time to mature emotionally or come into his own with respect to his gifts. Physical characteristics and vitality are often shown by the first house. People with red hair, for example, frequently have Mars in the first house, or someone who is remarkably attractive will have Venus in the first near the Ascendant. If the Sun is sorely afflicted but in the first house, especially close to the Ascendant, one would have the perseverance and fortitude to deal successfully with the requirements of a difficult life.

Seventh House

The position opposite the first house is the seventh. The seventh, one of the angular houses, but not as potent as the first and tenth houses, begins at the Descendant and extends in a southerly direction toward the Midheaven. All of it is above the horizon. Its first point, the line of the western horizon, was called the "duat," the entrance to the underworld, by the ancient Egyptians. The seventh house relates to all the significant others in the life of the native, especially the mate. So in the sense that the first house relates to the self, the opposite house, the seventh, relates to the "not-self"—those people who bear directly upon the self. People with whom one is not intimate nor even acquainted can be seventh house persons, if there is a direct exchange as with the people who flesh out bureaucracies, operate cash registers, look the native in the eye or somehow personally engage him or her. It is easy to see then that the seventh is also the house of enmity. The reasoning behind this notion is that one's enemy is intimately bound up with the native even if it is in strife. As a practical matter the seventh house relates to that part of the public affected by the native, as for example the people who read these words, in relation to this writer.

Second House

The second house is related to the financial condition of the native. Vedic astrologers attribute much more to the second, like food, family, even speech. Broadly speaking, one's resources, assets and especially cash are the province of the second house. The point that the Indians make about the second house is a good one: everything that the native can access as an asset is a second house matter. Westerners see the second house primarily as one's personal Department of the Treasury. The entire second house is below the horizon.

Eighth House

The house opposite the second is the eighth. The old lore is that the eighth house is related to other people's money; that is, the spouse's money and money gained through wills, legacies, insurance and broadly speaking, gains realized through losses. It is also known as the house of death. But since one-twelfth of the population has its Sun here and most of them are surely not associated with things funereal, nor have shortened lives, one must be careful about how to judge planets here. One could indeed be associated with the mortuary business, hunting, slaughterhouses or crime, especially vice, but also geriatric medicine, the floral business or be fascinated by the macabre and lugubrious in poetry and art. Unfortunate circumstances are often associated with the eighth house, but those associations are very much over-emphasized in the experience of this writer. In general, however, it is not a good house for the lights (Sun and Moon). More often this house emphasizes interest in the occult, myth, legend and their depiction, especially via film, as well as the supernatural and experiences that are neither good nor bad but extraordinary and beyond rational explanation. All of the eighth house is above the horizon.

Third House

The third house is primarily connected with siblings, elementary education, neighbors and short journeys. There are other things attributed to it by modern astrologers but these four are the oldest and undisputed. There is also a playful and mischievous quality about the third. People with many planets in it are often connected with children in their work. All of the third house is below the horizon.

Ninth House

The position opposite the third house is the ninth, a distinctly fortunate house that relates to the professions, especially the law, academia, philosophy, publishing and long journeys. Planets in the ninth house are generally enhanced. Both the third and the ninth relate to study and school, but the ninth is didactic, whereas the third relates to receiving instruction. The ninth house is entirely above the horizon. Some of the good things that accrue from placements in the ninth house come simply from its elevation. Planets high in the sky get fuller expression more easily than planets with less altitude above the horizon. Planets below the horizon are muted even more in comparison to planets above it.

Fourth House

The fourth house, an angular and therefore powerful house, is bordered by the meridian and extends from there up toward the Descendant in a southwesterly direction. It has dominion over the mother, houses and buildings, land, farms and broadly, the things that accrue to the native via his heritage and the final resolution or disposition of affairs. When evaluating the condition of the early life, one looks as much to the fourth house as the Moon. The fourth house, even if it is untenanted, gives some insight into the basic orientation of the native; that is, his psychological state in his heart of hearts is shown to some degree by the condition of the fourth house, whether it is unhelpful emotional baggage that has to be jettisoned over a long period, or a good start from a psychologically healthy mother. The entire fourth house is below the horizon.

Tenth House

The tenth house, directly opposite the fourth, is the most powerful of the angular houses and indeed the most powerful placement in the horoscope. It extends from the upper (southern) meridian in a northeasterly direction toward the eastern horizon. It is entirely above the horizon. Planets come to fruition in the tenth house and are altogether unrestrained there for good or ill. The Sun is at its best in the tenth house. The tenth house relates to career, the father and one's status in the public eye. Tenth house positions usually represent things earned and achieved, although occasionally a royal personage will have the Moon here, which represents an exalted position gained through one's family connections.

Fifth House

The fifth house is entirely below the horizon in the western half of the horoscope. It is a distinctly auspicious house that relates to children, especially one's own, amusements, games, various pleasures (major and minor), speculation, sports, gambling the state of being smitten and subsequent romance in distinction to marriage that is the province of the seventh. Clearly, fifth house matters can become seventh house matters, but this sweet place—the fifth—is a flower that has not fully opened, but shows much promise.

Eleventh House

The eleventh house, directly opposite the fifth, is entirely above the horizon in the eastern half of the horoscope. According to the old lore, it is primarily about friends, hopes, desires and opportunities. The affairs of this house generally improve with time. The eleventh occasionally relates to financial matters, but not in the sense of money earned; rather, it is about fortunate connections that benefit the native. The most striking example known to this writer is a secretary who received a $1 million bonus from her immensely wealthy boss. She has Jupiter in the eleventh.

Sixth House

The sixth house is directly below the western horizon. It relates to health, diet and medical issues, servants and people in subordinate positions. Planets are weakened here because celestial bodies in the sixth have just recently passed out of view under the western horizon. The overall state of the horoscope shows whether the native's health is poor, and when many planets occupy the sixth, the native attends to people in need. People in the medical profession from doctors, nurses and social workers, to laboratory and other technicians, frequently have many planets in the sixth. Animals are also the province of the sixth whether they are pets, performers or draught animals like horses, oxen or elephants. The sixth is a house of labor and service to others. The affairs of this house also improve over time.

Twelfth House

The house directly opposite the sixth, the twelfth is the most unfortunate of the houses. It extends from the eastern horizon in a southeasterly direction toward the upper meridian. It is entirely above the horizon. It seems counter-intuitive that the first daylight house should have negative connotations but it is not invariably so. Many people with planets in the twelfth are strongly inclined toward a spiritual orientation or a life of service that benefits others. More often planets in the twelfth are compromised. It is the part of the horoscope that points to incarceration, literal or figurative, defeat or great difficulty at the hands of one's enemies, and problems that are often one's own fault. Like the sixth it has much to do with hospitals but less medical and surgical matters than those that handle mental disorders, alcoholism, sanitoria and long-term recuperation from wounds or disease. Orphanages and other state instituitions are associated with this house. The twelfth relates to things that the native keeps secret or hidden. People with many planets here often deal in clandestine matters as a career. Planets in this house can be compromised; for example, those with Uranus here could have their original work used by others without proper attribution; their original works could also be stolen outright or misrepresented. The twelfth is not a good place for the lights, but for virtuous people committed to running their lives supremely well, even a path that seems like forty miles of bad road can take the native to the pinnacle of success. Mohandas Gandhi had the Sun in the twelfth house.

Chapter Five

The Planetary Aspects

The relationships between the planets are called aspects. Their interpretations go to a deeper level of character than the individual placements of the planets. An aspect is an angle between two bodies that brings them into a relationship (or no angle as in an exact conjunction). Aspects can be applying or separating. In an applying aspect, the faster planet is approaching the slower one. In a separating aspect, the faster planet has already made the exact contact with the slower one and is leaving the part of the zodiac where the aspect holds sway. Applying aspects are stronger than separating ones. The aspects are:

☌ conjunction
∠ semi-square
□ square
⚼ sesquiquadrate
☍ opposition
⚻ quincunx
⚺ semi-sextile
⚹ sextile
△ trine
∥ parallel
∦ contraparallel

Conjunction ☌

Planets in the same part of the zodiac in the same or nearby degrees are in conjunction. That is, the Moon at 12° Cancer and Jupiter at 15° Cancer are only three degrees from the same place on the ecliptic. Their natures combine. Conjunctions and oppositions are the strongest contacts between planets. They are strongest when they are within five degrees of the exact contact. Note that planets conjunct in the same constellation share the same element and the same quality.

Opposition ☍

Planets 180 degrees apart in opposite constellations are in an opposition aspect. If the Sun is at 19° Aries and Saturn is at 19° Libra, the two bodies form an exact opposition. Their natures combine. It is not necessary, however, for the planets in opposition to be in opposite constellations. For example, Mercury at 28° Gemini and Mars at 2° Capricorn are only four degrees from exact. The closer they are to an exact relationship, the more powerful the blend. Oppositions within five degrees of the exact contact are strongest. Planets involved in an opposition share the same quality unless the aspect is an out-of-sign opposition, just described.

Square □

Planets 90 degrees from each other are in zodiacal square, e.g., Mercury at 5° Virgo and Mars at 5° Sagittarius. If one of them rises at the same moment that another one culminates in the Midheaven, or nearly so, regardless of the number of degrees between them, they are in mundane square. Both types of squares are powerful relationships. Squares are especially strong when they are within five degrees of the exact contact. Note that planets in square aspect, unless the aspect is an out-of-sign square, share the same quality.

Trine △

Planets 120 degrees from each other are in trine, e.g., Venus at 17° Cancer and Pluto at 17° Scorpio, a potent but less powerful relationship than the conjunction, opposition and square. Trines are weak beyond five degrees from the exact contact. Note that planets in trine aspect, unless the trine is out of sign, share the same element.

Sextile ⚹

Planets 60 degrees from each other are in a sextile relationship, e.g., Mars at 3° Capricorn and Neptune at 3° Pisces. They are weaker than trines and lose effectiveness beyond an orb of three degrees. Note that planets in sextile aspect share neither quality nor element.

Sesquiquadrate ⚼

Planets 135 degrees from each other are in a sesquiquadrate relationship, e.g., Saturn at 7° Gemini and Mercury at 22° Libra. It is a square (90 degrees) and half a square (45 degrees) combined. Sesquiquadrates are very strong when they are within a degree and a half of the exact contact. Planets in sesquiquadrate aspect may share the same element, but not necessarily; e.g., the Sun at 19 Virgo and Uranus at 4 Aquarius share neither quality nor element.

Semi-square ∠

Planets 45 degrees from each other are in a semi-square relationship, e.g., the Sun at 5° Leo and Uranus at 20° Virgo. Semi-squares are very strong within a degree and a half of the exact contact. Semi-squares share neither quality nor element.

Semi-sextile ⊻

Planets in a 30 degree relationship are semi-sextile, e.g., Venus in 28° Taurus and Jupiter at 28° Gemini. This aspect is not particularly strong unless it is within one degree of the exact contact. Semi-sextiles share neither quality nor element.

Quincunx ⊼

Planets that are 150 degrees from each other are in a quincunx relationship, sometimes called an inconjunct, e.g., Mars at 4° Cancer and Venus at 4° Sagittarius, which is not particularly strong unless it is within one degree of the exact contact. Planets in a quincunx relationship share neither quality nor element.

Parallel and contra-parallel ∥ ∦

Planets are in a strong parallel relationship when their declinations are within one degree on the same side of the celestial equator. Planets are in a strong contra-parallel relationship when their declinations are equidistant within one degree on opposite sides of the celestial equator. Parallels and contra-parallels can exist between any planets regardless of their quality or element.

***

It is important to distinguish between some elements of western sidereal (Babylonian) and eastern sidereal (Indian) practices with regard to aspects because they are not the same and many people think that anything sidereal is bound to be equivalent from one system to the next. The Vedic school of sidereal astrology considers fewer aspects than those described above but allows enormous orbs of influence. Indian astrologers consider aspects from sign to sign. That is, any planet in Aries, say in 4° Aries, is, according to the Indian system, in an opposition aspect to any other planet in Libra, say 29° Libra, even though they would be 25 degrees removed from the exact opposition. A western siderealist would say two bodies so placed are in no relationship whatsoever. Conversely, constellation borders in Indian astrology can negate relationships western siderealists consider important. For example, an Indian astrologer would say that a planet in 29° Aries has no relationship with a planet in 0° Taurus because the constellation cusp forms a barrier to their integration into relationship. A western siderealist would see two planets separated by only a degree and call that circumstance a powerful conjunction pregnant with meaning.

The aspects themselves impart a quality to the planet combinations they comprise, but those qualities are much less important than the intrinsic natures of the planets in the relationships. Oppositions and squares in particular are regarded by some to be difficult, and sextiles and trines beneficial in themselves regardless of the planets involved; but as past masters like Charles Carter have rightly pointed out, it is hard to make something so negative out of Sun square Jupiter or so good out of Sun trine Saturn that the malefic nature of Saturn or the benefic nature of Jupiter are negated. The siderealists acknowledge only to a modest degree the so-called natures of the aspects per se. So many eminently successful and happy people have charts replete with what some schools consider severe afflictions, due to the number of squares and oppositions in their charts, that most siderealists consider the good versus bad aspect debate to be very much over-emphasized. An exception can be made for the Moon which does appear to handle most squares and oppositions badly. Mercury and Venus are likewise occasionally somewhat adversely affected by oppositions and squares depending especially on the dignities and debilities of the planets that make the aspects, but in general the sidereal school does not get caught up in the issue of aspect quality. Most practicing astrologers discover that, as a practical matter, the approach of Jupiter brings good fortune no matter the type of relationship; and likewise the approach of Saturn brings trouble no matter how that planet configures another. The aspects relate more to the reach of a body. Conjunctions, squares, oppositions and trines can be felt from farther away from partile than the other types of aspects.

Chapter Six

The Equatorial System and the Stars

The equatorial system is a grid system oriented to the Earth's pole and equator extended off the planet into space. The plane of the Earth's equator extended off the planet is called the celestial equator—hence the term, equatorial system. The terrestrial pole extended off the planet is called the celestial pole. The equatorial system is reckoned in two coordinates: right ascension and declination. They are directly analogous to terrestrial longitude and latitude, respectively. Right ascension corresponds to meridians of longitude extended off the planet and given a new name: hour circles of right ascension. Parallels of declination are analogous to parallels of terrestrial latitude extended off the planet. The unit of measure of right ascension is sidereal time that is measured eastward along the celestial equator from the vernal equinox; sometimes right ascension is measured in degrees of arc. Sidereal time is much preferred for astrological use. The horizontal axis of this system along the celestial equator is termed its *x* axis. The vertical axis along the celestial pole is termed its *y* axis.

The equatorial system is obviously a tropical system since right ascension is measured from the vernal equinox, but the equatorial system is not connected to the zodiac, and siderealists make no attempt to render right ascension into a sidereal format. It is essential, however, to update equatorial positions from one era to another as equatorial positions constantly change. The equatorial positions of the stars prominent in the horoscope of Martin Luther, for example, who was born in 1483, are radically different than their current positions rendered in equatorial coordinates (or tropical longitude). In the absence of almanacs with equatorial values for the era in question, the equatorial positions of bodies have to be calculated for eras prior to the present day, which is beyond the scope of this book but will appear in future works that follow this introductory book.

The other main reference system used in astrology is called the ecliptic system. Like the equatorial system, the ecliptic system is a grid system but oriented to the ecliptic plane and the ecliptic pole. The ecliptic is a plane that runs through the center of the Earth and the center of the Sun. The Earth orbits the Sun in that plane. The ecliptic pole is perpendicular to the ecliptic. The ecliptic system is reckoned in two coordinates: celestial longitude and celestial latitude. The positions of bodies along the ecliptic are measured in celestial longitude. The units of measure of celestial longitude are degrees of arc. Astrologers are familiar with the ecliptic system because the degrees of the zodiac are reckoned in the ecliptic system. The horizontal or ecliptic plane is termed the x axis of this reference system. Celestial latitude is also measured in degrees of arc perpendicular to the ecliptic plane above and below it. The vertical plane is termed the y axis of this reference system.

The angle between the ecliptic and the celestial equator is called the obliquity of the ecliptic. Obliquity means that the relationship between the two planes is neither parallel nor perpendicular but rather an acute (less than 90 degrees) or obtuse (greater than 90 degrees) angle. That angle slowly varies by almost three degrees over a period of 41,000 years. The current angle between the ecliptic and the celestial equator is an acute angle of approximately 23.5 degrees. Figure 2 illustrates the grids of the ecliptic and equatorial systems.

A place on a flat or curved surface like a map whether a map of a country or the sky, cannot be located without two coordinates, one horizontal and one vertical. If someone says that they live on the meridian through 122 west longitude, while that is helpful, one can't know without more information whether they live in San Francisco, California or Seattle, Washington, which are both on 122 West but separated by700 miles—or some other point on the 122 West meridian in Oregon or British Columbia. Neither terrestrial nor celestial longitude alone is sufficient to locate a point on a map oriented to the ground or the sky because both only address the *x* axis.

A weakness of standard horoscope layouts is that they show only the x coordinate. which tends to leave the astrologer with the impression that the y coordinate is not important, especially since the orbits of the planets, except for Pluto, are confined to the zodiac, which is a belt that runs eight to nine degrees on either side of the ecliptic. Similarly, astrologers speak glibly about declination, the y coordinate of the equatorial system but they rarely engage the x axis which is right ascension.

One must understand when speaking of stars that unless the stars are directly on the ecliptic or very close to it, their celestial longitudes alone will not make the planet relationships with natal planets that are supposed from a comparison of longitude positions of stars and planets. Even for stars on the ecliptic the discrepancy between an actual position versus an assumed position may be further compounded by the planets themselves that may be many degrees of celestial latitude removed in the y axis from their assumed positions on the x axis taken alone. This is easily illustrated by an examination of the night sky that shows conjunctions on a regular basis between the Moon and the visible planets and stars. Many of them don't look like conjunctions to the eye because the bod-

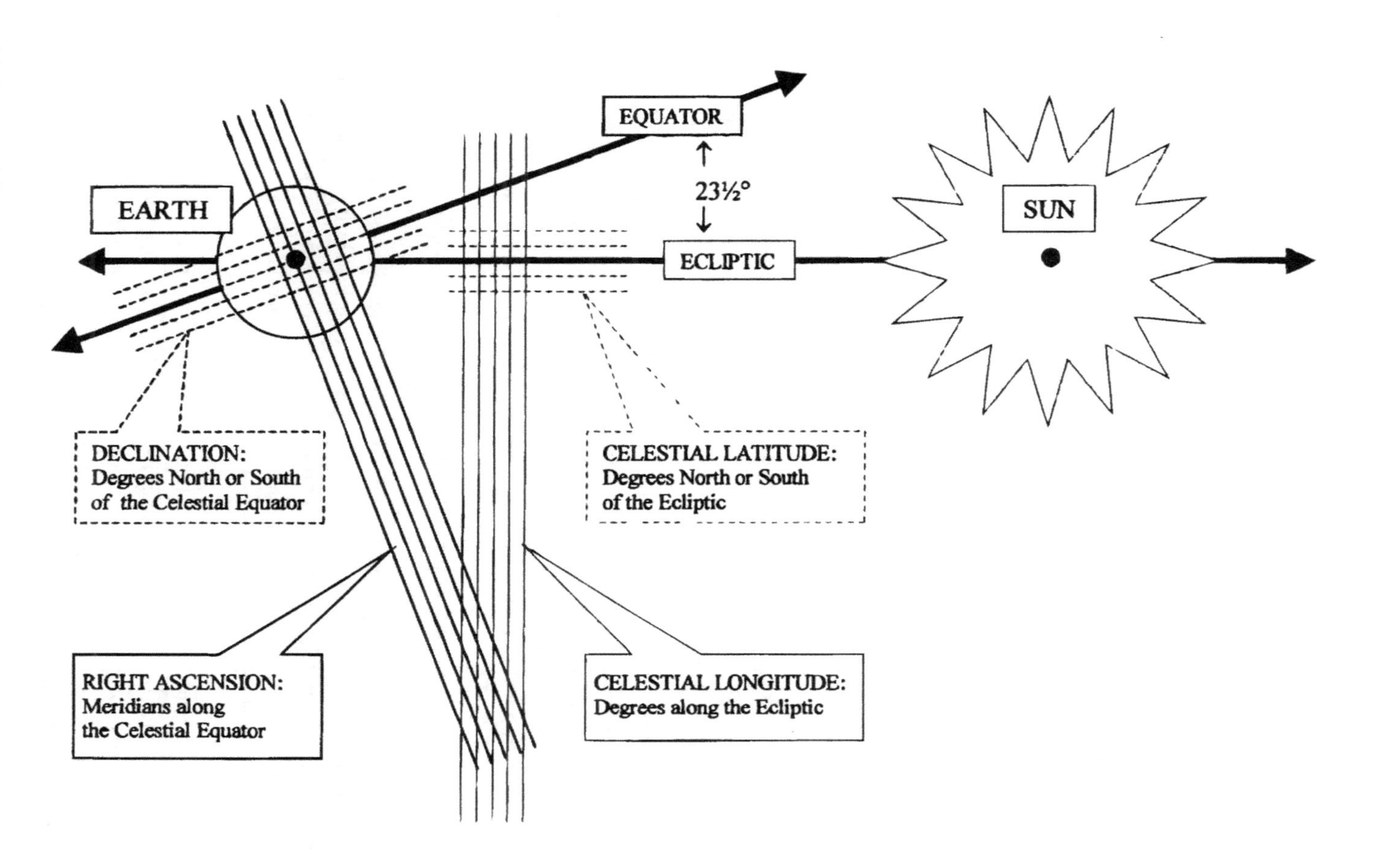
SOLAR SYSTEM GEOMETRY
EQUATOR
23½°
EARTH
SUN
ECLIPTIC
DECLINATION:
Degrees North or South
of the Celestial Equator
CELESTIAL LATITUDE:
Degrees North or South
of the Ecliptic
RIGHT ASCENSION:
Meridians along
the Celestial Equator
CELESTIAL LONGITUDE:
Degrees along the Ecliptic

ies are conjoined in only one coordinate, usually celestial longitude. For astrological purposes one cannot be so cavalier with stars. They must be conjoined in two coordinates for bodies to appear to occupy the same place.

In a similar manner the apparent positions of stars cannot be known without two coordinates. Only their actual (apparent) positions are meaningful. Since stars range all over the sky well beyond the ecliptic, their positions are commonly reckoned in terms of the equatorial system rather than the ecliptic system. Since most stars are not on the ecliptic, a star in a house via any house system is misleading at best and meaningless at worst. Stars that appear on the horizon or meridian at or near the birth or that culminate, rise or set with the lights and natal planets are noteworthy. Their apparent positions are the only criteria for judging their effect. That means that it is possible, indeed common, for a star that appears to be above the horizon when its celestial longitude is considered alone to be actually, literally, below the horizon when its celestial latitude is examined as well. Since the celestial sphere (a concentric half-sphere of the sky visible to an observer) is described in coordinates that are reckoned from the Earth, not the ecliptic, horizon and meridian phenomena are described in terms of the equatorial system, which does not bring the zodiac into play in the slightest. A tropicalist and a siderealist describing the horizon and meridian phenomena of planets and stars would use identical numbers and arrive at identical conclusions. Horizon and meridian phenomena are the times when bodies rise, culminate, set. and anti-culminate through the lower meridian beneath one's feet.

The equatorial system is actually no stranger to astrologers. The first problem in astrology is to determine the local sidereal time of the horoscope also called the right ascension of the Midheaven. That point is often abbreviated to R.A.M.C. from Right Ascension [of the] Medium Coeli from Latin, which means the right ascension [of the] middle [of the] sky. It is also called "the throne of heaven," or simply the meridian, upper meridian or cusp of the tenth house. Once the local sidereal time or R.A.M.C. of a time and place has been determined, the Ascendant and Midheaven values in the ecliptic system that are associated with that sidereal time are calculated from tables, but more commonly in this era, from a computer program. If a star rises, culminates or sets with a sidereal time within a few minutes of the natal sidereal time, it is angular, that is, the star is prominent at the cusp of an angle house: one, four, seven or ten. Proximity to the angles is what makes the effect of a star strong. A star or planet doesn't have to be visible to be potent but must be close to the horizon soon to rise, just having risen, soon to set, just having set or just about to culminate or just having recently culminated.

House attribution is not assigned to stars that are technically in the first house just about to rise or in the twelfth house just having risen. Likewise, a planet that has just passed from view and entered the "underworld" does not get a sixth house flavor. Nor does a planet close to the western horizon get a seventh house influence. The houses are over-emphasized in every branch of astrology at the expense of the planets and the stars whose meanings are not secondary to the supposed effect of a house.

It is important to note that a transiting planet does not culminate in a horoscope until its own right ascension (hereafter R.A.), not its longitude, is in the Midheaven. Only the Sun, because it is always on the ecliptic, is where it appears to be from its celestial longitude alone. In the same manner, a star or planet is not in the midheaven when its celestial longitude is the same as the longitude of the midheaven unless its celestial latitude is zero. Otherwise one leaves the world of the actual and starts to impart value to what is in effect over-simplified due to reliance on one coordinate when two are required to locate points in space or on the ground. If an important star rises, culminates or sets at or nearly the same time that an important body, especially the lights, simultaneously appear in the angles, that is an important event even if the bodies in question were not angular at birth.

The R.A. and declination (dec.) of a star can be determined from its celestial longitude, latitude and the obliquity of the ecliptic. The method and many others will be demonstrated in forthcoming works. For the past 300 years astronomical ephemerides published by governments have been available that provide star positions in an equatorial format, although seventeenth, eighteenth and some nineteenth century ephemerides are not widely available. Fortunately, modern general-purpose computer programs can supply the information which is often more accurate than what was printed several centuries ago.

For English speakers who want to avail themselves of the thorough information in a national ephemeris, the (British) *Nautical Almanac and Astronomical Ephemeris* has been published annually since 1767 and *The American Ephemeris and Nautical Almanac* has been published annually since 1855. They combined for the edition beginning in 1981 under a common title, *The Astronomical Almanac*. The texts of the British and American versions are now identical except for the title pages. These almanacs are generally available in big city libraries and university libraries. Current editions are available from the U. S. Government Printing Office. The astronomical information in a national ephemeris is extensive but a publication devoted to exclusively stellar information that is the most complete publication of its type in tabular form is titled *Apparent Places of Fundamental Stars*. This publication first appeared in 1941 and was printed annually as a reference book with updated star positions through the edition for 1999. Generally, this book can only be found at university libraries. The star data from 2000 onward are available online. The only astrological ephemeris currently available in book form that contains both R.A. and dec is *The American Sidereal Ephemeris*.

The Speculum

A star culminates in the Midheaven when its R.A. is the same as the R.A.M.C. whether the subject is a person or an entity like a business. A planet anti-culminates or appears in the Imum Coeli, that is, the "lower sky" or "lower heaven," from the Latin, twelve hours after it culminates in the Midheaven (M.C.). *The Imum Coeli* is more commonly called by its abbreviated, form, I.C. It refers to the cusp of the fourth house or lower meridian.

This book, because it is introductory, has little math in it, but the practical use of the equatorial system is shown here; it applies equally to planets and stars. What is wanted are the sidereal times when planets or stars rise in the East, culminate in the M.C., set in the West and anti-culminate through the I.C. Everything is referenced to the M.C. That means that a planet or star is said to rise or set when a particular sidereal time is culminating in the M.C. A planet rises when a particular sidereal time is in the M.C.; a star or planet culminates when its RA is in the M.C.; it sets when another sidereal time is in the M.C. and it appears in the I.C. with a sidereal time that is twelve hours greater than its R.A. The sidereal times that transit the M.C. when planets rise and set are particular to the terrestrial latitude of the place in question only. The rising and setting times of a body are functions of its declination and the terrestrial latitude of a place; thus a body will rise and set at different terrestrial latitudes with different sidereal times.

A quick note on sidereal time is necessary here. Sidereal time is not the same as civil time; sidereal time is a faster rate that is directly related to the rotation of the Earth. The Earth rotates on its axis in 23h 56m 04.09054s of mean solar time which is the legal time kept by the clocks of commerce, public places and your watch. Twenty-four hours of mean solar time is equal to 24h 03m 56.55536s of mean sidereal time. Sidereal time is reckoned from the moment of the Northern Hemisphere vernal equinox every year, usually on March 21, since the Gregorian Reform of the Julian calendar in 1582. At the moment in the Northern Hemisphere spring that the Sun's declination is zero, (on March 21 in most years) the value of sidereal time is 00h 00m 00s. Every day thereafter at local mean midnight the local mean sidereal time is 3 minutes and 56.5 seconds in advance of the previous midnight.

It is important to understand the quantities being manipulated by calculator or computer program; otherwise the astrologer is reduced to a button pusher who may not really know what he or she is doing; but for those who are not interested in knowing the mechanics of their art, they must at least be able to deal with R.A. and dec. in the form that a program will render it. A good general-purpose astrological program like Janus will print a traditional layout called a speculum in hours minutes and seconds of sidereal time in four columns marked, Rise, M.C. Set and I.C. The speculum for Albert Einstein is used here as an example. The data in this table (shown at right) are calculated for March 14, 1879 at 11:30 am LMT at Ulm, Germany (10E00, 48N24).

The Mercury row in the M.C. column shows that Mercury appeared in the M.C. when the sidereal time was 0h 12m 09s. The Mars row in the Set column shows that Mars set when the sidereal time of 0h 10m 26s was passing through the M.C. The difference is only 1 minute and 43 seconds of sidereal time, which is within a small fraction of a second of the same amount of civil time. They are therefore in a mundane square which cannot be seen directly from their respective zodiac positions, yet Mercury and Mars were positioned such that they were simultaneously angular when the horizon and meridian swept through those planets. Mundane squares, oppositions and conjunctions are not potential aspects but actual aspects since they operate whether they are actually in the angles

Body	Rise	M.C.	Set	I.C.
☉	17h 47m 48s	23h 36m 10s	05h 24m 32s	11h 36m 10s
☽	13h 06m 34s	16h 50m 52s	20h 35m 11s	04h 50m 52s
☿	18h 08m 08s	00h 12m 09s	06h 16m 11s	12h 12m 09s
♀	18h 36m 19s	01h 03m 41s	07h 31m 03s	13h 03m 41s
♂	15h 42m 40s	19h 56m 33s	00h 10m 26s	07h 56m 33s
♃	17h 00m 27s	21h 59m 48s	02h 59m 09s	09h 59m 48s
♄	18h 20m 13s	00h 18m 48s	06h 17m 24s	12h 18m 48s
♅	03h 20m 09s	10h 14m 27s	17h 08m 44s	22h 14m 27s
♆	19h 26m 30s	02h 24m 20s	09h 22m 09s	14h 24m 20s
♇	21h 17m 06s	03h 42m 43s	10h 08m 20s	15h 42m 43s

at the time of birth or become so later in the day. Stars are placed into an expanded speculum by hand when their R.A. and dec. values are taken from a reference work or caluclated by converting their celestial latitude and longitude into R.A. and dec. Relationships they make with planets then come to light that are real since bodies are described in terms of three-dimensional reality via the x and y coordinates of R.A. and dec. plus the component of time/date. Bodies that are within two degrees of arc, which is eight minutes of sidereal time of simultaneous angularity are tremendously powerful because they are local. Only people born within a degree or two of the forty-eighth parallel of latitude on the day Einstein was born had the close or exact Mercury-Mars mundo square. Whereas everybody on the planet born on March 14, 1879 had Jupiter opposite Uranus.

A quick summation of the speculum should dispel any uncertainty about how to use it. First, assume that the moment of birth is frozen in time. Einstein's Sun in the Rise column would have appeared on the Ascendant at his birthplace, if the Sun had been rising when he was born, when 17h 47m 48s of sidereal time was in the M.C. Actually the Sun rose on March 14, 1879 at Ulm with a sidereal time twenty-four seconds of sidereal time earlier than the value given here in the Rise column, but a speculum shows the relationships that obtain for the birth moment and no other. Again assuming a static condition, the Sun would have appeared in the meridian when the M.C. held 23h 36m 10s of sidereal time. Note that Einstein was born a half-hour before local mean noon. He was actually born thirty-nine minutes before true (apparent) noon, but a clock set to mean time severs the relationship between the Sun and true noon. In thirty-nine minutes of civil time the Sun traverses approximately six seconds of sidereal time but the value of the R.A. of the apparent Sun at noon is not what is wanted. The value of the R.A. of the apparent Sun at the time of birth is what is particular to the individual. In the same manner, if Einstein had been born at sunset, 5h 42m 32s of sidereal time would have appeared in the "Set" column if his 11:30 birth were transposed to the western horizon. Finally, at the I.C. column the Sun would appear at the cusp of the fourth house at the lower meridian when 11h 36m 10s appeared in the upper meridian. The value of the I.C. is twelve hours greater than the M.C. The point of reference of a speculum is the Midheaven in every case.

Unfortunately, computer programs give the positions of stars in terms of their celestial longitudes which is not helpful when the astrologer recognizes that a position in only one coordinate has very limited utility. An exception has to be made to the non-technical nature of this book that entails a formula, to demonstrate how to know when a star will rise and set. Obviously a star will culminate in the M.C. only when its R.A is the same as the R.A.M.C. of a horoscope, regardless of what its celestial longitude value happens to be. Celestial longitude is irrelevant when angles that have been determined in R.A. are at issue with both the meridian and especially the horizon. The factors that determine when a body—a planet or a star—rises or sets are its declination and the terrestrial latitude of a place. To find the sidereal time with which a star rises and sets the astrologer must find the ascensional difference (a/d) of the body. The a/d is the difference between oblique ascension and right ascension. Bodies only ascend rightly (at a right angle to the horizon) at the equinoxes when day and night or equal. At all other times they rise obliquely, that is, at some angle other than a right angle to the horizon. The modest formula to find the a/d that every astrologer should know is:

$$\text{Arc Sin a/d} = (\text{tan lat.})\ (\text{tan dec.})$$

Where lat. is terrestrial latitude and dec. is declination.

When the a/d is found it is added to 90 degrees if the declination of the body is north or subtracted from 90 degrees if the declination of the body is south. This rule is reversed for the Southern Hemisphere.

The a/d added or subtracted from 90 is then divided by 15, because 15 degrees of arc equals one hour of time, and the decimal portion of that operation is put into hours, minutes and seconds format. This is the diurnal semi-arc of the body that represents one half of the arc in sidereal time that the body is above the horizon at the latitude in question. To determine with what sidereal time (in the Midheaven) the body will rise, subtract the diurnal semi-arc from the R.A. of the body. To determine with what sidereal time (in the Midheaven) the body will set, add the diurnal semi-arc to the R.A. of the body.

With the natal speculum at hand, another powerful tool becomes available to the astrologer: primary directions. A preliminary example with Einstein's speculum shows the effect. The RAMC of Einstein's natal chart is 22h 56m 44s. His natal Sun has RA 23h 36m 10s. The arc between them is 0h 39m 26s.

23h 36m 10s RA Sun

-22h 56m 44s: RAMC

00h 39m 26s: arc of direction

Put 39m 26s into decimal form and divide by four because four minutes of sidereal time equals one degree of arc. A degree is taken as analogous to a year, thus,

$$\frac{39.43333}{4} = 9.85 \text{ degrees, i.e. near age ten}$$

For an 11:30 am birth at Ulm on March 14, 1879, the Sun matures by primary direction early in 1889. Primaries are strong for about six months. It is around age ten that Einstein began to accelerate intellectually and to show his promise. Very few adolescents are competent in the differential and integral calculus as he was by the age of fifteen. The Sun relates to illumination, awakening, consciousness, expansion and power. While he may not have been able to articulate it at age ten, that is when he would have begun to get a sense of his identity specifically, not merely as a function of his age.

One might be tempted to think as result of this little exercise that all one has to do is to count the degrees between the horizon and the meridian and a planet or star to know the dates when primary directions will mature. That is a grave error because the positions of bodies with respect to the horizon and meridian are mere approximations except in the equatorial system unless those bodies are precisely conjoined to the ecliptic. Many of those approximations will be wildly wrong and worse than worthless: they will be misleading if the astrologer falls into a classic apples and oranges trap by ignoring the units of the ecliptic system and the equatorial system. Dollars can't be added to euros or vice versa. One has to be converted to the other. In the same way, celestial longitude cannot be added to right ascension values. The rationale and use of primary directions, which are precise and not approximations, are explained in detail in the book that follows this work.

Chapter Seven

The Forty-five Planet Combinations

Sun-Moon

The Sun and Moon, known as the lights, are the most important bodies in a horoscope. When they are configured together, the self-esteem and strength of will of the native are enhanced. Such people are dynamic, self-involved, and anxious for attention; thus their talents are more likely to be on display than those without a Sun-Moon aspect. This is especially true of the opposition. Typical examples of the opposition are real estate financier Donald Trump (one degree); the best male voice since Caruso, Luciano Pavarotti (two degrees); vibrant singer Tina Turner (three degrees); and the late Senator Edward Kennedy (four degrees). The parents are also signified by the condition of the lights. With the opposition the parents are likely to be either profoundly mismatched or their relationship more strained than most. The native is more likely to experience higher highs and lower lows than others without this contact because these two most important bodies will experience transiting bodies simultaneously or nearly so.

The Sun-Moon combinations are active, ambitious and successful, although the New Moon, i.e. the conjunction, is least desirable unless it is strongly configured with a third body, preferably Mercury, Venus, Jupiter or Uranus. In the ancient world the day of the actual syzygy, the conjunction of the Sun and Moon, was considered the least promising day of the month because the night was completely dark; i.e., the Moon was not visible. Sometimes New Moon people don't achieve much in their lifetimes but the effect of their work tells later—for example, Karl Marx (born May 5, 1818 with a two-degree conjunction), whose socio-economic theory still affects the world. His work didn't get much traction during his lifetime; he was even supported financially through much of his life by his friend and collaborator Freidrich Engels. The lasting effect of the conjunction people is perhaps best shown by the long reign of the English monarch, Victoria I, who came to the throne in 1837 and died in 1901. She had the one and a half degree conjunction and gave her name to an entire era. Probably the premier American actor of the twentieth century, Marlon Brando, with a one-degree conjunction, is a good example of the emotional power in the conjunction, and its self-absorption. Often too much attention is lavished on the native. Conjunction people are usually very sure of themselves whether they know what they're about or not. Adrian Peterson, the great running back for the Minnesota Vikings, is so aware of his exalted status that he takes self-confidence into the stratosphere. He was born on the day of the New Moon. If such people have prodigious gifts, their self-image may appear to have no limit. Peterson has extraordinary athletic ability, symbolized by a very close Mars (dignified in Aries)-Pluto opposition. He won the National Football League Most Valuable Player award in 2012. The most troublesome manifestation of the conjunction is that it is the classic symbolism of narcissism. There is a fine line between being one's own favorite subject—which is true of most people—and someone who cannot see beyond themselves, empathize with or love someone else deeply. The great majority of the conjunction people surely do not cross that line but they may flirt with it; the narcissist crosses the line, especially if the conjunction is below the horizon.

People with these planets in square are often polemical, fighting against something, staking out positions, taking a hard line. Former President George Bush who railed against all things liberal has the square (three degrees); one of his constant critics, comedian Bill Maher, who railed against Bush, Trump and all things conservative, also has the square (three degrees). Carrie Nation, the nineteenth century temperance advocate, appeared at drinking establishments brandishing an axe ready to do battle with patrons and bar owners. She had the square only one and a half degrees from perfect. People with the squares are often brave and sometimes foolhardy. They tend to move against strong prevailing conditions and sometimes overturn them or are overcome by those forces. Eleanor Roosevelt, with the one-degree square, was a powerful voice for human rights and international cooperation, but Heidi Fleiss, with the four-degree square, served time in prison for running a high-end prostitution ring. Her customers were happy but the official public was not. Often people with the square arouse strong emotions and find themselves in the middle of controversy. There is more energy in the opposition and square than the other contacts, which is why the desire nature is especially strong when the two most important bodies come together in relationship. Only Sun-Mars and Moon-Mars are more consumed by desire than Sun-Moon.

The trine is much easier for its natives, especially the career path. Usually the parents of the native, if the combination is unafflicted, are well-matched, remain in relationship and provide a happy, stable home environment. Therefore, like Moon-Jupiter, taken by itself, Sun trine Moon is symbolic of a good start in life. Often it is a family matter: like father, like son or like mother like daughter as in the case of the singer Liza Minelli, daughter of the great singer/actress Judy Garland. The people with the trine are more generally loved or appreciated than the other types of contacts. The great musician Louis Armstrong (two degree trine) became a de facto ambassador of American culture. One of the great beauties of her time, actress Grace Kelly (two degree trine), was adored and envied by millions, and she appeared from the outside to lead a storybook life, especially when she married the Prince of Monaco. It is very characteristic of Sun trine Moon for there to be a conspicuous absence of internal conflict, other things not considered; and while it is not invariably true, the life path is often clear or reveals itself quite readily or naturally. Such people frequently know from an early age what they want to do or will become. Wayne Gretzky, the "Great Gretzky" (three degree trine) became an athletic legend as one of the greatest and most popular hockey players of all time. His circumstances provide a stunning array of qualities that frequently attend Sun-trine-Moon: robust health, extraordinary ability, remarkable popularity, wealth, love, happiness, children and stability.

Sun-Mercury

Mercury's maximum elongation from the Sun is slightly more than twenty-seven degrees at apehelion and slightly less than eighteen degrees at perihelion in Mercury's highly eccentric orbit. Thus the only standard relationships it can form are the conjunction, the parallel and contra-parallel. Orbs become a significant issue with this combination because it is so common. Mercury is always retrograde at the inferior conjunction when it is between the Earth and the Sun. Mercury is always direct when it makes its superior conjunction on the other side of the Sun from the Earth. Consideration of both the ecliptic system and the equatorial system complicates the matter further with regard to what constitutes a contact. A conjunction in right ascension appears to this writer, from experience, to be not less important than a conjunction in celestial longitude. Similarly, a conjunction in declination (a parallel) should render a conjunction in celestial latitude equally effective. The strongest relationships occur when there are simultaneous conjunctions in two coordinates.

First it must be understood that there is nothing unfortunate about Mercury retrograde. Otherwise people like Steve Jobs would have been hamstrung by their retrograde Mercury and Apple Inc., which he co-founded and guided into an immense powerhouse, would not be approaching a market capitalization of one trillion dollars. Likewise, Jeff Bezos, also with Mercury retrograde, among the wealthiest men on the planet, would have been confounded in his efforts throughout life. Instead he was valedictorian of his high school class, a national merit scholar and graduated phi beta kappa from Princeton with a double major in electrical engineering and computer science. The main arenas of Mercury are career and school. Mercury retrograde is misunderstood. It often appears in the horoscopes of people who see deeper and farther than their fellows into the true nature of things. Robert Frost, winner of four Pulitzer prizes and the poet Laureate of the state of Vermont, delivered a poem at the inauguration of President John Kennedy in 1961. Frost had Mercury retrograde. If a man of letters can succeed with Mercury retrograde, how can the fiction be upheld that the condition is a debility? The father of heart transplant surgery, Norman Shunway M.D. (and Ph.D.) had Mercury retrograde. He was the chief of cardio-thoracic surgery at Stanford

University Medical Center for decades. The supposed difficulty surrounding Mercury retrograde is one of the most widely held and utterly worthless notions in astrology when held up to the light of day and examined in large numbers. Since Mercury is much closer to the Earth when it is retrograde, one can make a case that the people who have it are smarter than the Mercury direct group. People with Mercury retrograde both near conjunction with the Sun or in parallel do appear to be a more independent, prolific and sometimes notorious group. The prodigious output of the novelist Barbara Cartland should have been compromised if her Mercury retrograde conjunction had been an impairment. Likewise, Apollo astronaut Buzz Aldrin should have been weeded out of the astronaut program if his Mercury retrograde conjunction with the Sun had reduced his effectiveness. Henry Kissinger would never have been plucked from the Harvard faculty eventually to become Richard Nixon's secretary of state if his head had been screwed on backwards due to his Mercury retrograde conjunction with the Sun. Harvey Milk, the first openly gay person elected to public office in the United States, should have been seen as somehow unfit for office if his Mercury retrograde conjoined to the Sun had hurt him. Michel de Nostradamus would have been dismissed as a fool, a fake and not worthy of lasting fame if his Mercury retrograde conjoined to the Sun were a problem instead of a blessing. Frequently, Mercury retrograde people, especially when the planet is with the Sun, say and do outrageous things or at least not what they're expected and exhorted to do. Princess Diana is a fine example. The independence of Mercury conjoined the Sun is quite marked whether it is retrograde or direct.

Mercury direct conjoined to the Sun is somewhat more conventional. But any contact between Mercury and the personal planets (Sun, Moon, Venus and Mars) makes the native distinctly cerebral, a wordsmith, possessed of oratorical ability and often with the Sun, gives excellent executive ability, like the former British prime minister, Margaret Thatcher, who had the direct conjunction. It is often literary like the great American writer Edgar Allen Poe who had the close direct conjunction less than a degree from exact, but it is occasionally mathematical like the astounding Scottish physicist James Clerk Maxwell, who also had the close direct conjunction. His ground-breaking work proved that electricity, magnetism and light are all manifestations of electromagnetic fields.

Marcian Edward "Ted" Hoff, with the one degree conjunction, was the principal inventor of the "computer-on-a-chip" microprocessor that launched the personal computer industry (and many other applications). Gordon Moore, one of the co-founders of Intel Corporation, called the microprocessor, ". . . one of the most revolutionary products in the history of mankind." J.P. Morgan, the man who put together General Electric in 1892 and U.S. Steel in 1901, and probably the most successful pure financier to come out of the United States, had the Sun conjoined to Mercury one and a third degrees from exact. Theodor Mommsen was among the greatest—perhaps *the* greatest—historians of the nineteenth century. He was awarded the Nobel Prize for literature in 1902. Mommsen had the conjunction less than a degree from exact. Ben Bradlee, the long-time editor of the Washington Post, had the two-degree conjunction. Bradlee's courage in pursuing the Watergate scandal when no other editor in the country would, was instrumental in bringing down Richard

Nixon. Bradlee's independence and integrity underscored the first amendment of the U.S. Constitution that guarantees freedom of the press at a time when the White House tried to hide its crimes under the veil of national security. The success of these individuals tends to put the lie to the notion that combustion (when the Sun is close to another body [see Sun-Venus]) is a serious debilitation, at least regarding Mercury.

The parallel is much the same in effect as the conjunction but when the bodies are north of the equator the effect is enhanced and its natives are luckier. When the conjunction occurs in south declination its beneficial effect is somewhat reduced, although more artists and people in the sample examined for this category who have achieved fame in the sphere of spirituality like Paramahansa Yogananda have the parallel in south declination.

The contra-parallel is a benefit to the people who have the Sun above the celestial equator and Mercury below it by the same amount like the poet Maya Angelou and the author and investigative reporter Bob Woodward, but the reverse can show ability unharnessed or wasted.

Sun-Venus

Venus's maximum elongation from the Sun is slightly more than forty-seven degrees at its aphelion and about forty-five degrees at perihelion because of its most circular orbit of all the planets; the aspects it can form are thus limited to the conjunction, semi-sextile, semi-square, parallel and contra-parallel. Like Mercury, Venus is always retrograde at its inferior conjunction and direct at its superior conjunction, but it should not be supposed that people with Venus retrograde will have trouble figuring out the planet that signifies eros. As a group, however, people with Venus retrograde at conjunction appear in this writer's sample to be more devoted to their work than the happy-go-lucky nature of most Sun-Venus people. For example, businessman Ted Turner, professional athlete Venus Williams, mutual fund golden boy Peter Lynch and theosophist Annie Besant all have retrograde Venus conjoined to the Sun. While they all are or were, good natured, decent people, they are much more known for their extraordinary work ethic than as social butterflies.

Sun-Venus is generally easy to engage, casual, and puts other people at ease because they are socially adept. Television personality Oprah Winfrey, with a direct Sun-Venus conjunction only one minute of arc from exact, could be the poster girl for this combination. It is also charming, sometimes artistic, still more often cute and sweet, but not invariably so if the conjunction configures other bodies contrary in nature. The wealthy socialite Leona Helmsley with a direct Sun-Venus conjunction less than a quarter degree from exact, was known as "the queen of mean," doubtless because Pluto also configured her Sun-Venus conjunction.

Most often Sun-Venus is playful, hedonistic, even self-indulgent. The Sun is overwhelming up close, however, and can damage planets near it, especially the Moon, Mercury and Venus. For this reason, despite their agreeable natures that should make relationships easy, the Sun-Venus people often struggle to make their marriages work or a good relationship is confounded by outrageous and unlikely circumstance.

The elongation of a planet from the Sun is a somewhat critical matter, although over-emphasized by those who claim that a planet close to the Sun is thoroughly compromised; and yet the effects of close conjunctions are noticeable, in particular regarding Venus. The condition of close proximity of a planet with the Sun is called combustion. There are many opinions regarding how close is too close. In the experience of this writer, if a planet can be seen, that is, if it is not lost in the Sun's glare, at sunrise or sunset, it is not combust. The reason for the various opinions about what elongation between the Sun and another body constitutes combustion is that the distance is variable. It depends on the declination of the body (whether north or south and how much), the angle between the ecliptic and the horizon (the time of year), the terrestrial latitude of the place, the seeing conditions of the locale—whether dry or humid—and the brightness of the body, which in the case of Venus varies a lot with her phase.

Venus is more inclined toward the arts than any other planet. When artistic gifts are allied with the energy of the Sun, success may prove unusually long lasting. For example, the great Irish playwright George Bernard Shaw and the superb British poet Percy Bysshe Shelley both had the one-degree direct Sun-Venus conjunction. Relationships with the Sun are basic. They color the character to a noteworthy degree. Kindness of heart, emotional tenderness and a sweet nature are commonly features of close Sun-Venus conjunctions. These qualities cannot be considered some sort of debility, although they do soften the nature and may incline the native toward the pursuit of pleasure or indolence, other things not considered.

But talent in the visual arts favors Venus far removed from the Sun—witness Picasso, Matisse, Manet, Renoir, Degas, Pollock, Raphael and Da Vinci. Often when the Sun and Venus are far apart they are in different constellations. When the Sun-Venus elongation is such that both bodies are in the same sign, Venus is most often not under the Sun's beams among the majority of the greatest figures in the visual arts like Vincent van Gogh. The elongation between his Sun and Venus was 11 degrees 36 minutes. The same situation applies in music. With few exceptions, the greatest composers, musicians and singers have Venus at some considerable remove from the Sun—witness Bach, Beethoven, Brahms, Chopin, Mozart, Schubert, Stravinksy, Gershwin, Toscanini, Johnny Cash, Mick Jagger, John Lennon, Verdi, Pavarotti, Menuhin, Miles Davis and Adele. The style of the work is unaffected by elongation. That is, the leading lights in their fields, both traditionalists for their eras and innovators, usually have Venus remote from the Sun. Even art *historians*, like the great Jacob Burckhardt, whose Venus was 19 degrees east of his Sun, show the affect. Thus, generally, the artists and the connoisseurs of art have Venus away from the Sun, while the gentle sweethearts have Venus close.

Venus is concerned with beauty, love and the more delicate parts of life. Sun-Venus is conspicuously kind, helpful, gentle, merciful and may do much to help one's community like the Indian mystic, Sai Baba, revered by many as a saint who had the direct conjunction less than a degree from exact.

The semi-sextile and semi-square generally produce more success and energy than the conjunction and parallel. Venus is best away from the Sun. Moreover, the semi-sextiles and semi- squares that are east* of the Sun produce bigger success and renown than when Venus is west of the Sun. The Renaissance master Michaelangelo had the semi-sextile less than a degree from exact. William Shakespeare, the greatest man of letters in the English language, also had the semi-sextile within a degree if he were born at any time on April 23, 1564, the day commonly assumed from his christening three days later. Both men had Venus east of the Sun. The semi- square has even more power. These natives typically embrace virtue, righteous causes and liberal politics. The 14th Dalai Lama and the assassinated civil rights leader Martin Luther King Jr. both have a semi-square between the Sun and Venus that is less than a degree from exact. Abraham Lincoln, the great emancipator, had the semi-square one degree out. President Bill Clinton and his vice president, now environmentalist, Al Gore, both have a semi-square between the Sun and Venus less than a quarter of a degree from exact. In each of these cases Venus is east of the Sun. President Jimmy Carter, who was less successful than Bill Clinton, has the semi-square one quarter of a degree out but west of the Sun. Chief Justice Earl Warren with a one degree Sun-Venus semi-square, wrote the 1954 Supreme Court opinion that ruled segregation in public schools unconstitutional.

Sun-Mars

This potent combination is notable for its aggressiveness, athleticism and daring. It is very strongly sexed. Both sexes have boundless energy, generally like to work hard and almost never shrink from conflict. There is an attraction to competition, contentious issues and open conflict, although Sun-Mars is able to sometimes resist being pulled into situations that avail its natives nothing, unlike Moon-Mars, which is virtually compelled to engage an opponent if it feels challenged. There is volition in the Sun but none in the Moon. The exception is when the honor of the Sun-Mars person is at stake. But their temper is spent as quickly as it flashes. Many people are intimidated by a cocked fist, literal or figurative, but Sun-Mars is incensed by such displays and may occasionally fly to arms when others would back down; more often, however, Sun-Mars is more formidable than malevolent. Yet opponents get the point that the native is ready to deliver a blow if pressed. Sun-Mars rarely bluffs and will challenge injustice to the delight of everyone who wishes they could summon the courage to do so. Thus Sun-Mars natives can easily attract allies who are encouraged by their example. The type makes a good soldier who fights in the front ranks, a good leader who leads from the front and someone who can work without allies or the protection of an organization.

---

*A body with greater celestial longitude than another is farther east than the body with a lesser degree. For example, if the Sun is at 0 Aries and Venus is semi-square the Sun at 15 Taurus, Venus is east of the Sun. If Venus were at 15 Aquarius, she would be west of the Sun at 0 Aries.

Many men with this contact live the fantasy life of most males, in that they are considered eminently desirable and take full advantage of it. The women with this combination have the desire nature of a man and exude it like an elixir that alerts all the men within a wider radius than other women can command. The conjunction is most obvious as the reputations of Catherine the Great of Russia and Mae West testify. Elizabeth Taylor, another Sun-Mars conjunction personality, turned heads in her prime, like they were on ball-bearings. Her allure was overwhelming. In addition to being quite demanding in the bedroom, women with Sun-Mars often wear the pants in the family. They may go outside the marriage to satisfy their lust. Sun-Mars girls typically find that boys' adventurous activities are more fun than the activities that engage most girls. Sun-Mars by itself is no indication of sexual orientation, although women with these planets in combination may display more athleticism than women without such contacts. These contacts usually symbolize fecundity; and within the modest radius of the simple life of this writer, male offspring are more common than females among its natives.

These contacts do not necessarily confer a sense of virtue in the native as evidenced by the partile Sun-Mars opposition in the horoscope of Alphonse Capone, the most notorious American gangster to date, who committed his first murder before age 20. It is a mistake, however, to attribute pure negativity to the opposition. The tendency toward living an extremely intense life accompanied by dissipation does appear to follow the opposition however. A good example is singer/actress Judy Garland with the exact opposition.

The direct, impatient, irreverent and sarcastic side of the contact shows clearly with the square in the horoscope of the great boxer Muhammad Ali. The strong Martian tendency toward mischief, and the rough and tumble side of life attended by danger is well displayed by Prince Harry, the younger son of Princess Diana and Charles, Prince of Wales. Prince Harry also has the close square. Willie Mays, a breathtaking talent and one of the greatest baseball players in the history of the game, has Sun square Mars two and a half degrees out. Just as important because of the problems that often attend Sun-Mars, Mays' Sun-Jupiter sextile, only seven minutes of arc from exact, symbolizes that his life has been directed through channels that can only be described as successful via the prodigious physical gifts that relate to Sun-Mars.

People with this contact who are not endowed with exceptional athletic gifts usually feel the need to engage in intense physical labor, even if it is via a form as mild as digging and tending a garden, which entails much more work than most people realize. Hunting is often embraced by these people. Sun-Mars likes to extend itself and may readily get deeply involved in casual pick-up games of basketball that quickly become serious efforts, a vitriolic exchange in debate in the halls of government or in the middle of combat literal or figurative. Sun-Mars gets its hands dirty, its uniform dirty and holds back nothing.

The trine shows best in terms of energy directed toward a just cause that must be forcefully pressed. Thus raw courage, one of the greatest of the virtues, finds ready expression in the symbolism of Sun trine Mars. Until Abraham Lincoln, no American president had shown the courage to engage Southern belligerency over the monstrous evil of slavery. Lincoln, with the two-degree trine, kept the American union from being broken up and rid the country of the scourge of slavery, but the effort cost more than 600,000 American lives during the Civil War. Modern social activist Michael Moore speaks out against the failings of American society and the American political fabric that requires more than a little courage. He does it out of sincere concern for the general welfare, not because he needs a field of action as a troublemaker. While some are irritated by his efforts it may be fairly said that his concern is patriotic. Other Sun trine Mars people like poet-philosopher Johann Wolfgang von Goethe display a burning desire for justice and fair play on a grand scale. Sun-Mars in some manifestations, may be heroic and a champion of the mistreated and dispossessed.

Sun-Jupiter

This is one of the most desirable contacts. It is more conducive to success in the world than in one's personal life, and the success it often brings can be severely compromised if the malefic planets are more powerfully positioned in the horoscope than the Sun-Jupiter combination. Examples thus extend from the Roman emperor Hadrian, who had the six-degree conjunction (with the Moon as well) and ruled at the height of the empire, to French monarch Louis XVI with the one-degree conjunction, who lost his throne and his head on a guillotine to a revolutionary mob.

It is usually liberal, generous, lucky, judicious, academic and occasionally associated with religion. These natives are frequently born to privilege especially, if the Sun and Jupiter are near the horizon or meridian. As a group they are integrous people who usually rise to the top even if they are not well-born. They gravitate toward the professions, government and big business to a noteworthy degree. Even when this is not the case, they are distinctly lucky, other things not considered. Singer/songwriter Bob Dylan, astronaut Gordon Cooper and actress Brooke Shields, successful since childhood, all with the conjunction, show the effect. The great quarterback Brett Favre, who led the Greek Bay Packers to two Superbowls, has the one-degree conjunction. He was the first man to pass 500 touchdowns (at the end of the 2017 season there was only one other quarterback—Peyton Manning—who had thrown 500 touchdowns in the entire history of the game). Very considerable success often attends this combination whether the endeavour of the native is athletic, artistic, business related or purely intellectual.

The huge success of Elvis Presley is a testimony to the power of Jupiter. He was born into poverty, became a truck driver and then exploded into fame on the basis of his singing voice, stage gyrations and general presence. Presley had the sextile less than a degree from exact. He harnessed the attitude of an entire generation and achieved stupendous celebrity, but died young although enormously wealthy yet desperately unhappy. Money can change almost everything, but he certainly showed that it can't buy love or happiness. Presley's good friend, James Brown, "the godfather of soul," was also the originator of funk, and distinctly influential with regard to the development of hip-hop and rap. Brown enjoyed a degree of success and renown in the black community similar to Presley's in the white community. He had the trine one-half degree from exact. At the height of his career, Brown finally woke up the white world to his extraordinary talent. He was born into extreme poverty and raised in a brothel with neither parent present. Despite two stints in prison he was lifted by irrepressible talent and drive into a life characterized by notoriety, popularity and what can only be considered spectacular self-expression, that few people realize. The angular planets in Brown's horoscope are dignified, which is a tremendous testimony to a big life, especially the Sun exalted in Aries at the Midheaven, which speaks to his ambition, the Moon in her own sign, Cancer in the Ascendant, which is testimony to his enormous popularity, and Saturn in his own sign, Capricorn, on the Descendant. That last position was quite remarkable in that he was married four times and mistreated many of the women and other associates in his life but was not called to account for it, nor did his mistreatment of others affect his popularity. The point is that a dignified planet in an angle manifests in the best possible way even when the native is less than virtuous with respect to the affairs of the house in which the dignified planet resides.

Sun square Jupiter is more inclined to embrace extreme positions, sometimes around religious issues. David Koresh, leader of the Branch Dravidian cult, had the square less than a degree from exact. Frank Sinatra, one of the most successful and popular entertainers of all time, had the square less than a degree from exact. He ran with a fast crowd and refused to throttle back his unrestrained life consistent with the square aspect. Bob Fosse, dynamic guru of contemporary dance, also had the square only a half-degree from exact. These types are quite sure of themselves and may believe they are on a mission. Ronald Reagan and George W. Bush, both with close Sun-Jupiter squares, struck many people as heavy-handed and arrogant. Just as many lead the wild, exciting life of a *bon vivant* and are envied by millions, like author Ernest Hemingway, who had the three-degree square. All of them are adventuresome and most suffer losses on foreign ground, which is a vestige of the old doctrine that all things connected by square carry negative energy. There is some modest truth to it that can be seen in real life, but the effect is not ironclad. In contrast to the example above, Edgar Cayce, known as the "sleeping prophet," had the less than four degree square. Cayce was probably the best known and most talented American clairvoyant of the twentieth century. He was a delightful and thoroughly virtuous man.

Sun trine Jupiter is usually more moderate than the square, although one should not depend on it to always be mild since both evangelist Billy Graham and convicted felon and Heisman trophy winner O.J. Simpson both have the one-degree trine. But in most cases this group is more relaxed and easygoing than the other aspect types. Prince William, who will probably some day be king of England, has the trine, as does his step-mother, Camilla Parker-Bowles. They are both cultivated, gracious and reserved, which is what most Sun-trine-Jupiter people display. The gentle, laid-back manner of singer Willie Nelson, who has the three-degree trine, is representative of the type as well.

The sesquiquadrate is just as fortunate and successful as the other Sun-Jupiter contacts and often remarkably to an extraordinary degree. Steve Jobs, co-founder of Apple, who became a billionaire and an icon in the computer industry, had the sesquiquadrate a quarter of a degree from exact.

The opposition is somewhat easier to handle than the square and is frequently spectacularly successful or notorious. These people often deal with big issues consistent with the expansive, far-reaching nature of Jupiter. Helena Petrovna Blavatsky, with the two-degree opposition, exemplifies the contact. She was a Russian-born writer, occultist and one of the founders of Theosophy, a spiritualist organization. She traveled widely throughout Europe and Asia and became an American citizen. Many people think she expressed a very high level of consciousness, but she was also accused of fraud. Her best known works, *Isis Unveiled* (1877) and *The Secret Doctrine* (1888) still sell modestly well. Jean Baptiste Joseph Delambre, the extraordinarily gifted French mathematician, astronomer, author and government official, had the opposition less than a degree from exact. He was born into poverty but lifted himself via unrelenting effort and prodigious ability into a highly respected and exalted position in life, which Jupiter craves. He played an important part in the development of the metric system and wrote an encyclopedic history of astronomy.

Jupiter, in its far-seeing capacity to take in the broadest expanse of events, trends and the flow of ideas, often shows a truly sagacious temperament with talent for analyzing and writing history. Many familiar names in this field show the Sun-Jupiter effect: Oswald Spengler (sextile), Arnold Toynbee (mundane square), Ibn Khaldun (inconjunct), Georg Wilhelm Friedrich Hegel (mundane square), Thomas Carlyle (mundane square), Thomas Babbington MacCaulay (zodiacal square) and Lord Acton (mundane square). Almost as common among the historians are these with Jupiter-Saturn aspects: Theodor Mommsen (mundane square), Edward Gibbon (mundane square), Leopold von Ranke (mundane square) and Samuel Huntington (mundane square), to name just a few.

Sun-Saturn

This combination, often dreaded as profoundly undesirable or at least unfortunate, is not inimical to very considerable success. In its positive manifestations, Sun-Saturn gives a conscientious, persistent and determined nature, anxious to find material and circumstantial security. It is usually acquisitive, and sometimes distinctly avaricious, as though having things constitutes a defense against the world. This tendency may also manifest as the inclination to put together extraordinary collections of things renowned for their rarity, value and sheer volume. A wealthy person known to this writer with the exact sextile collects apartment buildings (for profit); another collects hotels and motels; and yet another collects rare books. Raw land and buildings are seen as the safest bet by Saturnians. Hoarding may be a problem for this type.

People with this combination are, to a remarkable degree, on the prowl for advantage to exploit. They are practical, extremely industrious, astute, worldly and serious, somewhat inclined toward depression and to take on difficult and responsible positions. They are not deterred by high degrees of difficulty or labor-intensive undertakings; rather, they gravitate toward such endeavors. These natives are concerned with the world of facts primarily rather than flights of fancy. Its natives revere the past and often show a strong inclination for the study of history or indisputable scientific truth. They may be too attached to their work or seem quintessentially boring to frivolous people.

Many lawyers, politicians and business people have this combination who delight in the exercise of power. In general they have earned their positions, zealously guard their turf and seek to control events and other people rather than cooperate with them. They may collect people, in effect, who gravitate toward them out of conscious or unconscious deference.

Russian president Vladimir Putin, with the three and a half degree conjunction, tolerates no dissent in his government. Saturn tends to be absolutist in temperament. Insiders speak of Putin as effective and admire him for his success in imposing control over a large and diverse state. Outsiders speak of him as cold, ruthless and an unapologetic tyrant. Joseph Stalin, the brutal and absolute ruler of Russia for thirty years, also had the square, his less than a half degree from exact. He made no pretense of civility and ruled through fear. Fidel Castro, the Cuban dictator who also had the square almost exact to the minute, imprisoned and executed his political enemies with impunity. Cuban exiles in the United States speak of him as a monster and a thug, among the words that an editor would not expunge from a text. One should not, however, assume a bad character as a mater of course with this combination. Most people who have it are not evil but they are usually serious and extremely hard working with a strong sense of purpose. They may have to fight depression like the great novelist, Virginia Woolf, who had the less than half degree square. Yet, depending on what else is in play, Sun-Saturn natives may readily turn toward the dark side of life and embrace the dishonorable, the heinous and corrupt. The combination does not signify generosity, although the native may display generosity symbolized by other planet combinations. Much depends on the rest of the horoscope and other bodies that impinge upon the Sun-Saturn combination.

Many women who have Sun-Saturn combinations find that the men in their lives are not on their level in terms of character, intelligence, earning potential or refinement. Many such women are attracted to "bad boys" because they are perceived as sexy—and perhaps they are—but the women come to regret that such relationships have little else to commend them. Other Sun-Saturn women become involved with men who are decent and even honorable but without a trace of dynamism or remarkable qualities, such that the question may be posed, "How did that fabulous woman become involved with him?" If other planets in addition to Saturn, especially Jupiter, are involved with the Sun in a woman's chart, her mate may simply be considerably older than she is and quite likely he will be well off financially.

The father may be unfortunate, harsh, strict, or he may show little interest in the native; he may even be absent altogether due to divorce, abandonment, imprisonment or his early death. When the father is a generally positive figure in the life of the native he is likely to be a person who dispenses power and authority outside the household such as a professor, a military commander, a judge or some other type of imposing or domineering character. If the benefics also configure the Sun, the father is much more likely to earnestly engage the native, but he may be spread too thin and be overwhelmed by his responsibilities such that he is unable to adequately carry out his paternal role. Sometimes natives of this combination feel like they are virtually parents to themselves or their siblings. They are inclined to keep their own counsel. Sun-Saturn people often conceal deep feelings of inadequacy that only their husbands or wives may realize. They are usually very hard on themselves and remonstrate internally over exaggerated failings.

If the Moon configures Jupiter, the native may have a good family upbringing and a conscientious, attentive father. In such cases the Sun-Saturn contact is likely to manifest through the husband, the brother, male children or other near relations who bring difficulty, limitation and heavy responsibility into the life of the native. This is an important point to stress. There is usually contradictory symbolism in any horoscope that prevents complete, unrestrained manifestation of all the classic indications of any planet combination. Thus the father may be simultaneously strict, even emotionally inhibited or grievously wounded in combat, but loving, or absent through divorce yet the native knows unmistakably that he or she is loved.

Both liberal President Woodrow Wilson (four-degree opposition) and conservative Vice President Dick Cheney (two-degree square) are exemplars of the contact. Wilson was blocked by conservatives in many of his most important endeavors, particularly regarding the League of Nations. Cheney was reviled by liberals as virtually satanic, in particular regarding the spurious justification for the Iraq War. Their elevated and official status are juxtaposed the low level malice of Charles Manson with the two-degree square, who was the mastermind behind at least six murders, and Lee Harvey Oswald, with the three-degree opposition, who assassinated President John F. Kennedy. Sun-Saturn people sometimes seem distinctly mean-spirited or unlucky, but additional symbolism is required to produce that result because the contact is not inherently mean; rather, it is usually hard, pessimistic, efficient, objective and logical. If they are fortunate, they achieve through diligence, patience, unrelenting effort and an opportunistic attitude that drives a hard bargain. In a good horoscope a Sun-Saturn combination symbolizes someone who carries heavy responsibilities and sometimes, physical infirmities especially with regard to the eyes, the heart or the spine. In a harder one the Sun-Saturn personality coldly exploits opportunity and other people and thinks nothing of it. Sun-Saturn people are usually hard-minded and feel that they are operating according to the law of the jungle, that all is fair in love, war and business. Just as many Sun-Saturn types fight an uphill battle against hard circumstance and are models of rectitude. Therefore great care is required in delineating horoscopes that contain this pair. Success often comes late or may be only partially realized; or success may be wholly realized but then lost. The addition of Jupiter to Sun-Saturn may render the native profound, a good judge of men and someone who will work for the benefit of others.

Remarkably, Sun-Saturn often produces a superb comedic sense. Robin Williams, perhaps the quickest wit of his generation, had the sextile less than a half degree from exact. Jonathan Winters with the two-degree opposition and Woody Allen with the five-degree square show it well. Tom Waits, the poet/singer with the three-degree square, combines the comic with the lugubrious such that one doesn't know whether to laugh or cry upon hearing his work.

The trine is the least troublesome contact with this pair. It produces a workaholic, perfectionist tendency and the patience to persevere through difficulty that others consider too daunting. Actor Leonardo Di Caprio with the exact trine the very successsful producer/director Ron Howard with the one-degree trine, singer/musician Elton John with the two-degree trine and singer/ dancer Madonna with the four-degree trine show the effect. One should not get carried away by these examples and remember that the planets that comprise an aspect are more important than the supposed effect of the aspect. Sun trine Saturn doesn't become a "good" thing because the planets are trine. Otherwise, Marshall Applewhite, leader of the Heaven's Gate cult, would not be associated with the mass suicide of 39 people that he organized in 1997. Applewhite, with the two-degree trine, also took his own life, thereby reducing the Heaven's Gate membership to none.

Most Sun-Saturn people produce few children, especially few boys. They are often extremely diligent workers, intrigued by antiquity and all things hidden and obscure, who solve intractable problems like Jean François Champollion, with the two-degree square, who deciphered Egyptian hieroglyphs that opened up the iconography and paleography of ancient Egypt. Yet Sun-Saturn may also appear dull and unremarkable. It is slow to mature unless forced to mature early by circumstance and may not show itself to advantage until middle age.

Keith Duckworth, the outstanding British mechanical engineer who designed the Cosworth Ford DFV (for double four valve) Formula One racing engine, had the three and a half degree opposition in longitude; but it was less than one degree from exact *in mundo*. The Cosworth DFV won on its first start at the Dutch Grand Prix at Zandvoort in 1967. It powered 153 more Grand Prix victories, the most wins for a particular design by any engine manufacturer to date in Formula One. The DFV dominated the sport for seventeen years. Twelve Formula One driving titles were won with this engine and ten manufacturer's championships. Duckworth shows the best of Sun-Saturn, which happens most readily when Saturn is dignified as Duckworth had it in Capricorn. In his obituary he was described as ". . . multi-talented, super-confident, deep-thinking, forthright, stubborn. . . ." The latter three qualities are particularly Saturnian. Duckworth is a good example of how Sun-Saturn works out in real life, despite the odious qualities frequently attributed to it. Engineering is a common venue with this combination in a good horoscope. These natives are fascinated by the rules that govern how and why things work. A good Mercury facilitates that desire to a considerable degree: Duckworth had Mercury semi-square Venus less than a degree from exact which provides the intellectual horsepower to address questions that, in the end, are matters of physics. That he would succeed to an extreme degree was assured by his Jupiter sextile Pluto exact almost to the minute as well as Venus conjoined to Jupiter.

When both bodies are dignified, the benefits that accrue to the combination may be extraordinary if other factors lend support. José Miguel Cabrera Torres plays first base for the Detroit Tigers. He has the Sun exalted in Aries in a three degree opposition to Saturn exalted in Libra. He has won the American league Most Valuable Player award twice; he has been an all-star nine times; he won the triple crown (highest batting average, most home runs, most runs-batted-in) in 2012 which was the first time any player had achieved that distinction since 1967. His ten year salary commitment from the Detroit Tigers is worth 292 millions dollars. Not everyone with such a good Sun-Saturn aspect will realize success on this scale. Cabrera also has Mars dignified in its own sign, Aries, very closely quincunx Jupiter conjoined to Uranus, which is obviously symbolic of amazing athletic gifts and great good fortune combined. He also has Mars opposite Pluto in mundo only a degree from exact which is excellent for Herculean strength. The point is that the Sun-Saturn opposition doesn't hurt him. It's a benefit due to the exaltations of the bodies in the combination.

Simon Newcomb, long-time director of the Nautical Almanac Office at the United States Naval Observatory in Washington D.C., had the quincunx less than a degree from exact. He was also professor of mathematics and astronomy at Johns Hopkins University. He revised and improved all the major astronomical constants, most of which are still universally employed today. Ephemerides throughout the world, including the astrological ones, were based on Newcomb's *Tables of the Sun* from 1895 until 1984 when the slightly more accurate numerical integrations developed at the Jet Propulsion Laboratory in Pasadena, California superceded Newcomb's *Tables of the Sun*. The JPL ephemerides were based on better observations than those available to Newcomb, rather than any shortcoming in his methods. His work still has relevance in many areas and is considered an amazing achievement since it was done without electronic computers. Sun-Saturn people typically celebrate precision and order. In a good horoscope these natives gravitate naturally toward positions that allow them to exercise those qualities without arousing opposition or ill will.

It is noteworthy that on July 4, 1776, the date of the U.S. Declaration of Independence, the Sun was square Saturn and fewer than two degrees from exact. The success of the United States is therefore proof that Sun-Saturn people and entities can surmount all difficulties to reach the mountain top.

Sun-Uranus

This dynamic combination is on the whole lucky, innovative, entrepreneurial and inclined to operate with eyes-wide-open; thus they are perspicacious and primed for discovery. It appears constantly in the horoscopes of successful and powerful people who are both in the mainstream of society and at its periphery, often too much in advance of what is commonly accepted to be part of the establishment. Sun-Uranus people cannot abide pretense, injustice or tradition that restricts their freedom of action. They are strongly inclined to recognize intrinsic merit or fundamental relationships before the people around them and to remind others of it who may have forgotten.

Spanish artist Pablo Picasso, with the semi-square less than three quarters of a degree from exact, is a prime example. Sun-Uranus is detached, self-confident, independent and cool but in a completely unaffected manner. They see opportunity and take risks to exploit it like John D. Rockefeller with the trine that was exact almost to the minute. He built the first large American oil refinery in 1870 and was the principal player in the development of the American petroleum industry. Dwight Eisenhower, with the conjunction, rose from Kansas farm boy to become a five star general and supreme commander of Allied Forces in Europe during World War II as well as a two-term president of the United States. Sun-Uranus people are typically in the first rank of their professions like the superb actress Meryl Streep who has the exact conjunction. No mere movie star, she is clearly touched by the spirit of the muses of drama, Thalia and Melpomene, and therefore conveys apparently effortlessly her characters' natures so completely that she achieves what all actors strive for: utter credibility and emotional purity. The stunning face of actress Zooey Deschanel is classic eye candy. She has Uranus sextile the triple conjunction of Sun, Moon and Mercury. She is also a musician and songwriter. Versatility is often present with Uranus. Taking in her features is likely looking into a tulip and being entranced by the purity and depth of the color. The flower impels one's attention. In the same way, Zooey's beauty is consistent with the symbolism of Uranus which is typically exceptional.

Bill Gates, who founded a software empire and is one of the wealthiest people, has the three-degree square. Sun-Uranus people consistently make names for themselves for their original work. Henrietta Swan Leavitt, one of the most unsung heroines of the last 100 years, discovered entirely on her own the Period-Luminosity Law that allowed Edwin Hubble, two years after her death in 1921, to determine that the Andromeda nebula is a galaxy outside the Milky Way galaxy. Until Hubble's discovery nobody realized that the universe was bigger than the Milky Way itself. Leavitt's study of variable stars, (stars whose brightness varies regularly) was not merely a contributing factor but rather *the* determining factor that allowed the immense distances of extremely remote stars to be measured accurately for the first time. A graduate of Radcliffe College (which merged with Harvard in 1999), she began her astronomical career at Harvard Observatory in 1893 as an unpaid worker to catalogue and measure the brightness of stars. She was later paid thirty cents an hour to perform her critical work, the importance of which stands at the pinnacles of twentieth century astronomy. She had the Sun-Uranus conjunction less than a degree from exact. Hubble said that she deserved a Nobel Prize for her work. She was actually nominated to receive the Nobel Prize in physics after her death by persons unaware that she had passed on. Nobel Prizes are not awarded posthumously.

Sun-Uranus types are also distinctly non-conformist, well-exemplified by the French author Amandine Lucille Aurore Dupin, better known by her pen name, George Sand, who rebelled against the nineteenth century straightjacket that European women were forced into. Although mostly heterosexual (and the lover of the great Polish composer Frederic Chopin), she dressed as a man in public for years in protest of it. A free spirit in true Uranian fashion, she created a continuous sensation by her unconventional behavior that would not seem out of place in the twenty-first century. Sun-Uranus is often ahead of its time or at least in the vanguard of it. Sand had the square three degrees out. Most Sun-Uranus people, however, do not act in a deliberately bohemian manner for effect, yet they are the very essence of hip. Most of them are in disguise as ordinary people. The non-stop creativity and cutting-edge excellence of Yves St. Laurent made him one of the brightest lights among the very best twentieth century fashion designers. He had the square less than a quarter of a degree from exact. His work looked right, chic yet elegant. That is a tall order when much, if not most, new work in the fashion world looks like an exercise in the bizarre. St. Laurent is an example of what Uranus is about: original, outstanding and avant-garde, rather than merely different for its own sake. Uranus has substance behind its novelty. St. Laurent had something to say from childhood about fashion when he was cutting out his drawings into paper dolls when other children were playing with conventional toys. He was inspired and expressed himself accordingly via pencil and cloth in a manner that was clearly a calling, not a job, a check or a hobby, but pure art. The freedom-loving nature of these people shows most obviously through the artistic members of this group like the great musician Jimi Hendrix, who had the two-degree opposition. They are utterly natural and tolerant but defend their positions and principles quite fiercely. They are often "idea" people like the eighteenth century philosopher Immanuel Kant with the exact opposition, the twentieth century philosopher Jean-Paul Sartre with the three-degree opposition and the father of psychoanalysis, Sigmund Freud, who had the four-degree conjunction.

The influence is present in great scientists like the physicist Galileo Galilei who had the exact square. Galileo, however, through his own arrogance, ran afoul of the Catholic Church by espousing the heliocentric theory (whereby the Earth orbits the Sun), advanced by Copernicus and Kepler, in such a way that he clearly insulted the pope. The church found reason in Scripture to embrace the geocentric theory (whereby the Sun orbits the Earth). The position of the church was that the work of Copernicus was not objectionable as an hypothesis but Sun-Uranus people are not careful to avoid giving offense. Galileo was accused of venturing into religious interpretation outside his scientific jurisdiction. Sun-Uranus types can easily find themselves on the wrong side of a power struggle when their advanced views irritate entrenched authority. When Galileo was summoned to an audience before the pope, he was told to produce proof of the Copernican theory, which he could not, or suffer his tongue cut out of his head on the spot. Galileo was forced to recant his heretical (but correct) view of the Sun-Earth relationship, because of his own measureless conceit and foolish assertion that he was virtually the only person who knew anything. Sun-Uranus, especially in square, is usually close to a position like this where they are over the line, so to speak, or incur the enmity of others for their injudicious use of power.

In a similar fashion, Julian Assange who founded Wikileaks, which publishes data meant to be clandestine in order to embarrass governments, has made himself extremely unpopular, even despised, in some circles and a hero to some others. Unauthorized disclosures by Wikileaks of government secrets have probably put many people in jeopardy and have made information public that all governments intend to keep secret. Assange has Sun square Uranus less than one and a half degrees from exact. Typically these people are a law unto themselves, and they may be much maligned when their exploits run counter to public sentiment and simultaneously embraced by a large segment of society for the same reasons. It can fairly be said, in any case, that Sun square Uranus sparks controversy.

Sometimes the daring of the Sun-Uranus types succeeds without costing the native an unwelcome reaction. Thomas Jefferson, one of the founding fathers of the United States and its third president, had the three-degree square. He pursued an aggressive policy against pirates in what is modern Morocco, Algeria and Libya when he dispatched a task force of warships and marines against the Barbary Coast pirates in 1801 who had been preying on U.S. merchant shipping for nearly twenty years. The policy of much stronger nations than the U.S. up to that time had been to pay ransom and tribute to secure the freedom of captured crews, as well as ships and their cargos. Sun-Uranus people will have none of that.

Copernicus had the trine, as did the extraordinary scientist Marie Curie, who discovered radium and polonium. She was the first woman awarded a Nobel prize and won two of them (physics in 1903 and chemistry in 1911). The Italian philosopher, historian and law professor Giambattista Vico had Sun trine Uranus less than a degree from exact. His stunning intellectual prowess paved the way for modern complexity thinking that has powerfully influenced the modern world. Vico is best known for his magnum opus *Principi Di Scienza Nuova* (*Principles of New Science*) and for his *verum factum* principle, which flies in the face of Cartesian logic. Descartes maintained that the truth of a matter is verified by observation. Vico maintained that the truth of a matter is verified through its own creation because the mind perceives itself but it cannot make itself. Thus creation supercedes observation. The issue is important regarding logical rigor because it addresses the question: "How do you know that you know (sic) [anything]?"

The unconventional and outspoken actress Angelina Jolie has the sesquiquadrate less than a half degree from exact. She has made headlines since she was a teenager, both for her Oscar winning performances and her off-screen behavior.

The most prominent historian of science of the twentieth century was Otto Eduard Neugebauer, who had the opposition less than two degrees from exact. Frequently the Sun-Uranus people are the most outstanding in their specialties. They also tend to break new ground or go off in a direction that is either esoteric or uncommon. Neugebauer was initially a pure mathematician but became so fascinated by the mathematics and science of the ancient world that he devoted his life to bringing it to light. He shows the international tendency of Uranus. Neugebauer was born in Austria, educated mostly in Germany where he earned his Ph.D. and took on university faculty positions, went to live and work in Denmark after the Nazis made life uncomfortable for liberals, and then spent five enormously productive decades in the United States at the very fine Ivy League school, Brown University and later at the Institute for Advanced Study at Princeton. He was a superb linguist, at home in German, English, Danish, Latin, Greek and Akkadian and a man for all seasons typical of the polymath tendency of Uranus. His list of credits is very long. He may be best remembered for his *Mathematical Cuneiform Texts* with Abraham Sachs (1945), *The Exact Sciences In Antiquity*, (1951), *Astronomical Cuneiform Texts* in three volumes (1955), *Egyptian Astronomical Texts* with Richard A. Parker in four volumes (1960-1969) and his magnum opus, *A History of Ancient Mathematical Astronomy* in three volumes (1975). Charlie ("Yardbird") Parker was a brilliant American jazz musician. He had the Sun dignified in its own sign, Leo, in a two degree opposition to Uranus also dignified in its own sign, Aquarius. He demonstrated the determination of the fixed signs by many years of practice of up to fifteen hours per day which ultimately made him a master of improvisation. Those dignities and the opposition signify why his beautiful and innovative phrasing on the alto saxophone is revered as classic. He was a consummate artist who, with Dizzy Gillespie, was the father of bebop.

Sun-Neptune

This combination produces an idealistic, occasionally visionary temperament. In its best manifestation Sun-Neptune sees the big picture and is able to make its dreams real. Bill Gates, founder of Microsoft, with the six and three quarter degree conjunction, shows the effect. It is frequently humanitarian and philanthropic that Gates also demonstrates. Thomas Alva Edison, the inventor of the phonograph, the movie camera, the first practical incandescent light bulb, the stock ticker, and the printing telegraph, and holder of a staggering 1,093 patents, had the Sun-Neptune conjunction five and two-thirds degrees from exact. Sometimes these people appear to have a direct line to another world. The extraordinary 18th century Swiss mathematician Leonard Euler, one of the greatest mathematical geniuses of all time, had the four-degree conjunction. Notwithstanding the technical virtuosity of Euler, Gates and Edison, the contact is usually emotional, intuitive and overly sensitive and finds its most common expression in religion, spirituality, the occult, music and the dramatic arts. The various contacts are not substantially different in terms of quality. The exceptionally talented blues guitarist Freddie King had the two-degree conjunction. He combined the Texas blues with the hard driving West Side of Chicago sound that won over everybody in the 1960s and 1970s. He powerfully influenced Eric Clapton, Stevie Ray Vaughn, Dicky Betts, Jerry Garcia and many others. He is one of the three "kings" of the electric blues; the other two are Albert King and B. B. King. Joe Walsh, another brilliant guitarist (James Gang, Eagles) has the semi-square less than a degree from exact. Prominent British astrologer Walter Richard Old (Sepharial) had the six degree conjunction. Excellent British astrologer Charles Edwin Owen Carter, found that Sun-Neptune aspects are the most common signature of astrologers.

The father may be dominated by the native's mother or he may be irresponsible and abandon the family as was the case with President Barack Obama, who has the four-degree square; or there is little sympathy between the native and the father In some manner the father often either fails the native or appears weak. With additional affliction the father and or the native may have problems with addiction that range from drink and drugs to include food, gambling, vice and the many forms of deceit and manipulation, both legal and direct and illegal and indirect. Scandal often dogs Neptune. When Jupiter simultaneously configures a Sun-Neptune combination the native may be virtuous yet literally or figuratively still suffer paralysis. That was the case with Franklin Delano Roosevelt, with the two-degree square, who was struck down by polio in the summer of 1921 at age 39 when transiting Neptune opposed his natal Sun and squared his natal Neptune. People with Sun-Neptune may easily find themselves in a dependent situation.

Psychologists with the Ph.D. degree often have this contact, but psychiatrists who have the M.D. are typically more saturnine in this writer's experience and have it much less often. Noteworthy exceptions are Sigmund Freud and Carl Jung who were both medical doctors, but neither of them had a Sun-Saturn aspect. Jung (whose father was a pastor in the Swiss Reformed Church) had an exact Sun square Neptune aspect. Jung was fascinated by philosophy, the occult, the mystical and the world of the spirit—the things behind the veil of religion—which is the province of Neptune. He was also openly interested in astrology. Sun-Neptune is one of the primary astrological contacts. It is common among the biggest names in the art, e.g., John Dee, William Lilly (mundane square), A.J. Pearce, Walter Old, Alan Leo and Robert Hand (mundane square). The world of the imagination is much enlarged with Sun square Neptune whether the occult is embraced or not. The celebrated authors Rudyard Kipling and James Joyce illustrate the effect.

Musical talent is also common with this contact, for example, Wolfgang Amadeus Mozart (two-degree opposition), Dave Brubeck (one-degree trine) and Paul McCartney (one- degree square). Singers, some of whom are also musicians, and dramatic actors have it in large numbers. Buddy Holly (one-degree conjunction), k.d. lang (one-degree conjunction), Michael Douglas (one-degree conjunction), Sean Connery (one-degree conjunction), Susan Sarandon (two-degree conjunction) and Noel Coward (two-degree opposition) show the effect.

Sometimes issues that relate to the fantasy life of men are engaged by the Sun-Neptune people as evidenced by Hugh Hefner, founder of Playboy Magazine, who has the three-degree trine. Artists, also fantasy ridden, have this contact as well. Michelangelo, for example, had the one-degree trine.

Another characteristic feature of Neptune with any planet, but especially the lights, is to elevate its natives in status even though their efforts, if any, do not warrant the elevation; rather they are well positioned by circumstance and are carried more by good fortune than their own achievement. There is usually a price to pay, however, which may find the native trapped, seduced by the bait of a higher status life. The late Princess Diana, mother of the children of the heir to the British throne, is a fine example. She had Sun trine Neptune one degree from exact. Much of her work was focused on another characteristic feature of Neptune: charity. Former Pope Benedict XVI has the trine less than a degree from exact which makes a grand trine with his Midheaven degree. Two late American presidents, Harry Truman and Gerald Ford, had Sun conjunct Neptune. They both inherited the presidency, Truman via the death of Franklin Roosevelt and Ford via the resignation of Richard Nixon, who with a natal Sun-Neptune opposition himself, resigned in disgrace, trapped by his attempt to conceal his involvement in the Watergate scandal.

Sun-Pluto

The chief effect of Pluto in aspect to the Sun is to make the native distinctly private, sometimes even reclusive. Some of these natives develop well-practiced charm and grace as a practical tool but they still need a lot of time alone daily and may be distinctly disinclined to let other people into their worlds. Without enough solitary time they can be quite irritable and refuse to engage their friends, spouses and co-workers. The native is often not close to the father or sometimes the father is removed by death, imprisonment, divorce, prolonged military service; more often, the father is simply inaccessible or without enough interest in the native to sufficiently engage him. Austrian born body-builder, actor and former California governor, Arnold Schwarzenegger, has the six-degree conjunction. He has spoken of brutal treatment at the hands of his father who showed a marked preference for Arnold's older brother. There was no demonstration of patience or willingness to hear out the son on the father's part. Schwarzenegger said there was, in effect, a wall or barrier between them. He did not attend his father's funeral. Usually the father is innocent of gross ill treatment but the Sun-Pluto native may be isolated by illness or physical incapacity and the father may be powerless to help him. If the Sun is simultaneously configured with benefics, the father will usually be present during the early life of the native, and the native might love him and remember him well, even though the father would still (from the point of view of the Sun-Pluto person) be a distant or austere figure, but a formidable personality. Occasionally the father is an honorable man but the native suffers some stigma through his actions. Leonardo Da Vinci (1452-1519), perhaps the greatest genius of the Renaissance period, was illegitimate (during an era when that word and status were very significant); but his father took him in and his mother moved to another town. Da Vinci had the Sun in Aries, its exaltation, in a one and a half-degree square to Pluto in Cancer. The most successful producer/director in Hollywood, Steven Spielberg, was estranged from his father for decades but reconciled with him in middle age. Spielberg has the sesquiquadrate less than two degrees from exact. This is an important fact because it shows that, if the father survives, resolution of differences and reuniting with the native in adulthood can sometimes occur.

If the Sun is in Libra, the sign of its fall, or Aquarius, the sign of its detriment, and configured with Pluto, the patrimony is more often suspect and the native may never know his father. If a father is present at all in such cases he might well be a step-father. Sun-Pluto people may display a mean streak as a consequence of ill treatment at the hands of the father or bitterness over his absence. Sun-Pluto people are often reclusive, misfits who reinforce their loneliness by choice. They frequently have exceptional ability that they find difficult to integrate into the world. They are often secretive and go to great lengths to avoid prying eyes. These people usually hate crowds and confined spaces. John D. Rockefeller, the major figure in the rise of the American petroleum industry, had the three-degree square. His father, who was a sometime businessman and occasional charlatan, was indicted for rape, which may have induced the family to relocate. Rockefeller himself, one of the richest men in America, was notoriously avaricious (until the end of his life), intensely surreptitious and always tried to remain out of the public eye. Sometimes the opposite extreme shows itself and the Sun-Pluto person wants a great deal of attention but such effort makes them stand out in a negative way with their faults exposed, so that they are isolated anyway. Sun-Pluto is pre-eminently the signature of a loner. Shyness, therefore, is common with this contact and deep intimacy is usually hard to achieve for these people, especially with the conjunction. Sometimes the native eschews intimacy as undesirable; more often the native desperately wants it but doesn't know how to bring it about, or the efforts of would-be partners arouse formidable defenses that may take decades to breach and sometimes are never overcome. The problems can usually be traced to inadequate parenting—sometimes not, such that these people are simply a mystery. They both embrace their loneliness and are tortured by it.

The marvelous English blues guitarist Eric Clapton has Sun trine Pluto only one degree from exact. His mother was only sixteen at Clapton's birth and he never had a relationship with his biological father who was Canadian. He was raised by his grandparents and was unaware until his adolescence that the woman he took for granted to be his older sister was actually his mother.

The extraordinary German philologist, philosopher and author Friedrich Nietzsche (*Thus Spake Zarathustra*, *Beyond Good and Evil*) had the opposition less than a degree from exact. His father died when Nietzsche was four. Although brilliant, Nietzsche alienated most of his intellectual and academic contemporaries mainly by his attacks on traditional Christian morality as well as the underpinning of most Greek philosophy. His work is widely studied and has had a profound effect on modern philosophy, especially existentialism, although in his day he steadily painted himself into a corner of isolation, by his uncompromising stance toward the conventional and received wisdom of his day. He was so far ahead of his time that German conservatives tried to get his work banned.

Moon-Mercury

This excellent combination symbolizes intellectuals, wordsmiths, poets, teachers, orators, editors, publishers and modern-day minstrels. Its natives are clever, quick, and likely to do well in school; they are attuned to public sentiment and able to capture and reflect it in their work. These people wear well and remain in the public eye long after most people have had their moment in the Sun because Mercury is inherently youthful and childlike. Actors, athletes, artists and musicians are prime examples of this: Ringo Starr, Bruce Springsteen, Robert Redford, Whoopi Goldberg, Muhammad Ali, Danny DeVito and James Earl Jones all have the conjunction. On a more prosaic level, people who think on their feet and live out of a suitcase, as salesmen often do, have this planet combination. Mercury is mercantile. People who sell anything benefit from this combination. It is also good for office work, public relations, advertising, radio and television. It is very good for politicians who must communicate effectively with their constituents and be alert to the shifting winds of opportunity, intrigue and advantage. The late Cuban dictator Fidel Castro is a good example of Moon sextile Mercury. His was less than a degree from exact. He was a firebrand to the end, partly due to Mars square his Moon but his long public harangues are characteristic of the inexhaustible prolixity of the Moon-Mercury combinations. Moon-Mercury people are extremely active, sometimes frenetic and enjoy being in motion. They may excel as sprinters on the athletic field and dance well in many styles.

The square is more active and unconventional than the conjunction. It is distinctly likely to embrace causes and produce works that are new, odd and may evoke strong responses both pro and con. Martha Graham, perhaps the greatest choreographer to come out of America to date, had the square almost exact to the minute. Her *raison d'être* was pure emotion in movement. She made the world of dance stand up straight in awe. Mary Shelley, with the one degree square, wrote her macabre novel *Frankenstein* in 1817 when writing anything professionally was out of bounds for a western woman, much less subject matter best described as weird. Controversial works, that are later considered masterpieces, are almost the hallmark of Moon square Mercury. The writer-actor-director Orson Welles, with the two-degree square created one sensation after another in the 1930s and 1940s by his innovative work in film. George Lucas, also with the square did the same thing in the 1970s and 1980s through his Star Wars series. The outspoken and demanding but immensely talented singer Barbra Streisand flourished when she got executive control of her artistic endeavors. She has the two-degree square. Moon square Mercury insists on what it wants which is usually ahead of the curve. Natives of Moon square Mercury frequently find themselves in headlines as objects of widespread attention and controversy sometimes not even due to their actions but rather what befalls them. Austrian archduke Franz Ferdinand, with the square less than two thirds of a degree from exact, was assassinated in Serbia in 1914. His assassination sparked World War I that produced nine million combat deaths and toppled four empires.

The trine is more pliable, usually more popular but just as enduring as the other contacts. The soft and sweet lullabies of composer Johannes Brahms, with the two-degree trine, is a prime example. The smooth finesse of interviewer and commentator Barbara Walters with the exact trine further illustrates the effect. The work of the trine people is characteristically much loved and long appreciated. Singers Cher and Aretha Franklin, dancer-actress-comedienne Lucille Ball and the very long and distinguished career of violinist Yehudi Menuhin are classic exemplars. James Brown, a terrific singer and an equally amazing, indeed jaw-dropping dancer, had moves that were simply beyond all of his contemporaries. He was more than a showman, rather he was a fabulous artist. He connected with people so completely through his art that his performances induced people to get up and dance on the spot, no matter the venue. Brown had the two degree trine.

J.P. Morgan, after whom the present day investment bank is named, was perhaps the richest of the super ultra-rich of his day. He was widely considered a robber baron, completely unscrupulous and a *force majeur* in the rough and tumble of unregulated big business. He was actually a truly extraordinary businessman who understood how to wield financial power for constructive purposes and not merely as a form of self-aggrandizement. He had the Moon sesquiquadrate Mercury less than a degree from exact. His ability to perceive and exploit the potential of all enterprises, especially new technology, was amazing. Moon-Mercury people are exceptionally smart, quick, adaptable and unperturbed by the moral outlook of their day. These qualities are innate in them and do not require cultivation over time.

Gottfried Wilhelm Leibniz, the great German polymath and a contemporary of Isaac Newton, independently developed the calculus, much to the great irritation of Newton. Leibniz actually got into print with a paper on differential equations two years before Newton, but Leibniz's work contained no proofs. Moreover, it was later shown that Newton had developed the calculus in the 1660s, with proofs, ten years before Leibniz, but did not publish his work until twenty years later. Leibniz had the quincunx a half degree from exact.

The opposition produces pronounced effects. The works of the people who have it are often innovative in the extreme. Their work typically finds wide utility inasmuch as the Moon has affinity with the general public. Mercury is about the transmission of ideas first and foremost. Transportation, education and the direction of one's career are its secondary venues. Allied with the Moon, which pertains to the public at large, it's easy to see a Moon-Mercury relationship as symbolic of speech and hearing, even before reading and writing because emotion and speech precede the written word. Alexander Graham Bell, the inventor of the telephone, has to be considered the quintessence of Moon opposition Mercury. He had the opposition laid across the horizon less than a quarter degree from exact. He was issued the patent for the telephone in 1876 and founded the Bell Telephone Company that became American Telephone and Telegraph. Henry Cornelius Agrippa von Nettesheim (1486-1553), one of the greatest minds of the European Renaissance was a physician, ambassador, university lecturer, soldier and astrologer extraordinary. He had the opposition one degree from exact. The great Italian-American physicist and Nobel laureate, Enrico Fermi, also had the one-degree opposition. William Shakespeare, if he were born late in the day (of April 23, 1564), had the Moon in Virgo closely opposition Mercury in Pisces. He is *the* master wordsmith in English, the greatest playwright, a poet, actor and businessman whose popularity after 400 years has not wanted.

Moon-Venus

This combination may be the source of the "trines are good, squares are bad" doctrine that is so much overused in astrology; but that notion is nowhere else more distinct than with this pair. The soft aspects of Moon-Venus (conjunction, sextile and trine) are notable for the kind, pleasant, socially adept natures of its natives. The Moon has a lot to do with the general public. The people who are lucky enough to have the Moon with Venus are often the darlings of the crowd like actor James Dean with the sextile exact almost to the minute, and the universally popular and successful actor William Bradley Pitt (Brad Pitt) with a less than one degree conjunction. Albert Einstein with the two-degree trine was the best-known and most popular scientist in the world for forty years. Super model socialite and singer Carla Bruni (wife of former French president Nicholas Sarkozy) has the sextile two and three quarter degrees out. Her beauty, charm and grace are effortless and near legendary. Even the wide conjunction, like Amelia Earhart's six-degree conjunction, puts people in the spotlight as beloved figures if the combination touches the horizon or meridian. Earhart's Venus was semi-square the Ascendant. She was the first woman to fly the Atlantic alone. The popularity that characteristically attends Moon-Venus in soft aspects is sometimes also conferred on the hard aspects: the square and opposition; but the relationship problems of the hard aspect natives are far more common than what the soft aspects experience. Without affliction from other bodies, Moon-Venus is often remarkably good looking. This pair in good aspect is accommodating, gentle and believes that resolution of problems is always possible. Venus is symbolic of peace; with the Moon, her natives exude a quality best described as nice.

If there is affliction to a Moon-Venus combination, even from Jupiter, the native may be shy though successful, and may occasionally succumb to infidelity due to the expansive nature of Jupiter. The basic incompatibility in relationships of all kinds, that people suffer who have the square, is quite marked. Divorce is very common with it. Princess Diana is perhaps the best-known example. She had the square less than a degree from exact. The effect is the same even when the contact is wide. For example, Rudolph Giuliani, former New York mayor, with the seven-degree square and even the helpful nearby presence of Jupiter, has been divorced twice. When the marriage lasts, special circumstances often obtain but upon close examination the marriage is likely to have serious problems that would ordinarily bring divorce in their wake. For example, the infidelity of President John F. Kennedy, with the square less than a half-degree from exact, imposed extreme pressure on his marriage. If the special factors are praiseworthy, however, a Moon-Venus square can produce separation via unjust imprisonment, prolonged military service or extreme devotion to some high calling. Mohandas Gandhi, who had the four-degree square, entered into a marriage arranged by his parents at age 13. He and his wife produced four sons in their 61-year marriage. The clue that Gandhi's square would be an exception to the rule is that his Moon was dignified in her own sign Cancer, and his Venus was also dignified in her own sign, Libra. Still, he and his wife endured many years of separation due to Gandhi's years in law school in England, his long-time residence in South Africa fighting against racial injustice there, as well as his imprisonment at the hands of the British in India. This last and most important part of his career was played out as an Indian patriot through his repudiation of and disobedience to British authority in order to secure independence for India.

Sometimes there is racial prejudice or religious intolerance with Moon square Venus. A good example is Catherine de' Medici, queen of France (1547-1559), who was highly influential during the reigns of her three weak sons. She was instrumental in the development of policy directed against Protestants in France that resulted in large-scale persecutions and massacres. Before she was a factor in governmental policy, she had to endure the humiliation of being less favored in public and private than her husband's chief mistress. Moon-Venus is fertile in any combination. Catherine de' Medici, even with the four-degree square, had nine children.

The opposition is less severe although extenuating circumstances via other well-placed planets are necessary to mitigate the untoward effect of the opposition. When this is the case, the native may enjoy success and celebrity like comedian/actor Robin Williams and actor Al Pacino who both have the one-degree opposition. This writer has many examples of people with the opposition who are successful as serial monogamists but who never marry or even live with someone though they could have married. Some others are once burned and twice shy. That is, once divorced, they resolve never to marry again and live alone but don't give up romantic partners. Others, although married, wish they were not and only go through the motions of intimacy and commitment. Stephanie Lynn Nicks (Stevie Nicks), lead singer for Fleetwood Mac in their heyday in the 1970s, has the wide opposition with both bodies angular through the meridian. She has been married only once but has had many relationships, primarily with musicians. Her Moon at the Midheaven is a fine example of the *ecce homo* (behold the man) configuration which applies to the Moon when she appears on any of the four angles. In Nick's case it should be *ecce femina*. The *ecce homo* placement—especially at the Midheaven—puts a person on display often as a public figure, but in any case with a lot of exposure. She was a feminine ideal in her prime: sexy, beautiful, entrancing with a unique voice, envied and emulated by women, desired by men but appreciated by everybody as an artist. Known as much as a songwriter as a singer, she has had a successful solo career that is still in full swing (eight Grammys as a solo artist and one with Fleetwood Mac).

Moon-Mars

Moon-Mars is distinctly vigorous, direct, competitive, athletic and possessed of a compelling attractiveness that consistently turns heads. Moon-Mars people are often blunt. In general nobody has to wonder about their position on any score. Discretion, if they display it, will be due to a powerful Saturn, more likely connected to the Sun than the Moon.

The Moon in her capacity as the symbol of the early life and family frequently signifies a dysfunctional family when configured with Mars. When this is not the case, the Moon will be found to be simultaneously configured with the benefic planets Venus and or Jupiter. In such cases, one or both of the parents, but usually the mother, may suffer in health or die young but be much loved by the native. In similar fashion the combination of Moon-Jupiter or Moon-Venus with Moon-Mars has, with noteworthy frequency in the experience of this writer, been symbolic of many miscarriages on the part of the mother and sometimes the wife as well; but the children that complete the full gestation period and subsequently survive are deeply cherished by the mother of the native. The Moon is much related to the important women in the life: wife, mother, mother-in-law, sister, daughter, aunt, grandmother and important friends who are like sisters to the native. These people may be powerful figures and/or sources of difficulty for the native unless there are extenuating planetary circumstances to the contrary. The harshness of Moon-Mars may be ostensibly contained by a powerfully placed Jupiter, especially if the planet is angular and the Moon and Jupiter are conjoined, opposed or in mundane square (q.v.) to it. Even with the helpful presence of Jupiter, the Moon-Mars condition suggests few children, or problems with children that are out of the ordinary.

In the absence of help from Venus and Jupiter, the mother of the person with Moon-Mars may be a harsh, coarse, demanding person, possessed of a decided mean streak and be the dominant parent. Moon-Mars people are contentious and attract controversy like a magnet. They often make themselves distinctly unpopular due to their willingness to take on other people who have not asked for their opinion. It is harder for these people to control their aggressiveness than the Sun-Mars people because the Moon represents automatic, unthinking responses. Self-awareness is in the Sun, not the Moon.

On the other hand, the fighting and rebellious spirit of Moon-Mars will often adopt a worthy cause and will not give way on any score. Eleanor Roosevelt and Gloria Steinem, both with close trines, took courageous stands well ahead of public opinion at the time, the former with regard to human rights and the latter with regard to women's rights.

The libertine tendency is illustrated by Charles II of England, who had the square, as well as the novelist D. H. Lawrence, author of *Lady Chatterley's Lover*, who had the exact square. Moon-Mars is not inimical to artistic talent, as shown by musician Miles Davis, with the trine, and dramatist, Tennessee Williams, with the conjunction; they both showed the tendency of Moon-Mars to dance a fine line between the notorious and mere celebrity. While the trines are usually better, they are not as powerful as the squares. The willingness to take on the system is characteristic of Moon-Mars contacts and sometimes the square is better for the biggest tasks. For example, Mohandas Gandhi with the close square, took on the entire British Empire to secure Indian independence. Martin Luther King, who much admired Gandhi, had the square, and just as Gandhi did, stared down the intolerance and malevolence of racists and bullies on a staggering scale. Abraham Lincoln also had the close square. He was well known as a tremendously strong fighter and wrestler in his youth who was never deterred by bullies or long odds, but he always preferred to settle disputes without violence whenever possible. Significantly as a war president, he presided over the most extreme blood-letting in the history of the republic to date (800,000 Civil War deaths). King and Gandhi were both jailed dozens of times, both successfully persevered in their tasks, as did Lincoln, and like Gandhi and King, Lincoln was also assassinated.

The sexuality of the Moon-Mars people is overwhelming, which can be distinctly troublesome to the women with this contact who generally look only after they leap; that is, they tend to react virtually automatically to opportunities for sexual stimulation rather than to respond after at least some consideration and reflection. The men are often just as much out of control; witness John F. Kennedy with the close trine whose escapades were legendary but mostly secret during his lifetime. Moon-Mars is often obliged to extricate itself from trouble especially in early life because of its attraction to controversy, fighting, the "wrong people" and sex. It is independent, willful, selfish and often encounters trouble with women due to poor or inadequate parenting. The mother usually provides the bad example, but occasionally the father is the culprit since the Moon broadly relates to the entire family. When these conditions do not obtain the native receives injustice from the partner or may suffer physically from a congenital defect, debilitating illness, or an uphill fight against grinding poverty (especially with Saturn also involved).

Sometimes the native endures an all but impossible social battle such as a lower class intellectual may suffer against ignorant and hidebound people in positions of entrenched authority. If the bodies are dignified such as Mars in Capricorn opposite the Moon in Cancer, particularly with the Moon elevated over Mars, the untoward effects are much mitigated. Such a person might well excel as a military or political leader. Blue bloods or others born to privilege with this contact may act in a manner that endears them to the masses and be attracted to people of a lower social station than their own. If there are extenuating circumstances, generally the presence of Venus or Jupiter, a Moon-Mars native may be merely so full of energy, enthusiasm and a crusading spirit that he or she can run circles around other people and accomplish tasks too daunting for most people to consider. President Theodore Roosevelt, an extraordinarily dynamic and vigorous man, shows the effect. He had the Moon opposite Mars one and a quarter degrees from exact. Consistent with the influence of Mars, whether the Mars influence is suffered as violence or not, one's fate is often bound up with it somehow. Teddy Roosevelt as President William McKinley's vice president became president when McKinley was assassinated in 1901.

Moon-Jupiter

This is a superb aspect in any form. The Moon is symbolic of the family, thus with Jupiter, the greater benefic, the native gets a good start in life if the Moon is simultaneously free of affliction from the malefic planets. A Jupiter-Moon combination also suggests that the native and the parents, especially the mother, are invested with integrity, that the family history is an honorable and often a prosperous one. Obviously many people born to wealth and rank have this contact but many more people who are less well born have it too. All of them are generally talented, lucky and successful to a noteworthy degree. Jupiter-Moon is remarkably personable, enthusiastic and usually virtuous. It is also gentle, decent and generous, other things not considered. Those various other things can ruin parts of the contact and merely leave the native mostly successful and lucky, as in the case of the psychopath Adolf Hitler who had the two-degree conjunction.

Any contact with Jupiter is protective but one cannot be protected from everything especially if one lives a public life. William McKinley rose from chairman of the Ways and Means Committee in the House of Representatives to become a two-term president of the United States, but he was assassinated in 1901. McKinley had the conjunction a half-degree from exact. The contact is not a magical talisman; most of the time, however, a Moon-Jupiter conjunction is some species of wonderful. The Roman emperor Hadrian, who ruled at the time of greatest Roman power and expansion, had the conjunction a half-degree from exact. Talk show host Merv Griffin became immensely wealthy buying radio and television stations and had a great time doing it. He had the conjunction less than a degree from exact. President George W. Bush has the conjunction one and a half degrees from exact. Another talk show host who had a 30-year run in the business, Johnny Carson, had the two-degree conjunction. He was more than merely popular and a brilliant humorist, rather, an iconic figure. The very popular actress, Angelina Jolie, with the four degree conjunction appears to have everything one could possibly want, at least materially and circumstantially. Without the addition of other contacts to the combination, that is the basic affect of Moon-Jupiter: one's needs *and* desires are supplied in abundance.

The square is more active, occasionally contentious in the service of virtue and may feel impelled to insert itself into the major issues of the day. Malcolm X (Little), with the square less than a degree from exact, took a stand directly in the cross hairs of racial injustice but was struck down despite his courage and integrity. Mohandas Gandhi, with the square only a quarter of a degree from exact, suffered the same fate for his political activism to secure independence for India. Pope Francis (since 2013) has the six and a half degree square in zodiac, but it is less than one degree from exact in mundo. He is another example of the progressive thinking and good fortune that typically attends this combination. People with the square usually stand for something solid even if it seems to an outside observer that their lives are merely a celebration of creativity and freedom of expression, like singer/actress Cher Bono with the exact square, designer Giorgio Armani with the one-degree square and singer/musician Bruce Springsteen with the one-degree square. All three are wealthy.

The people with the trine are often widely celebrated whether high born or low. Toni Morrison, winner of a Pulitzer Prize and the first black woman to win the Nobel Prize for literature, has the trine only a quarter degree from exact. Charles, Prince of Wales, heir to the British throne, has the trine only a half-degree from exact. The benefit that accrues to him therefore bears directly upon his family connection as the son of a queen. More often, Moon trine Jupiter confers nobility of temperament and character, which is shown to good effect in President Barack Obama who has the trine two and a half degrees from exact. He had a good mother and grandparents who made a critical difference in his life when his father abandoned the family.

The opposition is hardly different in its tendency to confer wealth and power, except perhaps to enhance it still more. Ronald Reagan, a two-term president, had the opposition exact almost to the minute. The first Roman emperor, Augustus Caesar, who ended decades of civil war in the Roman world, had the opposition one and a half degrees from exact. Both Reagan and Augustus were almost beyond question the most powerful men in the world at the height of their power respectively. Oprah Winfrey is fabulously wealthy and successful by any measure. She has the opposition four degrees from exact straddling the meridian. Francois Hollande, president of France from 2012 to 2017 has the opposition less than a quarter of a degree from exact. While he is very bright, well educated and an expert politician, so are many people. It's important to be good at one's job but in general, in order to get to the top one must be good and lucky. The Moon with Jupiter makes its natives predisposed to exalted positions in life because in addition to being capable, they are also fortunate, often because they look good and/or are personable. They look right for the part. In a more raw and direct manner, people who engage in open, heated and dangerous competition are more likely to excel than their competitors who are without this aspect. A. J. Foyt, the first driver to win the Indianapolis 500 four times, has the five-degree conjunction. He also has the Moon sextile Venus only one and a half degrees from exact. Only two other drivers have won the Indianapoilis 500 four times (Al Unser and Rick Mears).

Moon-Saturn

The Moon is the most tender of all the bodies used in astrology. Its sphere of action is the home, family, the early life in general and the body. In combination with Saturn, the greater malefic, early poverty, dysfunctional and broken families, the early death of a parent and divorce suffered as a child or as an adult are common themes in the horoscopes of people who have this combination. The type of aspect appears to make little difference with a slight nod in preference of the conjunction. It bestows a dogged, very hard-working, duty-oriented quality that finds its natives working circles around other people, accepting responsibility and burdens early. The Moon-Saturn person usually takes more satisfaction from discharging duties and responsibilities than from pleasure, play and taking their leisure. Sometimes they feel guilty for even taking enough rest. Much depends on the rest of the chart, however, because Moon-Saturn people may, with additional affliction to the Moon, appear inert, lazy unproductive, painfully shy, socially maladjusted or without ambition. Their self-image is bad, their early environment usually difficult and they may also suffer serious health issues. People with multiple afflictions to the Moon often spend decades recovering from their childhood, sometimes in therapy. The child with Moon-Saturn must be handled carefully because it is the sign of a bad start in life. There is an inclination toward depression, a tendency to be the black sheep in the family and difficulty in getting along outside the family. Such people may benefit more from the friends they finally make, who will be much loved, and the golden hearts of their girlfriends and boyfriends.

If the Moon is simultaneously in some relationship with Saturn as well as Jupiter and/or Venus, the mother will often suffer in health yet be much loved; or the family may suffer grinding poverty yet hang together and be strengthened through the unremitting love of the parents and the adversity of being disadvantaged. Without help from the benefics the Moon-Saturn person may find the parents to be damaged goods, especially the mother, incapable of help, cold, undemonstrative, selfish and without much apparent interest in the native. The parents in such cases will probably also have Saturn with their lights (the Sun and Moon). Some combinations like the Moon in Leo with Saturn will make the mother overpowering and domineering; in some way with Moon-Saturn, the mother is a problem or fails the native. The mother of the native is also likely to be depressed, feel trapped in her marriage or resent her station in life, which spills over into her relationships with her children.

Remarkably, Moon-Saturn contacts are not inimical to success, as evidenced by producer/director Stephen Spielberg, President Bill Clinton, and actress Marilyn Monroe, all of whom have squares two degrees from exact. Spielberg's parents divorced when he was a teenager, which was very difficult for him. Clinton grew up without a father whose death preceded his birth and Marilyn Monroe's father was not part of the family and had no influence in her life except by his absence; moreover her mother was insane. Despite an inclination toward depression, Moon-Saturn contacts often symbolize implacable resolve, which is frequently the salvation of these natives. Yet early poverty and/or the death of a parent, family dysfunction, outright broken families, divorce in adult life and catastrophes that relate to one's personal life rather than one's professional life, are still the theme. The conjunction looks much the same: singer Elvis Presley, actress Sophia Loren and poet/singer Bob Dylan, who all have the conjunction, came out of distressed or impoverished backgrounds to succeed on a big scale.

Steve Jobs, who achieved spectacular renown for his work that put a computer in front of millions of people, was born to an unwed college student who put him up for adoption. He had the Moon sesquiquadrate Saturn one and a half degrees from exact which suggests the most fundamental of difficulties that relate to the relationship between the native and the birth mother: she didn't want him.

Actor Jack Nicholson, the 14th Dalai Lama and French monarch Louis XIV, the "Sun King," all have Moon opposition Saturn. Nicholson didn't know until he was an adult that the woman he thought was his older sister was actually his mother—the same experience of the musician Eric Clapton. Nicholson's father was never part of the family. Louis became king of France at age five on the death of his father. He was extremely autocratic and hard-working but bled France white by his wars. The Dalai Lama left his family at age five to begin his education to become a Buddhist monk. He became the Tibetan head of state at age 15 and has lived in exile in India since 1959 when China invaded Tibet.

Moon-Uranus

Men with this combination often have a strong, domineering or at least somewhat strange mother and or wife. The women often get involved with men who are not merely unusual but unlike any particular type and may even be distinctly weird, or very smart in some specialized way. Often in the same person there is a contrast between talent in math and science and interest in bizarre subjects that range from science fiction to the supernatural. The contact veers decidedly toward the uncommon, the unconventional and the far-out. It is consistently a sign of high intelligence, is frequently very talented, ahead of its time, perceptive and so exceptional that its natives may be easily misunderstood or considered unfathomable. Like all Uranian contacts, it is freedom-loving, bold, daring and associated with the leading edge of contemporary thought; thus its natives will adopt stances in opposition to the prejudices of the day and embrace anything that ensures justice for people at large.

Even those with the wide contacts like the author Louisa May Alcott, with the seven-degree conjunction, display the classic features of the contact. The publication of *Little Women* in 1868 brought her fame but she was also well known during her lifetime as an intellectual, an abolitionist and a strong advocate of women's suffrage seventy years before it became law. She embraced a philosophy called transcendentalism whose members included her friends Ralph Waldo Emerson and Henry David Thoreau. Screenwriter-producer Gene Roddenberry, creator of the Star Trek series, also shows the effect; he had the five-degree conjunction. French musician Erik Satie, with the three-degree conjunction, although classically trained, went off in his own direction that was described as musical surrealism. Germaine Greer, Australian author, academic, marxist and radical feminist, has the three degree conjunction. She, one of the earliest bra-burners, advocates a permanent state of revolution in order to constantly address the evils of hidebound society. W.D. Gann, the best stock market timer of all time, had the one-degree conjunction. No one has been able to duplicate his method.

The great dancer, singer and actor, Fred Astaire was, in his prime, the most amazing and profoundly gifted dancer of his time, which is highly characteristic of this combination to symbolize the exceptional and often the best in a specialty. Astaire had the opposition a quarter of a degree from exact. Occasionally there is nothing weird about Moon-Uranus, yet it is still exceptional as effortlessly cool, without trying to be, extraordinarily likeable without a shade of pretense and brilliantly successful in high pressure situations well beyond the abilities of most people. Joe Montana, one of the greatest quarterbacks of all time, has the one and a half degree conjunction (only a half degree from exact in right ascension) high in his chart. His ability to produce unlikely victories from near certain defeat was a characteristic feature of his football career from high school, through college at Notre Dame and twice as the most valuable player in the National Football League as he led the San Francisco 49ers to four super bowl victories in the 1980s and 1990s. Moon-Uranus people consistently stand out either as so far removed from the mainstream that they defy description (not necessarily in a good way) or as so remarkable that they evoke awe, admiration and appreciation in an extreme manner. The combination tends to produce a remarkable life. This is most likely if the combination is high in the horoscope or in one of the angular houses: the first, fourth, seventh or tenth. Montana has it in the tenth house. But this combination is valuable even when it is wide, below the horizon and in a cadent house. Tennis great Roger Federer, who has won Wimbledon eight times, has the five-degree conjunction in the third house. Federer's conjunction is closer in right ascension than longitude by a degree and yet another degree closer still when the combination appears on the western horizon.

Brilliant Irish author-poet-playwright Oscar Wilde, with the square only a half-degree out, was imprisoned for two years for his homosexuality that was considered an affront to public decency in the 1890s. Swiss psychoanalyst Carl Jung had Moon square Uranus less than a degree from exact. His mother was such an avid spiritualist that the family harmony was confounded by it. When Jung's professional friendship with Sigmund Freud (who had Sun conjoined to Uranus) broke in 1913, their original contributions had made them the most highly acclaimed figures in clinical psychology. Their differences were mainly about the nature of the unconscious which Jung thought extended to universally shared experiences and symbols now called the collective unconscious: a distinctly lunar point of view. Freud thought that religion was without inherent legitimacy but Jung considered it also a part of the collective unconscious. Freud thought sexuality was the motivation for virtually all behaviors; Jung felt that sex was one of several overwhelmingly important factors that comprise the drive for wholeness. The Moon is more about integration than the Sun that relates to hierarchical segregation and domination. Jung went on to explore the occult, including astrology. Mark Knopfler, the brilliant guitarist-singer-songwriter for the now disbanded Dire Straits, has the square two degrees out.

Moon-Uranus people are often the leaders of groups due to their original contributions. A large number of people in this writer's clientele who have Moon square Uranus have left their country of birth to live in the United States. The Moon relates to one's origins and Uranus to people, places and things foreign, thus ex-patriots. Most Moon-Uranus people characteristically love the out-of-doors; none more so than the square people who also feel wanderlust to a noteworthy degree. They often work for airlines, cruise lines, travel agencies or in some capacity that affords them the opportunity to exercise their desire to experience the new, the foreign or simply the wide-open spaces of their own country. They may live in many places as military families often do. It is quintessentially peripatetic.

The lightning-fast wit of comedian Robin Williams is a tribute to his Moon trine Uranus only one degree from exact. The arts are a magnet for Moon-Uranus. Jim Henson, who developed Ernie, Bert, Big Bird, Kermit the Frog and all the Sesame Street characters, as well as the Muppets, had the four-degree trine. He was a wellspring of creativity. The excellent French author and dramatist, Alexandre Dumas (père) had Moon trine Uranus five degrees from exact. His *Three Musketeers*, The *Man in the Iron Mask* and *The Count of Monte Cristo* are considered classics, one of the primary features of Uranus. That is, Uranus relates to things so fine, and beyond mere style, that their appeal is timeless. Uranian experiences in transit are usually excellent and often represent one's initiation into major chapters in life, such as when one graduates from the world of school to the world of work, one's first sexual experience, becoming a parent or a moment of flashing insight that sends the native into his destiny.

Natives of Moon opposite Uranus are quite extreme or they are thrown into extraordinary circumstances. Author Jack Kerouac, one of the primary exponents of the bohemian life that was first called the "beat generation" in the 1950s that blossomed into the hippie movement in the 1960s, had the opposition less than a degree from exact. He wasn't trying to be different for effect; he just answered to a different drummer. Alcoholism ended his life too soon. Princess Diana had the two-degree opposition. She was the first wife of Prince Charles and mother to Prince William and Prince Harry, one or both of whom will someday sit on the English throne. She refused to conform to the dimensions of the box that contained her life after her marriage. Her rebellion is a characteristic Uranian response to limitation, restriction and, right or wrong, the perception of injustice. John Belushi, the gifted wild man cum comedic actor/entertainer, had the opposition four and a half degrees from exact. His antics moved millions to uproarious laughter until a drug overdose ended his life early.

Moon-Neptune

Natives of this combination are strongly inclined toward the dramatic arts, music, religion and spirituality, drink and drugs and liberal politics. It is sometimes the sign of inherited wealth or at least being carried in life by the good will and effort of someone else. It can be distinctly licentious and succeed in gaining position and rank through underhanded means. It is a contact that may symbolize a home-wrecker or someone who is on the receiving end of the schemes of a home-wrecker. Some form of mental illness, more often of a family member than the native, is very common. The contact may symbolize a sneaky, deceitful and shameless hustler or a self-sacrificing, tender-hearted saint. It is often reclusive, may find meaning in service to the poor and dispossessed and is usually distinctly kind. Senator Edward Kennedy had the conjunction less than a half-degree from exact. The 14th Dali Lama has the one-degree conjunction. Many theatre people have this like the great character actor Dustin Hoffman with the one-degree conjunction: David O. Selznick, who produced *Gone With The Wind*, the highest grossing movie of all time (adjusted for inflation) had the three degree conjunction; actor Robert Redford has the three-degree conjunction; and German medical missionary Albert Schweitzer had the two and a half degree conjunction. One of the finest voices of her generation, Amy Winehouse had the four-degree conjunction. Her problems with alcohol led to her early demise at age 27. Addiction, the fine arts, unusual sensitivity to suffering and family dysfunction sometimes show up with this combination in a package; other times these qualities appear in part.

The square is not markedly different in effect. Actor Michael Douglas is not only a fine actor, he was born into an acting family with the square a third of a degree from exact. French sex-kitten Brigitte Bardot from the 1950s and 1960s became an avid animal rights activist, which is also characteristic of Neptune's desire to eliminate or mitigate suffering. She has the one-degree square. Comic genius Peter Sellers had the one degree square. The sinister side shows in the four-degree square of J. Edgar Hoover, former head of the Federal Bureau of Investigation who had dossiers on virtually everyone of consequence and used them to threaten public figures who had something to hide. Any Neptune aspect to the Moon may relate to addiction. Sigmund Freud, the father of psycho-analysis, with the five-degree square, was addicted to cocaine and tobacco for decades.

Moon trine Neptune natives may enjoy popularity that verges on cult status even if it is frivolous. The silent film star Rudolph Valentino, whose trine was only two minutes of arc from exact, experienced adulation in the 1920s on an heretofore unheard of scale that made him the most popular figure of his day. The great Italian operatic composer, Giacomo Puccini, was similarly mobbed by fans. Puccini had the one-degree trine. His *La Boheme*, *Tosca* and *Madame Butterfly* are still, more than a century after their composition, the most widely performed operas in the world. The best known and revered British prime minister since Disraeli, Winston Churchill, with the one-degree trine remains a towering figure, renowned for his political acumen, steely resolve, brilliant wit and fondness for drink. Martin Luther, with the two-degree trine, achieved enormous fame that has lasted five hundred years for his Reformation of the Catholic Church. Luther always thought himself a good Catholic even after he was excommunicated. Devotion, another Neptunian virtue, made him feel that the embrace of Scripture was more important than the authority of the pope or canon law. Robert Zimmerman, better known as Bob Dylan, achieved a staggering celebrity in the 1960s that still endures. His mind was tuned to the very essence of the era that was reflected back in his work. Really a poet at heart, he was inspired by forces even he admits that he doesn't understand and couldn't duplicate. Dylan has the three-degree trine. The highly developed Neptune people sometimes suspect that they are instruments through which higher forces work.

Former President Bill Clinton has the sesquiquadrate less than two degrees from exact. Like the opposition between these bodies, this Moon-Neptune aspect shows the tendency toward scandal despite the equally obvious talents of the native. Often there is misfortune with this planet combination that nevertheless has a silver lining if there is supplementary support. The best known, and perhaps most capable English astrologer of the last 500 years, William Lilly, had the sesquiquadrate less than a quarter of a degree from exact. He inherited two fortunes via the deaths of two of his three wives. He bought thirteen houses with half of what he inherited from the first wife. Jupiter added to this combination helped it considerably. Lilly had Jupiter square the Moon, slightly more than one degree from exact and Jupiter semi-square Neptune, also slightly more than one degree from exact, both of which are excellent for financial gain. The latter contact, Jupiter-Neptune, is commonly associated with unearned benefits. The excellent actor Robert Downey Jr. with the one-degree opposition went through drug abuse rehabilitation like it was a revolving door until he finally beat his addiction. The native is thus not invariably caught in an endless cycle of addiction, although entrapment, addiction, humiliation and scandal is often the signature of Neptune when it is afflicted. The brilliant post-impressionist French artist Henri Toulouse-Lautrec, whose works command millions today, drank himself to death at age 36. He had Moon opposite Neptune one degree from exact, and was born into a wealthy aristocratic family. Woolworth heiress Barbara Hutton had the three-degree opposition. She inherited $50 million in 1933 (the equivalent in purchasing power of $1 billion in 2011) but had a miserable life. Her mother killed herself when Barbara was a child; Barbara was totally ignored by her father; her only son was killed in an accident; she was married seven times; and was addicted to pills, hashish and alcohol for decades. At her death, $3,500 was left of the $50 million she inherited. Marilyn Monroe, also with the three-degree opposition, was perhaps the best-known American actress of all time. She was born dirt poor to a mother who was insane, and her mother was ultimately committed to an asylum. As a reuslt, Marilyn grew up in foster homes. Marilyn clawed her way to the top in Hollywood, became addicted to pills and died a mysterious death that was first ruled an overdose of sleeping pills. Some experts think she may have been murdered.

Moon-Pluto

The chief effect of Pluto in aspect to the Moon as a natal condition is to disturb the harmony and stability of the early family relationship. When this is not the case, it often happens with Moon-Pluto people that the mother is the dominant parent. If there are no other aspects to the Moon to mitigate Pluto's influence, the mother is often cold, remote, harsh, undemonstrative, or too self-involved. She may suffer poor health and be unable to help the native or she may be removed by an early death. Orphans, adopted children and illegitimate children usually have Sun-Pluto, Moon-Pluto or both conditions. Frequently, Moon-Pluto points to divorce, either of the parents, in the adult life of the native or both, especially if Pluto configures both lights. Most often a Pluto-Moon relationship simply means a lack of love, or an inadequate expression of love in particular from the mother, in a household where most other needs are supplied except adequate physical contact, affection and play. Difficulty in intimate relations as an adult is commonly the main consequence of this contact. Often Moon-Pluto children were unwanted and they know it. As adults, if the aspect is very close, they may not want to be touched and refuse, like Sun-Pluto, to let people into their lives or their partners complain that they are not let in far enough. Often the native has few friends. The Moon-Pluto person usually is not close to his siblings and may have little or no contact with them as an adult. Aspects of the Sun, Venus and Mercury warm up the Moon quite a lot so that people with these aspects to the Moon appear to be far more pleasant, clever, funny and socially integrated than the pure Moon-Pluto types. Still, they may strongly incline toward solitary conditions and need to be drawn out by others who urge them to play or to attend a group. Pure Moon-Pluto types fiercely resist social integration. They are often victims or bullies in a playground situation, more commonly the former.

Sometimes the effect is reversed and the mother of a person with a close Moon-Pluto aspect is herself rejected by the native, sometimes even detested, because of her neglect or things she has done that make her an outcast. Prostitutes, strippers and drug addicts consistently have children with

Moon-Pluto aspects. Strange to say, even though Moon-Pluto is generally alone and lonely, even within (an unhappy) relationship, unlike the Sun-Pluto contacts, the Moon-Pluto people usually don't want to be as reclusive as the Sun-Pluto people. Even so, they are often bachelors or spinsters anyway because they have great difficulty accommodating to another person, or they choose people who are also emotionally unavailable. When these conditions do not obtain because of configurations between the lights and Venus, which give warmth, empathy and suggest good relationships with the parents, Moon-Pluto contacts are sometimes symbolic of siblings with serious mental problems or trauma incurred by the death of siblings. Occasionally an apparently well-adjusted person with a Moon-Pluto aspect will become involved with a person who is so profoundly unavailable emotionally and sexually that the entire relationship appears untenable to an outside observer. In such a case the Moon-Pluto person will have recognized a suitable person upon whom to cast his projection to avoid owning it. No matter how charming the native may appear to be when he can't escape social interaction, he is still not inclined to be a social animal unless other planets join the combination, especially Jupiter.

Moon-Pluto aspects are more serious than Sun-Pluto. Men with these contacts are occasionally attracted to girls because they can't deal with women, or their mates are considerably younger than they are. Women with this contact are often childless or have many pregnancies but few children carried to term. If the benefic planets, usually Jupiter, also attend the Moon, the other extreme of Pluto is invoked: the child may live with the mother and ensure her comfort and support well into the adult life of the native and sometimes as a life-long condition. It is as though mother and child are siblings. Ordinarily the person with Moon-Pluto can't connect with the mother or she is an austere figure, but if the benefics are also in play, the native can't separate from the mother or only achieves it with great difficulty. This triple combination, Moon-Pluto- Jupiter, also appears in the horoscopes of people who are part of a remarkably close extended family that contains three or even four generations that is more like a clan. Occasionally they all live under one roof but even if they don't live together in the same household, their own households are extensions of the same family, unlike most Western households that are discrete and distinctly separate units comprised of only two generations: parents and their children.

The tremendous strength of the dignities and debilities can also ameliorate or exacerbate the effect of this aspect. For example, if the Moon is well placed in Taurus or Cancer, and in particular, if the Moon is higher in the sky than Pluto, the mother will simply be a formidable figure who takes her role seriously and applies herself conscientiously to it. If the Moon is in Scorpio or Capricorn, the mother may totally abdicate her responsibility to the native and off-load him to a relative. Occasionally with Moon-Pluto, family matters control the life or the native suffers inordinate restriction at the hands of overbearing parents. A classic example is Wolfgang Amadeus Mozart, whose life was to an extraordinary degree controlled by his parents, especially the father after the death of the mother. Mozart had the Moon conjoined to Pluto less than a degree from exact. People who go into the family business or feel obliged to follow the father in a military career or to excel in a career as the mother did frequently suffer extraordinary pressure from the family that is more like coercion.

George Washington, the first U.S. president, had the Moon square Pluto within a half degree. He had a distinctly strained relationship with his mother; some sources call it life-long animosity. John Lennon, the most creative of the Beatles, the greatest musical group of the post World War II era, had the square less than a degree from exact. While his father was at sea for extended periods during World War II, Lennon's mother went through a string of boyfriends that ruined her marriage. Young John was caught in the middle of his parent's dissolving marriage, his mother's boyfriends and multiple residences until some stability was achieved at the age of six when he went to live with his aunt. He was devastated at his mother's death when he was 17.

Singer and actor Frank Sinatra had the two and a half degree trine. His parents stayed together but his mother was known as a fiery personality and a part-time abortionist. Sinatra was married four times. Hugh Hefner, founder of Playboy magazine, has been married only twice. He was raised in a strict Methodist environment, which may explain why he has kept a virtual harem for the past 50 years. Hefner has the one-degree trine, which shows the propensity of Pluto go to extremes and to become impersonal and detached, perhaps genuinely jaded by sheer numbers.

The main figure of the Reformation, Martin Luther, had the two-degree opposition. His mother has been described as a harsh disciplinarian. She was also slandered as a whore and a "bath house attendant," the truth of which is hard to verify and probably false, but it shows how the mother of a Moon-Pluto native may become an object of scorn or derision whether deserved or not.

Mercury-Venus

This is an excellent contact in any configuration. Since Mercury at maximum elongation east or west, and Venus simultaneously at maximum elongation in the opposite direction, cannot be greater than 75 degrees apart, the only possible major aspects for this pair are the conjunction, parallel, contra-parallel, semi-sextile, semi-square and sextile.

Natives of this combination are artisans, intellectuals, sometimes both, as well as people whose skills unite body and mind into Nietzschean supermen and women. They are generally attracted to the fine arts but all forms of sophistication tantalize their sensitive natures. Literary skill is often prominent with it as well as those who can successfully maneuver through the business world in any capacity. Usually they display conspicuous integrity even in the rough and tumble of business. Mercury-Venus people appreciate the good ideas of others and learn, promote or keep those ideas in circulation as teachers and students. A teacher with a Mercury-Venus aspect doesn't merely recite facts but dispenses information in a manner that engages the interest of his or her students who become educated and made ready to express themselves in life effectively. Similarly, a master inculcates an apprentice by example with knowledge of technique, who in turn becomes a journeyman and then a master in his own right. Occasionally natives of this pair are such perfect conduits of thought and feeling that others experience their work seamlessly, viscerally, as though they were personally engaged in what is actually a vicarious experience. Eugene O'Neill, Pulitzer and Nobel Prize winner (for literature in 1936) and the greatest American playwright to date (*Long Day's Journey Into Night, The Ice Man Cometh, Mourning Becomes Electra, Desire Under the Elms*), appreciated and was influenced by the work of the great Russian author and playwright, Anton Chekhov, but O'Neill was a genius in his own right. His Mercury-Venus conjunction, three degrees from exact, is a classic example of the best of that pair. In a similar vein, the excellent American born (later British subject), Thomas Stearns Eliot (T.S. Eliot), had Mercury conjunction Venus straddling the Ascendant in Libra two degrees from exact. Eliot was among the best twentieth century poets in English and also a playwright, essayist, publisher, professor (although he had only a B.A.), literary critic, editor and businessman. He won the Nobel Prize for literature in 1948. Another fine example is Nora Ephron with the wide seven-degree conjunction. She went from reporter to columnist to essayist to the author of novels and screenplays and finally to movie director. She was charming, clever, wickedly funny, brilliantly insightful and popular among the artsy cum literary set. Johann Sebastian Bach had the two-degree conjunction. He is among the two or three best composers of all time (born March 1685), and with Mozart and Beethoven, one of the giants of the Enlightenment.

Venus contacts impart a degree of artistry to whatever planet she touches: with Mercury, ordinary narrative becomes prose and poetry; utilitarian considerations assume elegant proportions; and work is performed in a manner that is pleasing to the native's sense of taste, no matter how simple. People who have this pair, whether they are teachers or not, gently but skillfully guide and increase the understanding of others, especially children since Mercury relates to youth. Natives of this combination are often social butterflies, clever, quick and frequently blessed with a brilliant sense of humor. They write well, sometimes literally as calligraphers, and more often figuratively as effective communicators and masters of word-play; they speak well, frequently dance well and display amazing versatility. Actors, because they play radically different characters, show the broad range of the Mercury-Venus type. Kathy Bates, with the nearly exact conjunction, and Paul Newman with the one-degree conjunction, are classic examples. Engineers, who delight in not merely clever but beautiful solutions to technical problems, often have Mercury-Venus aspects. Clarence (Kelly) Johnson, the long-time director of the famous "Skunk Works" at the Lockheed Corporation, may be the finest aeronautical engineer to come out of the United States to date. He could give the correct figure of the wing loading of an airplane by a brief visual inspection without computation. He had the three degree Mercury-Venus conjunction beautifully complimented by Jupiter closely trine that conjunction. He was the main force behind the Lockheed Electra, the Lockheed Constellation, the P-38 Lightning, the F-80 Shooting Star (the first U.S. jet fighter) the U-2 spy plane the F-104 Starfighter, the C-130 Hercules, the SR-71 Blackbird (which has flown from the west coast of the U.S. to the east coast in less than an hour) and many others. The breathtaking lines of these beautiful machines illustrate how the principle, "form follows function," is an exercise in aesthetics as well as mathematics. The "once-in-a-generation" fashion designer Yves St. Laurent emphasized the aesthetic manifestation of this combination. He had the same combination as Johnson: Mercury conjoined to Venus (only five minutes of arc from exact in this case) trine Jupiter. Novelists and their publishers, whose works are revisited for generations, like F. Scott Fitzgerald, have this contact. He had the conjunction a degree and a half from exact. The contact is also distinctly symbolic of people who excel in handcrafts, whether they are famous or not, like sewing, knitting, weaving, crocheting, embroidery, dressmaking, tailoring and all textile arts. Yet the effect extends to other hand-eye skills that invoke the native's aesthetic sense. Both the mason who works in granite and the sculptor who works in marble usually have Mercury-Venus in some combination, as well as wood carvers and experts in cabinetry and joinery.

All the Mercury-Venus contacts appear to operate in the same way. As usual, the so-called minor aspects are not minor in effect when they are close. The eloquence of President Barack Obama is a contemporary example of the effect of the semi-sextile only a half-degree from exact. The extraordinary intellectual and greatest of the German poets, Johann Wolfgang von Goethe also had the semi-sextile a half-degree from exact. Both of them excelled in the classroom, which is typical of Mercury-Venus. The utterly clear, pure voice of the late singer Patsy Cline entranced millions who were moved by this daughter of the muse Melpomene. Cline also had the semi-sextile a half-degree out. Legendary actor Charlie Chaplin shows the timeless popularity of the contact. His semi-sextile was a third of a degree from exact.

The seven-time Formula One World Champion, Michael Schumacher, is the best open-wheel professional driver of his era. He has the most Formula One wins to date (ninety-one) of any driver in the history of the sport. The key to car control is not aggressiveness, although that trait is essential for a competition driver; rather, the most important elements are subtlety, quickness (in reaction to outside stimuli) and smoothness. Schumacher has the semi-sextile only two minutes of arc from exact. Mercury-Venus is a testament to quick reactions and reflexes; in short, the extraordinary coordination, which is innate and cannot be taught, that allows someone to negotiate a race course at 200 miles per hour and not merely survive but win. The career of the brilliant Brazilian driver Ayrton Senna da Silva was cut short by his death at the Italian Grand Prix in 1994 when he crashed at 190 mph. He was a three-time Formula One World Champion and is widely considered among the most gifted drivers of all time; as of this writing in 2015 he is third in Formula One wins with forty-one. Senna also had a Mercury-Venus combination, a six degree conjunction in longitude (but only two and a half degrees *in mundo* when the combination was on the western horizon). Senna's Mercury was retrograde but it didn't hamper his effectiveness. There are very few people capable of handling a car, at least under full race conditions, with a power-to-weight ratio better than a strong motorcycle. It is therefore beyond question that Senna's retrograde Mercury could not have impaired his ability to manage a car capable of 230 mph if Mercury retrograde were the debility that is widely supposed in some astrological circles. Component failure was suspected by the investigators of his fatal accident. The matter was never resolved. Jim Clark, "the flying Scot," was a two-time Formula One World Champion who likely would have been champion several more times except for his death in a Formula Two race in 1968. The cause of his fatal accident is unknown. Clark won twenty-five grand prix races in only seventy-two starts which is an astounding winning percentage. He also won the Indianapolis 500 in 1965. He is in the same class with Senna and Schumacher. Clark had a Mercury-Venus conjunction four degrees from exact which clearly is a signature of one who is possessed of extraordinary grace in action as much as in speech and manner. Typically and effortlessly natural, these people are a joy to engage or even to watch. They are quickly recognized for their poise, fearlessness and adroitness.

The semi-square is more vigorous than the other contacts as evidenced by former president Theodore Roosevelt whose enthusiasm and optimism are very characteristic of the contact. His was less than a third of a degree from exact. Mercury-Venus natives are often classic "do-gooders" anxious to improve things, to promote the general welfare, safety and happiness of the people within their purview. Roosevelt's advocacy of the Pure Food and Drug Act of 1906 is an important, though not spectacular, example of how that attitude manifests in real life. Those who have the semi-square are a bit edgy but they usually get away with it without giving offense. Actor Joe Pesci with the half-degree semi-square, director Oliver Stone with the less than one degree semi-square and model turned entrepreneur/businesswoman Martha Stewart all show the gutsy, ambitious desire to have an effect and to get things done that goes with this combination. Herman Melville, author of *Moby Dick*, was thought by some of his family to be insane, possibly because his works did not sell well or receive much critical acclaim until long after his death. He had the one degree semi-square. People who have Mercury-Venus combinations are very much in earnest and are quite put off by a poor response to their offerings.

The sextile is dynamic and lucky. At the moment that the Wright Flyer first gained altitude under its own power in December 1903 at Kitty Hawk, North Carolina, Mercury was sextile Venus only six minutes of arc from exact. That's a tenth of a degree. Mercury with Venus can be exhilarating as in the first moment of powered flight or in a moment of deep understanding after long effort, or when one succeeds in any intrinsically difficult endeavor. Mercury-Venus is instantly convertible, however, from matters of gravity into levity. It is active, clever, quick, playful and entertaining. Cheerleaders, who cavort, dance and help carry a mood, consistently have it. People whose business is concentrated silliness and fun also have it, like Walt Disney, who built an empire around a cartoon. He had the two-degree sextile. The brilliant American comedian, Chris Farley, had the sextile less than a degree and a half from exact. His quick wit and improvisational skill could turn any situation into instant uproaring joy. Mercury-Venus contacts rarely produce many children. Often there are none. The genius of American theoretical physicist Alan Guth is symbolized by his Mercury-Venus sextile only a half degree from exact with Mercury in the zenith of the horoscope. He produced the theory of exponential expansion of the universe in the first few billionths of a second after the Big Bang. It is known simply as "inflation," whereby the expansion of space increased briefly at the rate of ten to the ninth power, which is faster than the speed of light.

Mercury-Mars

This combination is present in the horoscopes of people with high intelligence, sharp tongues, and a quick, high-strung temperament. They are sometimes a bundle of nerves, but their problem-solving ability is often astounding. Mercury-Mars people can usually handle advanced mathematics or other demanding courses of study and they typically fill the ranks of graduate schools everywhere. They excel in debate and most areas that entail a high degree of difficulty. They can be overwhelming and may appear to hold back among people with lesser ability so as not to make such people feel uncomfortable; or they may ruthlessly humiliate lesser minds. A fine contemporary example of the conjunction is Bill Gates, who founded Microsoft, Inc. before he had even completed his bachelor's degree.

In mundane work a Mercury-Mars conjunction can signify flashing insight for people who are prepared by training and inclination to see beyond accepted limits. On the night of October 5-6, 1923, when Edwin Hubble discovered his first Cepheid Variable star in the M 31 Nebula (the Andromeda), transiting Mars was applying to the conjunction of transiting retrograde Mercury. They were separated by six and a half degrees in longitude on the night of the discovery but by only three degrees in mundo at the latitude of the Mt. Wilson Observatory in California. It was the Cepheids that provided Hubble with the realization that M 31 was beyond the Milky Way galaxy and thus a galaxy in itself. He also instantly realized that the universe was immensely bigger than had been previously thought, which was for many people in virtually all walks of life, the most mind-expanding event of their lives. Hubble's work ultimately led to the conclusion that the universe is expanding, that it may well be infinite, thus beyond "size" and that all galaxies are accelerating away from each other.

Robert Noyce, dubbed "the mayor of Silicon Valley," had a mind so quick that he was called "Rapid Robert" while an undergraduate. Noyce was studying college-level physics while still in high school. He had the two degree Mercury-Mars conjunction, steadied and rendered more formidable by the nearby addition of Saturn to the conjunction, eight degrees east of Mars and six degrees east of Mercury. He earned a Ph.D in physics and became one of the most important, influential and powerful players in the development of the semi-conductor and electronics industries upon which the world is utterly dependent today.

The downside is that under affliction this combination can be distinctly unstable. Even without affliction this pair can lead to nervous breakdown, especially in conjunction form, although intellectual prowess is more common. Much depends on the rest of the horoscope as to how this combination will work out. In a difficult map, Mercury-Mars can symbolize a distinctly troubled person. In a fortunate map, Mercury-Mars signifies prodigious ability. It gains most from Saturn, which lends stability and profundity to the mix. In fact, the three-way combination of Mercury, Mars and Saturn is a consistent signature of talent in math, physics or chemistry. Mercury-Mars natives, without assistance from some other helpful planet, may fly to pieces under stress or be unable to perform in an emergency situation. This is especially true of the square. Yet the doubtful quality of the square may be cool under stress but embrace extreme positions or perform heinous acts like the assassin Lee Harvey Oswald who had the close square.

The placement in the zodiac of some of these occasionally troublesome combinations is an important adjunct with regard to how they work out in real life. John Flamsteed, the first *astronomer royal* at the Royal Observatory at Greenwich, had Mercury exalted in Virgo square Mars in Gemini less than a degree from exact. The combination in Mercury's signs points to his brilliance rather than ill-temper. He vigorously defended his work, however, when he had to contend with the arrogance of Isaac Newton. Mercury-Mars thus is not invariably aggressive but almost always forthright. Flamsteed proved in 1678 the isochronous rotation of the Earth and supplied the best observations of the heavens in his day among his many fine achievements.

In spite of the trouble that often attends the square, other planets or combinations that touch the Mercury-Mars aspects will modify it substantially. The brilliant German physicist Wilhelm Conrad Röntgen had Mars square Mercury only four minutes of arc from exact but his Mercury was also conjoined to Jupiter less than three degrees from exact. Röntgen was awarded the first Nobel prize in physics in 1901 for his discovery of X-rays in 1895. He donated the prize money to his university and refused to take out patents on his discovery in order for the entire world to be able to benefit from it immediately in the form of diagnostic radiology. Only an advanced personality deeply infused in the spirit of goodness and generosity can do such a thing. Thus it is simplistic to evaluate any Mercury-Mars contact, indeed any combination, as though all natives are pure types without other contacts that impinge upon the combination; unless, of course, they are pure types.

In the same manner in another field of endeavor, the extraordinary American jazz musician and composer, John Coltrane, a great innovator and tenor saxophone virtuoso, was also well known for his generosity toward younger artists, his devotion to a musical ideal and his religious convictions. Coltrane had Mercury sesquiquadrate Mars and Mercury sesquiquadrate Jupiter. Coltrane's Mars and Jupiter were in a one and a quarter degree square. Both Mercury sesquiquadrates to this square were less than two-thirds of a degree from exact. Frequently mentioned in the same breath with Archimedes and Isaac Newton, the great German mathematician Carl Friedrich Gauss had the one and a half degree sesquiquadrate between Mars and Mercury. He also had the mundane square between Mercury and Jupiter (Mercury rose when Jupiter was in the I.C.) only five minutes of sidereal time from exact which is one and a quarter degrees of arc. Mercury-Jupiter is excellent symbolism for a stellar career; allied to Mercury-Mars, the two combinations are powerful symbolism for worldly success.

Among the pure types there is a distinct inclination toward impatience, a foul-mouthed tendency and an irascible attitude that may put Mercury-Mars people at odds with others who won't tolerate the native's uncivil manner. The opposition in particular often produces someone who ranges from the type of person who has no problem occasionally stretching the truth to an outright liar who constructs elaborate deceits. Common problem areas are education, which may be repeatedly interrupted or incomplete; the career, which may go nowhere despite remarkable ability; and travel accidents or problems that result from sports injuries. Occasionally people with the opposition are innocent but suffer from the deceit and manipulation of others. If Mars is elevated over Mercury the native is more likely to be mendacious, but much depends on sign and house position as well as other bodies that add to the combination. Mercury elevated over Mars is generally far less troublesome but the native may be a gossip. All these undesirable characteristics can be mitigated through meditation if the native acknowledges their existence.

Realistically, taking into account the large number of successful people who have them, oppositions and squares should not be considered "bad" in themselves. They are just strong, and if a strong aspect contains a classical malefic planet like Mars, untoward results may follow. But it is not due to the so-called "difficult" nature of the aspect; rather, it is the planet. So while there is a tendency for squares and oppositions to manifest badly or with difficulty, one must not take the supposed good versus bad quality of aspects as an inviolable rule, because it is frequently contravened. Richard Nixon, brilliant in school and as a politician, had the conjunction but was brought down because he broke the law, lied about it and was caught.

Conjunctions, sextiles and trines of Mercury-Mars are usually easier to handle than squares and oppositions because they are less forceful and more subtle. Master politicians like President Franklin Delano Roosevelt and one of the greatest English monarchs, Elizabeth I, both with the close trine aspect, enjoyed success in high stakes maneuvering in politics. Even with the trine, the impatience of Mercury-Mars may show itself. Roosevelt completed a history degree at Harvard in three years instead of four and passed the New York bar exam before he had completed his law degree at Columbia.

The exceptional mathematical ability of Amalie Emmy Noether is a testament to Mercury trine Mars three degrees from exact. Her Mars was in one of Mercury's signs, Gemini, and Mercury was in Aquarius, the sign of original work and discovery. She discovered two theorems that were fundamental to Einstein's Relativity Theory and elementary particle physics. She is somewhat better known as the foremost exponent of abstract algebra and number theory of her time. Her intuitive approach led to the underlying connections between algebra, geometry, topology and logic. She worked without pay in an academic position from 1908 until the University of Gottingen granted her a small salary in 1922, and even then, only due to the intercession of physicist Albert Einstein and mathematician David Hilbert on her behalf. Forced out of her academic position when the Nazis came to power in Germany, because she was Jewish, she came to the United States and taught at Bryn Mawr College in Pennsylvania.

Mercury-Jupiter

This combination tilts its natives toward an intellectual life and often a good education. Even when education is not emphasized these people are decidedly cerebral, usually successful, liberal and progressive. They excel in the law, politics, academia, publishing, literature, psychology, drama and standard religion practiced in the open, as well as esoteric spirituality like Free Masonry generally pursued behind closed doors. They also love to experiment, to take things apart and to revel in how they work. There are always exceptions. Richard Nixon graduated third in his class at Duke Law School but was distinctly conservative; he had the one-degree conjunction. French monarch Louis XVI, who loaned the American colonies large sums of money and resources at a critical moment during the American Revolutionary War, was neither an intellectual nor well educated, but he thrilled at mechanical contraptions. Louis had the one-degree conjunction. Giovanni Montini, better known as Pope Paul VI (1963-1978), had the two-degree conjunction. He was a remarkably intellectual and forward-looking pope who is more characteristic of Mercury-Jupiter in its standard manifestation as a man-of-letters.

The renowned academic and author, G. J. Toomer, who did the definitive translation of Ptolemy's *Almagest* from Greek into English and many other astronomical and mathematical works, has the two degree conjunction. He is equally at home in Greek, Latin and Arabic, which is also characteristic of the great breadth of the work of Mercury-Jupiter people. They tend to be far-ranging in their interests, or if their interests are singular or limited, the affect of their work still frequently extends beyond the limits, eras and the cultures into which they were born.

Singer/songwriter Daryl Hall's work is so good that his songs first performed thirty years ago are heard on the radio every day even now. He has the two-degree conjunction. Dr. John Dee, astrologer to Elizabeth I of England, was one of the most learned men of his day. He had the three-degree conjunction. William Blake, the eighteenth/nineteenth century British poet and painter, was so far ahead of his time that he was misunderstood by most of his contemporaries. Now he is seen as one of the brightest lights of the age. Blake had the four-degree conjunction.

The only disagreeable issue that relates to the conjunction is that it may produce a know-it-all attitude if afflicted by a third body.

One of the finest technical achievements of the eighteenth century was the solution to the problem of finding longitude at sea. British mathematical genius and polymath Isaac Newton once said that he thought the solution would never be found. John Harrison, a modestly educated English technical genius of a different sort, solved the problem by building the first marine chronometer, the most accurate clockwork in the world up to his time. Harrison had Mercury sextile Jupiter less than a degree from exact; although that is only one, admittedly important, part of an amazing horoscope, it does illustrate the technical virtuosity that often accompanies this planetary combination. Inventors and progressives typically have Mercury involved with Jupiter and or Uranus. Academics and physicists typically have Mercury involved with Mars and Saturn.

Harrison's solution is based on the fundamental relationship between time and place, familiar to astrologers. If the difference between a local time, which can readily be determined at sea if the sky is not overcast or stormy, and a standard reference (like the Greenwich meridian) is known, that difference in time between those two places equals the arc in longitude between one's position and the standard meridian, because four minutes of time equals one degree of arc. Nobody could make a clock that would keep accurate time at sea because the movement of a ship through the sea disturbed the movement of a pendulum suspended beneath every more or less accurate clock at that time, even if the clock were in gimbals.

Harrison had the Sun, Mercury, Venus and Neptune in Pisces and the Moon in that sign as well, if he were born in the second half of the day. He was so deeply involved with the spatial abstraction of clockwork design that he found it difficult to communicate his ideas in words, consistent with Mercury in its fall. Yet debilitated bodies in a good horoscope usually produce someone who thinks outside the box of what the planet is about in its standard form. That he was equipped to grasp the patterns associated with the abstraction of time reckoning was symbolized by Saturn square Neptune two and three quarters degrees from exact. Harrison's chart is a good example of the fault of simplistic horary thinking that would render his entire horoscope a disaster inasmuch as Saturn was square all the Pisces planets to a greater or lesser degree *in zodiaco* and *in mundo*.

The Saturn-Neptune square, in particular, isn't a debilitating problem in itself; it makes the need to understand complex issues insistent and gives the ability to differentiate between the apparent versus the true. In other words, Saturn-Neptune can see beyond the veil, beyond appearances to apprehend underlying principles or facts. The symbolism that promised success in his endeavor and made him rich (in addition to Mercury-Jupiter) was Jupiter mundane square Neptune. Jupiter culminated at his birthplace less than two minutes of sidereal time after Neptune set. That's less than a half degree. He was able to bring his ideas into form. Harrison's Uranus-Pluto mundo square (Uranus rose as Pluto passed through the IC) only one and a quarter degrees from exact at his birthplace, revolutionized navigation through his several inventions that were incorporated into the marine chronometer that gave an error of only one second per day. There are 86,400 seconds in twenty-four hours.

After laboring for thirty years to produce a pendulum clock that would work at sea, he finally abandoned the clock approach and redirected his study of clockwork design into a very large pocket-type watch more than five inches in diameter that weighed more than three pounds but was not subject to the rolling and pitching of a ship at sea. Watches were far less accurate than clocks until Harrison applied his prodigious talent to the development of this extremely accurate watch that incorporated most of the features in miniature that he had used in his extraordinarily accurate pendulum clocks. The watch was powered by a mainspring with temperature compensation that turned an escapement of Harrison's own design. It was the first watch that used a high energy, high frequency balance (that beat at five oscillations per second, which is 18,000 per minute). Harrison's "sea watch" kept Greenwich Mean Time* at sea no matter how far removed from the Greenwich meridian a ship might be. It was, in effect, a portable standard time meridian. Harrison had the most progressive of all planet combinations: Neptune-Pluto. Neptune culminated in the Midheaven of his horoscope slightly more than one degree before Pluto rose. The manifestation of that contact was that after the success of Harrison's sea watch, marine chronometers were adopted universally. They ushered in a new era of precision that saved thousands of lives and many ships and cargos that, until the advent of the chronometer era, were lost at sea every year due to gross errors in dead-reckoning navigation. The ideas behind Harrison's chronometer were employed (although much modified in particular by his contemporary Pierre Le Roy) until the advent of electronic navigation in the twentieth century.

Baseball player Ted Williams, the last man to hit .400 over the course of an entire season (.406 in 1941) had Mercury-sextile Jupiter less than a degree and a quarter from exact. Significantly, his Mercury was retrograde, but it didn't slow his fast rise to the highest tier of professional athletics or his entry into the Hall of Fame. His case is a good example of what Mercury retrograde very often *really* means: intense concentration. Like many of the great players, Williams was not merely extraordinarily gifted but a serious student of baseball. His swing was a thing of beauty and his place in the Boston Red Sox pantheon is secure forever.

The square is often less successful than the conjunction although not less capable, or if extraordinarily successful, the native may be tainted by bad decisions or unseemly associations. Immanuel Kant, who had a two-degree square, was the most influential thinker of the European Enlightenment. His contributions to logic, philosophy, and astronomy are hailed as the work of a genius. Kant's *Critique of Pure Reason*, his magnum opus, is an attack on traditional metaphysics, and while brilliant and extraordinarily profound (throughout eight hundred very dense pages), it wasn't as widely embraced in his lifetime as it is now. The celebrated singer/actor Frank Sinatra, with the three-degree square, though professionally very successful and wealthy, was dogged by allegations that he had ties to organized crime. The mysterious but extraordinarily popular Swedish actress, Greta Garbo ("I want to be alone."), retreated from the spotlight when the world could have been

---

*Local Apparent Time (LAT [sundial time or time o'sun rather than time o'clock]) was the civil standard in England in 1761 when Harrison's first "sea watch," commonly known as H4, underwent its first sea trials on a voyage across the Atlantic from England to Jamaica (H1, H2 and H3 were clocks). But Greenwich Mean Time was an *astronomical* standard that had been in place since 1675 with the establishment of the Royal Observatory at Greenwich thanks to the patronage of Charles II. Greenwich Mean Time (GMT) replaced the LAT of London in 1792 as the civil standard of the capital city. All English communities subsequently but slowly converted from their own LATs to GMT over the course of the next sixty years, with the cities adopting GMT first and the rural communities adopting it last.

her oyster. She had the square one degree from exact. Mercury-Jupiter tends to confer enduring celebrity, popularity and admiration, especially for one's written, spoken or sung works. Edith Piaf is still the most beloved songstress France has produced. Her works are heard every day though she died in 1963. She had Mercury mundane square Jupiter less than a half degree from exact. The British novelist, essayist, publisher, feminist and intellectual, Virginia Woolf, had the one and a half degree square. The excellence of her work was not confounded by recurring bouts of mental illness, although ultimately she killed herself. She also had Mercury square Neptune.

The success enjoyed by natives of Mercury trine Jupiter is quite remarkable and consistent. Arnold Schwarzenegger, with the zero degree trine, rose from modest circumstances to win the Mr. Universe bodybuilding title seven times, then went to Hollywood where he amassed a two hundred million dollar fortune in action movies and finally became governor of California. George Washington, with the two-degree trine, led American forces to victory in the American Revolution, became a two-term president of the United States and was also the richest man in the country for many years. Dwight Eisenhower, with the one-degree trine, also came from modest circumstances to become supreme Allied commander in World War II and two-term president of the United States. Samuel Clemens, better known by his nom de plume, Mark Twain, with the four-degree trine, may still be the most widely read American author of all time though in 2010 he had been dead for a century. The colorful former wrestler Jesse Ventura, with no formal training, education or experience, came out of nowhere in 1998 to win the governorship of Minnesota; he has the one-degree trine. Ginger Baker, one of the greatest drummers of his era, founded *Cream* in 1966, the first of the co-called "super groups." He has the four degree trine. A drummer must have an extraordinary sense of time, which Baker claims is the basis of his virtuosity, as well as exceptional manual dexterity. Mercury is symbolic of the hands. A Mercury-Jupiter aspect is an invaluable gift to a musician.

The opposition is also very successful. Writer/producer Aaron Spelling, with the one-degree opposition, still is the most prolific producer in the history of Hollywood. Pablo Picasso, with the one-degree opposition, was the pre-eminent figure in modern art during his lifetime with only one rival (Henri Matisse). Alain Prost, the outstanding French competition driver, is a four-time Formula One World Champion. He is currently second in all-time grand prix wins with fifty-one. He has Mercury opposition Jupiter less than a quarter degree from exact, which is extremely lucky. Obviously he is as talented as he is lucky to have won fifty-one times. His case is interesting because it illustrates how even so-called good aspects of Saturn can take the bloom off the rose of otherwise superb combinations. Prost has Saturn trine his Jupiter less than a degree from exact and Saturn sextile Venus, also less than a degree from exact. He is a member of a very select group and even though he survived a long racing career, and is in the first rank of the great drivers, he isn't the overall leader in wins and may be overtaken (whereas Michael Schumacher will probably not be overtaken). President Barack Obama, with the two-degree opposition is a terrific example of the eloquence and political skill that usually attends this combination. It is also, obviously very lucky and able. Mercury has a lot to do with the career of the native. Generally, all these people need is a chance to display their ability to be recognized. The noted seer of the early modern period, Michel de Nostradamus, had the opposition six and a half degrees from exact. If he were a fraud, his work would have long since been forgotten.

Thomas Alva Edison, the great American inventor who revolutionized the world via his prolific output of devices, procedures and scientific applications to industrial design, had Mercury mundo square Jupiter. His Mercury rose with a sidereal time of 16h 28m 13s and his Jupiter passed through the IC at his birthplace with a sidereal time of 16h 20m 11s. That difference, 8m 02s, is two degrees of arc, making this a very significant aspect.

James Dyson, the very successful and talented British inventor and master of industrial design, has the two degree quincunx. His products are used globally. His work serves to illustrate how the occasionally weird and generally pejorative opinions about the quincunx are without merit. Planets determine how aspects work out, not the other way around.

Among the people who have this who are successful but do not achieve fame, Mercury-Jupiter in any configuration gives a head for business, especially marketing skills. The native can generally maneuver an enterprise such that increased profits, market share and stock price are the results of their efforts. These people are usually "suits," i.e. office types who direct the work of others.

Mercury-Saturn

This combination has a reputation as an undesirable contact; in fact, in some circles it is considered a signature of stupidity. The opposite is true: Mercury-Saturn is among the most intelligent and gifted of planetary combinations. Its natives are extremely hard-working, like most planet relationships that involve Saturn. There is amazing perseverance and persistence, a fondness for order, and an appreciation for underlying patterns that illustrate the bounds, limits and laws of the physical world, indeed even cosmic laws, that are the underpinning of everything.

Albert Einstein, who discovered the relativity of time and the fabric of space-time, had the one-degree conjunction. His discovery was so enormously recondite that only physicists could grasp it for decades. Like many people with Mercury-Saturn, he had a slow start and didn't show his great promise until adolescence. Saturn is slow to mature. Edgar Cayce, the most gifted American psychic in the history of the republic to date, also had the one-degree conjunction. Saturn is profound. The great lawyer/statesman Nelson Mandela, unjustly imprisoned for twenty-seven years for his political convictions, had the conjunction less than two degrees from exact. His unshakable resolve, highly characteristic of Mercury-Saturn, made him the father of his country. Former President Bill Clinton was a Rhodes scholar before he went into politics; he has the five-degree conjunction. His father died before he was born. Clinton rose from poverty, in the determined manner of Mercury-Saturn people, on sheer will and talent. He has the five degree conjunction. Wyatt Earp, the frontier sheriff, gambler, teamster, buffalo-hunter, saloon and brothel owner and miner is best known as one of the principals in the shoot out in 1881, known as the "Gunfight at the OK Corral" at Tombstone, Arizona. Tombstone was a boom town that sprang up almost overnight on a huge discovery of silver. There, he and two of his brothers (one of whom was sheriff at the time) and Doc Holiday, an alcoholic dentist, turned gambler/gunfighter and friend of the Earps, killed several outlaws whose small time-criminal empire was in jeopardy due to efforts of the Earps to bring it to an end. The survivors of the criminal element subsequently killed one of the Earp brothers and permanently maimed another in ambushes. Wyatt was relentless in his pursuit of the outlaw gang and managed to kill three more of them against heavy odds. Wyatt had Mercury conjunction Saturn less than a degree from exact. He was intransigent in his unwillingness to retreat. It doesn't matter if the native is on the right or wrong side of the law or what the circumstances are: Mercury-Saturn people are stubborn, adamant and determined. They will not back down.

The mathematical prowess of Mercury-Saturn people is occasionally their most noteworthy quality. Urbain Jean Joseph Le Verrier, the man given the credit for finding the planet Neptune in 1846, had the sextile less than a degree from exact. His was a dexter sextile, i.e. Mercury, the faster planet, was east of Saturn. Le Verrier's specialty was celestial mechanics.

If a Mercury-Saturn aspect is thrown from a troublesome house, especially the eighth or the twelfth, and in particular if the aspect is a sinister square (whereby Mercury is west of Saturn), the result can be very difficult. For example, a person with Mercury in the twelfth house square Saturn in the second house, *exact to the minute*, was born strangled by his umbilical cord. This person lived but suffered irreversible brain damage from oxygen deprivation and was severely retarded as a result. His Mercury was not retrograde. He was institutionalized for fifty years because his day-to-day requirements were beyond the ability of his family to supply them.

In most cases the square is not less talented than the conjunction but excites controversy to a greater degree, often because its natives flout convention. Former Secretary of State Hillary Clinton has the all but exact square. She was an outstanding student as an undergraduate and in law school at Yale; she has been a devoted wife and mother; she forgave her husband's philandering; she was a fine senator in service to the people of New York; and a tireless and very capable secretary of state. But because she wanted a bigger life than a domestic one, and said so, she is a lightning rod for the anger and irritation of people who are put off by her ambition. Isaac Newton, who derived the laws of motion as well as the differential and integral calculus, had the one-degree square. Newton changed the world more profoundly than any other figure until Einstein. The calculus is the most powerful mathematical tool of all time. It created a sensation that swept the world and revolutionized problem solving. Newton was also irascible, reclusive, jealous and possessed of a fierce temper. Notwithstanding feats of great intellectual power, an extraordinary fault with Mercury-Saturn will sometimes show itself, especially with the square or opposition and usually if the combination is afflicted by another body: narrow-mindedness accompanied by stubbornness. This fault does not always attend the hyper-intellectual manifestation of Mercury-Saturn, although Newton, for one, displayed it to some degree despite his advanced thinking in general. Occasionally it appears as overcompensation toward a domineering parent. That is, the native dominated, rejected or in some way treated badly by a parent, resolves to never allow anyone to gain a position of power over him again and thus becomes defensive and closed which paradoxically manifests as aggressiveness. Joseph Alois Ratzinger, better known as Pope Benedict XVI (2005-2012), has the mundane square (Saturn rose at his birthplace two minutes of sidereal time before Mercury conjoined the lower meridian) slightly more than one half degree from exact. He is extremely conservative as the ultimate guardian of the Catholic faith; but he is also an intellectual, an academic, a writer and a linguist. Throughout his career he has been strict and exacting as an enforcer of Catholic ritual and dogma, so much so that he is widely regarded as quintessentially doctrinaire. If either body is badly placed in its fall or detriment, ill will or a sour, critical, nasty attitude is very common when this pair is in square. Such people generally respond to irritation and stress not with grace but with impatience, aggression and sarcasm. They are readily criticized for their meanness.

More artistic types have the trine, but there are also many very strong technical types with the trine. Director-producer-writer Steven Spielberg has the trine less than a degree from exact. While he down plays it, his Mercury-Saturn trine suggests that he's enormously wealthy and successful because he's very smart. Emile Zola, the French author of 20 novels and strong critic of injustice within the French government, had the one-degree trine. The Russian genius, Dmitri Menedeleyev, who developed the periodic table of elements organized by atomic weights, had the three-degree trine. The result of his work is probably hung on the wall of every chemistry class in the world.

The opposition produces marked effects that evoke hard feelings and may occasionally be distinctly incendiary in nature. Henry VIII of England with the opposition almost exact to the minute dismantled the power of the Catholic Church in England in order to obtain a divorce. He also confiscated the property of the abbeys, many of which lie in ruin even today. Henry's efforts produced a level of antipathy unequalled in England until the English Civil War, a hundred years after his death. The great jazz trumpeter Miles Davis had a distinctly irascible personality that created tension and turmoil almost everywhere he went. Davis had the zero degree opposition; yet the opposition between these planets speaks to the basic, even minimalist nature of his mature works that are at once profound and deeply satisfying. The best American actor of the twentieth century, Marlon Brando, with the three-degree opposition, was legendary for his temper tantrums when he didn't get his way.

The horoscope for the Federal Reserve Bank of the United States (December 23, 1913 at 6:02 p.m. EST at Washington D.C. [the time was found by Bill Meridian—it was broadcast over the radio in 1913]) has a Mercury-Saturn opposition less than a degree from exact. That aspect symbolizes the responsibility of the "Fed" to determine monetary policy, control interest rates, promote price stability, limit inflation, prevent deflation and promote full employment of the entire country.

Mercury-Saturn is also common in the horoscopes of engineers, especially mechanical engineers. Leonardo da Vinci with the five-degree opposition is the foremost medieval example. Ever practical, these people find how to render the abstract and merely conceptual into concrete reality. The aspect symbolizes control *per se*; people as well as the organizations that have it tend to be both strict and to limit the behavior of others. President Barrack Obama has the wide six-degree opposition. He attracts the vilification of hidebound conservatives who oppose his every policy, maneuver and statement despite the obvious merit of most of them. Sometimes the native is on the receiving end of harshness, misplaced blame and injustice, yet engages those harsh elements to mollify them rather than evokes them through his own arrogance or ill-advised behavior.

Mercury-Uranus

Many astrologers have this planet combination as well as their clients. Such people are also receptive to other occult arts and advanced ideas in general. Mercury-Uranus tilts decidedly to the left but not invariably so, as evidenced by the conservative president Ronald Reagan who had the five-degree conjunction. He took astrological advice for decades and was known as the "Great Communicator." John Locke, considered the father of modern liberalism, had the four and a half degree conjunction with both Mercury and Uranus trine Jupiter. Locke was a physician and a philosopher (*An Essay Concerning Human Understanding*) who very strongly influenced eighteenth century Enlightenment thinkers. His ideas about the necessity of the separation of church and state, religious toleration and the notion of government by the consent of the governed, deeply influenced Thomas Jefferson, James Madison and Alexander Hamilton to the extent that Locke's philosophy made its way directly into the United States Declaration of Independence though he was a life-long British subject. Locke therefore is a classic example of the advanced thinking and the freedom-loving, radical positions—for their time—characteristic of the combination.

Mercury-Uranus has oratorical ability, dramatic ability of a high order as shown by the actor Leonardo Di Caprio who has the conjunction less than a degree from exact, and literary ability as shown by Nobel Prize winner (for literature) William Faulkner who had the sextile only eleven minutes from exact. The amazing and inspired Indian mathematician Strivinasa Ramanujan had the two-degree sextile. He was compared by his collaborators at Cambridge to the Swiss mathematical genius Leonhard Euler. Ramanujan's originality and staggering mathematical prowess put him in a class beyond almost all of his contemporaries. His work has been applied to the study of black holes though he died more than forty years before they were discovered. Charles Dickens, one of the most popular British authors of all time, also had the two-degree sextile. Reform and the redress of grievance is a recurring theme with this combination that Dickens embraced in particular in his greatest works: *David Copperfield*, *Oliver Twist*, *A Christmas Carol* and *Bleak House*. Ability in languages frequently accompanies any Mercury-Uranus combination. The native is often bilingual or may be obliged to study languages due to a career in the diplomatic service. People who take degrees in history are required to study several languages in order to be able to read primary source material in the original vernacular. People who teach languages commonly have these planets prominent in their horoscopes.

With the single exception of Wallace Stevens among the greatest American poets, all of them have Mercury involved with at least one of the three outer planets, Uranus, Neptune and Pluto, especially Uranus and Pluto. These contacts suggest that the poetic turn of mind can both sense fundamental truths about life and transcribe them into language that is both accurate and aesthetically pleasing better than people without these contacts. Consistently the most common aspects among the poets between Mercury and Uranus and Mercury and Pluto are the conjunction, semi-square and sesquiquadrate with a modest sprinkling of sextiles and trines.

The outstanding Italian physicist Alessandro Volta had a three degree Mercury-Uranus conjunction. He discovered several fundamental electrical laws and developed the first electro-chemical battery that could produce a constant electric current. In consideration of his work with electricity and his Mercury-Uranus conjunction, it is perhaps noteworthy that the color of Uranus is electric blue. The unit of electric potential, the volt, is named in honor of him. He also studied the chemistry of gases and isolated methane in 1778. He was a lifelong academic and held university faculty positions for nearly fifty years.

This type feels imprisoned in a cubicle, the military or a corporate hierarchy—unless they have rank and freedom of action. The contact is original, advanced and often a champion of individual rights. It is headstrong, independent and imbued with a strong sense of justice, irony and occasionally flashing insight. These people are not impressed by tradition, or what passes for prevailing wisdom and they may be a thorn in the side of those who expect agreement or deference. They have a particular talent for making themselves unpopular, although often for legitimate reasons, not because they have a contrary response to every established condition, but rather only those that are clearly in need of modification or elucidation. Mercury has a lot to do with education and vocation; with Uranus, natives of this pair are attracted to particularly engaging work that affords them opportunities to express their individuality, especially in areas that relate to new and advanced thinking.

French author, philosopher and feminist Simone de Beauvoir with the one-degree conjunction shows the effect, as well as the brilliant German mathematician and astronomer, Johannes Kepler, who confirmed and correctly modified the heliocentric theory of Copernicus. Kepler had the three-degree conjunction. Another well-known mathematician/astronomer, William Marshall Smart, had the one-degree trine. His *Textbook on Spherical Astronomy* has been a classic for eighty years and has run to six editions. Usually the Mercury-Uranus people demonstrate extraordinary ability wrapped in conventional clothing that nevertheless often lifts them above their fellows. They are disdainful of poseurs, extravagance and display and let their work speak for itself. Professor Smart taught at Cambridge University and the University of Glasgow.

The people with the square are very clever but may ruffle feathers due to their unwillingness to play the "go along to get along" political game. Bobby Kennedy aroused a hornet's nest of enmity as attorney general in his fights with FBI director J. Edgar Hoover and organized crime; he had the two-degree square. The greatest English monarch of the modern period, Elizabeth I, steered the English ship of state through the violent tensions of the Reformation without becoming subject to any faction or aligning England with any other state that could have compromised English independence; she had the two-degree square. The celebrated British statesman and author, Winston Churchill, known for his wit, oratory and deep political insight that often cut against the grain, also had the two-degree square. The father of modern independent India, Mohandas Gandhi, had the mundane square a third of a degree from exact. Like Bobby Kennedy with the zodiac square, Gandhi was an implacable enemy of the *status quo ante* that was invested in tryanny and corruption. He devoted his life to addressing institutionalized repression of an entire nation and, by extension, all such people everywhere. The work of British-American author and playwright, Christopher Isherwood, with the four-degree square, was also devoted to social and political freedom consistent with the nature of Mercury-Uranus. The great Czech author and intellectual, Franz Kafka, wrote in German (Die Verwandlung [The Metamorphosis], Der Process [The Trial], Das Schloss [The Castle], Das Urteil [The Judgement] about realism and surrealism combined in the same works, as well as alienation, anxiety and the absurd. His work is among the most compelling and engaging social commentary of the 20th century. He was a lawyer who worked for insurance companies and wrote voluminously at night. Kafka had Mercury square Uranus less than a half degree from exact. These planets in any combination give voice to the complexities and stresses of life that is often eloquent, beyond merely insightful and penetrates to the most profound and fundamental issues that nearly everyone feels yet may struggle to express coherently. The headstrong, outspoken and breathtaking beauty Austrian born actress Hedwig Eva Marie Kiesler (Hedy Lamarr), was also an inventor. She was often described as the most beautiful woman in the world and was also considered a genius by many people, including one of her lovers, Howard Hughes, who put his resources at her disposal. She co-invented a device that quickly changed communication frequencies in electronically controlled devices that kept them secure from jamming. She was granted a patent for the device in 1940, although her idea didn't become practical until the advent of the transistor. Lamarr had Mercury (retrograde) square Uranus fewer than three degrees from exact. Her patent (now expired) is in every cell phone and computer used today.

Social activism and a deep sense of goodness that may manifest via politics, appears with the trine (although it is not absent from the other aspect types). President Abraham Lincoln, with the trine less than a degree from exact, is a compelling example. Taking a stand against the monstrous tyranny of slavery describes the essence of the contact. The same is true of President Woodrow Wilson's efforts to found a league of nations that ultimately saw the light of day in the form of the United Nations. Wilson had the two and a half-degree trine. President Lyndon Johnson, with the three-degree trine, pushed his "Great Society" social program through Congress to further the lives of still disenfranchised black and poor people. Uranus always stands for freedom, excellence and the best manifestation of an idea; with Mercury, one's thoughts, words and deeds are harnessed to classic virtues unless there are afflictions to the combination. Jim Thorpe, who won the pentathlon in the 1912 Olympic Games at Stockholm, is even today considered one of the finest athletes of all time. He was in a class by himself. Thorpe had Mercury trine Uranus exact to the minute if he were born near noon. He was so fast that some of his records were not equalled more than fifty years after he set them, when training and conditioning afforded to athletes was of a much higher order than early in the twentieth century. Mercury's wings are attached to his feet and a winged helmet, in the symbolism of the ancient world, which is meant to convey swiftness. Since Uranus is typically exceptional, it is easy to see how that planet connected to Mercury is frequently related to one who can run like the wind. Thorpe later became the first great halfback in the National Football League in the 1920s. He also had Mars conjunction Pluto, but that relates more to strength and martial ability than speed.

People with this combination commonly embrace positions that are opposite the standard position of the day. Uranus is like this in any combination. For example a person with Venus-Uranus may be polyamorous, whether homosexual or heterosexual instead of singular with respect to partners. More commonly, such people frequently get involved with someone from outside their cultural matrix or a foreigner. A person with Mercury-Uranus embraces ideas and positions that run counter to the prevailing condition of the day. Such a person might well embrace the sidereal zodiac in a largely tropical milieu or play the devil's advocate in a sea of consensus.

In general, Mercury-Uranus sees things in non-standard ways. Malala Yousafzai, the youngest person to win the Nobel Peace Prize (in 2014 at age 17) took a stand against the tradition in her native Pakistan that mitigated against education for girls—at least the poor and disadvantaged ones—and was shot in the head by the Taliban for her efforts. She survived and has become an international celebrity for education for women and girls. Malala has the opposition less than a degree from exact. She is a classic example of how Mercury-Uranus emphasizes education, radical ideas (with respect to a culture or an era) and especially how this aspect symbolizes people who will stand up to injustice when it's not easy or convenient to do so. Annie Besant, one time leader of the Theosophical Society, had the exact opposition. The Theosophical Society is the ultimate Uranian organization: non-sectarian and devoted to the advancement of understanding. The astounding French artist Henri Matisse, the greatest colorist of the twentieth century, whose works ranged from impressionism to near abstraction, had the opposition only a half-degree from exact. Alexander the Great, one of the greatest and most innovative military captains of all time, had the two-degree opposition. Adolf Hitler, renowned for his oratory, had the six-degree opposition, which should serve as a reminder of the extremes that may be embraced by misguided natives of this combination.

Mercury-Neptune

This combination is mainly concerned with idealism, music, the theatre, traditional religion as well as non-traditional heightened spiritual awareness, the occult, fashion and the arts. At its best, Mercury-Neptune is supremely virtuous and connected to high levels of consciousness. At its worst, the combination relates to deceit, mental illness and drug-induced stupor.

Total faith in Scripture versus religious bureaucracy that deviated, he felt, from Scripture was the basis of Martin Luther's quarrel with the Catholic Church hierarchy that produced all the Protestant faiths. Luther's conjunction, only two minutes of arc from exact, is typical of true believers. Some others with this contact are reluctant to disclose their spiritual positions. Neil Armstrong, the first man to walk on the Moon had the conjunction less than a degree from exact. He has always refused to discuss his religious views except to say that he is a "deist," that is, one who believes in a higher power without any denominational trappings or priesthood. Mercury-Neptune is apparently privy to the unseen world in a genuine manner. Its natives gravitate toward spirituality quite naturally and even when not religious in a standard sense they are frequently "sensitives" who leap-frog past mere intuition into the realm of pure thought, feeling and energy. Once the great composer Ludwig van Beethoven said of Johann Sebastian Bach, that his name should not be [merely] Bach (which means "brook" in German) but Ozean ("ocean" in English). Bach, one of the greatest composers of all time and the man who brought polyphonic music into vogue, had the three-degree conjunction. He was utterly brilliant, prolific and inspired by a great ocean of energy that washed over and through him and emerged as music. These people fairly consistently handle artistic endeavors much better than they do regular, uninspired, everyday life. Often the memory is very poor, especially if Mercury is in its fall or detriment. People with this conjunction often feel betrayed by their poor recall or inability to explain what they do actually understand, but can't find the words or means to express what they know at a symbolic or non-verbal level, that somehow becomes confounded in transmission to the logical, verbal world. A state of infuriating befuddlement is not uncommon with this contact, made better by a simultaneous association with Saturn: the only prophylaxis against Neptune.

Gabrielle Sidonie Colette, the notorious author of 50 novels, including Gigi, which was made into a popular American movie, had the nearly precise square. She is still the most popular female author France has produced even though she died more than 50 years ago. Her work was tender, vivacious and insightful in an uncommonly true to life manner that struck a nerve in the public consciousness. The work of the great jazz musician Miles Davis, with the square less than a degree from exact, is a musical corollary of thought and feeling so fundamental that it feels naked. Art is an external demonstration of internal feeling, but to produce a rendering so fine that it is widely embraced is inherently difficult, which is why art is celebrated. Mercury-Neptune speaks to its creation. Singer/songwriter and poet, Bob Dylan has the square less than two degrees from exact. He is connected to the wellspring that all artists drink from—which even he allows that he does not understand—like the actress Audrey Hepburn with the two-degree square and singer Jim Morrison of the Doors with the three-degree square. Extreme religious fervor may attend this pair in all its combinations, but those with the square have the most trouble with it as witnessed by David Koresh, leader of the Branch Dravidians, whose paranoia evoked an armed governmental response to his own armed fanaticism. In contrast, the idealism and compassion of President Abraham Lincoln, with the less than four-degree square, was instrumental in amending the most glaring flaw in the United States Constitution. President Donald Trump has the three degree square which points out the necessity to interpret the horoscope, rather than to merely recite standard interpretations, because he is neither religious nor virtuous, artistic or musical, but well-known for taking liberties with facts. Trump is an extreme example of the effect of a sinister square whereby the faster body is west of the slower one. That is, he has Mercury in Gemini square Neptune in Virgo. A dexter square, whereby the faster planet is east of the slower one, is far more likely to work out well; that would be the case if he had Mercury in Virgo square Neptune in Gemini. The unique musician, Malcom John Rebennack, better known as Dr. John, The Night Tripper, has the semi-square less than a quarter degree from exact if he were born in the late morning or afternoon. His embrace of jazz, New Orleans culture and the bizarre is so complete that his reputation immediately evokes images of great music, Cajun, Creole and Voodoo themes and the wild, creative and artistic lifestyle that frequently attends this planet combination.

The trine is not always a good thing in itself. Jim Jones, leader of the People's Temple movement, had the nearly exact trine. He was an ordained minister gone bad. Nine hundred people committed suicide (with him) on his order in 1978. John Hinckley with the two-degree trine, shot and nearly killed President Ronald Reagan in 1981. Hinckley has ever since been confined to a mental institution. Many more people with the trine have been successful in the dramatic and performing arts and businesses, like the playwrights Oscar Wilde with the trine only a quarter of a degree from exact and George Bernard Shaw with the two-degree trine. Politicians who seem at first unremarkable but redeem themselves by their cool and accurate assessment of affairs also have it, like President Dwight Eisenhower.

The opposition is very potent and, as with the musicians, its natives have affinity for translating distinctive qualities of energy into form via color, texture, cut and drape that are pleasing to the eye and evoke feeling and mood from their style and constituent materials. Fashion looks "right" if the stylist can translate the energy of long term contemporary transits into form. The fashion genius Christian Dior, with the opposition only nine minutes of arc from exact, shows the effect. Director Robert Altman with the half-degree opposition did the same thing on film. Wolfgang Amadeus Mozart with the one and a half-degree opposition, was a child prodigy who played professionally before royalty at the age of five, and astonished the world with his creativity and virtuosity. He played the clavier, harpsichord, piano and violin in the classical style and died at age 35 after producing more than six hundred works. Political figures who have this may sway the public with their smooth oratory even if they are short on facts and long on agenda like President Ronald Reagan with the two-degree opposition. Reagan was a successful actor before he took up politics.

The manner in which an aspect manifests depends very much on the sum total of all the contacts that impinge upon the combination. The beautiful actress Lindsey Lohan has been the poster girl for going off the rails. She has the quincunx one minute of arc from exact, which is certainly good symbolism for the dramatic arts. If there is further affliction to Mercury or Neptune, however, it may also symbolize instability or one who is unable or hard pressed to apply herself to everyday tasks. Lohan's Neptune is sextile the Midheaven exact to the minute, which is once more good for someone who needs to be able to step into character as an actress must do, but it also produces people who sometimes feel lost out of character, i.e. in themselves in ordinary life. Her Neptune is sesquiquadrate her Venus only three minutes of arc from exact which suggests exotic sexuality but trouble via friendships and romance as much through selfishness as bad choices.

Lohan's Neptune is semi-sextile Saturn only thirteen minutes from exact which suggests confusion about how her life could both unravel and become so entangled that it could sometimes seem unmanageable. A Saturn-Neptune aspect is often a good thing unless one or the other planet is simultaneously afflicted by another malefic. Saturn-Neptune people are also inclined to avoid problems by throwing themselves completely into their work or they may be inclined to avoid their problems through indulgence in drink and drugs. Lohan's Neptune is sextile Pluto only nineteen minutes from exact and the Pluto is trine the Midheaven from less than a degree out. That both removes her from the mainstream as a person singled out by fame and fortune and simultaneously thrusts her back into it as an object of envy and desire, without friends and allies but rather with poseurs, hangers-on, sycophants and other false friends.

Lohan's Mercury is trine Saturn less than a degree from exact, which as yet has apparently availed her nothing except to make her intransigent about addressing the disturbing elements in her life, perhaps because, in turn, Saturn is semi-square Mars less than a degree from exact. Mars-Saturn tends to make her feel like a victim, yet she gets little sympathy because she is inclined to work her own destruction with regard to relationships of all kinds due to Mars in her seventh house. Mars is trine the Moon less than three degrees from exact. Moon-Mars is classic symbolism for family problems, and her difficulties with her parents are well-known. It is also symbolic of unbridled lust and, failing that, of at least near total willingness to take foolish chances and to run through "stop signs" of all kinds. The trines and sextiles definitely do not render this train of connections into something overflowing with benefit, but rather, taken merely as connections between planets and angles, into dissipation and a long series of major and minor train wrecks that add up to bad judgment, general confusion and squandered opportunities. All these contacts explain why her Mercury-Neptune quincunx is a problem to her and more difficult than what most people experience with it. That is, the planets that comprise her quincunx pick up a lot of baggage. All the malefic planets are connected through the Mercury-Neptune quincunx. Fortunately she is young enough to rebuild her life, and if eventually chastened by indulgence, she may well turn it around and return to her excellent early form.

Transcendent figures who are conscious of a higher reality may also have this. At a dark hour in the history of France, Joan of Arc inspired the French to fight back hard against British imperialist ambitions during the Hundred Years War in the fifteenth century that threatened the whole of France. Joan was a devout, peasant girl of only 19, who claimed to be summoned by the voices of long dead saints when she was captured by the Burgundians and executed by the English. She is the national heroine of France. Neptune contacts are consistent with clairvoyance and especially clairaudience. Joan had Mercury opposite Neptune two degrees from exact.

Mercury-Pluto

The chief effect of Pluto in aspect to Mercury as a natal configuration is to strongly incline the native to delve deeply into issues that are hidden from view or lost, forgotten, legendary and sometimes taboo. It makes the native privy to secrets and affords its natives a point of view well ahead of that of their contemporaries. It occurs often in the horoscopes of academics who want to understand things at the level of first principles, or historians who must be able to read primary source material in the original (often dead) languages. It is so wedded to secrecy that persons with this combination often have security clearances and may be literally attracted to espionage; or they are attracted to the secrets of the physical world that can only be apprehended by experiment and intense intellectual labor. People with this combination frequently have an affinity for laboratories, research and development like the extraordinary French scientist Louis Pasteur with the two-degree square. John Bardeen, co-inventor of the transistor in 1947, had the three and a half degree conjunction. He shared two Nobel prizes in physics, one for the transistor in 1956 and the other for superconductivity in 1972. He was a professor of electrical engineering and physics, but his most important work was done in a laboratory rather than a classroom.

Consistent with the tendency of Pluto to embrace opposites, this combination is common in the horoscopes of people with learning disabilities as well as those who make their living teaching those so afflicted—usually children—or treating cognitive, reading and writing problems. Language is a powerful theme with this combination. Scholars who have recorded American Indian and Eskimo languages in danger of dying out and those engaged in linguistics, lexicography and philology usually have these planets in some combination (although fluency in many languages, most often their contemporary renderings, is usually a trait of the Mercury-Uranus combinations). People with Mercury-Pluto are remarkable as exceptionally persuasive communicators and speakers or the reverse: they may be remarkable for the poor quality of their communication skills, to the extent that such individuals could be imprisoned by autism. Often when the upside prevails, the Mercury-Pluto natives have political as well as oratorical and literary ability which center around justice, truth and fair play. Abraham Lincoln, with the four-degree conjunction, perhaps the greatest American president to date, is the best example. The brilliant Italian mathematician and physicist, Galileo Galilei, with the one-degree conjunction, illustrates a quality about this combination that Lincoln also exemplified: these people push the envelope of the issues of their day and address matters that other people would like to ignore. They are not merely bold and outspoken but they excite the desire of others to know the nature of the physical world or moral and ethical issues that engage everyone at more than a cerebral level, rather a gut level.

These natives may find themselves in positions that require that they weigh life and death decisions. President Harry Truman, with the one-degree conjunction, had to decide whether or not to use atomic weapons to hasten the end of World War II. These people consistently embrace unpopular issues and find themselves in the arena of life to a greater degree than most people. Truman also brought a storm of protest onto his head when he ordered the integration of the United States military forces in 1948. Even without consciously trying to attract controversy the Mercury-Pluto people find themselves at odds with conventional wisdom that sets them apart from and often above the herd. This was particularly true of the English naturalist Charles Darwin (*On The Origin of Species*), born the same day as Abraham Lincoln (February 12, 1809), who outraged Christian fundamentalists when he connected all the primates (i.e., homo sapiens and the anthropoid apes) on an evolutionary scale.

Sometimes Mercury-Pluto veers toward the absurd yet is still embraced. The English mathematician and author Charles L. Dodgson, better known by his pen-name, Lewis Carroll, wrote timeless comic fantasies for children, (*Alice's Adventures in Wonderland, Through the Looking Glass*) that do double duty as satire that are just as popular with adults. He had the three-degree square. True to Pluto's nature, Carroll's delightful romps came from within the mainstream (academia) but they are about a life outside it. Equally removed from the mainstream and as much embraced in a clandestine manner, was the business of Heidi Fleiss who ran a high-end call girl operation until she was arrested in 1993. She has the square only a quarter of a degree from exact. Mercury has a lot to do with one's business or job, and with Pluto, the native's interests and vocation are sometimes not merely secret but out-of-bounds.

Pure research, especially conducted individually—that is, without the benefit of a staff or company resources—is a characteristic feature of Mercury square Pluto. Ralph Nelson Elliot who developed Elliot Wave Theory, widely used by stock market timers throughout the world, had the three degree square. Elliot Wave Theory is organic in the sense that it is not so much an invention as a discovery of underlying patterns in the real world. Hidden realities are the *sine qua non* of Pluto. Jeff Bezos is the chairman and CEO of Amazon Inc. He is the wealthiest man alive in 2017, with a fortune in excess of 100 billion dollars. He has Mercury (retrograde) mundane square Pluto a quarter degree from exact if he were born at 12:01 AM and less than twentieth of a degree from exact if he were born at 11:59 PM on 1/12/1964. His birth time is unknown. Only the Moon may have a closer contact; otherwise, Mercury-Pluto is the closest aspect in his chart (Mercury sets when Pluto is in the I.C.). This combination speaks to someone who thinks outside the box, who ventures into areas unexplored. Bezos speaks of heavy equipment manufacture in outer space and colonization of planets. He has taken steps to bring these things about; it is not idle talk.

Mercury trine Pluto is more accepted or protected when it takes on prejudice, injustice or discloses the ugly truth about a matter that has heretofore been considered a sacred cow. Eleanor Roosevelt, with the one-degree trine, played this aspect of her horoscope to the hilt. As First Lady she constantly used her position to bring attention to the outcast, the powerless, the poor and disenfranchised. She visited hospitals, schools, asylums and prisons, places considered inappropriate for a person in her station in life. She was an advocate for civil rights (and a member of the N.A.A.C.P.), as well as the rights of working women and migrant workers. This may seem relatively tame now but it was radical in the 1930s and 1940s. The basic yet haunting quality of poet Carl Sandburg's work that stirs the pot of the psyche is testament to his Mercury-Pluto trine two and a third degrees out. He won three Pulitzer Prizes.

Sometimes this combination is displayed in the horoscopes of pure mathematicians like Andrew Pollard Ogg, who has the trine only a quarter of a degree from exact. He earned his Ph.D at Harvard and taught at the University of California at Berkeley for many years. Ogg is not inaccessible, unfriendly or weird but his work is so complicated and intrinsically difficult that, except for other mathematicians, he is thoroughly insulated from the rest of the world.

The notoriety of people with Mercury-Pluto prominent and/or in very close aspect is expanded with the slightest concomitant contact from the benefic planets. The short life of Henry McCarty, also known as Henry Antrim, William Antrim and William H. Bonney, but best known as Billy the Kid, attests to the staying power of the contact. He is known to have killed at least five men by himself, although some sources claim he killed twenty-one with others in gang battles; but his name was emblazoned across newspapers throughout the United States and even Europe in the 1870s and 1880s due to his gun fights and escapes from jail and imminent execution. His exploits had earned him legendary status 140 years ago that still endures. Billy had Mercury sesquiquadrate Pluto less than a degree from exact with Venus loosely conjoined to Mercury (but applying) seven degrees from exact; his Mercury was also applying to the quincunx to Jupiter from two degrees out.

Still seen as radical are the artistic works of Spanish genius Pablo Picasso, who had the four-degree opposition and the political ideas of the first ruler of Communist China, Mao Tse Tung who had the six-degree opposition. If there is affliction to this opposition it will occasionally bring down its natives as experienced by President Richard Nixon, who had the two-degree opposition. He had Mars conjunct Mercury, and thus both Mars and Mercury opposed Pluto. Though brilliant, he was unprincipled and was toppled by his willingness to approve secret, illegal activities to undermine his political enemies.

Venus-Mars

This combination is good for Mars but hard on Venus. Its natives are lusty but often ruin their relationships due to thoughtlessness, a wandering eye, a demanding attitude and a selfish, inconsiderate attitude toward partners. Venus is gentle, sensitive, delicate, sweet, loving and alluring. Mars is carnal, forceful, unsophisticated, possessive and driven by lust. The marriage of the two is often a bad match. Women with this combination may find the men in their lives to be clods or possessed of a "slam-bam, thank you ma'am" attitude; or the women themselves may give in to their own desires without restraint. The partners of the Venus-Mars person sometimes suffer outright mistreatment. Henry VIII of England, who was married six times, is a classic but extreme example. He divorced two of his wives who were apparently innocent of any significant fault, and he may have had one of them poisoned; two others were beheaded by his order; one died shortly after childbirth; and the sixth survived him. Henry had Venus trine Mars. He also had Venus trine Saturn. His case is enough to dispense with the supposed unerring goodness of trines.

When there are simultaneous relationships with other planets that can mitigate the difficulties that often attend this combination, a Venus-Mars contact may manifest as lust for life, fondness for nature, and the outdoors, vigorous play, sport that entails speed and risk, as well as strong appetites in general for food, drink, games and pleasure. The work of people who are artistically inclined who have this contact is extremely vivid well exemplified by the great Dutch impressionist Vincent van Gogh who had he two-degree conjunction.

Childhood is often difficult due to inadequate outlets for play or bad treatment at the hands of the parents or bullies in the neighborhood. There is the great risk when Venus is closely configured with Mars, Saturn or Neptune that pleasures may become indulgences. The native may be tantalized more than most people by at least some of the seven deadly sins such that mere indulgences may expand into the territory of the classic vices: chief among them are lust and gluttony in which latter case food and drink come under the same head. These faults may ruin their friendships and marriages as much as the tendency of the Venus-Mars natives to bring trouble into their lives through selfish disregard of the feelings of others. The overall makeup of the horoscope will determine if the native must endure the pain and sorrow of an afflicted Venus or inflicts it himself. The Venus people in one's life are those who are liked and loved: one's children as much as one's siblings, friends, lovers and mates. There is some risk to the children of the native with all the Venus-Mars contacts even if the native is as sober as a judge. Actor John Travolta, with the exact square, lost his young son to accidental death. Parents who have this contact should think twice about signing off on their minor children entering the military.

The native is often bold in his or her expression of affection. Women with Venus-Mars combinations may become impatient with their would-be but polite or timid lovers and make the first move

*Roosevelt also had Venus inconjunct the Moon, which is quite fertile, less than a quarter degree from exact.

themselves. The contact produces a decidedly emotional disposition and the work of the people who have it evokes a similar response that is distinctly colorful, lively, and moving as evidenced by the nearly exact trine in the horoscope of Wolfgang Amadeus Mozart. Mozart's trine also shows the harsh treatment and undue influence of at least one of the parents, sometimes both of them. That is, the people who love the native or should act responsibly and affectionately toward him, are at the same time sources of difficulty for him. Former President Bill Clinton, with the conjunction, is a good example of the family problems that characteristically accompany this combination. As a teenager Clinton was sometimes in the position of having to literally defend his mother (who was a widow) from her difficult boyfriends and from his step-father when she remarried. His problems with fidelity and subsequent scandal as an adult are well-known. Separation due to circumstance when there is no problem between the mates is common. Venus-Mars combinations do not necessarily make their natives fertile despite their ardor, but they are commonly better parents to their own children than the parents who parented them.

Apparently it is helpful to the native to have Venus elevated over Mars, especially in the case of the opposition, as the example of former President Jimmy Carter and many other examples attest. In cases like these, love triumphs over adversity and the relationship remains active and affectionate into one's elder years, but even in the cases wherein Venus appears undamaged by Mars in terms of harmony with the mate, tragic separation or the early death of the partner is all too common. When Mars is elevated over Venus, these aspects are more likely to produce relationship problems, but there needs to be more adverse symbolism to produce a tragic result. The native may suffer the trauma of divorce even when this pair is closely configured in a so-called good relationship. For example, President Ronald Reagan had the sextile only a third of a degree from exact with Mars higher in the sky than Venus. He was quite shaken when his first wife, actress Jane Wyman, divorced him, but his long and harmonious marriage to his second wife, Nancy, clearly showed that one does not have to replay the most extreme part of the symbolism of difficult combinations. Usually, however, difficult combinations do play out at least once and most often earlier in life than later. If planets are in their dignities, the untoward affect of this combination is generally lessened even if Mars is elevated over Venus and the planets are in square. For example Carla Bruni, the Italian-born super model heiress and socialite, has the two degree Mars-Venus square, but she is more a heartbreaker who lands on her feet when her relationships end than one who is devastated by relationship problems. She has Mars exalted in Capricorn elevated over Venus in her own sign, Libra. In the end, despite the tendency of some people to beat the drum of this planet combination as mainly symbolic of sexual athleticism, Venus-Mars people are often hurt *by* the people they love. In turn, Venus-Mars people just as often hurt the people *whom* they love, sometimes even literally—physically—as with Donatien Alphonse Francois de Sade, who had the two-degree Venus-Mars square. Still, this combination is frequently a wonderful ride, especially for the men who have more success with ladies than most of us. Mick Jagger, for example, lead singer for the Rolling Stones, has the one-degree trine. The trine usually works best with this pair.

One of the great beauties of the current age is Welsh actress Catherine Zeta-Jones, who has Venus trine Mars less than a quarter of a degree from exact. Her extraordinary face, coupled with her unspoken, unintended, yet smoldering sensuality, make her such a compelling attraction as to be a modern day Helen of Troy. The case of Zeta-Jones brings up an important point: Venus-Mars people, especially the women, without making the effort, may attract attention that they don't want, or at least they may attract more attention than they can handle. Zeta-Jones is in a long, stable marriage; she is a mother; she is utterly natural and without affectation; and yet because she is a classic example of what Americans call, "drop-dead gorgeous," she evokes envy and appreciation that few people experience. It's easy to get the mistaken impression that such people are trying to produce an effect. Venus-Mars women learn quickly not to deliberately create an effect because they do it naturally without trying. Venus-Mars people have animal magnetism that goes beyond good looks. If these natives are also exceptionally stunning, they could find it hard to lead a normal life, except perhaps in the movies.

Venus-Jupiter

The combinations that involve the two most fortunate planets, Venus and Jupiter, appear in the horoscopes of those who are lucky, favored, popular and often talented, although that last quality is by no means assured. When good fortune and ability are combined, this combination frequently takes people to the top of their professions. Natives of this pair are generally gracious and generous. They are social creatures who love to dispense benefit and good will in many forms, not least financial, but their specialty is joy, fun and play. They are smooth, warm and friendly like talk show host Jack Paar with the four-degree conjunction and Eleanor Roosevelt with the five-degree conjunction. They may also be edgy but endearing like singer/poet Tom Waits with the conjunction only seven minutes from exact, and the late actor-comedian John Belushi, with the conjunction less than a degree from exact. Belushi's behavior both professionally and personally knew no bounds, which is often typical of this combination that inclines toward excess, extravagance and indulgence.

Money and success usually go with this combination. Director Steven Spielberg has the conjunction less than one and a third degrees from exact. Even the wide aspects, especially if they are prominently placed high in the horoscope, are tremendously fortunate. Eddie Arcaro, the only jockey to win the Triple Crown (Kentucky Derby, Preakness and Belmont Stakes) twice, had the six-degree conjunction high in his horoscope. He is widely regarded as the greatest jockey in the history of American Thoroughbred racing. Woolworth heiress Barbara Hutton had the seven-degree conjunction very high in the horoscope. American soldier Chris Kyle served four tours of duty in Iraq. He was known as "the Legend" for his prowess as a warrior, symbolized by his six degree Mars-Saturn conjunction. In stark contrast to Mars-Saturn, Kyle also had a five degree Venus-Jupiter conjunction. His popularity, not merely within the military, but among civilians who saw his combat record as nothing less than heroic, was perhaps the greatest of any of his contemporaries. Notwithstanding his association with violence, he was a highly principled man as well as a devoted husband

and father. Ironically, after surviving his service in Iraq, Kyle was murdered by a disturbed combat veteran after he had returned to the United States.

The square magnifies the effects of most combinations. If they are extreme in conjunction form, they may go off the map in square form. Venus symbolism relates to one's love life, among other things. Venus is not as sexual as Mars, but many Venus-Jupiter people see themselves as artists or connoisseurs of horizontal dancing. One of the greatest basketball players of all time, Wilt Chamberlain, claimed to have had sex with 20,000 women. He was 7'1" tall and his playing weight was 300 pounds. He holds many scoring records and is considered the strongest man ever to play the game. Chamberlain had the one-degree square. The greatest seventeenth century European monarch, Louis XIV of France, had the square one and a quarter degrees from exact. His bedroom appetite was legendary and every woman within his purview, married or not, was fair game for him. Few people go to such extraordinary lengths but the native is not likely to settle down with his high school or college sweetheart and live happily ever after in an undisturbed state.

Talk show host Larry King, who has been married eight times, shows the effect. He has the square less than a degree from exact. Sometimes the native is not inclined toward variety, divorce or promiscuity, yet the effect will show in other ways. For example, the very talented singer/actress Dolly Parton, who has the square only ten minutes of arc from exact, is also known for an extraordinary abundance of femininity. The bigger issue is that she is known for evoking smiles, pleasure, and admiration as an artist: typically the stock in trade of this combination.

Venus-Jupiter people are often patrons of the arts, as well as artists themselves. One of the founders of the impressionist movement, Edgar Degas, and the greatest talent of the Northern Renaissance, Albrecht Durer, had the three degree square. Venus-Jupiter people are not invariably agreeable as attested by Nicolo Machiavelli with the four degree square, and Saddam Hussein with the five degree square. In most cases Venus-Jupiter natives are like the Duchess of Cambridge (wife of Prince William of England) with the nearly exact square, and Tina Turner and Pope John Paul II have the three-degree square: they are charming, engaging, much loved and enjoy good fortune and high status on an epic scale. Jupiter square Venus may incline its natives to be too self-indulgent, especially regarding alcohol, pleasure in general and sporting pastimes, but as the examples show, much depends on the rest of the chart. The enormous celebrity and wealth of actress Angelina Jolie is a testament to her two and a half degree mundane square with Jupiter in the Midheaven and Venus on the Ascendant.

The trine people are not less celebrated than those with the square but they usually have less tumultuous lives. That is not an ironclad rule, however, as attested by the suicide of talented and popular musician Kurt Cobain, who had the one-degree trine. Even people whose works and positions are initially considered controversial are eventually embraced as the public catches up to ostensibly radical positions that are actually grounded in justice. Once considered a radical feminist, Gloria

Steinem, with the half-degree trine, was reviled by those who would not confront their gender prejudice. Now her position is widely seen as courageous and virtuous. The very popular and altogether virtuous Paramhansa Yogananda, whose *Autobiography of a Yogi* has been a best seller for decades, had the one-degree trine. In a similar vein, philosopher Immanuel Kant wrote brilliantly about ethics and what constitutes the right way to live; he had the trine less than a half-degree from exact. Issues that relate to goodness, justice, virtue, *joie de vivre* and love in full bloom are the recurring themes of Venus with Jupiter. Occasionally somewhat like Venus-Neptune, Venus trine Jupiter is symbolic of a large family, especially if the Moon is also involved. Isaac Singer, whose several patents founded the Singer sewing machine company and subsequent fortune, fathered twenty-four children by several wives and mistresses. He had Venus trine Jupiter, one degree from exact.

James Dyson, who made his fortune (three billion pounds sterling) largely on the strength of a revolutionary vacuum cleaner design, has the sesquiquadrate less than a degree from exact with Venus exalted in Pisces.

The opposition is not different in mode than the other aspects. Its natives push just as hard for what brings benefit to others as a natural expression of their own natures. President Teddy Roosevelt acted in the best interest of the country and held back nothing of his vigorous nature in the process. He had the opposition three degrees from exact. Venus opposite Jupiter is a celebration of self-expression. It often manifests sexually, but artists enjoy the effort perhaps more than anyone else because their works are more lasting than most other endeavors. Goethe's Faust is still read and studied passionately. Goethe had the one-half degree opposition. The same is true of the great American novelist Toni Morrison whose works are staples of high school and college classrooms. She has the two-degree opposition. The music of Quincy Jones and the fiction of Victor Hugo, who both have the three-degree opposition, are the successful result of an internal need to express oneself with unbridled enthusiasm and consummate technique.

Venus-Saturn

This contact has a terrible reputation as inimical to happiness and affection, which is far too strong and by no means invariably the case. All too often, however, the partner is difficult and cold, does not satisfy the native sexually or is a poor provider. Sometimes marriage occurs late or the partner dies early. Frequently the partner is older than the native. Venus-Saturn concentrates the affections to an extraordinary degree but it often produces an unsteady love life unless one or both planets are well placed in the zodiac. When the love life is stable it sometimes happens that Venus-Saturn denies children to the native or there are serious problems around children. For example, the first American president, George Washington, was happily married for 40 years but fathered no children (probably the result of having contracted smallpox as a young man). He was step-father, however, to his wife's two children by a previous marriage. Washington had the conjunction three and a half degrees from exact with Venus exalted in Pisces. Bill Gates, the founder of Microsoft, has the one-degree conjunction in Libra where Saturn is exalted and Venus is well-placed in her own sign. Happily married, he has fathered three children; both Saturn and Venus are dignified. Martin Luther, the main force behind the Protestant Reformation, also had the conjunction in Libra only a half-degree from exact. He eventually married in middle age and fathered five children, which started the tradition of marriage for the Protestant clergy. Less well placed, this combination frequently works out badly in terms of delay, dismay, distress and divorce. George Gordon, Lord Byron, one of the greatest English poets of the Romantic Period (Childe Harold's Pilgrimage, Don Juan), had the conjunction two and a half degrees from exact in Aquarius. He lurched from one wife, mistress and affair to another without lasting effects, except emotional damage in his wake. In other cases there are both children and apparent stability, but a lack of mutual understanding or profound incompatibility such that both partners are deeply unhappy. In situations like this the unremitting stress is likely to eventually manifest physically, in particular as a herniated disc in the lumbar and or sacral regions, which is the location of the first or root chakra. This can also happen if a homosexual or bisexual person is locked into a heterosexual marriage.

The sextile is no different from the other aspects. Actor Paul Newman was married for 50 years to actress Joanne Woodward. He had Saturn exalted in Libra sextile Venus in Sagittarius less than a degree from exact. Well-placed planets with this pair are symbolic of success in love but the action of a third planet can alter the effect substantially. Famed ladies man Giacomo Casanova had the one-degree sextile with both bodies well disposed. He had Venus exalted in Pisces and Saturn dignified in Capricorn. But his Venus was also less than a degree from the sesquiquadrate to Uranus in Libra, so he was driven by his desire for variety and could not be faithful for long, but his renown as a great lover is legendary.

President Franklin Delano Roosevelt had the square only one minute of arc from exact. He was unfaithful to his wife Eleanor who had borne him five children.* When she discovered his infidelity, their sexual life together ended immediately and permanently, although they stayed married and remained close friends. Former heavyweight champion Muhammad Ali has the one-degree square; he has been married four times. Playwright Eugene O'Neill, the first American playwright to win the Nobel Prize for literature (in 1936), also had the one-degree square. His Venus is well placed in its own sign, Libra, but Saturn is in its detriment, Cancer, one of the worst places for Saturn. The province of Cancer is the family. O'Neill was married three times and fathered three children. One of his children was a suicide, another suffered from schizophrenia and he disowned his daughter Oona when, at age eighteen, she married the silent film actor Charlie Chaplin. Chaplin was O'Neill's age at the time: fifty-five.

Joan of Arc was a virgin by reputation until she was raped while held captive by the English and then burned at the stake. She had the one-degree trine. Diana, Princess of Wales also had the one-degree trine with both planets well placed in their own signs. Saturn was in Capricorn and Venus in Taurus but Venus was in a zodiacal square with Mars, and Pluto was also closely square Venus in an aspect relationship called a mundane square (q.v.) only two degrees from exact. Together, Mars and Pluto assaulted her Venus trine Saturn relationship, symbolic of her unhappiness within her marriage and its subsequent destruction. Abraham Lincoln had the four-degree trine. His wife Mary was the first presidential wife who was considered a liability due to her mental instability (although she had predicted he would become president many years before the possibility presented itself). Lincoln had Venus exalted in Pisces and Saturn in Scorpio. His marriage held together though his wife became a source of difficulty to him, although earlier in their life together she had been a conspicuous benefit to his career. The loss of three of Lincoln's four sons, who preceded him in death, was the main symbolism of Saturn trine Venus. There was additional pressure on his Venus from a close trine to Neptune and a two-degree mundane conjunction of Venus with Pluto (due to Pluto's extreme south celestial latitude and declination). Sometimes the marriage is stable and a source of great joy to the native, but the children are drug-addicted, criminal or a source of grief, dismay or disappointment. Other times the children are exemplary and the marriage is a disaster. Yet, other times there are no children. The untoward effect of the combination is usually countermanded by well-placed planets. Thus the dignities, debilities and houses are the key to how this contact works out, as well—as always—as other bodies that touch the combination. Trines do not contravene the intrinsic natures of the planets that comprise them.

The iconic French singer Edith Piaf had Venus opposition Saturn within six degrees with neither planet dignified. Despite the nearly exact sextile of Jupiter to her Venus she suffered many losses in her intimate relationships, some of them tragic. It cannot be emphasized enough that the planets in their dignities are the best prophylaxis against the difficulties of this combination. Trines do not contravene the intrinsic natures of the planets that comprise them.

Venus-Uranus

This combination has long been regarded as the "gay" aspect, but most people who have it are not gay in this writer's experience. A large number of the horoscopes examined (about a third), however, are gay. That may be statistically significant, but one cannot say without a huge sample and a control group. What is consistent about this contact is that its natives are distinctly likely to become involved with friends and lovers of a different race, religion, national origin or cultural matrix than their own. They are quintessentially eclectic, broad-minded and don't observe barriers that limit interaction between groups. For example, affluent, protected, well-educated, suburban, white boy falls hard for sultry Cajun goddess who has been reared in the school of hard knocks. There are endless variations on that theme. Catholics with this combination may marry Jews, often to the consternation of both families; Japanese-Americans marry Irish-Americans; or the native marries a foreigner. Queen Victoria I of England, for example, married a German. She had the three-degree trine. Sometimes the native leaves home to live a life as an ex-patriot.

The conjunction, square and opposition produce the most marked results. It is usually uninhibited, liable to try anything at least once, resents attempts to limit its social or sexual expression and often has trouble remaining faithful. People with this combination are tremendously attracted to the freshness of new relationships. When that freshness is gone, so is the excitement for the Venus-Uranus people, and whether there are problems in the relationship or not, this type generally wants to move on or may begin to stray when a relationship has, for them, become stale. It is quite daring and may also appear grossly insensitive toward partners. People who have been hurt by them consider them shallow. For their part, the Venus-Uranus people generally don't feel jealousy and don't understand why anyone should feel it. Actor Warren Beatty, with the two and a quarter degree conjunction, may hold the record for bedding the greatest number of Hollywood starlets and other beauties between 1955 and when he finally married in 1992. His marriage has been stable, however, since then, which illustrates that other factors can contravene even a strong wayward trait but that everything plays out in its own way and in its own time. The Renaissance genius Leonardo da Vinci had the two-degree sextile. He had a voracious homosexual appetite that was too flagrant to hide, which caused him to leave some towns in order to void being charged with sodomy. He was charged in some venues, however.

Sometimes the native has many marriages and is faithful or faithful in all but one or two of the marriages. Actress Elizabeth Taylor, who had the very close conjunction, was married eight times. Sometimes the noteworthy condition among those with this contact is that the partners are not separated in age by merely a few years but an entire generation, such that the pair, standing side-by-side, appears as an unlikely combination. Often Venus-Uranus people who are involved with partners who have better characters, are better looking, more interesting, earn a better income and are more intelligent than they are, will still leave relationships with these talented and virtuous people because they become bored after several years of apparent stability and happiness. The partners are frequently without fault. Uranus is freedom-loving and unconventional in the extreme. Every planet combination it makes has that quality about it. Contacts with Saturn moderate the roving eye that sees life as a buffet. Contacts with Jupiter make the Venus-Uranus tendencies worse because Jupiter inclines toward expansion. Sometimes people with this contact do not display its classic characteristics but their mates do who may appear odd or they fervently embrace some form of counter culture or they, and not the native, are unfaithful. Furthermore, among the group that is faithful, their partners often precede them in death suddenly or unexpectedly.

Frequently this contact speaks to class differences in countries where that is still an issue like England or especially India. Tony Blair, former British prime minister, has a very close square. His wife is beautiful, gracious, accomplished, well educated and successful in her own right. She is clearly exceptional in true Uranian fashion. Yet she was born into working class circumstances. He is upper class.

Very commonly the native is irascible to a noteworthy degree. Their short fuses may make them hard to be around, and they have a hard time tolerating people who judge them. They also commonly feel that people remain in relationship for the wrong reasons, but that they, the Venus-Uranus people, have the courage and honesty to leave a relationship that has become mired in obligation, fear of abandonment, routine, guilt or some manner of neurosis. People without this planet combination generally can only imagine the Venus-Uranus turn of mind and do not entertain it unless they are inclined to cheat on a partner. The Venus-Uranus people are open about it. Uranus, like Aquarius, is characteristically casual and detached. While this quality is attractive to many people, those same people may be dismayed to find that the ties that bind for the Venus-Uranus people are more casual and detached than what most other people feel.

Venus-Uranus often has an outstanding aesthetic sense. Gertrude Stein, with the close opposition, appreciated, purchased and promoted abstract impressionistic art long before it became the rage. She was a connoisseur of art, an avant-garde intellectual, and the essence of hip, cool, malin, but just herself, unaffected. This type also likes the altered state of intoxication as an amusement rather than a crutch. They are usually quite willing to experiment with anything new or unconventional. The great benefit of the contact is its open-minded and generally liberal tendency; but its natives are criticized as capricious and unwilling to acknowledge barriers that keep most people in their places.

Sometimes the most noteworthy thing about Venus-Uranus relates to the children of the native, even the number of them. Swiss mathematical genius Leonard Euler fathered thirteen. He had the quincunx less than a degree from exact.

Venus-Neptune

This contact has several manifestations that incline toward one or the other planet. In some people it is subtle, virtuous, highly cultivated, refined, romantic and tender. In others it is distinctly licentious and likely to be caught, trapped or blackmailed as a result; its natives may be deceitful, especially in matters that relate to sex and dogged by scandal; occasionally there are problems around drugs and alcohol. Neptune, as a first-class malefic, often enlarges the scope of a bad habit into a vice. Venus has a lot to do with the things that bring pleasure to the native. There are many pleasures, of course; sex is only one, yet infidelity is fairly common with this contact or its natives are cuckolded themselves. Thus uncommon devotion to the mate is as common as betrayal. Usually the native displays one tendency or the other, rather than devotion to some and debauchery on the side.

There is a strong tendency toward artistic expression in music, art, sculpture or drama. Some people with this contact are students of the occult in its various forms, but fundamentalist religious positions are more regularly embraced. When the religious element is not evident, the native is inclined toward fantasy as most Neptunians are, yet whoever or whatever constitutes "the other" in the life, is often idealized. Venus-Neptune in its purest form is an euphoric or utopian state of mind that is perfect and therefore hard to realize in form or circumstance. An artistic rendering of a form or an idea, however, can be perfect from the point of view of the artist and thus deeply satisfying. The striving toward that end motivates many of these people.

Occasionally the mate or one's children are not robust or may be chronically ill. People with this combination are likely to display kindness, understanding and support toward their loved ones that is exceptional. Most of these people are incurable romantics, including the men who wouldn't admit as much under any circumstance. But Venus-Neptune is an all too common indication of disillusionment in love. The strongly religious people who have this contact appear to fare best in that department of life. Many women with this pair confess to daydreaming constantly about romantic and sexual situations that are the stuff of which pot-boilers and page-turners are made.

Enrico Caruso, probably the finest voice of the modern era, had the conjunction less than a degree from exact. The most public divorce of the last fifty years was endured by half by the heir to the British throne, Charles, Prince of Wales. He has the conjunction two and a quarter degrees from exact with Neptune in Virgo, its detriment, conjunction Venus in her fall, also in Virgo. The debility of both bodies is the clue that the combination is fraught with trouble for the prince during at least part of his life, which in most cases manifests early. His case illustrates another feature of this planetary combination: its natives often choose people with whom they are mismatched. Former President Jimmy Carter, with the conjunction only one and a half degrees from exact, shows the other side of this contact. He is a deeply religious man who has been happily married for more than fifty years. He has admitted to merely lusting after women "in my heart." Former President Bill Clinton, with the wide conjunction at four and a quarter degrees (but with Mars nearby), was the focus of an epic sex scandal that tarnished his presidency and brought his (unsuccessful) impeachment because he lusted with more than his heart. Clinton also has Neptune in its detriment conjunction Venus in her fall.

The irrepressible and popular singer Tina Turner has the square only a quarter of a degree from exact. She didn't fully blossom until she got out of a bad marriage. One must not be too quick to judge a planet relationship, however, by the supposed nature of the aspect. The most popular American evangelist to date, Billy Graham, has the square one and a quarter degrees from exact. He was happily married for more than 60 years. As an idealist and a distinctly virtuous man, he displays one of the most wonderful qualities about Venus-Neptune: the tendency to see the best in people. Post-impressionist French artist Paul Gauguin had the square one and two-thirds degrees from exact; he abandoned his wife and five children to give himself over completely to his art and went to live in Tahiti. The contact is good for art in general whether there are relationship problems or not. The Spanish surrealist Salvador Dali had the sextile less than a degree from exact. The most famous British novelist to date, Charles Dickens, had the zodiacal square two and a quarter degrees from exact; he eventually separated from his wife who had borne him ten children. The great American jazz pianist Thelonius Monk had the mundane square exact to the *second* if he were born at noon EST at Rocky Mount, North Carolina on October 10, 1917. Venus had a right ascension for setting there that day at noon of 20h 36m 48s of sidereal time. Neptune was at the IC at the same moment. Therefore, the Venus-Neptune contact was very close, no matter what his time of birth that day. He has influenced several generations of musicians and brought pleasure to millions who have heard his work.

Venus-Neptune is both pleasure-loving and pleasure-producing. The people who have it are often looking for situations that allow them to indulge that tendency, more than most people, in any way that they can manage it. A notable number of Venus-Neptune natives have large families. King George III (one-degree conjunction) fathered 15, and composer Johann Sebastian Bach, (four-degree conjunction) was father to 20, by two wives.

John Milton (*Paradise Lost*), English poet and scholar, had the trine one half-degree from exact. He is a marvelous example of the exquisite delicacy of feeling and idealism characteristic of this combination at its best. The same qualities can be attributed to Raphael (Sanzio) of Urbino, one of the brightest lights in art of the Italian Renaissance. He had the trine less than one and a quarter degrees from exact. Both Queen Victoria I and jazz great Miles Davis had the trine one and a half degrees from exact. In their own ways in different worlds, they shared an emotional sensitivity of a high order. In the queen it was contained; in the musician it was expressed in full measure.

Mia Farrow was divorced by Frank Sinatra when she refused to allow him to dictate the terms of her career. She has the one-degree opposition. George Harrison, the best guitarist of the Beatles, and actress Uma Thurman both have the two-degree opposition. They are both superb and sensitive artists and both have been divorced

Venus-Pluto

The chief effects of Venus configured with Pluto are to accentuate sexuality to the extent that the person with this aspect exudes it constantly and unintentionally, and also to make relationships hard to maintain; that is, sex is easy but relationships are difficult, both developing them and making them last. Most people with this combination tend to be skilled lovers (unless Saturn is part of the combination) but they are also often demanding and difficult or they make along series of bad choices in partners. Once a connection is established, it is never really over, and relationships that appear to be long dead show themselves to have been merely dormant after they quickly revive. Actors who get a lot of attention for their attractiveness often have this combination. Antonio Banderas, with the three-degree square, shows the effect.

Pluto usually has a mirror opposite effect as well. Teresa of Avila had the square less than a degree from exact. She had visions, heard voices and reformed the Carmelite Order that emphasized poverty, austerity and solitude. Many people with this combination are painfully shy. As with most Pluto contacts, the issue of loneliness looms large with Pluto-Venus. In the majority of cases examined, when sexuality is given free expression, these people tend to hold the objects of their affection in their spell with sex. An odd effect, which manifests less often, is that the Venus-Pluto person will not allow anyone to get close to them except sexually, but if Saturn also enters the equation, the native may not have a sex life at all or have an aversion to it that requires therapy to put right. Many prostitutes have Venus-Pluto aspects. Another odd manifestation of this contact is that its natives are frequently befriended by or somehow become associated with misfits or outcasts. The native, who may not count himself or herself among this group, may notice this pattern and be puzzled by it.

In most cases the nature of the attraction is dark, which only serves to make it more compelling. This combination is occasionally a sign of early sexual activity, sometimes rape, various forms of abuse and non-standard sexual practices some of which were formerly considered deviant, but are now regarded as merely among the many sexual orientations. Most people with this contact tend toward fairly extreme forms of old-fashioned debauchery or none at all. Pluto strongly inclines toward extremes and not a middling display of its nature. Clandestine sex, unusual partners, many partners, infidelity, bizarre practices, overwhelming desire, rocky relationships and celibacy are the standard nexus of this contact.

Sarah Ferguson, former Duchess of York, ruined her marriage by her infidelity. She has the three-degree conjunction. Yet the great English monarch known as the "virgin queen," Elizabeth I, had the opposite reputation, with the four-degree trine. She had very little contact with her father, Henry VIII, who had her declared a bastard. Her mother was executed when Elizabeth was only two. Estrangement from one's natural intimates, one's parents, is the theme, which may extend to siblings and would-be intimates as an adult. Elizabeth never married and there is only speculation about any romantic life she may have had, though she was constantly surrounded by people who attended her person. The lack of intimacy in Elizabeth's life, despite being the focus of attention, reveals the often ironic nature of Pluto. Venus-Pluto contacts manifest in unusual ways even in the lives of people who are apparently well-adjusted, stable and successfully running their lives. George Bernard Shaw, the great Irish playwright, (*Pygmalion, Man and Superman*, *Saint Joan, Heartbreak House*) was married for forty-five years to a woman with whom he had a completely platonic relationship. He also had intense "affairs" by letter with women he never met in person. Shaw had Venus square Pluto less than a degree from exact. His critics complained that his plays were sexless.

It is not uncommon that the native has very little interest in sex and communion with friends, and often, when this flip side appears, those with this combination cannot find a sexual outlet either because they are unattractive or so disagreeable in temperament that others are either afraid of them or will not put up with them. Also common are inadequate outlets for sexual expression due to the physical incapacity of the partner, disinterested partners and profound emotional incompatibility such that one feels loneliness within a relationship, though he or she might sleep (fitfully) inches from the partner. Unless Pluto-Venus aspects are wide and separating, the people who have them tend to get one or the other polar opposite and not much in between. Sometimes both conditions obtain at different times in the same life. Some people in this writer's clientele with Venus-Pluto aspects who described themselves as sex addicts, wife-swappers or partners in open marriages as young adults, now in their forties, fifties and beyond have no interest in any sexual activity, although they don't lack partners or would-be partners. This last behavior predilection is far more common in women than men, in the experience of this writer.

The combination tends to be unsatisfying unless it is attended by other bodies, especially Jupiter or Mercury. It all too often leads to bachelorhood or spinsterhood, few or no children, unrequited love or a tortured emotional life due to unsatisfied desires. It can be entirely devoted however, taken to another extreme, and present in the horoscopes of women who have never slept with any man other than their husbands. Yet another manifestation of this contact is a decided interest in tantric sex. Sometimes nudism is embraced by these people. Pluto consistently makes extreme whatever it touches for good or ill, in an all or nothing manner that manifests as compulsive attraction or total rejection.

Unusual but noteworthy artistic works are a common manifestation of this contact. Jackson Pollock, foremost exponent of abstract impressionism, had the two-degree opposition. His work left many people perplexed and confused. Some experienced a visceral reaction against the entire genre. Many were amazed, stunned, even exhilarated and felt like his work evoked feeling that they were hard pressed to describe. Such is the task of art. Salvador Dali, the marvelous Spanish surrealist, had the same effect as Pollock, although Dali's work was perhaps more obviously bizarre than Pollock's, which was simply hard to make out as something distinct. Dali had Venus semi-square Pluto less than a quarter of a degree from exact. The brilliant jazz trumpeter and singer Chet Baker had the two-degree quincunx. His haunting yet compelling work and brilliant improvisations, especially with Gerry Mulligan, still arrest the attention and seduce the sensibilities of almost everybody upon hearing his work, after more than sixty years.

Mars-Jupiter

This combination appears in the horoscopes of powerful, aggressive and usually successful people. It has affinity with politics, the boardroom, ground-breaking discoveries made or advanced, and opinionated, overbearing, energetic and dynamic people. The native is often a leader or finds himself thrust into the center of controversy, disputes or dramas that involve dueling for power. Lawyers, brokers, developers and financiers—the "wheeler-dealers" of the world— consistently have this combination. Usually members of this group speak their minds, often take unpopular stands that are later shown to have merit and are known for embracing polemics. There is not much difference between the trines and sextiles and squares and oppositions with this contact, except that the trine people are able to exert power and remain popular more easily than those with the hard aspects. In addition, the trine people are more commonly associated with passive income as owners of buildings, established businesses or inherited wealth. The square people make money out of whole cloth but they also spend extravagantly and may create problems for themselves due to their difficulty in saving for a rainy day. Mars-Jupiter people are frequently associated with some endeavor so completely that their names become almost eponymous with their specialty. One invariably thinks of golf when one hears the name Arnold Palmer; he has the trine. One thinks of social criticism wrapped in comedy one when hears the name Bill Maher, who has the square; he was fired by a major American television network for his uncompromising positions. If Mars is very strong in the horoscope the tendency of this combination to find excuses to be violent or to pursue extreme and ill-advised courses of action is quite marked. Even when these people are right about an issue that needs revision or reform or they are ultimately proven correct—in contrast to a mistaken or obsolete policy in place at the moment—they are usually too impatient and wanting in respect of tact and diplomacy to bring about their aim easily. The irony is that when the ideas of the Mars-Jupiter people are ultimately implemented, the ideas that they championed are often exactly what they could not sell earlier due to their too strident approach.

The tendency for these people to wield power and to be associated with government, whether they are controversial or not, is particularly common with the conjunction as evidenced by Winston Churchill, Lyndon Johnson, Queen Elizabeth II, Richard Nixon, Tony Blair and Gordon Brown. But presidents and would-be presidents also have the trine—for example, Bill Clinton and John McCain. Somewhat more commonly the trine people are associated with the arts; for example, novelists Stephen King and Upton Sinclair, singer Stevie Winwood and actor Leonardo Di Caprio all have the one-degree trine. Mars-Jupiter is the sign of a champion, the victor in combat or one who can successfully display prowess in whatever manner is his forte. Even people who have done little or nothing to get or maintain themselves in a position of power are often born to it. The English queen, Victoria (1819-1901), had the one-degree sextile. She was not aggressive or mean-spirited (although a difficult mother to her children) but certainly the most powerful woman in the world at a time when Great Britain was the strongest nation on the planet economically and militarily. The opposition is particularly noteworthy in the horoscopes of people who are bold, advanced or take big risks. When Queen Elizabeth I of England defied Spain and its great armada in 1588 she took on what, at the time, was the world's greatest military power. Sigmund Freud placed his reputation in jeopardy, and was roundly castigated by his peers, for suggesting that sexuality played a pivotal role in the development of the psyche. Both Elizabeth and Freud had the opposition. Martin Luther, who launched the Reformation, took an enormous risk when, in effect, he challenged the pope and resisted the entire weight of the Catholic Church. He lived in hiding for years because, as a heretic, his life was in danger. He had the four-degree conjunction. His sincerity cannot be doubted. Mars-Jupiter is very much in earnest.

Like Luther, Mars-Jupiter people are often reformers, or modern and radical to some, but effective in their approach. They typically make money easily. Billionaire industrialist John D. Rockefeller, also with the four-degree conjunction, is a good example of the strength of Mars-Jupiter contacts).

The stupendously wealthy banker J.P. Morgan also had the conjunction fewer than four degrees from exact. These people often have access to extraordinary resources, yet they are just as often associated with raw power and bold, forceful self-expression. Mars-Jupiter generally holds back nothing and can readily embrace extreme positions to prosecute its agenda, sure of the merit of its position.

There is often athletic ability and the native may rejoice in sport or strenuous activity for its own sake rather than for reasons that relate to a health regimen. These people are usually uninhibited, great fun and live life to the fullest. They are also strongly inclined to take action when silence or inaction would be more conducive to the resolution of matters at hand. In general they are not interested in resolution, but rather in overcoming opposition. Impatience and ill-advised or thoughtless actions are the fault of this combination. Boldness, energy and the willingness to take on everybody are its strong suits. Schemers can successfully induce them to action by appealing to their sense of honor, patriotism and often greed. They commonly become parents unless Saturn simultaneously configures Mars, but even then the number of children is likely to be lessened and not denied altogether.

Mars-Saturn

This combination does not preclude success, but it does have a bad name among astrologers since the two classical malefic planets are combined. It inclines toward forceful measures, even violence, either delivered or suffered and highly disciplined endeavors that require careful planning, practice and execution like the study of martial arts, the actions of a hostile takeover artist in business and especially the military. The combination demands diligence in order to succeed but the freedom conferred by discipline may bring huge rewards. Most people are not willing to undertake the daunting tasks that Mars-Saturn requires and in most cases their lives are unremarkable until they do. In the absence of help from other bodies, many Mars-Saturn natives may appear aimless yet selfish rebels without a cause and too ready to display their temper. Many people with this combination are looking for a fight or situations that allow them to indulge their desire to engage an opponent to satisfy their nature. Others need to prove to themselves that they can hold up in combat.

Mars-Saturn combinations in their best manifestations are displays of controlled, directed power toward some practical end. In spire of the often harsh nature of the combination, unless other bodies configure this pair, especially Jupiter, the native is sometimes wanting in respect of the classical masculine virtues: courage, initiative and strength. However, *with* Jupiter added to this combination, it is symbolic of those who exercise restraint and control but are capable of directing overwhelming power toward worthy ends; yet they are altogether contained regarding lesser things; *without* Jupiter, Mars-Saturn people often display a mean streak or a hard edge that may make them inveigh against progressive ideas in a distinctly atavistic fashion. Social commentator Glenn Beck and vice presidential candidate Sarah Palin have the two-degree conjunction. Mars-Saturn appears in the horoscopes of those who thrive in organizations and bureaucracies because its natives derive strength and protection from those organizations. It is common among those who forcefully maneuver their way to the top like Rupert Murdoch, the billionaire media mogul, who has the opposition. Prosecuting attorneys who delight in punishing the guilty often have a Mars-Saturn combination prominent in their horoscopes; their criminal prey also have it.

The trine in particular will frequently find people with this combination in positions of command, such as a military officer who has authority over enlisted men. Unless configured with the lights, if either body in this combination is dignified, it will often bring honor to the native, especially in military matters. For example, Lieutenant Commander Wade McCluskey led the SBD Dauntless dive-bombers from the USS Enterprise without fighter cover that found and attacked the Japanese aircraft carriers at the Battle of Midway on June 4, 1942. Desperately low on fuel, McCluskey's correct decision at the pivotal moment in the search for the Japanese carriers proved decisive in the battle that turned the entire war at sea against the Japanese. All four aircraft carriers of the Japanese task force—Kaga, Akagi, Soryu and Hiryu—were sunk (with their complement of 332 airplanes) at the Battle of Midway by the planes of three American carriers, Enterprise, Hornet and Yorktown. These particular Japanese carriers were four of the six that had launched the planes that had attacked Pearl Harbor in 1941. The native may not escape unscathed even with the trine: after dropping his bomb, McCluskey was shot through the shoulder while pulling out of his dive. When he landed, with all but bone-dry gas tanks on Enterprise, his Dauntless was found riddled with several dozen bullet holes from Japanese anti-aircraft artillery. He was awarded the Navy Cross and his squadron received a presidential unit citation. McCluskey had Saturn in his own sign, Capricorn, trine Mars less than two degrees from exact. He also had Jupiter trine Pluto less than a degree from exact, which indicated the far-reaching effect of his actions, and Jupiter sextile Uranus which is supremely lucky; it also gives the ability to improvise or think on one's feet, even in the air.

Lieutenant Alexander Vraciu, the number four ace in the U.S. Navy (nineteen victories), shot down six Japanese planes at the Battle of the Philippine Sea on June 19, 1944. Like McClusky, Vraciu had Mars trine Saturn (three and a half degrees from exact at noon on his date of birth), but with Mars dignified in its own sign, Scorpio, conjoined to the stinger in the Scorpion's tail. This trine is also a mundane square much closer in right ascension than the trine in longitude. At his birthplace Mars set only two minutes and thirty-eight seconds of sidereal time before Saturn passed through the IC there. That's slightly more than a half degree. Vraciu was such an incredible warrior that when he was shot down by the Japanese months later over the Philippines, after he was rescued by Philippine Resistance fighters, he became the commander of a 180-man Philippine guerilla unit. Vraciu was awarded the Navy Cross and the Distinguished Flying Cross due to a clerical error. He was nominated for the Congressional Medal of Honor that as of yet has not been bestowed. The fifth Japanese carrier that had launched planes that attacked Pearl Harbor in 1941, the Shokaku, was sunk by U.S. dive bombers in the Battle of the Philippine Sea, the biggest aircraft carrier engagement of World War II (fifteen U.S. carriers versus nine Japanese carriers), which is also known as the "Great Marianas Turkey Shoot."

Despite the exploits of warriors that evoke patriotic admiration, the combination is often merely hard and may stop at nothing to get what it wants. Octavian, later known as Caesar Augustus, the first Roman emperor, had the close conjunction with neither planet dignified. He was brilliant, sophisticated and a master politician but completely ruthless: several thousand political enemies were murdered on his orders over the course of four decades as the absolute ruler of the Roman Empire. The wars he waged also led directly to the deaths of many hundreds of thousands at least; more likely millions.

The general orientation of the horoscope can point this combination in a radically different direction while staying true to the symbolism of the bodies. The great blues guitarist Eric Clapton has the exact trine between Mars and Saturn. His devotion to his art manifested as constant practice, but the subsequent freedom of expression he earned through the discipline of practice made him a master musician. A polymath, Leonardo Da Vinci had the trine one and a half degrees from exact. Better known now for his artistic gifts, in his own day his attention to military matters by design and invention found wide application. Most people who have Mars-Saturn in any combination are tightly wound, controlled or repressed. The people who have it in combination with many positive elements in the horoscope run a tight ship and keep strict accounts. Those with more difficult symbolism may take many years to come into their own and recognize their purpose in life. Until then many of them work at a level well below their inherent ability to the dismay of everyone who can see their potential and most serious failing: self-discipline. Some people with this combination are exceedingly pleasant and gentle. Such people, especially women and children, must be carefully and consistently protected because this combination is as often the sign of a victim as an assailant. The brutal Russian tyrant, Czar Ivan IV ("The Terrible"), responsible for innumerable tortures and executions, had the three-degree square.

These combinations, however, may confer great benefit depending upon what else is in play in the horoscope and especially upon other bodies that may configure the Mars-Saturn combination. Norman Shumway, the man primarily responsible for the research that resulted in heart transplantation, first made his reputation as a surgeon whose specialty was pediatric cardiac surgery, i.e., repairing congenital defects in the tiny hearts of infants and children. Shumway had Mars opposite Saturn; his Sun-Neptune-Jupiter T-square configured his Mars-Saturn opposition. Watchmakers and jewelers also have this combination. Their work is done under magnification with small parts attended by high stakes when a gem is cleaved. Precision work on a still smaller scale is characteristic of this combination. A machinist who operates a turret lathe that cuts steel to a tolerance of a thousandth of an inch will typically have a Mars-Saturn combination. A scientist with this combination, known to this writer, works in units of micro-radians; another in angstroms.

The most important work of astronomer Henrietta Swan Leavitt's life was her, "1777 Variables in the Magellanic Clouds," published in *The Annals of the Harvard College Observatory* in 1908, that established what is known as a "standard candle" (of brightness). She examined many thousands of stars to a high degree of precision. Henrietta had Mars opposition Saturn fewer than three degrees from exact. It was only through her exceedingly careful, patient and then brilliant conclusions based on this work that the standard candle allowed the staggering distances of galaxies to be realized for the first time. In a similar manner many Mars-Saturn natives are extremely exacting in their work which others, less inclined in that way, may find exasperating. The Mars-Saturn people may have a hard time "letting go" when relaxation and play are the order of the day; or when given the option to play or work, they continue in their work. The tendency toward exactitude, precision and measurement that serves to illustrate natural law is one of the most common and obvious manifestations of Mars and Saturn combined. It appears in all of the various aspect relationships of this pair, although this writer finds it mostly in the conjunction and opposition.

Nostradamus, the renowned sixteenth century French seer, had the three-degree conjunction. He was a student of what the great Lilly called "art," that is, the astrological art. Too often this combination is misconstrued as a signal that the native is a potential axe murderer or some other species of problem personality. Only rarely is that true; much more often the native may seem hard, abrupt and more at home with data than people; even that much is not assured because the strength of a body in the horoscope depends to a great extent on its position; therefore one should not expect an unfriendly nature as a matter of course from this combination. The very popular comedian Billy Crystal has the less than three-degree conjunction, but his conjunction is not angular and does not configure the lights. Likewise, the much-loved singer, songwriter and artist Joni Mitchell's four-degree conjunction is not connected to her Sun nor angular. The combination is best away from the lights. The character may be corrupted if both lights configure Mars and Saturn together or the native may be afflicted with serious physical debility. The simultaneous presence of Jupiter involved with Mars and Saturn in some manner, will generally preclude the worst of its possible difficult or unwelcome manifestations.

Men with Mars-Saturn combinations rarely father many children, especially boys, or the boys are not robust; sometimes, though strong, the boys are lost to accident or combat. This tendency may be mitigated by the addition of Jupiter to the mix. Men with Mars-Saturn combinations are often without progeny altogether. They may undergo vasectomy without reservation. Women with this combination are not necessarily infertile, but their husbands may be, and like the men, they are parents to few boys, boys with health problems, serious character failings or boys who suffer serious injury by accident or combat.

Still and all, this combination must signal the astrologer to evaluate the horoscope with great care. For every Eric Clapton with a close Mars-Saturn trine, who makes a success of his life, due in part to the loving grandparents who raised him, there is a John Dillinger who lost his mother at age three and was severely beaten by his father as a child on a regular basis. Dillinger had Mars trine Saturn less than one and a quarter degrees from exact and grew up to become a bank robber and murderer who was himself killed by U.S. government agents. Yet he was also a genuine *Robin Hood* in that he gave money he had stolen to people who had lost their farms and houses to banks during the Great Depression of the 1930s. His target was always the banks and bankers, not the man in the street. It is also noteworthy that Marilyn Monroe, a vivacious and famous actress and model, had Mars trine Saturn less than a degree from exact. Her mother was committed to an insane asylum when Marilyn was a child, and Marilyn never knew her father, grew up in several foster homes, was raped at age eleven, and never had children. Her death, ruled a suicide by a drug overdose, has long been suspected to have been murder since her demise in 1962. Trines do not convert aspects between malefics into sweetness and light. This axiom is brought home in an extreme manner by Joseph Stalin, the Russian dictator who had the trine less than a degree from exact. Stalin was directly responsible for the deaths of many millions of innocent Russians who aroused his paranoia. He made Ivan the Terrible look like an amateur. Stalin is in the first rank of the most heinous murderers of all time.

Mars-Uranus

This planet combination is brilliant, innovative, daring, extraordinarily creative and usually lucky. It also appears commonly in the horoscopes of notorious, headstrong, demanding people. This type is not a team player and needs to be the boss or to work alone. It can be extremely irascible like the brilliant chess master Bobby Fischer whose trine was exact to the minute and extremely egotistical like Napoleon Bonaparte whose military genius is without peer during the modern era; Napoleon's trine was a half-degree from exact.

There is often the need for excitement that goes beyond the limits of what most people consider fun. This combination is adventuresome and appears in the horoscopes of people who will jump out of perfectly good airplanes for amusement. It extends as well to mountain climbing, scuba diving, competitive skiing, racing and exploration of all kinds. This combination has special affinity with things mechanical like cars. Mars is attracted to the element of danger; combined with Uranus, activities that entail risk are tantalizing to an extraordinary degree. The combination is commonly, but not invariably, symbolic of people who are sexually aggressive, bold and forceful in pursuit of their interests. They get away with it too, especially if Venus or Jupiter is also in the mix. This applies to both sexes.

People with this aspect are serious about their work and inclined to break new ground. Medical missionary Albert Schweitzer, who worked mostly in Africa, took the view that the good life is spent in service. His Mars-Uranus square was exact to the minute. Johannes Kepler, who discovered that the planets orbit the Sun in elliptical rather than circular orbits, also had the square only one half-degree from exact. He was guided by the data for the positions of the planets that satisfied an equation for an ellipse. Mars-Uranus is concerned with what is true or possible, and these natives thus take exception to convention that strikes them as perverse, spurious or pretentious. The combination is very inventive and typically much more interested in the new and the future than the past. Alexander Graham Bell, who invented the telephone almost single-handedly, had the square two and a half-degrees from exact. Born in Scotland, he emigrated to America as a young man, which illustrates the common tendency of this combination to travel and or to become an ex-patriot. This is one of several combinations known for wanderlust.

Notwithstanding the serious inclinations of these people, they are often strongly attracted to counter-culture movements much like one of the earliest bone fide hipsters, the author Jack Kerouac, who had the exact square. Sometimes these people are deliberately weird to make a point, especially the artistic types like the nineteenth century French poet Charles Baudelaire, who dyed his hair green during an era that was very much more judgmental than today; he had the three-degree square. Artists who are at the stylistic pinnacle of their fields often have this like Michelangelo and Victor Hugo who both had trines. Knowledge of technique that exceeds the standards of the day will sometimes propel these people past their fellows. Sometimes the extraordinary public impact that often accompanies this contact makes people rich and famous like Oprah Winfrey who also has the trine. Fred Astaire, arguably the best dancer of his era—but certainly dancing on the mountain top with the best of the best with Nuruyev, Nijinsky, Pavlova and perhaps Gene Kelly—had the mundane square of Mars and Uranus less than a degree from exact. His Mars was also trine his ascendant less than a degree from exact, symbolic of extraordinary athleticism, and that same Mars was mundane square the Moon less than two degrees from exact. Thus this triple combination of Mars mundane square Uranus *and* the Moon (which are in a very tight opposition) were symbolic of excellence that went off the scale in an artistic cum athletic endeavor that left people who saw him awestruck.

Actress Katherine Hepburn was the very essence of this combination in conjunction. Her independence and unconventional nature is the signature, and she was forceful and direct but not unkind. Sometimes the conjunction is absurdly funny. Steve Martin and Robin Williams both with close conjunctions show the effect. They are unique, exceedingly quick, imitate nobody and fine exemplars of original talent. Mars-Uranus doesn't follow any style or school of thought; others follow them. Sometimes the work of these people seems so far out that they may be regarded as mysterious like L. Ron Hubbard who founded Scientology; other times they may seem more conventional but the path that leads to their objective is outlandish, unlikely or outrageous like Arnold Schwarzenegger, Austrian born governor of California and Jesse Ventura, the wrestler turned governor of Minnesota. These three all have the conjunction.

The American swimmer Michael Phelps is the most decorated Olympic athlete of the modern period (since 1896) and perhaps of all time. He has won twenty-eight medals (23 gold) over three Olympic Games. He has the quincunx within a degree. As the best American swimmer to date he is a fine example of physical prowess that frequently attends this combination. It helps that he also has Mars mundane square Pluto also only a degree from exact. Although some of his wins have been in relays, he shows the tendency of Mars-Uranus to symbolize individual exploits. These people are usually not team players. If not the best in their specialties they are usually in the first rank of their chosen pursuits.

The opposition is the most difficult combination with this pair. It may symbolize a wild personality at best or a mean-spirited, arrogant person particularly if close; some distinctly dastardly people have the opposition like the serial killer Ted Bundy. Yet the hair-trigger temper and impulsiveness of the contact often displayed by natives of this planet combination can appear in any of its aspect combinations. The notorious gunslinger and gambler, John Wesley Hardin may have been one of the fastest guns in the Old West. He reputedly killed forty-two men, although only twenty-seven have been confirmed. Hardin had the conjunction less than a degree from exact. Sometimes Mars-Uranus is celebrated as a romantic, free-ranging quality but it is worth noting that Hardin, for one, was a brutal, heartless killer who spent much of his life in prison. After release from prison he was murdered in a card game. In a good horoscope this opposition may well manifest as a formidable personality who may intimidate without malice or intent. This was true of the great blues singer/musician Chester Burnett, better known as Howlin' Wolf, whose intensity was as powerful as his singing voice. He had Mars opposite Uranus less than a degree from exact.

Mars-Uranus is always a potentially extreme combination. Mars was conjunct Uranus at the Midheaven at the moment that the first atomic bomb used against the Japanese exploded over Hiroshima. Between sixty and eighty thousand people were instantly vaporized at that moment (8:15 a.m. JST, August 6, 1945). By December 1945 the death toll due to the effect of radiation is estimated to have brought total mortality from the blast to 150,000 people.

Mars-Neptune

This combination is strongly inclined toward intense expression of emotional and psychic energy. It occurs in the horoscopes of artists of all types and especially actors, singers, musicians, writers of fiction and science fiction and those who embrace the occult arts. Aaron Thibeaux ("T-bone") Walker, master guitarist, singer and songwriter, had the conjunction less than a degree from exact. He pioneered the electric blues and the jump blues and heavily influenced B.B. King and Jimi Hendrix. Walker's influence on the music of the last seventy years is nothing less than pervasive. Michel de Nostradamus, the sixteenth century seer, is a good example of the Mars-Neptune quality; he had the opposition. Luciano Pavarotti, the greatest tenor of his era, had the close square, and actor Paul Newman had the close trine. There is not a great difference between the so-called good and bad aspects. Just as many of the scoundrels have trines as those with impeccable reputations have squares.

People who frequent health clubs and gyms, especially the weight-lifters who like to look at themselves in mirrors, have this combination. Neptune exaggerates everything including strength and the appearance of strength. Many people who are not vexed by this combination show one of the consistent features of Neptune: they are carried in life by the efforts of others and/or they enjoy an exalted position as an accident of birth that neither achievement nor virtue appear to warrant. People who are tormented by the Mars-Neptune configurations often achieve more in life.

This is one of the occasionally "kinky" contacts. Its natives are particularly lascivious and even perverse without the addition of other planetary factors that can mollify its more extreme manifestations. It inclines far more toward the masochistic than the sadistic side of the spectrum. The major fault of the combination is that it consistently appears in the horoscopes of people who have problems with alcohol, drugs, food and sometimes all three. Neptune is addictive and the most insidious malefic. It seduces its victims via pleasure that subverts their strength and makes them dependent.

Many of the women with this combination don't display its undesirable qualities, but their husbands may be blind, handicapped, badly wounded in combat, and occasionally ineffectual even if able-bodied. They may also drink to excess or smoke marijuana daily, both of which reduce their output. The men usually produce few offspring, especially boys.

Notwithstanding its undesirable qualities, Mars-Neptune people are members of a highly imaginative group. They have a good head for line, color, and fashion. Designer Christian Dior, with the trine, is a superb example. The wealthy art collector Peggy Guggenheim built one of the most fabulous collections of modern art in the world that encompassed works primarily from Europe and the Americas. She had the one degree conjunction. Johann Gregor Mendel, an ethnic German born in Moravia (modern Czech Republic), was an Augustinian monk who did ground-breaking work in the 1850s and 1860s on garden peas that demonstrated the laws of genotypic inheritance. The importance of his work was not appreciated or even recognized until decades after his death. He is called the "father of genetics." His Mars-Neptune square, less than a degree from exact, illustrates the intuitive leap necessary to apprehend things that cannot be seen directly but inferred about some underlying reality (i.e. what would later be called "genes"). Gregor Mendel, the father of genetics with the very close square illustrates the intuitive leap necessary to apprehend things that cannot be seen directly but inferred about some underlying reality (i.e., what would later be called "genes"). More often, like most Neptunian issues, those with this combination have exceptionally well developed feeling tone and intuition. They tend to favor fine arts and philosophy more than the world of hard science. Music, drama and literature are the most common venues in which its natives excel—witness Alexandre Dumas (père), Ernest Hemingway, Billie Holiday, Willie Nelson, all denizens of Mars-Neptune.

Mars-Neptune can be distinctly mean, under-handed, even cruel. Sometimes it is a signature of criminal intent. Charles Manson, with the conjunction less than a degree from exact instigated a murder spree and may fairly be termed a psychopath. O.J. Simpson, with a close trine, was acquitted de jure of murder but never escaped the general public's de facto conviction and has had repeated run-ins with the law ever since. Several of the greatest military captains in history have this, such as Alexander the Great with a one-degree square; Charles Martel, *the hammer* (who defeated the Muslims in France at Tours in 732 and rolled back would-be Muslim expansion into Europe) with a three-degree square; and Napoleon Bonaparte with a three-degree conjunction. While they were brilliant tacticians and very successful in the field, their ambitions cost the lives of millions. Mars and Neptune are malefics, a term that is too often downplayed as an antiquated notion. They commonly require extenuating circumstances when together, via the helpful rays of other bodies, to work out well.

Ernest Henry, the Swiss mechanical engineer responsible for the 1913 Peugeot that won the Indianapolis 500, had Mars trine Neptune less than a half degree from exact. His double-overhead cam, four valve per cylinder, pent roof combustion chamber design subsequently became the pattern for the modern racing engine, including the Millers, the Offenhausers, the Cosworth Fords and most modern manufacturers of racing and many passenger internal combustion engines to the present day. The modern Ford Cobra (passenger car) engine has the same internal layout as the 1913 Grand Prix Peugeot, except that the Peugeot was an enormous in-line four cylinder engine and the Ford is a much smaller (but much more powerful) V-8. Henry also had Mercury conjoined to Mars and the Moon in Gemini opposite the Mercury-Mars conjunction, which is, taken together nothing short of brilliant. In a manner reminiscent of Mendel, sometimes technically inclined people, who are not artists in the conventional sense, but who have Mars with Neptune, can see into machinery conceptually. Henry's designs were so technically advanced that they have been described as if they were extra-terrestrially inspired.

Literalist religious fervor of any stripe that sees only one way and simplistic solutions to complicated and variegated issues, frequently accompanies this combination. Mars-Neptune can be turned from a limited evangelical orientation, however, by additional benefic contacts into an idealistic and humanitarian, universal quality, well exemplified by Eleanor Roosevelt who had the three-degree opposition. It must be kept in mind though, that planets frequently display both the obverse and reverse sides of their natures, often in the same life at different times. Neptune in its positive rendering usually manifests as devotion to a person, an idea or faith as well as exquisite sensitivity to subtleties that often manifest as art, and with Mars, extremely vivid and unrestrained forms of art. The negative manifestation of Neptune, all too common with Mars, is addiction, obsession and extraordinary self-indulgence, particularly sexual indulgence. Perhaps the greatest blues guitarist of his generation, Eric Clapton, has had extreme struggles with drink and drugs that nearly ruined his life; devotion to his art brought him back from the brink of total disaster. Clapton has the quincunx less than a degree from exact.

Steve Jobs, the man who brought Apple back from the edge of bankruptcy and maneuvered it into one of the most advanced and successful companies in the world, had Mars opposite Neptune, a degree from exact. He was known as "the terrorist" for his harsh and demanding behavior toward subordinates. He mellowed somewhat with age but was known as a hard man to work for, notwithstanding the praise heaped upon him at his death.

Mars-Pluto

The chief effect of Pluto configured with Mars is to incline the native toward endeavors that involve force or the threat of force. Careers in the military and police forces occur frequently with this contact; even security guards have it, and like the other two examples, they are prepared to invoke force to discharge their responsibilities. Gang leaders who rule through fear and intimidation have this contact too. It is common in those who excel in athletics. Mickey Mantle, New York Yankees center fielder who won the American League Most Valuable Player award three times, had the trine less than a degree from exact. He was an iconic figure to an entire generation of post-war Americans. People with this combination do not, however, invariably act like they are looking for opportunities to exercise their aggression. There are two sides to all the Plutonian contacts. This combination is often easy to recognize because many people who have it act like they have a surplus of testosterone. Many Mars-Pluto natives delight in competition, and in particular in crushing their opponents through means fair or foul. Sometimes the native is not a particularly aggressive person but must dispense discipline or corporal punishment, such as a headmaster or some other kind of taskmaster. In some manner or another Mars-Pluto people are associated with violence, harshness, cruelty or meanness either on the giving or receiving end, but more commonly they dish it out.

There is also a rebellious, anti-establishment quality that isn't looking for a fight but won't back down from one either. These people display tremendous courage and indomitable will in the face of adversity. Mohandas Gandhi, with the one-half degree opposition, was a pacifist, yet he led the effort to secure Indian independence. He was many times severely beaten and jailed for his efforts. The late Princess Diana had the four and a half-degree conjunction. She was a gentle, decent and generous person who found her purpose in service to others but refused to look the other way and passively accept the iniquities of her marriage. United States Secretary of State Hillary Clinton, who served as secretary of state during the first Obama administration, has the conjunction less than a degree from exact. The great benefit of this contact is drive. It will not accept defeat. Women with this combination may be just as aggressive as the men and are sometimes masculine in demeanor and appearance, especially if this pair is angular. When the combination is far removed from the angles the women may have extraordinary femininity but extraordinarily compelling sensuality that is effortless and unaffected. Actress Scarlett Johansson with the two-degree square shows the effect. She was voted sexiest woman alive in a major national magazine at ages twenty-one and twenty-eight. Ernest Hemingway, who loved the outdoor life and embraced masculine themes, had the four-degree square.

This aspect is most conspicuously aggressive when it appears in or near the superior angles (Ascendant and Midheaven) or makes an aspect to an angle. With only modest additional symbolic support, the native is likely to display war-like qualities and to conduct his activities as one might conduct military maneuvers. When this combination is remote from the angles, the native may be charming, yet there is still likely to be continuous association with violence, hunting or the military if the aspect is close. For example, John F. Kennedy saw combat in World War II, was seriously injured, became commander-in-chief as president and was assassinated. He had Mars semi-square Pluto only nine minutes of arc from exact. Napoleon Bonaparte, the greatest military captain of the modern period, had the trine less than a degree from exact. Similarly, Peter the Great of Russia had the trine less than a third of a degree from exact. He made Russia into a world power, mostly at the expense of the Swedes and the Turks. Martial arts master Bruce Lee had the square less than a half-degree from exact.

When very prominent in the horoscope this pair may be loud, sometimes coarse and full of anger, despite an otherwise good character. Even when well-spoken or quiet and apparently reserved, Mars-Pluto may be a troublemaker who finds satisfaction in making other people squirm or suffer. This type of person must be met head-on or scrupulously avoided as he will steamroller anyone who lacks the will to take him on. It can easily manifest in a criminal manner, but this is by no means assured and usually requires further affliction. Persons with it are generally fearless and they sometimes look for avenues of expression that entail so much risk that most people would consider the exploits of the Mars-Pluto native dangerous. If this combination appears in the horoscope of a political figure, much good can come of it if the native is a champion of the people because such a person will be relentless in the pursuit of worthy goals. Many ostensibly meek people have this contact but their courage and resolve in the face of violence and danger are unshakeable, much to the consternation of their opponents. If the lights are involved with Venus, the daring of the Mars-Pluto person is below the surface but will come as a bigger surprise when it shows itself. In tightly controlled Saturnine personalities, a Mars-Pluto contact may manifest as tremendous physical strength or the capacity to work much harder and longer than other people.

It is conspicuously noteworthy that the Battle of Marathon (September 12, 490 B.C. Julian), was the defining engagement that saved Greece from being completely ravaged and incorporated into the vast Persian Empire. The Persians had amassed an enormous army in a punitive expedition against the Greeks for their support of rebellions against Persian authority in what is now Turkey. The unlikely Greek victory at Marathon allowed the Golden Age of Greece to blossom into full flower, and subsequently the whole of the West. It was fought when Mars, extraordinarily powerful in his own sign, Aries, and retrograde, opposed Pluto four and a half degrees out in longitude. However, as both bodies were well off the ecliptic and the equator (Mars had south latitude and declination and Pluto had north latitude and declination), their relationship was such that they came into an all but exact opposition in mundo at the latitude of the Plain of Marathon on September 12, 490 B.C. At noon at Marathon on that day probably as the combat was underway,

*The Entscheidungsproblem was posed by the mathematician David Hilbert in 1928 that relates to the logic of whether or not a statement is universally valid.

Pluto rose with a sidereal time of 5h 40m 32s and Mars set with a sidereal time of 5h 39m 25s. The difference, one minute and seven seconds, is a trifle more than one-quarter of a degree of arc. Thus the full force of the Mars-Pluto opposition was concentrated at the latitude of the Plain of Marathon when the sons of Greece were fighting for their little states that became both the well-springs and standard-bearers of Western Civilization. It was truly a David and Goliath situation.

The Greeks, who were outnumbered by Persian infantry by at least two to one—some sources think it was much more of a mismatch—but fighting, indeed *possessed* with their backs to the wall, on home ground, routed the Persians in what is the first recorded double-wing envelopment in history. Mars was sextile Uranus, which was also retrograde that day, by less than a half degree which produced that innovative tactic.

In general, it is crucial to control the center of a formation in massed combat, but the Greeks turned that idea on its head. The Greek hoplites fought in their customary and devastating phalanx formation but they deployed their flanks in eight ranks each while their center, spread thin to cover the big Persian formation, was in only four ranks. The Greeks charged the Persian line at the run in full panoply as the fighting began, but the Greeks gradually gave ground in the center as the superior Persian numbers began to tell. Then the Greeks advanced their heavy wings, wheeled and fell on the then encircled Persians from the flanks. The Greeks, typically heavily armored and armed with heavier weapons than most adversaries, fared best in the mélée of hand-to-hand fighting. The lighter armed and armored Persians were hoping to decimate the dense Greek phalanxes with arrows, slings and other missile weapons. The Persians, because they became encircled and were unable to maneuver, suffered the greatest disaster that can befall an infantry force: panic, which spreads through an afflicted force like wildfire. Ancient sources give Persian losses as greater than six thousand killed. The Greeks lost 192 Athenians and eleven Plataeans. The city state of Plataea, to the everlasting gratitude of the Athenians, had sent a thousand hoplites to supplement the nine thousand man Athenian force.

Famous poet and playwright Aeschylus (*Prometheus Bound, The Oresteia [trilogy], The Persians, Seven Against Thebes, Myrmidons*) considered his participation in the Battle of Marathon, the high point of his life. Aeschylus was wounded at Marathon and his brother was killed there. He was thirty-four or thirty-five at the time (born 525 B.C.) which underscores the gravity of the situation facing the Greeks. The Greek army was not merely a force of farmers and young men pressed into service. All classes and ages were there, not only out of necessity in accord with the military obligation of free men (until the age of sixty), but as a point of honor. If the Greeks had lost, not only would their political freedom and institutions have been destroyed, many of them would have been slaughtered outright and their wives and children enslaved.

It was from this engagement that the now-famous herald, Pheidippides, was sent hurrying nearly twenty-five miles to Athens to warn the civil authorities not to surrender if the Persian fleet appeared offshore. The Persian fleet subsequently did appear offshore ready to make an amphibious assault on Athens but for the arrival of the Greek army to thwart the attempt. Before the battle Pheidippides had run from Athens to Sparta (a distance of 150 miles) and back to appeal for Spartan assistance against the Persians. The Spartans arrived too late to participate in the battle. The weary Greek force, after their victory, was on a forced march back to Athens to block a Persian assault on the city from the sea. According to Plutarch (*On the Glory of Athens*), more than five hundred years later, Pheidippides ran that grueling twenty-five miles, gave the message, "We are victorious." to the assembled city government officials, collapsed and died on the spot of exhaustion. Obviously his pace was too fast, if the account is true. He would have outrun his extraordinary but over-extended capacity in the same way that a horse can be run to ground by a rider who does not consider the limits of his mount. Mars-Saturn and Mars-Uranus can both be extremely difficult, harsh and violent but Mars-Pluto is an overwhelming force that pulls out all the stops and then finds superhuman reserves, that nobody knew they had, like the badly outnumbered but desperate Greeks at Marathon, Pheidippides himself, or the woman who *picked up* the corner of a car that would otherwise have crushed her child. She embodied the essence of the contact at its most extreme in that what she did is considered impossible, yet there are many instances of such feats of strength. In a good horoscope the combination may show itself as an heroic influence, especially in high stakes situations. In a bad one it may be cruel, nefarious, dishonorable and can only be taken out by a similar force. In a combat situation where there is usually a winner and a loser, the winner wins an amazing, memorable victory and the loser endures an horrific loss.

Jupiter-Saturn

These people have enterprising, principled and usually conservative natures. They may found businesses, schools of thought and standards against which others measure themselves. They are stubborn, adamant, even intransigent about maintaining old, established positions. With the addition of other bodies to this combination they may be simultaneously far-seeing and willing to modify old strategies to accommodate traditional values to new realities, but in most cases they are resistant to innovation and change and remain true to an original vision. The best of them, however, are nothing less than the pillars of their eras. The alliance of the greater benefic with the greater malefic gives a temperament very much in earnest, intent on material security and dedicated toward establishing structures to that end. Thus, Jupiter-Saturn is solid, dependable and able to withstand the slings and arrows of outrageous fortune. Its natives consistently become members of established, entrenched authority although they may begin life on the outside looking into a good 'ol boy network. Because the attitudes and things symbolized by this combination are lasting, that longevity is responsible for the major fault of this combination: its natives usually insist that they know best in all matters of consequence. They are likely to be judicious and fair-minded, but also distinctly judgmental. They don't see that their point of view is limited if it has been successful. They rarely compromise on issues that relate to religion and spirituality or morality and ethics. Generally, interference by a third body with the Jupiter-Saturn pure type is required to make it deviate from its otherwise intractable, old-fashioned positions.

Jupiter-Saturn is a house built upon rock; it has long been called for good reason the "foundation combination." Its natives are extremely hard working, their efforts are enduring both in idea and physical form, but success usually comes slowly to these people. Still, slow or not, their efforts set the stage for those who come after them.

The father may have little success in his career or less success than his ability may appear to warrant. He may also be defined by his job and role in life that make him seem a dreary figure; yet his entire family may depend on him completely but take him for granted. The native may be inclined toward depression, and will at least be serious and may shoulder heavy burdens but not always get the reward that he deserves, much like workers, supervisors and occasionally middle management that perform the most critical, intrinsically difficult and demanding tasks, yet upper management gets the (undeserved) credit for it. Ever practical, Jupiter-Saturn people typically align themselves with authority and power and become long-term employees or bureaucrats. Jupiter-Saturn is generally not dynamic but rather it is quietly competent, persevering and tends to build up a fund of knowledge and experience that eventually makes its natives indispensable.

Frustrated in their desire to run an operation the way that they know it could and should be run, they will sometimes strike out on their own. The combination does not deny success although it usually comes late in life and may not completely satisfy the native. Some people with this pair become famous for their expert knowledge as authorities in their own right. They understand systems analysis and know how to exploit economies of scale. Often they appear cold, detached and unapproachable and only their personal intimates know what motivates them. If other factors support it, some with this contact lead exciting lives who embody the spirit of the age in their work. They are standard bearers to whom everyone can relate. They are concerned with quality, not quantity, the expression and maintenance of excellence, high standards and a stable environment conducive to such things.

Fine examples of the conjunction are the murdered songwriter/musician John Lennon, probably the most talented member of the Beatles, with the half-degree conjunction; Vice President Richard Cheney with the one-degree conjunction; ground-breaking Italian physicist Galileo Galilei with the two-degree conjunction; the greatest man-of-letters in the English language, William Shakespeare, with the three-degree conjunction; and President Barack Obama with the five-degree conjunction.

The sextile acts somewhat better than the other aspect types, but not invariably; as usual, much depends on what else is in play. Mark Zuckerberg, co-founder of Facebook, has the sextile less than a half-degree from exact. His fortune had reached $25 billion by age 26 and is growing. Gottfried

Wilhelm Leibniz was never wealthy but a co-founder of the calculus, and many other singular mathematical discoveries that have always been uncontested and are much used today. He also had the close sextile less than three quarters of a degree from exact. Leibniz was also a philosopher, a physicist, quadrilingual, a prolific author and a lawyer.

The people with the square may make their mark in a time of crisis. In AD 69 following the suicide of the emperor Nero, there were four Roman emperors in a single year, three of whom were deposed or killed by the next one until the fourth, an army general, Titus Flavius Sabinus Vespasianus, secured the throne and brought stability back to the Roman government. Vespasian had Jupiter square Saturn less than one and a third degrees from exact. He also took measures to return Rome to fiscal responsibility after the excesses of the deranged Nero. Vespasian ruled for ten years and embarked upon a huge building program, most notably the Coliseum, the largest amphitheatre in the Roman world by far, which is still standing mostly intact today. The great French King Louis XIV had the square one and two-thirds degrees from exact. His name is eponymous with an entire period of cultural refinement and style. George Bernard Shaw was an outstanding example of excellence in nineteenth and twentieth century English theatre whose works are classics and the epitome of his time. He had the square less than a degree from exact. James Butler Hickok, better known as "Wild Bill" Hickok, achieved enduring fame as a gunslinger who killed thirty-six men between 1861 and 1876 when he was murdered. His reputation as a some-time lawman and full-time tough guy would not warrant the renown he still enjoys except that he had a Jupiter-Saturn square, exact to the minute (with both planets exalted) at noon at his birth in 1837. Jupiter-Saturn is the quintessential benchmark aspect that makes people stand out for their exploits. Sigmund Freud was the dominant figure in psychiatry until his death in 1939 and for a long while afterward. His work was the model for psychoanalysis, the "talking cure." Freud had the two-degree square. His approach toward sexuality, the major theme of his work, tilted decidedly toward the idea that men naturally dominate women.

The trine people are known somewhat more fondly than the square people. Carl Jung, the other major figure in twentieth century psychiatry until his death in 1961, had the trine less than a half-degree from exact. Jung's approach to sexuality tilted decidedly toward gender equality. French author Jules Verne (*Twenty-Thousand Leagues Under the Sea, Around the World in Eighty Days*) expanded the genre of adventure stories into science. His work is extremely popular even today though Verne died in 1905. He had the trine less than a degree from exact. Model Christie Brinkley is a natural phenomenon, virtually an institution in itself. She is a classic "face" that can sell anything by virtue of her ability to stop men in their tracks. She has the one-degree trine. Biochemist James Watson ushered in a new era in biology along with his collaborator Francis Crick when they discovered the double helix structure of the DNA molecule in 1953. Watson has the trine less than three degrees from exact. The work of John Bardeen, who with Walter Brattain and William

*National Association for Stock Car Auto Racing, although there is nothing "stock" about these cars, which typically produce 700 to 800 horsepower.

Shockley invented the transistor at Bell Laboratories in 1947, changed the world profoundly, consistent with the far-reaching effects of Jupiter-Saturn combinations. Bardeen had the trine less than a degree from exact with Jupiter precisely in its exaltation degree (15° Cancer 00'). He is the only person to date who has won two Nobel prizes in the same field (physics).

The opposition does not differ markedly from other aspect types. Jean François Champollion cracked the code of hieroglyphics in the early nineteenth century that opened up the world of ancient Egyptian art, documents, statuary and monuments. He had the one-degree opposition. Scottish novelist Robert Louis Stevenson (*Treasure Island*, *The Strange Case of Dr. Jekyll and Mr. Hyde*), one of the major men-of-letters in English of the past century and a half, had the opposition one and three quarters degrees from exact. His work is still widely read, although he died in 1894. Robert Johnson, the king of the Delta Blues, inspired what later became known as rock and roll. His life is an extreme example of one who sets standards. His amazing guitar virtuosity is still studied intently by serious musicians, although he died in 1938 at age twenty-seven. He had the two-degree opposition. Johnson's case is a good example of how talent can be obscured or lurking as potential until the right direction, example or correction via training comes into play that allows that potential to appear in mature, coordinated, exemplary form. Johnson's technique was considered abominable until he was put right by the constructive criticism of two almost unsung masters: Son House and Isaiah Zimmerman, also known as Ike Zinnerman [sic]. Neil Armstrong, the first man to walk on the Moon, further illustrates the tendency of this contact to be present in the horoscopes of people who do ground-breaking and sometimes dangerous things. Armstrong's opposition is less than two and a half degrees from exact. Even the wide aspects have a good deal of power. George Washington, general and president, had the opposition six degrees from exact.

Jupiter-Uranus

In general this is one of the best planet combinations. It is distinctly fortunate and powerful. It should not be supposed, however, that the trines and sextiles insulate the native from trouble, nor that the squares and oppositions incline the native toward ill-advised use of power. Jupiter, the greater benefic, configured with dynamic Uranus signifies discovery, success in new endeavors, an innovative approach to old ones and a cutting edge orientation continuously in search of new territory to explore literally and figuratively. It exceeds existing limits both conceptually and in ordinary ways. It will not grant tacit acceptance even in areas considered sacrosanct, like religion. These people tend to ignore or find wanting all dogma, credo and doctrine that would restrict their free ranging turn-of-mind. In the rare instance where this is not so, severe affliction from the malefic planets (Mars, Saturn and Neptune) will be connected to this combination or the lights. These natives subscribe to the position that eventually it will be possible to do the (currently) impossible. One only needs to know how to do it. Jupiter-Uranus is the ultimate open-minded combination. They are thus often ahead of their time. It is a lucky, dynamic, progressive combination that finds its natives marshalling forces and harnessing resources that other people don't understand.

The seventeenth century French genius, René Descartes, made staggering contributions in analytical geometry, theoretical physics, metaphysics and philosophy that left his contemporaries reeling. He had the conjunction less than a degree from exact. Robert Noyce, owner of sixteen patents, shared the patent for the integrated circuit that is used now globally. He co-founded Fairchild Semi-Conductor in 1957 and Intel Corporation in 1968. Noyce had the five-degree conjunction in longitude, but Jupiter and Uranus appeared together in mundo on the eastern horizon of his birthplace separated by only two degrees. Singer/actress Eartha Kitt had the conjunction only ten minutes of arc from exact. Her inimitable voice and style carried her through career slumps that would have ruined many other performers. Fearless, she even spoke out forcefully against the Vietnam War at the White House in the presence of President Johnson and the First Lady. Though heterosexual she was equally adamant about gay rights. Bob Fosse with the one-degree conjunction was a major force in the world of dance. His sexy, jazz dance style won him particular fame for his choreography of *The Pajama Game*, *Damn Yankees*, *Cabaret* and *Chicago*, all classics of American theatre. The late Steve Jobs, chief executive officer at Apple, Inc., had the conjunction less than four degrees from exact. His inimitable management style constantly emphasized innovation and excellence in design that left his competitors playing catch-up. One of the greatest blues guitarists of all time, Stevie Ray Vaughan, had the conjunction less than a degree from exact. Some people call him hands-down the very best; others place him in the first rank of a very select group with a handful of members. The birth data of the great Hunkpapa Lakota chief, Tatanka-I-Yatanka (Sitting Bull), is not known beyond March 1831. There was a month-long Jupiter-Uranus conjunction then that was at three degrees remove when the month began and a degree and a half remove at the end of the month. Sitting Bull was fiercely independent and fought the U.S. Army for decades to avoid giving up the nomadic life of the Plains Indians. He was renowned for his physical courage, spiritual purity, great wisdom and strong resolve. His life is a clinic in what Jupiter and Uranus combined is all about when it operates at its best. Usually the combination is thoroughly virtuous. Sitting Bull organized the Sioux, Cheyenne and Arapahoe resistance to the U.S. government that culminated in the total annihilation of Lieutenant Colonel George Armstrong Custer's battalion of cavalry at the Battle of the Little Big Horn in Montana in June 1876 (Custer's Last Stand). Sitting Bull had a vision of the victory before Custer attacked the Indian encampment.

The tremendous creativity of singer/songwriter Paul McCartney, who has the semi-sextile only eight minutes from exact is testimony to Jupiter-Uranus. Nicolas Copernicus with the one half degree semi-sextile is typical of the counter-intuitive quality of the combination. He deduced the correct nature of the Sun-Earth relationship without experimental proof, which flew in the face of Scripture, though he was himself a canon of the Catholic Church, as well as a physician, mathematician, diplomat, economist, translator and classical scholar.

Guglielmo Marconi, who is given the most credit for development of wireless telegraphy, i.e., radio, had the semi-square less than one and a quarter degrees from exact. He shared the Nobel Prize for physics in 1909. Nikola Tesla, who invented alternating current, had the semi-square 21 minutes from exact. Alternating current powers the entire planet today. George Harrison, the best pure musician of the Beatles and the most under-rated of the group, had the semi-square only nine minutes of arc from exact. His musical creativity and virtuosity were superb.

The sextiles of this combination are extraordinarily valuable components in the horoscopes of politicians especially if they are bone fide patriots. Such people consistently enjoy the moral high ground and thus unassailable leadership positions as attested by George Washington and Mohandas Gandhi both of whom had the sextile one and half degrees from exact.

The square people often have to fight their way into positions of power and even then may be obliged to continue the fight. Lee Iacocca, who rose from engineer to sales executive and finally to president of Ford Motor Company, has the square less than two degrees from exact. He didn't get along with Henry Ford II and was fired in 1978 when the Ford Motor Company made a profit of $2 billion (when a profit that large was a major achievement). Iacocca was then recruited by the Chrysler Corporation that he steered from the brink of bankruptcy back to profitability. Actress and model Brooke Shields has had extraordinary professional success since age twelve. She has the square one and three quarters of a degree from exact. Jupiter and Uranus together represent the confluence of talent and good fortune. From the outside these people often seem to lead storybook lives.

Alan Turing, the amazing British mathematician and cryptographer, had the mundane square fewer than two and a half degrees from exact; Jupiter and Uranus were also the only two angular planets in his chart and thus the most powerfully placed bodies in his horoscope. He illustrates the decidedly advanced, inventive, even prescient quality, of this combination. His 1936 paper, "On Computable Numbers, with an Application to the Entscheidungsproblem,"* contained the seminal idea which is the basis of the architecture of all modern electronic computers. He was instrumental in the decipherment of the code of the German "Enigma" machine during World War II which was the primary German military code during that conflict. The Germans considered it an unbreakable cipher. Turing's work allowed the allies to read German secret plans and ordinary daily orders as well and as readily as the Germans did. He was utterly brilliant with five planets in sidereal Gemini (Sun, Mercury, Venus, Neptune and Pluto) and the Moon in Virgo conjoined to the South Node of the Moon. Either of the Moon's Nodes in Mercury's signs brings out the best they have to give. The South Node, when it operates well, enhances the native's sensitivity to the point of making a leap beyond intuition into pure abstraction. Turing was probably a genius. He earned a Ph.D at the Institute for Advanced Study at Princeton. He is also considered the father of artificial intelligence.

The trine frequently represents the most profitable combination of this pair. Television talk show host Jay Leno has the trine a quarter of a degree from exact. Entrepreneur Richard Branson, who put together Virgin Airlines and other businesses, has the trine only eighteen minutes of arc from exact. Financier and real estate mogul Donald Trump has the trine only twenty-seven minutes from exact. All three are multi-millionaires. Henry Ford (founder of Ford Motor Company in 1903) was a *billionaire.* He had the three-degree trine. Former Presidents Franklin Delano Roosevelt and George W. Bush both have the one-degree trine. Obviously this combination is symbolic of people in positions of considerable power. Both presidents are especially notable for projecting American military power to foreign shores.

All of these trine examples speak to power, success and financial gain but often those things are incidental to the life and not the aim or primary focus of it. Occasionally the contact symbolizes a mind or special talent that addresses issues far beyond the capacity of most people to conceive, much less perform. Isaac Newton, who developed the calculus, the most powerful mathematical tool to date, who discovered universal gravitation, the laws of thermodynamics and other physical laws, had the one and a half degree trine. Very much depends upon what else is in play in the horoscope. Many people with this are merely lucky and fond of esotericism. Even those for whom money is their god will occasionally surprise the truly material and jaded among their acquaintances, at the display of a distinctly progressive side that inclines toward the new, the advanced, the non-traditional and scientific. Some people imprisoned by their station in life may yearn to indulge their taste for travel and adventure, but unlike Moon-Uranus that can actually go there, contacts with Jupiter mean travel is formal and less authentic. The desire to expand and explore will find some outlet in the lives of Jupiter-Uranus people, no matter how content, contained or confounded their lives appear to be from the outside.

Mark Spitz, who won seven gold medals in swimming at the 1972 Olympics, has the sesquiquadrate only six minutes of arc from exact. Nobel Prize winner Marie Curie had the sesquiquadrate 17 minutes from exact. Obviously very few people experience success on this scale.

Prince Charles, heir apparent to the British throne, has the opposition only two minutes of arc from exact. His advocacy of organic and other advanced farming techniques is a classic example of the forward thinking that attends this combination. These people are often ahead of their time. Frequently even those who are not well born who are lucky enough to have this combination rise from modest circumstances and go to the top on pure ability, like Napoleon Bonaparte who had the opposition three and a half degrees from exact connected to the Sun by an aspect called a mundane square (q.v.). Likewise Albert Einstein, the greatest scientific mind since Isaac Newton, was born into middle class circumstances and changed the world via relativity theory. He was much distressed to realize that his work also led directly to atomic weapons. It is sometimes forgotten, however, that his Nobel Prize in 1922 was for the photoelectric effect, which made television possible. Einstein had the opposition less than four degrees from exact. Einstein illustrates one of the most powerful feature of this combination: the tendency to go beyond the envelope of the paradigm of the day. He asserted that resolution of intractable problems cannot be achieved by the level of thinking that created them; such resolution requires a higher level of insight and wisdom than is presently understood.

Jupiter-Neptune

Jupiter-Neptune is lucky and to a noteworthy degree carries its natives through life whether they appear to deserve the ride or not. It is present in the horoscopes of people who have inherited wealth and or political power. Lawyers often have this contact, as do people who benefit from lawyers. Yet it is a feature in the horoscopes of people who receive governmental aid legitimately but may have difficulty getting off welfare. It is also in the horoscopes of hustlers who may feign mental illness to receive state aid, or who misrepresent their financial condition and thus illegitimately play a system to their advantage. This happens both in the worlds of high finance and destitution. In the horoscopes of people of high integrity these contacts symbolize sympathy toward the poor and oppressed and willingness to help them. It is good for raising and receiving money that has not been earned for charitable as well as fraudulent purposes. This combination is consistently present in the horoscopes of those who ride a wave of business expansion and discovery by simply being in the right place at the right time. Unfortunately the so-called good and bad aspects are no consistent guide as to the honorable versus dishonorable manifestations of this combination. Only the horoscope taken as a whole will yield that answer.

Many people with this pair in some aspect are powerfully attracted to spirituality and religion, but it also is the sign of one who may merely professes such interest for reasons of his own. Addiction and devotion are both distinctly Neptunian qualities as opposite poles of that planet's axis. A Jupiter-Neptune person could be a compulsive gambler, a sanctimonious con-artist, a brilliant financier or a saint. These people are often deeply intuitive but they may be deluded if there is severe affliction from other bodies, especially Mars, or bad stars. The native is frequently interested in the dramatic arts as an actor, playwright or producer.

Benjamin Disraeli, the progressive British prime minister and author, had the conjunction one and a half degrees apart. He became wealthy via marriage but also pushed bills through Parliament that substantially improved the lives of all British subjects. Actress Katherine Hepburn also had the one and a half-degree conjunction, and her dramatic skill made her a classic in the world of film in her own lifetime. The sincerity, goodness and efforts on behalf of the poor and downtrodden everywhere made John Paul II (1978-2005) the best-loved pope of all time; he had the two-degree conjunction. President Franklin Roosevelt, with the three-degree conjunction, did everything he could via governmental policy to relieve the distress of millions of Americans who were desperately wanting during the Great Depression of the 1930s.

Charles Mingus, master of the bass and piano and a prolific composer (more than 100 albums and hundreds of scores), was among the most important American musicians of the twentieth century. He had Jupiter sextile Neptune one and a half degrees from exact. Both bodies in that sextile were quincunx Uranus, each less than a degree from exact, which is spectacularly creative, especially in an avant-garde manner in the fine arts. He was classically trained on the double bass but went off in new directions aptly described by a line in a song by Donovan, ". . . . Mingus, mellow, fantastic. . . ." (Donovan, *Sunny Goodge Street* from the Fairytale album, Castle Music Ltd., 1965).

People with the square take an active role in addressing the needs of the dispossessed, which often raises eyebrows when they come from exalted stations in life. Princess Diana with the three-degree square is a case in point. Chief Justice Earl Warren presided over the Supreme Court that struck down the separate but equal premise of segregated education in 1954. He wrote the opinion, which paved the way for better educational opportunity for African-Americans in the United States. Warren had the square less than two degrees from exact. Pope Paul VI (1963-1978) took a more active part than his predecessors in implementing church reform that touched all Catholics and even non-Catholics. He had the one-degree square. Aaron Spelling, a successful television producer, had the best sense of any of his contemporaries with regard to what shows would be popular. It made him immensely wealthy. He had the square less than a third of a degree from exact.

The trine is indistinguishable from the square in its effects. John D. Rockefeller, with the trine less than two degrees from exact, raised the Standard Oil Company into such a staggering power that the federal government declared it a monopoly and broke it up in 1911. Rockefeller was more wealthy individually than many countries. Edgar Cayce, a famous American psychic, was never wealthy and often hard put to get by but his enormous gift brought untold benefit to thousands. He had the trine less than one and two-thirds degrees from exact. Michael Moore, the popular social activist whose desire to put right what is wrong finds form in film, has the one-half degree trine. Martin Luther King Jr. had the trine only a quarter degree from exact; his life was sacrificed on the altar of racial justice. The Italian physicist Alessandro Volta had the trine less than a quarter of a degree from exact. He was an unreservedly religious man despite his scientific work that was the focus of his life. He also enjoyed good fortune and high rank as a university professor. He was made a count by Napoleon in recognition of his scientific work. There is typically no conflict in these natives between the sacred and the temporal.

The opposition is immensely powerful. Financier J.P. Morgan was so wealthy that he loaned the United States government money to help curb the financial panic of 1907. Morgan had the opposition only 18 minutes from exact. Queen Elizabeth II of England has the opposition one half-degree from exact, and her distant relative, King Henry VIII of England, had the one-degree opposition. In both cases their wealth and positions in life are inherited, a characteristic feature of the Neptune combinations. James Janos, also known as Jesse Ventura, former governor of Minnesota, has the three-degree opposition. While he is an interesting man, prior to becoming governor, he had no experience as an officer of government by experience, education or training beyond a term as a small town mayor. Ventura shows how Jupiter-Neptune can elevate someone, even a professional wrestler like Mr. Ventura had been, to positions of power and rank.

Jupiter-Pluto

The chief effect of Pluto configured with Jupiter is to put people into contact with wealth and or power. Sometimes they are born to it, although most often those born to advantage have Moon-Jupiter. The Jupiter-Pluto people usually earn it. Bank officers often have it as well as financiers, industrialists and other fabulously wealthy people. Since, however, there are always more Indians than chiefs, many Jupiter-Pluto people work as bank tellers, clerks, brokers and managers in the financial services community but their stock in trade is the use and accumulation of money. People in high positions in government or bureaucracies are also likely to have this pair in some combination. It relates to power on a big scale and accelerated growth, often of a genuine spiritual kind at the high end or secular power at the low end, and sometimes both. If this combination is in the angles or configures the lights, the desire to expand one's business and grow one's interests and sphere of influence is so great that its natives are considered remarkably ambitious to succeed. People with this combination may win against heavy odds like those who win contests or lotteries, but most often, people with this combination have good financial sense and make fortunate investment decisions. They may sell the rights to a ground-breaking invention or through a lucky opportunity that favors talent and insight, find themselves in the right place at the right time to seize authority to dispense and control money, power and favor. Often these people have very good lives. Bill Gates, with the one half-degree conjunction and $50 billion dollar fortune is the premier example. Mick Jagger, the much celebrated lead singer/songwriter for the Rolling Stones has amassed a fortune of several hundred million dollars. He has the one-degree conjunction. Academy Award winning actor Tom Hanks has the three-degree conjunction and a similar fortune. Yet Mohandas Gandhi had the two-degree conjunction. Neither money nor power were his aims in life, rather justice and independence for his country. His virtue and reputation however made him the most influential man in India. Pablo Picasso had the five degree conjunction in zodiaco that was only a half degree from exact in mundo when this pair appeared on the western horizon. He was a millionaire and the most successful artist of the twentieth century.

Similarly, the great physicist Albert Einstein did not aspire to wealth or power but his influence and reputation like Gandhi's were overwhelming. Einstein had the three-degree square. The immensely wealthy and successful Hollywood producer Steven Spielberg has the square less than five degrees from exact. The brilliant Italian electrical engineer, Guglielmo Marconi, became rich from his patents for wireless telegraphy, better known today as radio. He had the trine less than two degrees from exact. Secretary of State Henry Kissinger was enormously powerful in the Nixon administrations. He also has the trine less than two degrees from exact, but the contact is not a guarantee of virtue. Assassin Lee Harvey Oswald had the trine less than two degrees from exact. Mass murderer Jeffrey Dahmer had the one and one half degree trine. Afflictions to this combination can pervert it.

The opposition is no different from the other aspects. It has good and bad people who are wealthy and or powerful. British Prime Minister Margaret Thatcher has the opposition only a quarter of a degree from exact. Saddam Hussein, had the opposition less than a half degree from exact. The greatest American driver in any class of automobile racing is Richard Petty, who has two hundred NASCAR* wins, a figure that will probably never be exceeded. He has Jupiter opposition Pluto fewer than four degrees from exact in longitude (three degrees *in mundo*). The Jupiter-Pluto combination speaks to the extreme nature of his achievement and that in his prime he was the best of the best. No other driver is even close to Petty's record. The Jupiter-Pluto relationship also speaks to Petty's wealth, largely from endorsements and ownership of racing enterprises.

Jupiter-Pluto people can be, but are by no means invariably, extravagant. Sometimes they are frugal, even cheap, but manage to amass wealth well beyond what one would guess their financial condition to be from the external conditions of their lives. Jupiter-Pluto is just as often distinctly avaricious, materialistic and anxious to be among the "right sort of people," i.e., others with money and status, and they are frequently autocratic if other factors support that tendency. Yet, occasionally in the same people at different times in their lives, Jupiter-Pluto is a common sign of philanthropy on a huge scale. Consistent with the rapid advance this aspect symbolizes, that most unusual person, the spiritual adept, who has attained a level of awareness that makes the material world pale in comparison, will likely have this combination. Even when this is not evident the Jupiter-Pluto people are generally conspicuously generous and paternalistic. They consistently gain favor and respect and rise to positions of prominence in their fields of endeavor from which they operate quietly to advance their specialties. Jupiter-Pluto people usually revere truth, scholarship, and virtuous works that they try to advance for the general good. Thus, while it is not absolutely assured, they are known to combine virtue and power and direct it at issues that are related to social justice, so that they appear to be reformers, but their orientation is broader than that. Jupiter-Pluto in its highest manifestation is a marriage of the temporal and the sacred. It sees the big picture, is both progressive and appreciative of what has already been established as classically good, and is at the leading edge of technology.

Saturn-Uranus

This combination, comprised of slow moving bodies, is common to many millions of people for extended periods. Thus, it does not show marked effects unless the aspect is close, configured with other bodies especially the Sun or Moon, or is near the strongest parts of the horoscope: the horizon and meridian. Otherwise, almost everybody born in the most recent conjunction years, 1897, 1942 and 1988 would show the effect to an extraordinary degree which is demonstrably not the case.

Saturn represents the structure of the life, the things that don't change, the fixtures and constants in the life. Uranus is eternally evolving, unfolding and developing: a constant work-in-progress, except that sometimes the change symbolized by Uranus is sudden, radical or extreme.

The people with this combination are reformers, renovators and modernizers who make important changes and improvements that can completely alter the direction of an enterprise. This group is essentially independent and innovative without abandoning a conservative base, yet they are often headstrong, willful and impatient. They see past mere formalism to the deeper ideas behind structures that have not changed since a mold was first cast although external conditions may have changed. Therefore they consistently know better than the uninspired or hidebound people they work with, especially their bosses, the best course of action to resolve an issue that confounds essential issues with external conditions. Saturn-Uranus natives may be know-it-all types which does not endear them to others. They can ascertain the direction of long-term tendencies before other people are aware of the new realities. For that reason they are usually best on their own or the boss of others. They can exploit opportunity, see weakness in argument and devise solutions to keep organizations intact and invested with merit. When they are not wholly independent agents they work from the inside of an existing structure as opposed to Jupiter-Uranus that thinks outside the box. Pope Paul VI, one of the recent modernizers of the Catholic Church, had the conjunction less than a degree from exact. Singer Barbra Streisand is demanding and impatient in the manner of this combination. She also has the conjunction less than a degree from exact.

Agatha Christie, with the semi-square two thirds of a degree from exact, is the best selling author of all time. She wrote 80 books and short story collections and 12 plays that have sold 2 billion copies in 45 languages. As an author she controlled every aspect of the creative process. Saturn-Uranus is insistent about having a free hand. Its natives like the element of surprise, and as a writer of mysteries, she constantly supplied the unexpected. Alan Guth, the physicist who alone conceived the Inflation Theory of the earliest moments of Creation, has the semi-square less than a half degree from exact. He also exemplifies the inclination to conceive the inconceivable or at the very least the unlikely and the unexpected, given already understood facts or the unsuspected resolution that ties together disparate elements of a conundrum. Before the four basic forces of nature: gravity, the electromagnetic force, the strong nuclear force and the weak nuclear force had resolved into absolute law in a barely imaginable instant, the speed of light was not the speed limit of the universe. It was during the few billionths of a second before those forces were absolute that the universe expanded faster than the speed of light. Saturn-Uranus grasps structural complexity in matters large and small, simple and profound. It is similar in effect to Saturn-Neptune but more singular and original.

When the aspect is very close the native can stand out as the best of his or her generation in their specialty. The superb voice of singer/actress Julie Andrews delighted millions in her prime. She has the sextile seven minutes of arc from exact. Luciano Pavarotti whose golden voice was the best of his era had the sextile only two minutes of arc from exact.

Thomas Hobbes, a seventeenth century English man-of-letters (*Leviathan* and translated Thucydides' *History of the Peloponnesian War*), and one of the greatest English philosophers, had

Saturn sextile Uranus less than a half degree from exact. He asserted the necessity of an absolutist sovereign power but one that owed its existence to the consent of the governed. He is in the first rank of the most important figures in modern political philosophy and one of the first empiricist philosophers. In the manner typical of this combination, he took hold of both ends of the political spectrum, whereas most people are one of two flavors: liberal or conservative. He was the first to espouse "social contract" theory, whereby limited governmental authority and order and limited civil freedom of action exist side by side.

Cast from the same mold as Hobbes, Edmund Burke (*A Vindication of Natural Society; A Philosophical Enquiry Into the Origin of Our Ideas of the Sublime and Beautiful; Reflections on the Revolution in France*), the eighteenth century Irish statesman, lawyer, author, philosopher and Enlightenment thinker, had the square less than a degree from exact. He was sympathetic to the American Revolution but not the French Revolution (because the French Revolution was open-ended—almost a celebration of radicalism and disorder during the Reign of Terror). He was critical of British imperialism in India and Ireland but served in the English House of Commons for nearly thirty years. He is considered the philosophical father of modern conservatism but often broke with his colleagues to embrace classical liberal positions. He espoused the idea that philosophical principles must be incorporated into government policy; otherwise government becomes an instrument of tyranny. In effect he addressed the question, "What is the optimal relationship between the individual and the state that simultaneously ensures civil liberties and the ability of the state to exercise authority?" Saturn-Uranus people often wrestle with issues that pit freedom versus power.

Peter Drucker, called the father of modern management, had the square one degree from exact. He was an academic, a prolific author and long-time independent consultant to big business and government, who accurately foresaw our current business situation. He is considered the most important figure in business management of the last one hundred years. Proclus, one of the last neo-Platonist philosophers of Late Antiquity (and certainly the most important), was also a lawyer, mathematician and teacher. He had the square one degree from exact. His influence in the Christian and Islamic worlds was profound for many centuries after his death in A.D. 485 and helped maintain the stature of Platonic thought for a thousand years.

Sir Alexander Fleming M.D., who discovered penicillin in 1928, had the trine only seven minutes from exact. Until the advent of penicillin bacterial infections exacted an immense toll of death annually throughout the world. Hundreds of millions of people and their descendants are alive today because of the work of this man who was given his head to pursue his interests, in his own laboratory. He was awarded the Nobel Prize for medicine in 1945. Polish genius Nikolaj Kopernik, better known by the latinized form of his name, Copernicus, deduced alone and contrary to the accepted doctrine of the day, that the Sun is the center of the solar system rather than the Earth. The astronomical revolution he fostered drove one of the biggest nails in the coffin of medieval thought. He had the sesquiquadrate one degree from exact. Another Pole, Karol Wojtyla, better known as

Pope John Paul II (1978-2005), had Saturn opposition Uranus less than two thirds of a degree from exact. He completed the modernization of the church initiated by Pope John XXIII, but really implemented by Pope Paul VI and himself. He was a conservative man to be sure, but more than wise enough to be sufficiently progressive to keep the church relevant in a changing world.

Saturn-Neptune

This combination is tremendously hard working, usually talented and often successful, yet many of its natives are also libertines like the English king Charles II and the American president John Kennedy. It has affinity with music and art on the one hand and politics and organization on the other. The great gift of the contact is the ability of its natives to see the order that underlies abstraction; and its fairly consistent manifestations are psychological or mathematical insight and sometimes an artistic tour de force. These people see the fundamental patterns in the purely mundane that may provide elegant and ideal solutions to intractable problems.

Occasionally the rise of the careers of these people represents a return to justice and order from a period of crisis and confusion. The English king Charles II came to the throne following the death of Oliver Cromwell, the pre-eminent figure of the English Civil War. Charles had the two-degree conjunction. Abraham Lincoln was president of the United States shortly before, during and for a week after the American Civil War. Lincoln had the three and a half-degree conjunction. Lincoln shows the tendency, along with President John Kennedy, to suffer martyrdom or at least severe censure, or even exile such as endured by Charles Stuart, later Charles II, in the course of the career. Kennedy had the wide conjunction at five and a half degrees but it was at the top of his horoscope: the strongest position in the chart, where Lincoln had it too.

Often these people are at odds with those in the church who assert denominational superiority, or they maintain that God is (infinitely) bigger than any religion and abandon organized religion altogether, though they be spiritually inclined. The works of the brilliant Irish author James Joyce (*Ulysses*, *Finegan's Wake*) were for many years banned (and burned) in England and the United States. Joyce had the three-degree conjunction. He drank heavily and was at war with the Catholic Church from the time of his youth. The amazing American poet Edgar Allan Poe, (*The Raven*, *The Pit and the Pendulum*, *The Fall of the House of Usher*), had the conjunction four degrees from exact but close to a very powerful position in the horoscope (the lower meridian). Poe's works rank even higher now than they did in his lifetime (1809-1849). He also drank to excess and like Joyce illustrates another quality of Saturn-Neptune in combination: it inclines toward a morose even lugubrious turn of mind. But this is not invariably the case. One of the greatest conductors of the twentieth century, British born Leopold Stokowski, had the two-degree conjunction. Modern orchestral standards are his legacy. He is best known to the non-classically inclined for his work on *Fantasia* for Walt Disney. He was the long-time conductor of the Philadelphia and New York Philharmonic orchestras.

Edwin Hubble, one of the greatest American scientists (and man for all seasons), had the square less than a quarter degree from exact. He discovered that nebulae are actually galaxies (island universes) and by extension that the universe is immensely bigger than had been previously supposed and that it is expanding. This combination is excellent for discerning the order of over arching concepts that are so big that they are hard to conceive, which in turn inclines its natives toward an ecclesiastical turn of mind. Mikolaj Kopernik (Copernicus) 1473-1543, who was a canon of the Catholic Church (also a medical doctor, mathematician, astronomer, translator and economist) who broke with millennia of tradition and supposition and asserted that the Sun is the center of the solar system. He had the quincunx less than a half degree from exact. His capacity to conceive correctly, without experimental proof, the geometry of the solar system is highly symbolic of the inclination of this combination to grasp abstraction that exists not merely as an ephemeral notion or potential but as concrete reality. He was soundly vilified by the leading intellectuals of his day who insisted with exquisite sanctimony and much vitriol over what they claimed was the self-evident reality that the Sun orbits the Earth.

Saturn-Neptune often shoulders heavy burdens and gains much respect for it. Jawaharlal Nehru, founder of a political dynasty and India's first prime minister, had the square only a third of a degree from exact. Jean-Baptiste Poquelin, better known by his pen name, Molière, is still France's premier playwright after more than three hundred years (*Tartuffe ou L'Imposteur*, *L'École des Femmes*, *Le Bourgeois Gentilhomme*). Moliere's insight into human nature was magnificent. He had the square less than a degree from exact and may have worked himself to death. Samuel Clemens, also better know by his pen name, Mark Twain, had the square less than a degree from exact as well. He stands in the first rank of American men-of-letters for his perspicacity that so vividly, delightfully and accurately portrayed emotion, motive and spirit that his works (*The Adventures of Tom Sawyer*, *The Adventures of Huckleberry Finn*, *A Connecticut Yankee in King Arthur's Court*) have become classics. Peter Drucker, whose *The Practice of Management* that appeared in 1954 became a bible in the field, had the two-degree square. Jack Welch, former chairman of General Electric, called Drucker "the greatest management thinker of the last [the twentieth] century." Two English queens, Victoria I (less than one-degree square) and her great, great granddaughter Elizabeth II (two-degree square), have the close contact which is symbolic of the gravity of the positions they hold and, in another sense, how they are captives of their station in life.

Donald Trump, the forty-fifth president of the United States has the mundane square. It's the closest aspect in his horoscope. His Saturn rose with a sidereal time of 0h 23m 41s and his Neptune was in the I.C. only eight seconds later, when 0h 23m 49s of sidereal time was in the M.C. Eight seconds of sidereal time is less than four hundredths of a degree. He was at odds with the American government even before he took the helm and continued, intransigent, once he was president as though his own government was his enemy. Saturn-Neptune, in its less than desirable manifestations, assumes for itself status, ability and wisdom that is unwarranted. Worse, the Saturn-Neptune combinations in their negative manifestations represent the inclination to undermine established authority; in Trump's case, the so-called "deep state."

The father usually looms large in the lives of these natives as a figure of considerable consequence to be pleased, or whose expectations the native feels obliged to fulfill or exceed. The outstanding actor Henry Fonda, father of the fine actress Jane Fonda, was a difficult, cold and demanding figure who held his daughter in his thrall far into her adult life. She has the opposition, less than six degrees in mundo, but with Saturn sextile the Sun from less than one degree out. The celebrated author and intellectual Louisa May Alcott had the trine one and a half degrees from exact. She was educated at home by her father until she was sixteen but was profoundly influenced by him throughout her life. She died the very day he was buried. Phillip II of Macedonia was a great warrior but a remote and largely absent father who would have been extremely difficult for any son to live up to, but he was eclipsed by his son, Alexander III (the Great). Alexander had the three-degree trine.

Henry Ford, the founder of the Ford Motor Company had the opposition only a half degree from exact. He employed a moving assembly line to radically reduce the cost per unit of building cars which, equally radically, increased productivity. Ford thus invoked the very essence of this combination at its best: Saturn-Neptune conceives the ideal way to do practical things. Niccolo Machiavelli, the brilliant Italian author, playwright and diplomat, wrote the first work of modern political science (*The Prince*) which is essentially a handbook on how to maintain oneself in a position of political power. It is the fulcrum of realism and idealism. Machiavelli had the three-degree opposition. Wolfgang Amadeus Mozart had the opposition seven and a half degrees out but the Sun and Mercury were also conjoined to Saturn which adds a lot to an otherwise too wide combination. Mozart was a genius, but dominated for many years by his father; yet as all great musicians do, he could transpose feeling into exquisite form that rang so delightful and true that his works will be forever embraced.

Saturn-Pluto

The chief effect of Saturn configured with Pluto as a natal condition is to make the native fight against authority or to disparage or ignore it, sometimes to his detriment. Often these people are a one-man demolition crew or they are rebels without a cause especially if this combination appears in the angles or is connected to the Sun. These natives are prone to ignore tradition and to found new traditions themselves. Saturn and Pluto in some combination generally show themselves at crisis periods in world politics when new realities are forced onto the old order and the status quo is dismantled, dismembered or reconfigured. Typically, in a manner similar to Saturn-Uranus, people born with the Saturn-Pluto combination are sure that they know better then their fellows the true nature of problems and the right courses of action to fix them.

The father in the horoscope is primarily signified by the Sun and Saturn. The Saturn-Pluto group tends to rebel against their fathers, to reject his authority outright, or the father is missing through early death or divorce. Even when he is present, usually his influence in the family dynamic or his virtue—sometimes both—are secondary to the mother. Unless there are contacts with the lights and or Venus between father and daughter, women with this contact tend not only to have a less than exemplary relationship with their fathers, but also to divorce or outlive their spouses. In a natus in which the father's influence is wanting or absent altogether, the native is often insecure, aimless, uninspired or irresponsible until he suddenly finds within himself his own *raison d'être*, apparently self-generated. Until then, Saturn-Pluto people seem often to be contrary, dissatisfied and fighting everyone, paradoxically looking for guidance but accepting none because nobody can equal the legitimacy of the father. Even when this pattern is not obvious, the Saturn-Pluto native fights against the system, breaks new ground or erects new standards.

Many people never get to the self-generating stage and are best placed in positions that make an asset of their natural desire to root out obsolescence or disorder to impose new order and direction. Occasionally in the mirror image of Pluto contacts, Saturn-Pluto natives are willing to have order imposed upon them and thus to find satisfaction externally because they can't do it internally. Most children want structure, stability and direction as they are quite aware that they cannot generally establish those conditions for themselves. It is the job of the parents, especially the father, to establish authority, justice, stability and to be an example of the right way to live. When the balance is not right the native may feel himself a prisoner in a rule-bound world and therefore inclined to become an outlaw, or the native may lack all restraint and act as though any curb is an imposition or injunction to be opposed.

Queen Victoria I of England shows the effect as the eponymous figure of her time. She had the conjunction less than a degree from exact. Her father died when she was eight months old. She was headstrong and willful and though she loved her husband Prince Albert dearly, he died young and was never her equal as consort to the queen. Léon Foucault, the brilliant French physicist who invented the gyroscope, determined the speed of light to within one half percent of its true value (150 years ago) and devised the first experimental demonstration of the rotation of the Earth, had the conjunction less than one half degree from exact. His father died when Foucault was nine. Though formally educated, Foucault went off in his own direction in physics unaffiliated with a university. Herman Melville, author of Moby Dick, had the conjunction less than three degrees from exact. Melville was twelve when his father died. The teenage Melville worked at conventional jobs as a clerk, teacher and farmhand but said that his life really began when he signed onto a whaler bound for the South Pacific. Melville deliberately thrust himself into the maelstrom of life that completely overturned his formerly prosaic and bucolic existence without much preparation, help or guidance from his father.

Edward Snowden, who released hundreds of thousands of secret U.S. government documents in 2013 in his capacity as a National Security Agency analyst, has Saturn conjunction Pluto only a degree from exact. His efforts have made him a fugitive, reviled by millions, although a hero to some. He took it upon himself to flout convention, authority, his loyalty oath and the law to assume for himself, legitimacy and authority. His acts have certainly compromised espionage networks but exposed a heretofore unknown policy of massive domestic surveillance that is Orwellian in scope. The country is divided over whether to thank him or jail him if he can be apprehended. Snowden also has Mars opposite Neptune that are both connected to his Saturn-Pluto conjunction by trine and sextile respectively. Mars and Neptune ratchet up the level of damage from a nuisance or loose cannon to a catastrophe and a criminal act. His statements, if they are to be believed, indicate that his motivation is patriotic. Even if that is true, his Saturn-Pluto combination underscores how people with this combination are inclined to think that their own judgments in matters large and small supercede established authority. Certainly the virtue of individual acts perpetrated against what the native perceives as injustice is sometimes borne out in time, especially in reaction to a tyranny; probably most of the time it is not borne out, especially if the perception is misconceived, and in particular if innocents suffer as a result of the actions of a hothead or a fool who mistakes freedom for license.

Nikolaj Kopernik (Copernicus) was ten when his father died. Copernicus created a sensation that became an astronomical revolution with his heliocentric (Sun-centered) model of the solar system that ultimately demolished and replaced the old geocentric (Earth-centered) model. He had the square less than two and a half-degrees from exact. Carl Jung produced a similar sensation in psychiatric circles by opening up the world of consciousness to the collective unconscious. Jung had the square less than two thirds of a degree from exact. He clashed with his father, who was a pastor. Formal religion could not supply the self-knowledge that was the object of Jung's search which many independent people embark upon. As a young man, religion was too limiting for Jung's revolutionary temperament. As an older man he came to appreciate the spirit behind religion.

The "Sun King," Louis XIV ascended to the throne of France at age five following the death of his father Louis XIII. Shortly after coming of age he assumed for himself the task of governance without ministers, which was without precedent. Louis had the trine only a half degree from exact. The renowned British intellectual Bertrand Russell was orphaned at age three. Though a brilliant mathematician, his works on philosophy, religion and morality—too advanced for his day—caused him to be denied a passport, imprisoned during World War I for his pacifist views and dismissed from academic positions more than once. Russell had the trine less than one and a third degrees from exact.

Queen Elizabeth I of England was born into a deadly Protestant-Catholic controversy as the Reformation gathered strength. She had infrequent contact with her father, Henry VIII, did not live in his household and was eventually declared a bastard by his order. Thus in her case she did not reject her father but was kept at arm's length by him and was eventually rejected by him as his legitimate issue. Occasionally it is hard to tell who rejects whom. She was a brilliant though autocratic politician who steered the English ship of state through an extremely perilous period. She had the wide seven-degree opposition in zodiaco (q.v.) but it was only two degrees from exact in mundo (q.v.). Mikhail Gorbachev, the most enlightened Russian leader of modern times, presided over the dismantling of the Soviet Union. He had the opposition one and a half degrees from exact.

Another notable Russian, Dmitri Mendelayev, had the opposition less than three quarters of a degree from exact. His father died when Mendelayev was 13. He is the greatest Russian chemist to date (1834-1907). He developed the periodic table of the elements organized by atomic weights. He correctly predicted that empty positions in the periodic table would be filled by elements that were unknown in his day. The tendency of the Saturn-Pluto people to bring into general awareness heretofore unknown parts of the real world is quite marked. This opposition, in an undeniable manner, puts the lie to the still popular notion that the so called "bad" aspects, especially the most powerful of them—the squares and the oppositions—are likely to produce undesirable results. While sometimes true, it is usually not true, even with combinations that involve the malefics as in this case. Rather, squares and oppositions are merely strong, which can work out badly depending on what else is in play in the horoscope; but they are not signals that the native is doomed.

This combination is best away from the angles or configured with Jupiter or Mercury, which will turn its action toward things constructive, once the old order has been torn down, or toward an investigation of the fundamental components of substances and ideas, once they have been deconstructed. If this combination appears in the angles, the native is far more likely to merely break and destroy things that have outlived their usefulness or to fight against them.

Uranus-Neptune

This is another of the slow moving planet combinations common to huge numbers of people for extended periods. Yet this contact is a dumb note in the lives of many of its natives because all such combinations require close proximity or connections to the lights or the horizon and meridian to show marked effects. Even then, sometimes people with close aspects do not show the contact to good effect due to the greater influence of more powerfully placed planets in their horoscopes. The conjunctions and all the aspects that follow in regular order are one hundred seventy-one and a fraction years apart. Everyone, therefore, born in 1650, 1821 and 1993, as well as the adjacent years, has the conjunction to a greater or lesser degree.

This contact at its best symbolizes powerful but subtle forces that relate to exalted, idealistic and refined levels of thinking and feeling that are particular to the outer planets. For example, during the first decade of the twentieth century when these planets were opposed, two of the major issues of the day revolved around the debate about the reality (or not) of the unconscious in psychology and atomic theory in physics. "If the unconscious exists," the question was posed, "how can it be consciously known; and if atoms cannot be seen, even microscopically, where is the evidence that they exist?" Uranus and Neptune are associated with high levels of consciousness that relate to the unseen world and may verge on the supernatural. Natives of this combination are idealistic, daring and often scientific. It goes well beyond all contemporaneous thought—no matter the era at hand—to embrace issues of justice and the classical virtues, which are never dated but often ignored. Most of all it symbolizes the awakening of the insistent need to respond to a request from deep within the self for expression that threatens the defenses of petty egotism. Many natives put the question to themselves, "What would my life be like if I ran it perfectly?" Yet the contact is rarely religious in a conventional sense. It often produces surprising results that benefit society in a widespread manner. Sometimes the results are partial. Sir Richard Burton, for example, who had the conjunction only one minute of arc from exact, translated *A Thousand Nights and One Night* (The Arabian Nights) from Arabic to English. He was an extraordinary linguist, explorer and soldier but he was also violent, headstrong and bigoted.

Clara Barton, who had the one half degree conjunction, founded the American Red Cross. Known as "the angel of the battlefield," she nursed both Union and Confederate soldiers during the American Civil War and was among the first women to demand equal pay for equal work from an uncomprehending male authority structure. Louis Pasteur, a French national treasure who was the foremost biologist of the nineteenth century, proved the germ theory of disease. He had the conjunction less than two and a half degrees from exact with the Sun, Mercury and Venus also bound up in the Uranus-Neptune conjunction.

Financier J.P. Morgan, who put together U. S. Steel, the first billion dollar corporation, had the semi-sextile less than a degree from exact. He took astrological advice from the noted astrologer Evangeline Adams. The celebrated British poet Algernon Swinburne had the one-degree semi-sextile. His rarefied work was considered among the best of his day as well as scandalous during the Victorian period.

The distinguished American intellectual Ralph Waldo Emerson had the semi-square less than a half degree from exact. His advocacy of the doctrine of transcendentalism offended many people with strong, conventional religious convictions because he contended that religious authority stems from individuals rather than the Bible. Nostradmus, a sixteenth century occultist, and Alexander Graham Bell, the nineteenth century inventor of the telephone, both had the one-degree semi-square.

Uranus-Neptune is typically a practical combination. Noted geographer, cartographer, mathematician, astronomer and man for all seasons, Gerard Mercator, had the sextile only six minutes of arc from exact. The map projection that bears his name has been in use for nearly 500 years. The prolific author Alexander Dumas had the sextile less than a half-degree from exact. Composer Johann Sebastian Bach had the sextile one and a half degrees from exact. The originality, color, spirit, depth and clarity of Bach's work is a testimony to Uranus and Neptune combined.

The amazing Polish born scientist Marie Sklodowska Curie, had the square only seven minutes from exact. She and her husband and collaborator Pierre Curie and professor Henri Becquerel, were the first people to identify and study radioactive elements in the 1890s. She pioneered the use of radiation to treat cancer. Sigmund Freud, the father of psycho-analysis, had the square less than a degree from exact. His best known work, *The Interpretation of Dreams* (Die Traumdeutung), is a testament to the search to find clarity in the nebulous. Uranus square Neptune is nothing if not insightful in an uncommon manner. It is also a basic lesson in the intrinsic nature of Neptune which is commonly abstract, abstruse and arcane, but those things are brought into the light through association with Uranus, helped a lot by the power of a square.

The esoteric and profound French author, essayist and critic, Marcel Proust, had the two-degree square. His magnum opus, *A la Recherche du Temps Perdu* (Remembrance of Things Past, or as it is sometimes translated now, In Search of Lost Time) in seven volumes (1913-1927), was described as the best writing of the twentieth century. The British author H. G. Wells, virtually the father of science fiction (*The War of the Worlds*, *The Time Machine*), had the three and a half degree square in zodiaco that was less than one and a half degrees out in mundo (q.v.). One can readily grasp time travel as the sort of interdimensional, paranormal element that Uranus-Neptune evokes. This combination usually speaks to ideals, excellence, the artistry of ordinary life and the exceptional that is nonetheless grounded in actual truth. Yet if there is hyper-aggressive symbolism in the horoscope, like Osama bin Laden's Mars-Pluto square, then his one-degree Uranus-Neptune square will manifest not so much as an independent idealist but as a radical ideologue intent upon pressing an agenda. Before he fostered and coordinated the attack on the World Trade Center at New York on September 11, 2001, he had became *persona non grata* in his own country (Saudi Arabia) for his strident and intransigent views concerning politics and religion.

John Maynard Keynes, British economist and architect of temporary deficit spending as the only viable response to economic depression, had the trine only a quarter of a degree from exact. William Wordsworth, poet laureate of England late in his career, had the trine less than three-quarters of a degree from exact. He was a classic intellectual intent on addressing the deeper questions in life. Samuel Johnson, the greatest English man-of-letters of the eighteenth century had the two-degree trine. The best known exemplar of the trine is Pablo Picasso who had it one and a half degrees from exact. Significantly Freud with the square describes the true relationship between motivation and behavior. Picasso with the trine displays it non-verbally in his art, often apparently disjointed contextually as dreams are; but Picasso's abstractions are no less real than dreams that are hard to follow. Ultimately then, paradoxically abstract, Picasso was a realist. Uranus-Neptune combinations always address the real world.

Writer, actor and director Woody Allen has an odd, but distinctly insightful and comedic take on life that is thoroughly entertaining. He is not merely a writer of screenplay but a consummate artist. He has the sesquiquadrate one half degree from exact. Gloria Steinem, renowned author, feminist and intellectual has the sesquiquadrate less than three quarters of a degree from exact.

The greatest dramatist in the English language is William Shakespeare. He had the opposition only a quarter of a degree from exact. His work is a feast and celebration of intelligence, subtlety, beauty, pathos and feeling presented as art, and thus a classic manifestation of Uranus and Neptune combined. The tendency of this combination to produce many writers and intellectuals is shown by others with the close opposition: Simone de Beauvoir, Peter Drucker, Samuel Beckett, W. H. Auden and Robert Penn Warren.

James Madison, the fourth president of the United States, had the quincunx aspect only four minutes of arc from exact. He was the principal author of the United States Constitution and the Bill of Rights, which were, along with similar French treatises of the eighteenth century, the most radical documents in defense of political freedom adopted as governmental policy since Classical Greece. Neal Cassady, one of the main contributors to the ethos of the beat generation (with Jack Kerouac and Allen Ginsberg) had the quincunx only six minutes from exact.

The recently deceased blues artist, Riley B. King, better known as B.B. (for Blues Boy) King, was among the highest elite of his art. He had Uranus quincunx Neptune exact almost to the minute. He was one of the brightest lights as a singer, songwriter and master guitarist over a career that spanned sixty-five years. His influence is pervasive, his technique was impeccable and his personality was a delight. Uranus is original and creative; allied with Neptune which is often musical and or theatrical, the result is often beautiful, entertaining, even entrancing especially if the lights are also involved with the combination. King had the Sun opposite Uranus less than a half degree from exact.

Another great contemporary musician, Prince Rogers Nelson, had Uranus mundane square Neptune, exceptionally close in his horoscope. In his case they were simultaneously angular (Uranus culminated in the M.C. as Neptune rose) forty-eight seconds apart which is less than a quarter of a degree. It is the closest aspect in Prince's chart. The combination speaks to musical virtuosity, excellence in composition and a strong inclination toward the theatrical in both art and regular life, all of which were conspicuous elements of his life. Like B. B. King, Prince was extremely personable and kind, qualities that don't always attend the extraordinary popularity that both men enjoyed, but they do usually attend contacts between Uranus and Neptune. Leonardo da Vinci also had the Uranus-Neptune mundo square. His was less than a quarter of a degree from exact. His artistic and engineering skill in several media is among the best of the best. His name is probably the one first mentioned when the 15th century Renaissance comes to mind. The extraordinary subtlety that can translate both emotional and intellectual energy into form is extreme with this combination. Yet another example of Uranus mundane square Neptune is well exemplified in the horoscope of Leonard Euler, the best mathematician of the 18th century. Euler's was less than a quarter of a degree from exact in superior angles: Uranus rose when Neptune was in the M.C. These people are superbly equipped to grasp the subtlety of abstraction, some of it hiding in plain sight. Music and mathematics are often connected although few musicians are good mathematicians. More often the mathematicians display a strong musical sense. Euler's staggering output and contributions to the integral calculus and analytic geometry put him in the first rank of the most gifted mathematicians since Archimedes.

If both of these planets make close aspects to angles but not each other, the effect is still similar to a translation of light (whereby the influence of two planets in aspect is imparted to a third one) since the horizon and meridian are intimately intertwined as the most powerful positions in a horoscope. American inventor Thomas Edison, who built the first research and development laboratory, had Uranus quincunx his mid-heaven only a third of a degree from exact; his Neptune was at the nadir square his horizon, also only a third of a degree from exact. His amazing achievements are a signature of imagination and fantasy made practical by inspired technical innovation.

Somewhat like the Jupiter-Saturn aspects that confer lasting notoriety, Uranus-Neptune contacts also often impart a legendary quality to the exploits of its natives. This is especially true if other planetary factors lend support. Molly Ludwig Hayes, the daughter of German immigrants, has enjoyed such status since 1778 as Molly "Pitcher." She had Uranus quincunx Neptune less than two thirds of a degree from exact, Jupiter trine Saturn less than two degrees from exact and Mars semi-square Pluto less than one degree and three quarters from exact. Her husband, William Hayes, was a member of the 4th Pennsylvania Artillery that played an important part at the Battle of Monmouth (New Jersey) on June 28, 1778. It is known as the longest battle of the American Revolutionary War, fought on a brutally hot day.

During the Revolution many wives followed their husbands and performed extremely valuable services, not least, cooking, sewing, nursing and bringing water to soldiers in particular on the day of this battle when many men succumbed to heat stroke. When her husband was wounded and carried away, she put down her pitchers of water and manned his cannon for the remainder of the battle. Monmouth was a slug-fest where General Washington rallied his men after a subordinate general had ordered them to retreat. Washington, who rarely swore, is said by eye-witnesses to have rustled the leaves of the trees with his withering language as he laid into the commander who had failed to press a tactical advantage against the British. In the course of halting the retreat Washington was repeatedly exposed to enemy fire which spurred his men back into the fight by his example: "Follow me!!" When the Americans re-engaged, the British advance was stopped and pushed back. The battle ended at nightfall. Monmouth is called a draw but the British left the field in the middle of the night. During the battle, Molly had a British cannon ball pass through her legs which tore off the lower portion of her skirt and petticoat, but, unfazed, she continued loading, firing and swabbing her canon as though nothing had happened. After the battle she was presented to Washington who issued a warrant on the spot to make her a non-commissioned officer. She was known as "Sergeant Molly" for the rest of her life as much as by "Molly Pitcher."

Uranus-Pluto

The chief effect of Pluto configured with Uranus is toward independence, iconoclasm and revolution. These people are extremely willful, often far ahead of their time and inclined to take drastic action. The person with this contact prominent in their horoscope doesn't care what people think or finds the widely held positions of the day vapid. Sometimes these natives go through life incognito and some embrace a radical approach to everyday life. If the combination occurs in the angles, the native will display original talent that could make him the envy of his peers and occasionally a revolutionary who espouses political freedom. Edgar Cayce, the renowned American clairvoyant, had the square less than one and three quarter degrees from exact with Uranus in the Ascendant and Pluto at the Midheaven. His amazing abilities obviously demonstrate that human beings are capable of astounding sensitivity; but notwithstanding that ability, very few people regularly manifest it. The combination speaks to the exceptional, the extraordinary and the inexplicable.

If this pair configures the lights, the behavior of the people who have this aspect may be so unorthodox that they could have a secret life far removed from what they appear to be. If it is cadent or succeedent, the storms that gather about the native's head are likely to be less tumultuous than if the lights are angular and connected to this combination. Then these people will be leaders or outcasts, depending on the constellations emphasized and other factors. In the main, Uranus-Pluto in any combination is a wild, unorthodox departure from whatever constitutes an accepted norm. It is also distinctly related to the supernatural, the other side of life to which people gain access usually via divine grace or raising their consciousness via education and living a virtuous life. That breakthrough sometimes manifests as breakdown, especially in the West where it is uncommon. It is inherently difficult, a shock to the system and requires careful management.

The people with this combination are occasionally so unmanageable, yet undeniably brilliant, that it is hard for them to integrate their talents and insights into regular life. Their insights are valuable, but they have tremendous difficulty making any sort of compromise and would rather forego great efforts and difficult enterprises than have to endure outside interference. Uranus-Pluto is inventive, innovative, independent, unpredictable and usually high-strung. They are astute observers of human nature and frequently blunt in their assessments of others. They tend not to respect law, tradition and custom or are inclined to contrive new ones. They are commonly rash, impatient and may mistake freedom for license to the extent that they may believe that just ends warrant unjust means. Social justice and revolutionary fervor are favorite themes with this combination. Still, no matter what theatre in which it plays out, Uranus-Pluto is a brilliant combination in particular if it configures the lights and is often symbolic of discovery as well as enormous and unconventional talent.

The birth year of Socrates is not known with certainty. He was Plato's teacher but wrote nothing himself. Plato is the foremost philosopher in the Western tradition, but that tradition really takes wing with Socrates; and Plato, almost certainly, would have deferred to Socrates, especially since Plato was in his twenties when Socrates was executed. Plato in his *Apology* (from the Greek απολογια, which means "a defense," especially a verbal defense in court, not an apology as it is understood in English) puts the words in Socrates' mouth that he was seventy years old when he was charged with impiety (not believing in the gods and declaring it openly). He was charged via the supposed impiety with the subsequent corruption of the youth of Athens in 399 BC. Plato also wrote, speaking for Socrates, that he (Plato) was present at the trial. From that statement and the one in which Socrates gave his age in the *Apology*, most older scholars have assumed that Socrates was born in 470 BC or 469 BC. The birth place, Athens, is not contested.

Some newer sources assert that the birth year was 467 BC on the basis of Standley's *History of Philosophy* which also supplies a date: 6th Thargelion, third year of the 77th Olympiad, which is May 20, 467 BC. The year began with the summer solstice in ancient Greece when the archons were not fiddling with the chaotic Greek calendars for political purposes. It is not known for sure if the Olympiads were continuously observed in an unbroken fashion from the first one in 776 BC. If the 467 date is right, it curiously repeats in mundo what the 470 and 469 BC dates display in zodiaco. On May 20 (6th Thargelion), 470 BC at noon, Uranus in hyper-intellectual Virgo was one degree and sixteen minutes beyond the exact zodiacal square to Pluto in the stinger of the Scorpion's tail. On May 20, 469 BC at noon, Uranus in Virgo was three degrees and forty-three minutes beyond the exact zodiacal square to Pluto in far-seeing Sagittarius, the sign of the prophet. It is also noteworthy that the mundo square between Uranus and Pluto on May 20, 469 BC at Athens was less than eight minutes of sidereal time from exact, which is less than two degrees of arc. At noon on May 20, 467 BC the right ascension and declination of Pluto were such that it rose that day at Athens with a sidereal time of 10h 24m 30s; Uranus culminated that day with a sidereal time of 10h 29m 00s. The difference, four minutes and thirty seconds of sidereal time is one and one eighth degree of arc.

It appears in this case not to matter what the year is. Mundane squares are not less potent than the zodiac squares; they may even be more powerful than the zodiacal variety because they are particular to a narrow range of terrestrial latitude, whereas the zodiac squares apply broadly to everybody born during the period of the operational orb of the combination. The Uranus-Pluto squares in zodiaco and in mundo were in play at Athens for four years. Everybody had it but the people whose lights plugged into that combination would have displayed it most obviously and powerfully. The Sun threw squares from inquisitive, childlike sidereal Gemini to Uranus and oppositions to Pluto closely on and near May 20 for four straight years. A free thinker who questions everything is almost a signature for Uranus-Pluto. The addition of the Sun to that pair to produce a T-square would make such a person the leading progressive light of his day who would be overwhelming in debate and a major thorn in the side of hidebound people. Socrates' unwillingness to compromise his principles regarding the trumped up charges brought against him guaranteed his demise. His enduring fame rests on his admonition to "know thyself," i.e. to seek self-knowledge; and his position that the unexamined life is not worth living, are two of the cornerstones of Western thought. Significantly, in respect of solid squared up foundations in life, he had been a stone mason at one point in his career and a hoplite who distinguished himself for valor in at least three engagements. Probably Socrates was the foremost exemplar of Uranus and Pluto in combination of his day, which placed him above his fellows, and which may be why paradoxically, the corruption of Athenian society was thrown back at him as though he had been the perpetrator of what was wrong with it. Until his trial and execution, he chose to live in poverty in his later years dispensing wisdom to those who had the ears to hear it, in particular his pupils Plato and Xenophon.

The fame of the great Scottish philosopher and man-of-letters David Hume (*A Treatise of Human Nature*) is still strong after three hundred years. He was a Socratic-like thinker who angered religionists when he questioned their assumptions about the nature of God. His observations about the relationship between cause and effect, which he showed doesn't necessarily follow, moral truths that cannot be proven through induction and that rational self interest can be superceded by passion, were both brilliant and confounding to the traditionalists of his day. He had the Uranus-Pluto conjunction less than a quarter of a degree from exact.

The superb French author Henri René Albert Guy de Maupassant (Boule de Suif, Pierre et Jean) had the conjunction in longitude less than a half degree from exact. He wrote masterpieces effortlessly and prodigiously in the 1880s, was extremely popular and successful but was eventually committed to an asylum after a suicide attempt. The Dutch impressionist master Vincent van Gogh had the conjunction in right ascension (q.v.) only one minute of sidereal time from exact. He was quadrilingual, taught languages, worked as an art dealer, bookshop assistant, missionary and finally, for the last ten years of his life, as an artist. He produced seven hundred drawings and eight hundred oils but sold only one in his entire career, though his staggering talent has been long recognized since his death. His work is universally recognized now and is the most sought after in the world. He was in and out of sanitoria several times during the last three years of his life. Because Van Gogh suffered from depression, his death by gunshot wound was ruled a suicide in 1890; however, recent research provides compelling evidence that he was accidentally shot by young boys who were teasing him. Samuel Johnson, the subject of the first modern biography (*Boswell's Life of Johnson*) was one of the giants of English letters in the eighteenth century. His *Dictionary of the English Language*, and other books, essays, criticism and long time editorship of several magazines made him the indisputable cock-of-the-walk of his day. It is fitting that his two-degree conjunction is on the western horizon, symbolic of the "other" or the "not self" (the eastern horizon represents the self), i.e. everybody else. People with western horizon emphasis have an affect on the public at large. Johnson made a huge impression on the entire English-speaking world.

The undeniably strange, but gifted English mystic and author William Blake, had the square only one half-degree from exact. Thomas Jefferson author of the Declaration of Independence, third president of the United States and perhaps the greatest intellectual to occupy the White House, had the mundane square (q.v.) only four minutes of sidereal time from exact (which is one degree of arc). Edgar Cayce, the greatest American psychic to date had the zodiac square one and two-thirds degrees from exact.

The late and wonderful Pope John Paul II had the trine less than a degree from exact. He was a breath of fresh air to an institution in need of revitalization. The amazing English author David Herbert Lawrence (*Lady Chatterley's Lover, Sons and Lovers*) had the trine less than a degree from exact. He was also a poet, essayist and critic whose work was so far in advance of his time that it was mistaken for pornography during his lifetime. The trine stands out as a common feature among liberals and those who excel in the liberal and fine arts: Eleanor Roosevelt, William Wordsworth, Richard Wagner, Franz Lizst, Frederic Chopin, Ezra Pound, Michelangelo Buonarroti, Edgar Allen Poe and Charles Dickens, to name just a few.

The Italian-American genius, Enrico Fermi, winner of the Nobel Prize for physics in 1938, had the opposition five degrees from exact in zodiaco but that combination was half again as close at two and a half degrees in mundo. Fermi directed experiments at the University of Chicago in 1942 that resulted in the first controlled nuclear chain reaction. He was an important figure on the Manhattan Project that developed the atomic bomb. The French classical scholar and extraordinary linguist, Jean-François Champollion, had the four-degree opposition in zodiaco but which was only seventeen seconds of sidereal time from exact in mundo (which is .007 of a degree of arc!). He was primarily responsible for cracking Egyptian hieroglyphs and dating the Denderah zodiac to the Roman Period (which previously had been thought to be much older than the Roman Period).

Neptune-Pluto

This combination has the longest period of any planet pair. The conjunctions are 493 years apart. Therefore, everyone born in AD 1398-1399 and AD 1891-1892 had it. It is far more common however, during the modern period, when the combination forms the waxing sextile and the waning trine. These two aspects form when Pluto is near its perihelion (closest distance from the Sun) which is also when Pluto is inside the orbit of Neptune that for twenty years makes Neptune the planet farthest from the Sun. Pluto was last at perihelion in 1989 and 1741 before that.

Neptune and Pluto are in a 3:2 resonance that is stable. Pluto orbits the Sun twice in nearly the same period of time that Neptune requires to orbit the Sun three times. Yet Neptune and Pluto pace each other when Pluto is at perihelion and for more than eight decades (four decades each on the applying and separating side of perihelion) near that event. Therefore the mutual aspects they make at and near the time of Pluto's perihelia repeat for eight decades. This behavior is characteristic of no other pair of planets.

There are usually two and sometimes three phases when the mutual aspects between Neptune and Pluto wane or pass out of orb entirely for a period of decades before coming back into exact relationship again. For example, Neptune came into an exact sextile with Pluto for the first time in the twentieth century in 1950 and made exact contacts in subsequent years through 1956 when the exact to the minute sextiles began to wane and were not made again until 1976. The last exact to the minute of arc Neptune-Pluto sextile in the twentieth century was in 1986. The next exact to the minute sextile reforms in 2026 and the final one is in 2032 but the eighty year period of the Neptune-Pluto relationship is all part of a single long-term recurring aspect.

Neptune was trine Pluto exactly in 1704 and made ninety-two more exact to the minute trines in the eighteenth century until the last one in 1785. Furthermore, among the years in which there was no exact to the minute Neptune-Pluto trine, Neptune came to within one degree of the exact to the minute trine with Pluto in ten additional years between 1702 and 1787 and some years in the middle part of the eight-decade cycle. There were nine more years during the eighteenth century cycle between 1700 and 1788 and some years in the middle part of the cycle when Neptune and Pluto came to within two degrees of the exact trine. The sextile periods produce fewer exact contacts through the eight-decade span of recurring contacts. The current Neptune-Pluto sextile that runs from 1950 to 2032 has forty-six exact to the minute sextiles. Among the years in which there was no exact to the minute sextile, there were/will be eighteen years between 1948 and 2033 and some years in the middle of the cycle that have a Neptune-Pluto sextile that comes to within one degree of the exact contact. There are an additional sixteen years between 1946 and 2034 and some years in the middle of the cycle that have a Neptune-Pluto sextile that comes to within two degrees of the exact contact.

There are two basic reasons for this behavior: first, Neptune's orbital eccentricity is very small due to its nearly circular orbit, exceeded only by Venus, such that the variation in Neptune's distance from the Sun varies very little between its aphelion and perihelion. In contrast, Pluto's orbital eccentricity is very large. Pluto's distance from the Sun varies between 29 and 49 AU (Astronomical Units; one Astronomical Unit is the mean distance of the Earth from the Sun: 92, 960,000 miles). Neptune and Pluto are close to the same distance from the Sun at and near Pluto's perihelia. Second, Newton's second law of motion requires that Pluto's speed increases as it approaches the Sun and decreases as it recedes from the Sun. Pluto therefore temporarily moves at an orbital velocity near its perihelion that is not radically different than Neptune's mean velocity. The waxing sextile and waning trine do not constitute the recurring Neptune-Pluto aspects forever. Due to the libration* of the ellipse of Pluto's orbit, the long-term recurring aspects between Neptune and Pluto two thousand years ago and during the first millennium BC were the semi-square and sesquiquadrate. The waning trine began to become a long-term recurring aspect in the eighth century BC, sharing emphasis then with the waning sesquiquadrate, until the trine finally displaced the long-term status of the sesquiquadrate in the first millennium AD. In similar fashion, the waxing sextile slowly displaced the waxing semi-square as the other long-term recurring aspect between Neptune and

Pluto, which was not complete until early in the second millennium AD.

The chief effect of Pluto in combination with Neptune is to make its natives incline toward independence with respect to religion and spirituality. During the periods when it holds sway, religious dogma, credo and doctrine is found wanting, hollow and without merit, and to some, even absurd when some independent thinkers grasp that it is arrogant beyond measure to assume that one understands or has a corner on the Creator. It is thus a very progressive combination in general but tends in particular to weaken the influence of formal religion. Yet it deepens the resolve of those who have it to achieve spiritual awareness, but generally of, for and by themselves and not infrequently, via pagan, forbidden or at least unsanctioned methods. Its natives are modern and forward looking for their eras and the most courageous of them attack hidebound forms that elevate the letter of the law over the spirit of it. People with the close contacts are usually open to evolutionary developments or they at least understand and don't fight them. Neptune-Pluto periods are often, though not invariably, tumultuous characterized by deep insecurity and anguish surrounding the dissolution of the old under the onslaught of the new.

Because Neptune-Pluto combinations relate to deep spiritual currents to which everyone is connected, their effects are more pervasive than Saturn-Pluto, which usually entails political reshuffling. Neptune-Pluto combinations symbolize change in the prevailing attitudes of society as a loosening of the restrictions that impede advances. Institutionalized religion has been the main obstacle to secular advance. The arbiters of religion, under the supposed auspice of divine sanction, try to contain all new developments within their purview. Neptune-Pluto aspects often appear when old religion is weakened and formerly heretical attitudes and practices lose the onus of prohibition, or even become legitimized. Orthodoxy is a casualty of both Uranus-Neptune and Neptune-Pluto contacts.

The effect of this combination in individuals is often quite rarified and subtle but profound in scope. John Couch Adams, an English mathematical prodigy, produced the very complex calculations in 1843 that showed where an unknown body had to be that was perturbing the predicted, but incorrect, positions of Uranus; but he couldn't persuade the then Astronomer Royal or anybody else to train telescopes on that position in the sky. Adams was a newly-minted graduate of Cambridge at that time (first in his class in mathematics) but George Biddle Airy, the Astronomer Royal, dismissed Adams' efforts due to his youth and inexperience. Adams had Neptune square Pluto less than a quarter of a degree from exact. The exceptional French mathematician/astronomer Urbain Jean Joseph Le Verrier produced similar calculations three years later. He quickly managed to direct the attention of German astronomers to the planet Neptune on September 23, 1846 who found the planet telescopically on their first attempt. Le Verrier had Sun trine Uranus less than two degrees from exact, which is better for reaping the benefits of discovery than Neptune-Pluto. The British scientific community was tied in excruciating knots of frustration over the matter, having lost what could have been British priority in the discovery of Neptune. Adams eventually became professor of astronomy at Cambridge and later turned down the post of Astronomer Royal.

Clyde Tombaugh, the excellent American astronomer who discovered Pluto in 1930, had Neptune semi-square Pluto less than a quarter of a degree from exact. He also had the two degree Jupiter-Uranus sextile. Tombaugh, later in his career, made several very clear, distinct, well documented UFO sightings that the U.S. government made no effort to refute. Neptune-Pluto is strongly inclined to become aware of deeper, heretofore unknown and unsuspected or underlying realities that upset the mistaken or incomplete prevailing wisdom and the people who insist on it.

The discovery of the DNA molecule in 1953 during the first phase of the current long term Neptune-Pluto sextile unveiled the fundamentals of life at a biological level for the first time. These had heretofore been a mystery with which religion allied itself. People with Neptune-Pluto combinations are receptive to the occult and mysteries in general, but they are committed to the proposition that they can have conscious awareness of what has been illusory and beyond apprehension, until—they think—now. One could even say that they have a stronger faith than those who sought refuge in formalism, ritual and vicarious religious experience.

The conjunction of 1891-92 witnessed the beginning of the installation of an electric grid that eventually completely electrified the civilized world. That revolution freed up more hours that had formerly been devoted to human and animal physical labor than any other since the beginning of recorded history. It also ushered in an era of unparalleled ease and with respect to communication.

The long term trine of Neptune-Pluto that was in play for almost the entire eighteenth century was symbolic of the European Enlightenment and the ascendancy of the calculus in particular and science in general. The Enlightenment primarily sounded the death knell of the iron grip of institutionalized religion on the minds of men and women in the West. The Enlightenment was also the culmination of a political ideal that saw the first pure republic of the modern era come into being (the United States) on a large scale even though the antecedents of such a government are British and ultimately Roman and Greek. Representative government emphasizes the value of the individual, which frees up the expression of talent, individual initiative and enlightened self-interest on a scale greater than what other governmental forms can offer. It is these conditions protected by law that make an era progressive which makes the acceleration of secular advance general. Ultimately secular advance is itself found wanting which evokes on a broad front the two most important questions that human beings can pose: "Who am I?" and "What is this (world)?" Institutionalized religion cannot answer those questions because they require faith that may be misplaced or misinterpreted by the arbiters of institutionalized religion. Those ultimate questions can only be answered through one's own efforts to connect with the Divine and thus to know whereof one comes and to what purpose. Therefore, somewhat ironically, even though Neptune-Pluto eras are noteworthy for the weakening of formal religion, they also symbolize the quest for the true nature and meaning of existence. These eras incline toward a post-religionist orientation or at least one that revises the old paradigm. For some individuals the combination is neo-spiritual as the old form is dropped to reveal an altogether new vista. This is most likely, in an individual, if the Neptune-Pluto combination is connected to the angles or the lights.

The long-term Neptune-Pluto sextile that lasted for eighty years between 1460 and 1540 brackets both the initial fierce reaction against the Reformation of the Catholic Church and the High Renaissance that came bounding out of northern Italy and Gutenberg's printing press in Germany. Equally noteworthy, the European discovery of North and South America during this period produced a wild free-for-all and land grab that was unprecedented in its scope. This mainly European expansion also increased the reach of the Christian faiths, curiously at a time when they were in tumultuous competition for hearts and minds. Finally, the surge in artistic and scientific sophistication was so spectacular during this period that it seemed, in comparison to earlier periods, as though Europe had almost been standing still. The proliferation of all endeavors caught up in Neptune-Pluto periods is quite marked because Pluto itself is extreme and Neptune knows no bounds; thus the effect of the two together escapes containment and cannot be limited except by force and repression. Such attempts, however, only increase the pressure against those who would deny the power of an authentic natural force, such that the forces of repression come to be seen as old-fashioned at best and tyrannical at worst.

Further, the Neptune-Pluto opposition during the 1640s, during the Thirty Years War, was symbolic of the failure of Catholicism to contain and crush Protestantism. It especially symbolized the culmination of the doctrine *cuius regio, eius religio* ("whose realm, his religion" that is to say, whoever has the power to rule determines the religion of the realm). The Treaty of Westphalia in 1648, that ended the Thirty Years War, also marked the end of the papacy as a de facto secular power able to wage war or employ surrogates supposedly in God's name.

*A libration is a regular, periodic oscillation; this one has a period of 19,500 years.[6] Stated differently, the rotation of the ellipse of Pluto's orbit is not a complete rotation. It is an oscillation. The long-term recurring aspects between Neptune and Pluto change approximately every two thousand years. During the lifetime of Jesus of Nazareth, the long-term recurring aspect between Neptune and Pluto was the semi-square. This two-thousand year cycle [See, Arnold Toynbee, *A Study Of History*, (Oxford: Oxford University Press, 1955) 7:421, n.2] may well reflect the life span of religions until they become so heavily institutionalized that the original spirit behind the movement becomes hidebound that requires a reformation, if the religion is to live or that after two millennia a religion may begin to wane.

Chapter Eight

Political Figures

One should start with an outline that takes account of the salient features of a horoscope. Although everyone looks at a horoscope in his or her own way, an analysis of basic factors at the beginning facilitates a good overall interpretation. Astrological symbolism should be examined according to a hierarchy of factors. Following are some short interpretations that could form the basis of a more comprehensive analysis. The most important elements are:

1. The condition of the "lights," i.e. the Sun and the Moon.
2. The condition of the horizon and meridian, especially the ascending and culminating degrees known as "the angles" or "superior angles." Planets near the angles are called angular.
3. The meaning of any significant stars near the angles or the lights.
4. The closest planet relationships.
5. The houses that receive great emphasis.

Barack Obama

Barack Obama, forty-fourth president of the United States, was born August 4, 1961 at 7:24 p.m. AHST at Honolulu, Hawaii (data from birth certificate). He is the first person of mixed race elected to the office.

He has the Sun in Cancer, a gentle, nurturing constellation that is renowned for its patriotism, loyalty and devotion to family. The only relationship with the Sun is the square to Neptune that makes him highly idealistic and unusually sensitive to the needs and feelings of other people. Sun-

Barack Hussein Obama
August 4, 1961
7:24 p.m. AHST
Honolulu, Hawaii
21°N19' 157°W52'

*Sidereal – Campanus

8h 54m 07s: RAMS
8h 56m 21s: RA α ♋
9h 00m 03s: RAA☉

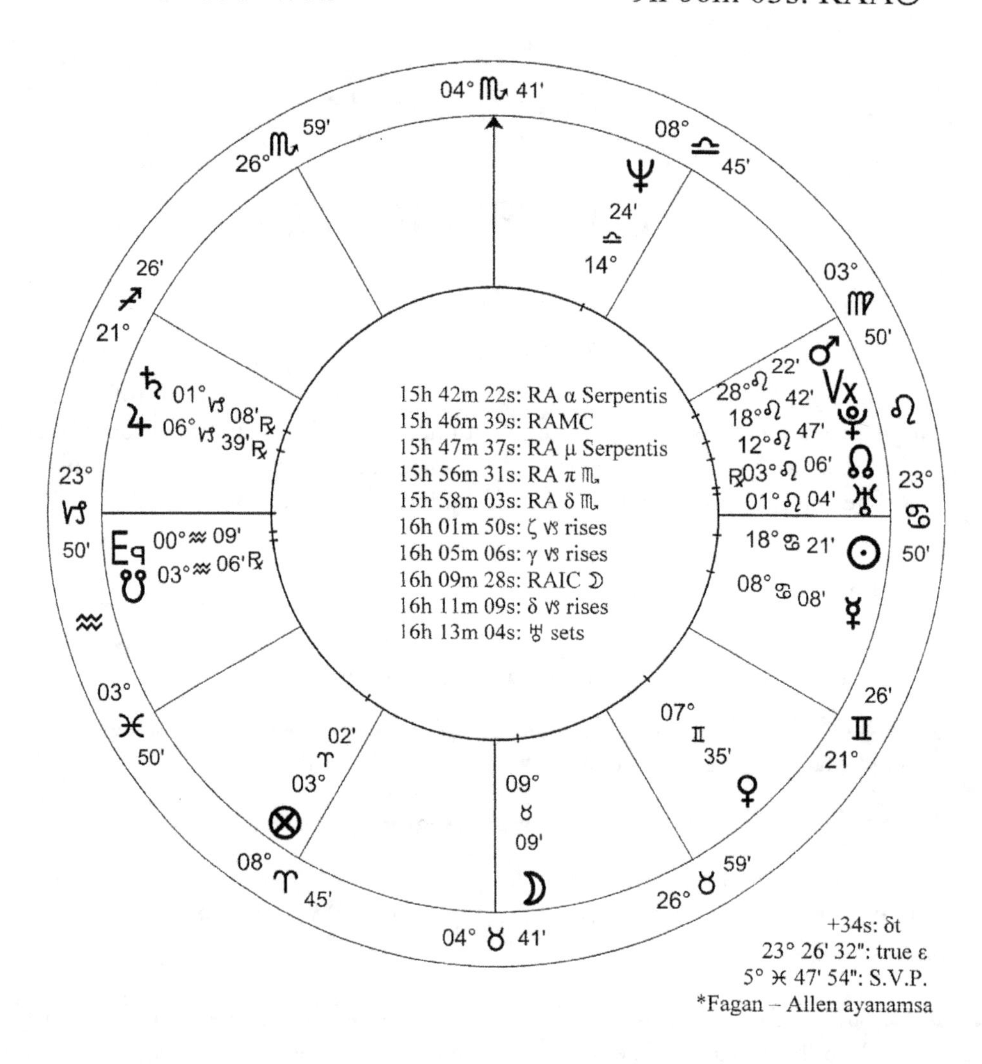

Neptune also weakens and lessens the influence of the father, especially since Neptune is elevated over the Sun. Many liberal presidents and candidates have had Neptune high in the sky in their horoscopes. That placement is compassionate and symbolic of a politician who tries to implement policy that benefits people at large rather than policy biased openly in favor of business. The criticism leveled at people with Neptune so placed is that they are "not tough enough."

Mr. Obama has the Moon square Pluto three and a half degrees from exact; but the Moon is exalted in Taurus, its best placement, which confers his gracious and agreeable manner. The Moon is also trine Jupiter which is extremely lucky and symbolic of someone in a position of authority. His father's abandonment of the family is shown by Moon square Pluto, but his exalted Moon and its trine to Jupiter is the symbolism for his devoted mother and grandparents. The Moon is symbolic of the family, especially on the mother's side. He has the Moon mundane square Uranus less than a degree from exact. That is, the Moon passed through the lower meridian when Uranus was on the western horizon. That is the sign of someone who leaves the birth locale and circumstances and lives an exceptional, unconventional or high status life.

The Sun and the Moon are the planets closest to the horizon and the meridian respectively. This means that his life, family and character are on display to an extraordinary degree; in other words he is famous for his achievement, virtue, intelligence and his history.

He has Capricorn rising which symbolizes early poverty, and later, that he has a strong desire to impose structure, order and law for constructive purposes because Saturn, the planet associated with Capricorn, is conjoined to Jupiter. Capricorn rising has no illusions and would recognize, as a practical matter, that the best way to fulfill one's potential is to get a good education. Jupiter and Saturn together frequently manifest as an interest in government, the tendency to create systems, institutions and schemes to harness resources. Jupiter-Saturn is the ultimate foundation combination; its natives create laws, businesses and conditions that outlive them and yet endure like timeless virtues. Jupiter is opposite Mercury within a degree and a half, which is an excellent combination that indicates he is very smart, well spoken and well educated (B.A., Columbia; J.D., Harvard). Jupiter is quincunx Venus less than a degree from exact which makes him generous, affable, kind and much loved. He has three planets and the North Node of the Moon in the seventh house. The first house is the self; the seventh house is the "not self," especially the mate, but strictly speaking everybody else and in particular those who engage the native directly. A loaded seventh house means that all eyes are on him. He is the golden boy, the "go to guy," the one who gets the ball when the game is on the line.

There were no bright stars rising, culminating or setting at his birth moment but the two bodies next to arrive a few minutes later at the lower meridian and the western horizon respectively, the Moon and Uranus, brought two important stars in tow. The gamma star in Capricorn, known as Nashira, rose at Honolulu one degree before the Moon transited the lower meridian. The derivation of most star names is from Arabic. Nashira is from "Al Sa'ad al Nashirah," which translates to *the fortunate one*. While that star rises every day at the latitude of Honolulu it is a highly auspicious omen to have it rise when the Moon is simultaneously in the meridian. Less than two minutes before Uranus set in the West, the delta star in Capricorn, known as Deneb Algedi, rose at Honolulu. Deneb Algedi is from "Al Dhanab al Jady," which translates to, *the tail of the Goat*. The ancient lore is that it gives glory, fame, wealth and authority. Connected to Mr. Obama's Uranus, this star suggests that Obama's fame and authority would come as a shock or be a "first."

Martin Luther

Martin Luther, was an Augustinian monk and the main figure of the Protestant Reformation. While Luther was the most important religious figure of his day, his socio/political influence since his death has been still greater. He maintained that in order to be a good Christian one must personally read Scripture and to facilitate that objective he translated the Old and New Testaments of the Bible into German. His work was such a tremendous spur to literacy in Western Europe that within a century of his death in 1546 ordinary people were fast becoming literate in numbers that were unheard of in all of recorded history. Literate people quickly become educated people. Educated people are hard to govern in an absolutist manner because their eyes have been opened to the facts of the world and the thinking of others. Thus the long-term effect of Luther's work was an increasing level of political freedom simultaneous with the second information revolution invoked by the printing press (in 1454). The first information revolution was the invention of writing itself.

The source for Luther's birth time, according to his friend Phillip Melanchthon, was Luther's mother. According to her, Luther was born November 10, 1483 (O.S.) at 11:00 p.m. at Eisleben, Germany. Municipal clocks in the fifteenth century didn't have minute hands, but most of them chimed the hour, quarter and half hours. Eleven o'clock was probably the chime closest to the birth. In addition, the time standard was local apparent time, which is the same as sundial time. The local mean time equivalent of 11:00 p.m. local apparent time for this Julian calendar date is 10:46:13 p.m.

The Sun is in Scorpio, a powerful contentious quality that is often a magnet for controversy. The fixed constellations (Taurus, Leo, Scorpio and Aquarius) are the most formidable of the sidereal signs. They have the strongest resolve and determination to complete a task once they are sure that their position has merit. Therefore, from the very outset it is clear that Luther was a figure possessed of strength, courage and power, the hallmark of Scorpio. The two main planet relationships with the Sun are the semi-sextile with Jupiter and the semi-square to Pluto. The Sun-Jupiter contact is only two minutes of arc from exact and therefore very strong. It means that he was lucky, virtuous, likely to be successful in his endeavors and to survive a showdown with entrenched, hidebound authority, since Jupiter is protective. The Sun-Pluto semi-square made him different than his fellows, a loner and especially a rebel. Furthermore, with the Sun in the fourth house, Pluto's semi-square

Martin Luther
November 10, 1483
11:00 p.m. LAT
Eisleben, Germany
51°N32' 11°E33'

*Sidereal – Campanus

2h 40m 05s: RAMC
2h 35m 04s: RA β Perseus
2h 24m 56s: α ♌ rises

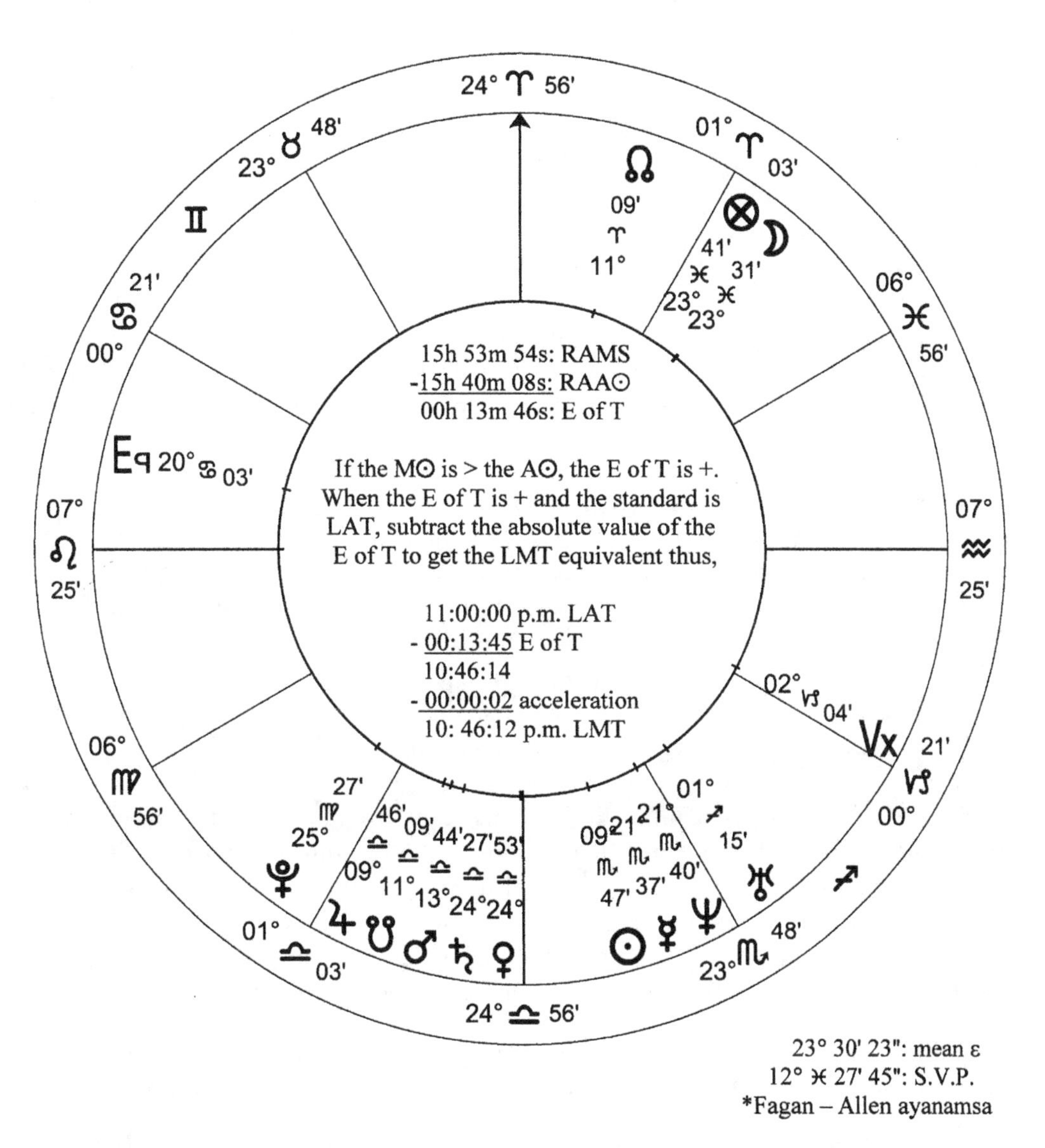

to the Sun, less than a degree from exact, made him deeply introspective.

The Moon is in Pisces, a good place for the Moon because both the Moon and Pisces are tender, subtle, kind and gentle. Pisces in its positive manifestations has affinity with religion, spirituality and the dramatic arts. It is therefore no surprise that Luther became a monk though he was actually in law school when a near death experience turned him toward the priesthood. When he entered the Augustinian order he already had earned a bachelor's and a master's degrees. The Moon makes several close relationships; the most important is the opposition to Pluto because both lights then are configured with Pluto. Pluto is usually the "odd man out," the non-conformist, the rejected one or one who rejects a position. Pluto with both lights is highly symbolic of one who was doubly inclined to be unable to suppress rebellious behavior in particular regarding religious matters.

Particularly galling to Luther was the practice of "indulgences" whereby one could purchase, with the coin of the realm, absolution of sin, even those not yet committed. He felt that such a practice was an extreme violation of the true task of the church: the saving of souls. He was thus primed to take a stand that pitted him against the entire weight of the Catholic Church. The Moon is closely trine Mercury conjoined to Neptune which makes him an intellectual, an academic and genuinely pious. The Moon is even more closely configured with Saturn and Venus, both by a quincunx relationship. The quincunx to Saturn made him serious, disciplined and duty oriented. The quincunx to Venus gave his work wide appeal inasmuch as there is no more popular combination than the Moon with Venus.

Venus and Saturn are also very close to the meridian which strengthens them to a considerable degree especially since they are both very well placed in Libra. The meaning is that he was motivated by love of God and a sense of obligation that he could not ignore. The rising constellation was Leo, the sign of authority, clout and the will to lead. With the Sun and the rising sign in fixed signs Luther was a formidable adversary who could not be deterred from his aim. The brightest star in Leo, Regulus, rose at Eisleben at 10:44:54 pm local apparent time. Western astrologers had recognized several centuries before Luther's time the extraordinary significance of having Regulus on the Ascendant. It means that its natives are born to something special in life. Regulus had also been considered a two-edged sword for centuries because in high European latitudes it rises when the beta star in Perseus, Algol (Ra's al Ghul, the Demon's head), culminates. Algol has been considered a spectacularly unfortunate star, connected to death and misfortune on an epic scale. It is noteworthy therefore that before the enormously violent reaction to the Protestant Reformation that lasted for a hundred fifty years, largely brought about by Luther, he was condemned as a heretic, anathema and excommunicated from the Catholic Church. Algol culminated in the meridian (the cusp of the tenth house) at Eisleben at 10:55 pm local apparent time on the night Luther was born.

Luther's third house is crowded with four planets and the south node of the Moon. A house so emphasized has great importance. The third house relates to elementary education among other things. That was his most important legacy. People need to be able to walk before they can run. One must be able to access the world of ideas to join it. Westerners came en masse to the world of ideas, facts, books, sophisticated abstraction and the freedom that knowledge confers because he admonished them to read the Bible. After that people read everything they could get their hands on and the information spigot could not be turned off.

George W. Bush

George W. Bush, forty-third president of the United States, was born July 6, 1946 at 7:26 a.m. EDT, New Haven, Connecticut (data from birth certificate).

Mr. Bush came into office as the darling of conservatives and some moderates but left office reviled by all the liberals, moderates and many conservatives with the lowest approval rating to date since that sentiment has been polled.

Mr. Bush's horoscope is noteworthy for the assault on the angles by the four malefic planets. He has Saturn in its detriment, Cancer, which suggests more than the standard problems between the native and the parents, especially the father. Saturn is square the meridian two degrees from exact. Without Jupiter simultaneously making an aspect to the meridian, Saturn alone is commonly a signature of failure in one's endeavors unless there are extraordinary extenuating circumstances that are not present here. Neptune in its detriment, Virgo, is sextile the Ascendant less than one and a quarter degrees from exact which suggests that he tends to fool or delude himself about facts. Neptune is also closely semi-square Venus which is symbolic of an indulgence that may become a vice, and accordingly, he drank to excess for a number of years. Mars is sesquiquadrate the Midheaven less than a tenth of a degree from exact which is symbolic of a heavy-handed attitude toward business and government that could also be described as belligerent. Pluto is three degrees below the eastern horizon in terms of celestial longitude but its true location in three dimensional space as described by its equatorial coordinates (right ascension and declination) place Pluto forty-five seconds of time above the Ascendant. Pluto therefore is all but precisely angular in the horoscope. People with that placement are consistently autocratic and will not tolerate opposition or positions that deviate from their hard line. These qualities are exacerbated by the presence in the Midheaven of the first magnitude star Achernar (Al ahir al Nahr, "The end of the river."), the brightest star in the constellation Eridanus. Ancient authors claim that it relates to those who attain public office and embrace religion. Achernar is six minutes of sidereal time from Mr. Bush's natal Midheaven which is one and a half degrees of celestial longitude.

He has the Sun in Gemini in the twelfth house. Gemini is usually distinctly intellectual but in a horoscope like this one in which the angles are bombarded by the malefics, and the Sun is in a difficult house, the twelfth, the major faults of Gemini are likely to show themselves: Gemini can be superficial, shallow and short-sighted. He has the Sun square the Moon three degrees from

George Walker Bush
July 6, 1946
7:26 a.m. EDT
New Haven, Connecticut
41°N18' 72°W55'

*Sidereal – Campanus
6h 55m 23s: RAMS
6h 56m 29s: RA ε Can. Maj.
6h 59m 52s: RAA☉
7h 06m 11s: RA δ Can. Maj.

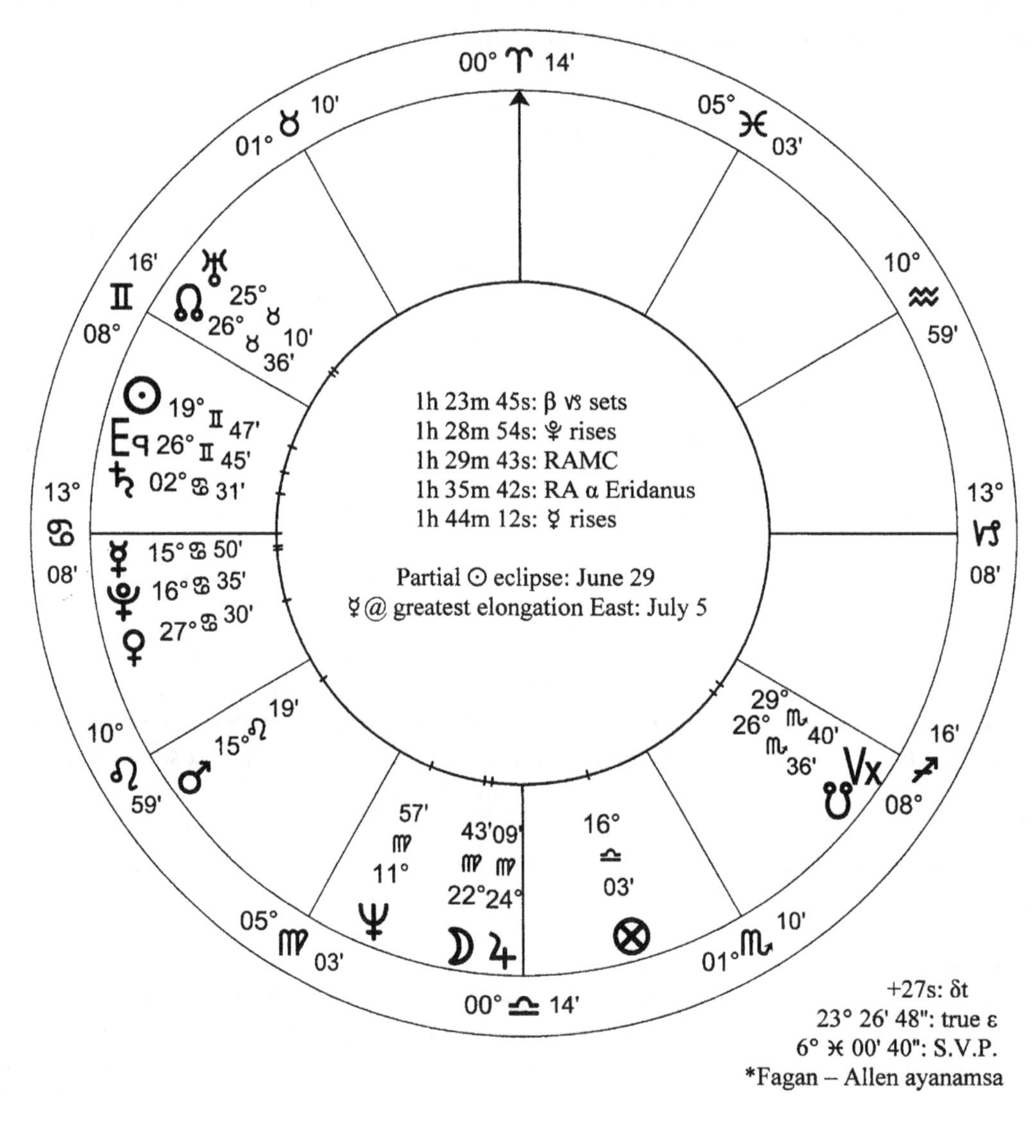

exact and Sun square Jupiter less than four and a half degrees from exact. Sun square Moon is the symbolism for following in his father's footsteps into the presidency. It also emphasizes the family ties in general such that family influence is telling even into adulthood. Sun square Jupiter is quite fortunate but the square frequently shows itself as irresponsible, headstrong and injudicious if other factors support misuse of power. Its natives often mistake the freedom to exercise power for license to assert that ends justify means, or the limits of power are not acknowledged with unfortunate results. This tendency to ignore authority other than one's own and to vault over any and all opposition that present obstacles to one's plans is also very characteristic of Jupiter trine Uranus, only a degree from exact. Usually that is a very good aspect but it can exacerbate tendencies to have one's own way at all costs.

The Moon is conjoined to Jupiter in Virgo less than one and a half degrees from exact in celestial longitude, but the conjunction in right ascension is only four seconds from exact. That is so outrageously lucky that he could lose the popular vote by more than 500,000 votes and still win the presidency on a Supreme Court imposed technicality. But good fortune and good judgment are not always partners. Contrary to what many people have concluded about the man, with the Sun in Gemini and the Moon in Virgo, he is very likely far more intelligent than most people believe but was hamstrung by his failings, not least of which was his poor speaking ability. He has Mercury conjoined to Pluto which is the right symbolism for a poor speaker especially if it is afflicted. Mercury is semi-sextile Mars a half-degree from exact. The so-called minor aspects are quite potent if they're close. Mercury is associated with the twelfth house as well as its ruler. The twelfth is a difficult house that tends to damage its associations.

There are three planets in the first house, Mercury, Venus and Pluto. The first house is about the self. That's not a bad thing but two of the three are afflicted: Mercury by the semi-sextile to Mars and Venus by the sextile to Neptune which is itself debilitated in its detriment, Virgo. Thus he would present a picture that says in effect, "This administration is all about me." He said as much with statements like, "I am the decider." It didn't play well except to his political base. He may have looked like a formidable figure to that group but to many others he merely seemed arrogant. He has three planets in the third house: the Moon, Jupiter and Neptune. The Moon-Jupiter conjunction is very fortunate. Many people with this are born with silver spoons in their mouths and receive every advantage the family can buy or provide. He went to the best schools (B.A., Yale; M.B.A., Harvard) but the presence of Neptune in the third house may compromise that achievement since he was admitted to Yale as a legacy (his father graduated from Yale); and one generally is not admitted to Harvard Business School with a C average as an undergraduate.

Chapter Nine

Great Minds

Isaac Newton

Isaac Newton may be the greatest physicist/mathematician in recorded history. He was born December 25, 1642 (O.S.) at 1:00 a.m. LAT at Woolsthorpe, Lincolnshire, England. His biographers have stated that he was born an hour or two past midnight (See, Frank Manuel, *A Portrait of Isaac Newton* [Cambridge: Belknap Press, Harvard University Press, 1968], 23. His primary directions, an ancient technique with a sound astronomical rationale (see chapter six, "The Equatorial System"), strongly suggest that the earlier time is correct or nearly so.

When Newton was born the Julian, or Old Style, calendar was still in effect in England. His Christmas Day birth in the Julian calendar (December 25, 1642) corresponds to January 4, 1643 in terms of the New Style, or Gregorian calendar in general use throughout the world today. The time standard in effect then was local apparent time; that is, clocks were set to local apparent noon, a varying standard. Local Mean Time was nowhere in place at that time anywhere in Christendom nor probably within the confines of the nation of Islam which bordered the Christian world then as now. An hour after local apparent midnight equates to 1:05:39 a.m. in terms of local mean time. The horoscope set up for that time at the birthplace gives an Ascendant of 0° 52' Libra. That is particularly noteworthy because Libra is renowned for its artistic skill for which Newton was not known. But it also is very close to the brightest star in Virgo, Spica at 29° 06' Virgo, one of the most fortunate stars in the heavens. Spica appeared on the horizon at Woolsthorpe in Lincolnshire three minutes and nine seconds before at 1:02:30 a.m. local mean time. Two and a half minutes earlier than that the last part of Virgo rose which is more appropriate to a genius in mathematics.

Isaac Newton
December 25, 1642 O.S. (January 4, 1643 N.S.)
1:00 a.m. LAT
near Woolsthorpe, Lincolnshire
England 52°N48' 00°W37'

*Sidereal – Campanus

7h 56m 14s: α ♍ rises
7h 59m 23s: RAMC

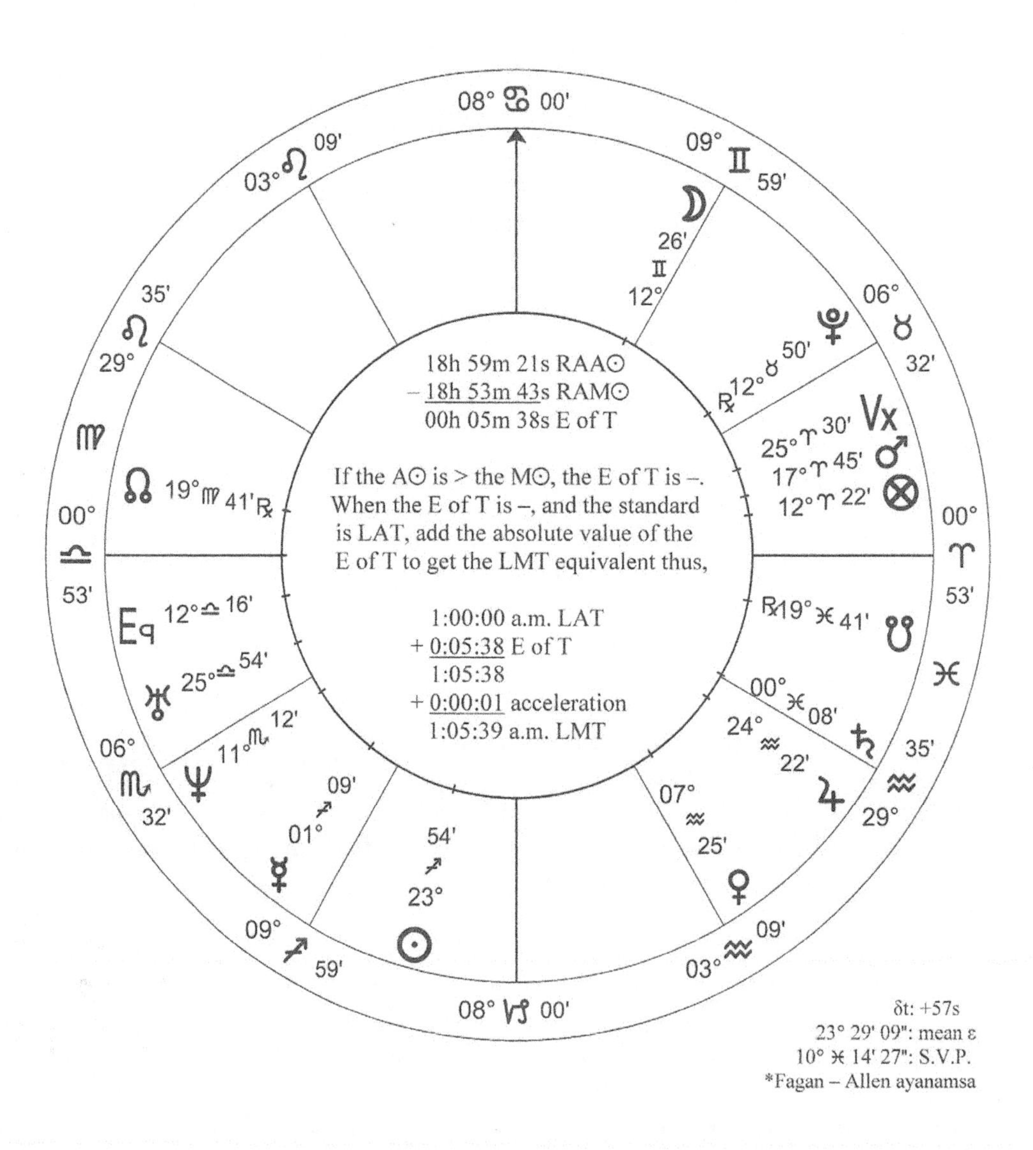

δt: +57s
23° 29' 09": mean ε
10° ♓ 14' 27": S.V.P.
*Fagan – Allen ayanamsa

One must wonder what is the astrological signature of the greatest mind since Archimedes. Newton derived the laws of motion, universal gravitation and invented the calculus. He is far more likely to have Virgo in the Ascendant, the most intellectual of all the zodiacal types, than Libra. He is also likely to have the end of Virgo rising because that is the location of Spica, the most important star in Virgo. Spica goes off the scale in terms of the benefits that accrue to people who have it rising or culminating. The North Node of the Moon in Newton's horoscope is also in Virgo. It has long been recognized that the best places for the Nodes are Mercury's constellations Gemini and Virgo. Virgo rising, if indeed that is the case for him, Spica rising as well, which is certainly a fact if he were born near 1:00 a.m. and the Node in Virgo would all combine to produce a hyper-intellectual of such prodigious power as to be commensurate with his achievements.

Newton's Sun was in Sagittarius, called the sign of the prophet in the ancient world. All the mutable constellations Gemini, Virgo, Sagittary and Pisces are distinctly cerebral and live in the world of ideas; the latter two particularly in the world of the imagination and the abstract. Gemini, Virgo and Sagittarius are conspicuously academic in a formal sense. Newton was a graduate of Cambridge University, joined its faculty and was associated with that great school for much of his life. Sagittarius is expansive, far seeing and hungry for understanding. The main aspects to the Sun, the two-degree sextile to Uranus and the less than one half degree sextile to Jupiter both support an orgy of intellectual expansion, exploration and innovation. He also had the Sun mundane square (q.v.) Mars one and a half-degree from exact which supplied his extraordinary energy. He worked 20 hours a day, barely ate, often slept in his clothes and never married. Newton's Moon was in Gemini. The Moon relates, among other things, to the automatic inclinations of the native without forethought. With Gemini and Virgo that inclination is scholarship. Newton studied constantly. When his mother died he inherited enough money which, with his university position secured, allowed him to pursue his intellectual interests exclusively. In addition to mathematics and physics he was deeply interested in chemistry, history and alchemy to the surprise of some, probably most, of his contemporaries.

Newton's Mercury is at first glance another surprise because it's in Sagittarius, the sign of its detriment. Debilitated bodies don't always operate badly but they do operate in a manner other than their standard mode. Mercury in Sagittarius doesn't know closure. It is open-ended and rambles on incessantly about matters that are not decided or settled. A better-placed Mercury learns a system, a discipline or a set of axioms that is complete. Newton's Mercury was square Saturn a degree from exact so he was obsessed with questions that were not resolved until he applied his talents to them. Without Saturn, a debilitated Mercury is often a daydreamer who cannot apply himself easily to tasks because his orientation is away from the object: either out the window or internal reverie. Saturn focuses intense attention on the object. Newton's Mercury also configured Mars by sesquiquadrate one and a half degrees from exact. Mercury-Mars combinations are extremely penetrating and consistently a sign of high intelligence. Mars and Saturn together directed at Mercury is a signature of prodigious talent for and inquiry into the fundamental facts of physical reality.

He had Jupiter mundane square Pluto (q.v.) less than a degree from exact. That is, Pluto set when Jupiter was in the lower meridian. Jupiter-Pluto operates financially for some people (to their great benefit) but the best manifestation of it is when its natives experience accelerated growth in terms of extraordinary ability, consciousness or both.

Albert Einstein

Albert Einstein, is the greatest mind in physics since Newton. He was born March 14, 1879 at 11:30 a.m. LMT at Ulm, Germany. The source for the data is from Michel and Francoise Gauquelin in *Birth And Planetary Data Gathered Since 1949*, Series A, Volume 2, Men of Science (Paris: Laboratoire d'Étude Des Relations Entre Rythmes Cosmiques et Psychophysiologiques, 1970), 75.

Einstein's Sun is in Pisces in the tenth house, the strongest position for it, elevated over all the other bodies. It means he is likely to find full expression of his essential nature and probably enjoy high status and possibly fame if other factors support that condition. The Sun in Pisces is a dreamer, one who lives in the abstract. Pisces has ready access to the unseen world and may get access to secrets, or it may employ fantasy and speculation as tools instead of fanciful toys. Pisces is sometimes at a loss, however, to navigate through regular life effectively without a strong Saturn because Saturn relates to here and now, the practical and the concrete. The closest contact with the Sun is the semi-square to Neptune only thirty-eight minutes of arc beyond exact. It makes him a visionary and strongly reinforces the tendency of the Sun in Pisces to get beyond logic into the realm of the intuitive and the conceptual. The Sun is sextile Pluto one and a quarter degrees from exact. This makes him a bit of a loner and misfit somewhat disinclined to adopt conventional or accepted wisdom. Since the Sun is elevated over Pluto he would get away with the sometimes awkward or strange responses that Plutonians frequently evoke.

Einstein had the Moon in Scorpio, the worst place for the Moon, but the Moon was trine Venus in Pisces which is the best place for Venus, two and a half degrees from exact. He and his first wife were incompatible. Their marriage ended in divorce after the birth of two sons. Outside his household, Moon trine Venus made him the most the most popular scientific figure in the world for four decades.

He has Gemini rising which is the right symbolism for an intellectual. The planet associated with this Ascendant, Mercury, is the main feature in Einstein's horoscope that is symbolic of his great mind. At first glance, the conjunction of Mercury and Saturn, while that is beneficial, doesn't look extraordinary. It gives a fondness for order and structure, sometimes mathematical ability and is common in the horoscopes of engineers and people who are able to understand how things work. Ordinarily one cannot expect much from Mercury in Pisces, its worst venue. Generally the people who have that placement do better in the arts than in school.

Mercury is about axioms, propositions, formulae and the nuts and bolts of techniques of all kinds.

Albert Einstein
March 14, 1879
11:30 a.m. LMT
Ulm, Germany
48°N24' 10°E00'

*Sidereal – Campanus

23h 26m 43s: RAMS
23h 36m 10s: RAA☉

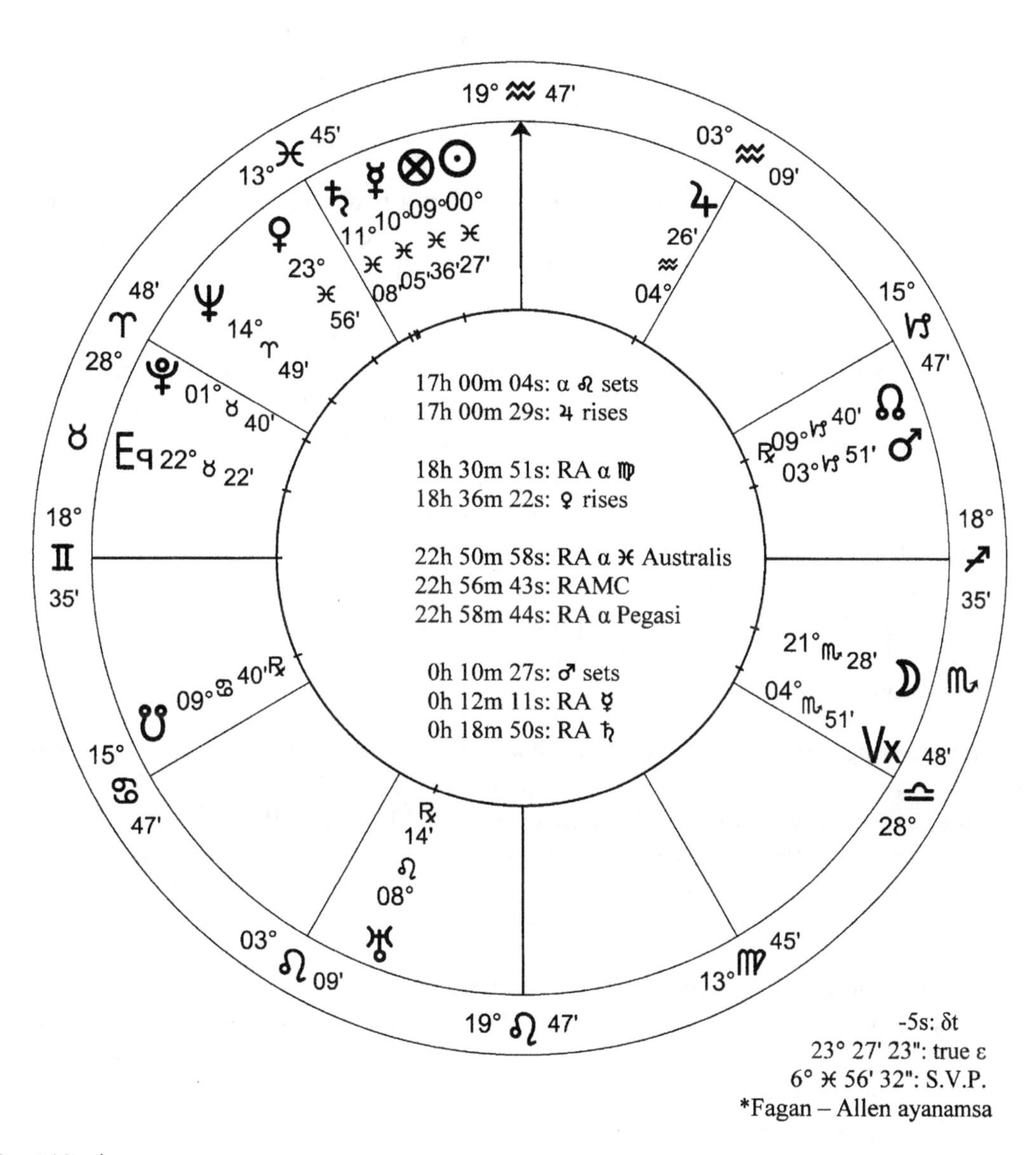

Mercury is a studious, head-down, exercise in logic and rationale. Pisces as a head-up quality that gravitates toward imagination, fantasy, intuition and possibilities, is not friendly to the set piece that Mercury embraces. Rather, Mercury in Pisces natives gravitate toward an unstructured mental orientation. They often resist the regimen of school that feels like confinement. Einstein hated learning by rote and felt that standard methods of instruction did not facilitate his education.

Like Newton whose Mercury was in its detriment, Sagittarius, Einstein's Mercury was similarly debilitated in its fall, Pisces; and like Newton, Einstein's Mercury operated therefore in a non-standard manner outside the box, as it were. Saturn finds endless application in Pisces of its tendency to find the natural order of things or impose one, but without additional influence from another planet, the conjunction of Mercury and Saturn in Pisces can symbolize a confused mental state that is at once profound and yet may struggle to express itself with facility.

The key to Einstein is the closest aspect in the chart: Mercury mundo square Mars. Mercury-Mars is intensely penetrating, sharp and quick. It is not apparent here in the ecliptic system but it is plain as day in the equatorial system. Einstein had Mars exalted in Capricorn, the strongest place for Mars. Mars has no ecliptic relationship with Mercury, since they are separated by sixty-six degrees and fourteen minutes which is not even a weak sextile, but rather a non-event. Yet Mars set in the west when 0h 10m 26s (0 hours 10 minutes and 26 seconds) of sidereal time was passing through the Midheaven at Ulm; Mercury culminated in the Midheaven when 0h 12m 09s (0 hours 12 minutes 09 seconds) of sidereal time was in the meridian at Ulm. In other words, Mercury and Mars were simultaneously angular separated by one minute and forty-three seconds of sidereal time, which is less than a half degree of arc. Both Mars and Saturn applied so closely to Einstein's Mercury in its fall that he could apprehend the underlying order of the highly abstract. The result was the special theory of relativity that demonstrated that the speed of light is a constant but that time is literally relative, therefore inconstant, and a function of the speed of an object. That time is apparently variable (for high speed phenomena) seems counter-intuitive and yet the conclusions arrived at through debilitated planets are likely to give pause or surpise.

It is an interesting exercise to compare Newton and Einstein. Newton had Mercury debilitated in its detriment, Sagittary, square Saturn and sesquiquadrate Mars. The laws he discovered apply to slow speed phenomena. Einstein had Mercury debilitated in its fall, Pisces, conjoined to Saturn and mundane square Mars. The laws he discovered relate to high speed phenomena. The work of both men changed the world more profoundly than any others since the beginning of the modern period around AD 1500, and perhaps more than any other personalities in recorded history.

Einstein's work might have been an obscure footnote or an obtuse convoluted dissertation that gathered dust because nobody could understand it, except for the Sun in the tenth house, which guarantees that the native will get attention for his efforts. In addition, Jupiter was sesquiquadrate the Ascendant in Einstein's chart only a degree from exact which made him distinctly lucky; and

Venus was trine the Moon which made him popular.

Finally Einstein's natal Midheaven was flanked by two important stars: Markab and Fomalhaut. Markab, the alpha (principal) star in Pegasus, is only two minutes and one second of sidereal time (one half degree of arc) east of Einstein's meridian. It symbolizes that honor, rank and money accrue to the native. Nearby in right ascension but far away from northerly Pegasus in declination is the very southerly Fomalhaut, the alpha star in Pisces Australis. Fomalhaut is one and a half-degrees in right ascension to the west of Einstein's natal meridian. The ancient lore is that Fomalhaut is a very fortunate star that gives enduring fame but carries with it some form of malevolence. That would be atomic weapons which came directly out of Einstein's famous equation $E = mc^2$.

Nikola Tesla

Nikola Tesla was a profoundly gifted electrical engineer and an amazing inventor far ahead of his time. According to his biographer he was born at midnight July 9/10, 1856 at Smiljian, Croatia to Serbian parents. (See, John J. O'Neill, *Prodigal Genius,* Albuquerque: Brotherhood of Life, 1994) 17; originally published by Ives Washburn, New York).

Educated in Europe, he lived for almost sixty years in New York City. More than 700 patents were issued to him and he is best known as the father of alternating current, which has been adopted globally. The idea of a rotating magnetic field—which induces alternating current and is the idea behind all polyphase induction motors—came to him complete, in a single moment. Tesla sold many of his patents to George Westinghouse, whose company became a major player in the business world as a result. Tesla was at one time employed by Thomas Edison, who was a strong advocate of direct current to supply large electric networks. Tesla won a fierce competition with Edison by demonstrating the superiority of alternating current generation and transmission. As a result, Tesla formed his own company and became a millionaire. Many of his other inventions are widely used today; the Tesla coil is a component of radios and televisions.

Tesla had four bodies in Gemini: the Sun, Mercury, Venus and Saturn, and two in Virgo: the Moon and Mars. With six bodies in Mercury's constellations he was so cerebral that an ordinary life was impossible. There is no sexuality in Mercury. It is concerned with dry facts, scholarship and knowledge of technique. Mercury is voracious for information; its natives have "know how" that sets them apart from their fellows that other people copy. Tesla never married nor is he known to have had a girlfriend. He lived in hotels for most of his adult life, took his meals alone and was extremely private, almost a recluse, due to the angularity of Pluto in the first house. He was not irascible, however, due to his Sun-Venus conjunction which can warm up even a Plutonian if other factors support. Gemini is youthful, child-like, playful and eternally curious. Like children they stay entranced by new things even as they age. The most important relationship with the Sun was a two and a half degree trine to Neptune which made him a visionary and also illustrates one of the

Nikola Tesla
July 10, 1856
12:00 a.m. LMT
Smiljian, Croatia
44°N35' 15°E16'

*Sidereal – Campanus
7h 11m 31s: RA δ ♊
7h 12m 15s: RAMS
7h 17m 13s: RAA☉
7h 25m 24s: RA α ♊

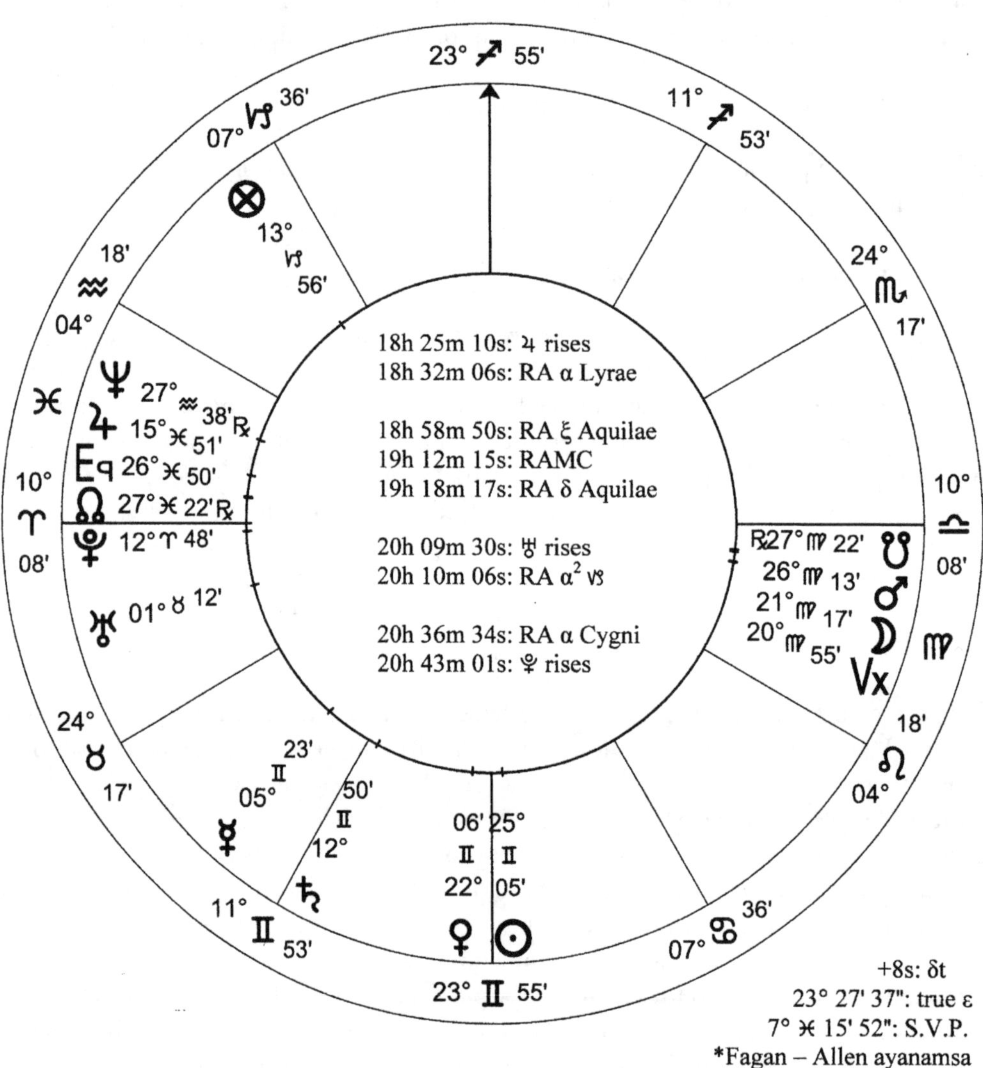

+8s: δt
23° 27' 37": true ε
7° ♓ 15' 52": S.V.P.
*Fagan – Allen ayanamsa

☿ at greatest elongation West (20° 27'): July 13

main features of the three great technically inclined minds used as illustrations here (Newton, Einstein and Tesla). All three of them had their Suns configured with the outer planets. Their powers of imagination were beyond merely formidable; they were probably inspired and may have played out their lives as agents of progress and betterment for the human race. Their purely intellectual abilities were staggering, but they were simultaneously intuitives, which seems clearly a good alliance because the pure thinkers are generally not inspired and the pure intuitives are not grounded.

Tesla had Sun square Mars less than a degree and a quarter from exact and Moon conjoined to Mars five degrees out. Ordinarily one might reasonably expect a distinctly aggressive person from a Mars contact with both lights, but Venus conjoined to the Sun squares both the Moon and Mars which softens what would otherwise be a gruff and quarrelsome nature. Yet Venus square Mars does compromises one's love life and friendships which may be harsh, unrewarding, full of trouble or simply absent if there is too much Gemini and Virgo as here. The result of the Mars placement was that he, like Newton, worked around the clock, sleeping very little and indulging himself not at all except for his wardrobe, the maid who changed his sheets and the chef who prepared his meals. That his efforts would bear fruit could be inferred from the fact that forty minutes before he was born the fabulously fortunate alpha star in Virgo, Spica, set at his birthplace in mundo conjoined to his Moon separated by less than a degree. The old lore about Spica is that if it configures the Moon the native will enjoy success through inventions.

The Moon in Virgo is a student, a reader, an experimenter and tinkerer. These natives may start out taking apart a clock and then graduate to the engine of the family car—removed, disassembled, understood and sometimes improved—and before long they are writing code in a new computer language they have devised or into pure mathematics or they have all but taken up permanent residence in a laboratory. Sometimes Virgo people are observed giggling with unconcealed delight at understanding something new. Mercury, the planet associated with Gemini and Virgo was near its maximum elongation (farthest from the Sun) West that was reached on July13. Mercury is best away from the Sun especially when Gemini and Virgo are emphasized. The Sun dominates everything it touches thus with Mercury at considerable remove from the Sun, the native enjoys independence of thought that may take him far afield from what his contemporaries consider normal or reasonable. Many people didn't know what to make of Tesla who was constantly dealing with the fantastic, the amazing, even the bizarre. He had Aries rising, which is ambitious, full of pride and inclined to think that they are people to be reckoned with whether it is true or not. Often it is true. Tesla's fights over patents with Guglielmo Marconi and Thomas Edison were legendary, lasted for years and probably cost him a Nobel Prize. Even so, he was a truly extraordinary figure whose legacy supplies light and power to the entire planet.

Chapter Ten

Notorious

O.J. Simpson

Orenthal James Simpson was born July 9, 1947 at 8:08 a.m. PST, according to his birth certificate. He won the Heisman Trophy in 1968 as the nation's best football player and enjoyed considerable success playing professional football from 1969 to 1979. When his football career ended due to injury, he successfully transitioned into acting, announcing athletic events and endorsements.

Simpson's success is very characteristic of Sun trine Jupiter less than a degree and a quarter from exact, particularly with Jupiter angular at the IC, which substantially enhances the benefit that accrues to the aspect. The Sun is in Gemini, which is intelligent, light-hearted and playful. Until he was arrested on suspicion of murdering his wife in 1994, his public image was spotless and his popularity boundless. He was seen often on television endorsing products and in movies. The factors responsible for success in the film and entertainment industry are his Moon in Pisces trine Mercury only a degree from exact. Pisces is closely allied with the dramatic arts, make-believe and amusement. He was a perfect fit as a pitch-man who could deliver a message and evoke the desired response: to buy a product. All of this follows from Moon-Mercury which is the right symbolism for a good looking, agreeable, well-spoken and athletic man with enormous name recognition.

In addition to Sun trine angular Jupiter and Moon trine Mercury, Simpson has a significant boost from the alpha star in Leo, Regulus, that rose at 8:29 a.m. PST, twenty-one minutes after birth. Regulus is a powerful star, symbolically speaking, but it has a reputation for being a two-edged sword that can boomerang on the people who have it prominent in their charts. At slightly more than a five-degree remove, it is too far from the Ascendant to have a huge effect. Therefore, his celebrity in football at San Francisco was local until he attended the University of Southern California, which is far enough south of San Francisco (34N04 versus 37N47) that his horoscope equated there puts Regulus within two and a half degrees of his Los Angeles Ascendant.

In his Anima Astrologiae, William Lilly, the most celebrated Western astrologer of the seventeenth century, quoted Guido Bonatti, the most celebrated Western astrologer of the thirteenth century, who described the influence of Regulus:

> "That thou see in Diurnal Nativities, whether Cor Leonis be in the ascendant, that is to say in the Oriental Line or above it one degree or below it three degrees; or whether it be in the tenth in like degrees, without the Conjunction or Aspect of any of the Fortunes; for this alone signifies that the native shall be a person of great note and power, too much exalted, and attain to high preferment and honors, although descended from the meanest parents . . . and yet still whatever of all this happens, it signifies that the Native shall die an unhappy death; or at least that all his honors, greatness and power, shall at last suffer an eclipse, and set in a cloud."[7]

Bonatti's admonition about Cor Leonis, the heart of the Lion, better known contemporaneously as Regulus, serves as an alert that despite Simpson's good fortune through his late forties, his life might eventually go terribly wrong. By moving to Los Angeles Simpson may have invoked the supposed effect of the star. His renown initially came through athletics due to the prominence of Mars, his most elevated planet, in the tenth house and the closest aspect Mars makes: a mundane square with Pluto that doubles as the closest aspect in the chart. When Mars rose Pluto was in the lower meridian less than an eighth of a degree from exact at San Francisco. At Los Angeles the Mars-Pluto mundo square is powerful too but on different angles. There his Pluto sets in the West as Mars anti-culminates through the I.C. within one quarter of a degree of the exact to the second contact. Mars-Pluto combinations give sexual and athletic prowess, but an inclination toward conflict and violence if other factors support that manifestation.

While many millions of people are born with Regulus in the Ascendant, many fewer millions have Mars at the same time elevated over all other bodies and so closely configured with Pluto. Fewer still have the beta star in Perseus, called Algol or Medusa's Head, all but precisely conjunct the Midheaven. The local sidereal time of Simpson's horoscope is 3h 05m 22s. The right ascension of Algol for July 1947 was 3h 04m 43s. Algol is therefore 39 seconds of right ascension from Simpson's Midheaven, which is less than a sixth of a degree. He was born under Algol.

Vivian Robson (1890-1942), author of *The Fixed Stars and Constellations in Astrology* and a solid twentieth century astrologer, described Algol thusly:

"It causes misfortune, violence, decapitation, hanging, electrocution and mob violence, and gives

Orenthal James Simpson
July 9, 1947
8:08 a.m. PST
San Francisco, California
37°N47' 122°W25'

*Sidereal – Campanus

7h 07m 01s: RAMS
7h 11m 59s: RAA☉

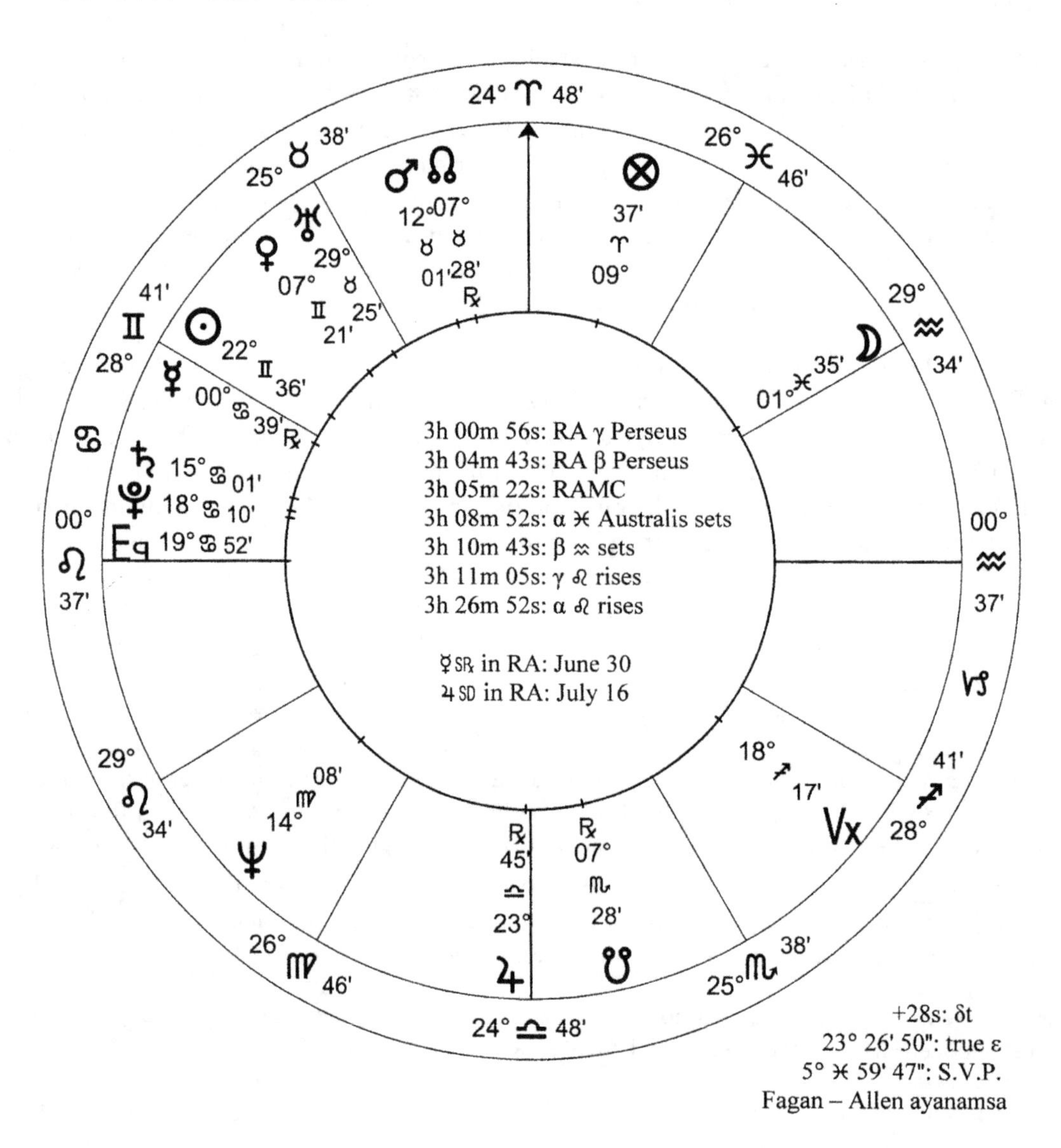

a dogged and violent nature that causes death to the native or others. It is the most evil star in the heavens. . . . If culminating, murder, sudden death, beheading, prone to murder and mischief. . . . With Mars or if Mars be elevated over the luminaries when Algol is angular, the native will be a murderer who will come to an untimely end."[8]

When police arrived at the scene of death of Nicole Brown Simpson, they found her head almost completely severed from her body. In O.J. Simpson's chart, Algol is angular. Mars is elevated over both luminaries and it is also the most elevated body in the horoscope, all of which fulfills the requirements to produce the worst result.

This writer has observed many people live through Regulus on the superior angles of their horoscopes without adverse effect. Because the great majority of them are Americans born in the parallels of the thirties and mid forties of north latitude, it appears that Regulus gets at least part of its bad reputation from its mundo square relationship with Algol which is much closer through higher European parallels, that is also the provenance of the lore. In the modern era the Regulus-Algol relationship is exact at 50N25 which is the latitude close to Plymouth, England, Frankfurt am Mein, Germany and Prague, Czech Republic. In addition, when Regulus culminates in the midheaven, the alpha star in Libra, Zubenelgenubi rises in mundo square with it. Zubenelgenubi has a bad reputation too. Robson says of it, "It causes malevolence, obstruction, an unforgiving character, violence, disease, crime, disgrace and danger of poison." The Regulus-Zubenelgenubi mundane square is exact at 49N30, which is a latitude higher than Paris, lower than London.but significantly higher than any latitude in the lower forty-eight contiguous United States. At San Francisco there is no relationship between Regulus and Zubenelgenubi. They rise and culminate in mundo (q.v.) separated by twenty-seven minutes of sidereal time; that is six and three quarter degrees which is far too loose to be of any consequence.

Bonatti wrote his Liber Astronomiae more than seven hundred years ago at Forli, Italy (44N13) when the Regulus-Algol relationship was exact at 46N30, thus distinctly strong at Forli. Currently, Regulus rises when Algol culminates at 50N30 as Regulus's declination continuously decreases and its right ascension continuously increases due to precession. Bonatti may not have had much of a local tradition to draw upon to separate the intrinsic natures of stars. Ptolemy's Almagest was translated into Latin for the first time only about a century before Bonatti became a working astrologer; and without a computer he had a much smaller sample size to examine than a modern astrologer.

Regulus's influence has apparently been intermingled with those of Algol and Zubenelgenubi with which it is configured through the high forties and low fifties of north latitude that makes its mundane squares with those two stars a factor through Europe, especially through the latitudes of the killing fields of World Wars I and II. Its influence through lower latitudes that contain the United States where it has no mundane square relationships with Algol and Zubenelgenubi and where it generally acts without such overwhelming deleterious effects, should bring relief to American astrologers who worry about the effect of Regulus. Algol's reputation continues unmodified, although the star by itself is not enough to produce the worst. It must be combined with a planet, especially Mars, Saturn or the Sun to produce the most undesirable effects. Furthermore since Algol has almost twenty-three degrees of north celestial latitude in the constellation Perseus, even in temperate terrestrial latitudes it rises, culminates and sets in each case with different zodiacal constellations. Its celestial longitude alone then is only a gross approximation about its true position and a reminder of how astrology should not be over-simplified by drawing conclusions about stars from only one coordinate.

Simpson's angular Jupiter is directly opposite Algol, only a half-degree from exact in right ascension to the star that dominates the horoscope. That is easily construed as extraordinarily lucky for someone accused of a capital crime related to Algol's reputation. Accordingly, Simpson was acquitted of murder, which was widely assailed as a miscarriage of justice by whites and cheered by blacks who remember all too well the thousands of lynchings of black men, especially from the end of the U.S. Civil War in 1865 until the 1960s. Simpson's life has been a kind of hell, however, since his acquittal and he now resides in prison for armed robbery.

Simpson has three planets in the twelfth house: Mercury, Saturn and Pluto. The twelfth house has long been regarded as associated with incarceration if it is heavily tenanted by malefic planets. However, modern examination of traditional house meanings brings them into question. The longest reigning English monarch, Queen Victoria, had five, six, or seven planets in the twelfth house, depending on which of several popular house systems are employed. She certainly did not suffer inordinately in her long life. Considered dynamically the twelfth house region is simply very strong such that the meanings of the planets in those areas have great strength. Either way, Simpson's twelfth house planets appear to be inimical to his interests.

Jeffrey L. Dahmer

Jeffrey L. Dahmer was a serial killer and sex offender. He killed at least 17 young men and boys. He was born May 21, 1960 at 4:34 p.m. CDT in West Allis, Wisconsin (data from birth certificate). His murders were ghastly. Dahmer dismembered and ate his victims. Body parts were found in his refrigerator when he was arrested. He also had sex with his victims, both alive and dead.

One can rightly expect immense affliction in a horoscope like his. The Sun was in Taurus, which is innocent enough in itself although well known for its fondness for the pleasures of the flesh. The Sun was square Pluto less than three degrees from exact and the Sun was sesquiquadrate Saturn slightly more than two degrees from exact. Saturn and Pluto together with the Sun incline the native toward a dark, gloomy and reclusive turn of mind. Many people have that pair with the Sun, however, and display no pathology. Dahmer's Moon was in Pisces on the Descendant. Pisces lives in the world of the imagination to an extreme degree and takes its cues from the planets that

Jeffrey L. Dahmer
May 21, 1960
4:34 p.m. CDT
West Allis, Wisconsin
43°N01' 88°W00'

*Sidereal – Campanus

3h 54m 37s: RAA☉
3h 58m 05s: RAMS

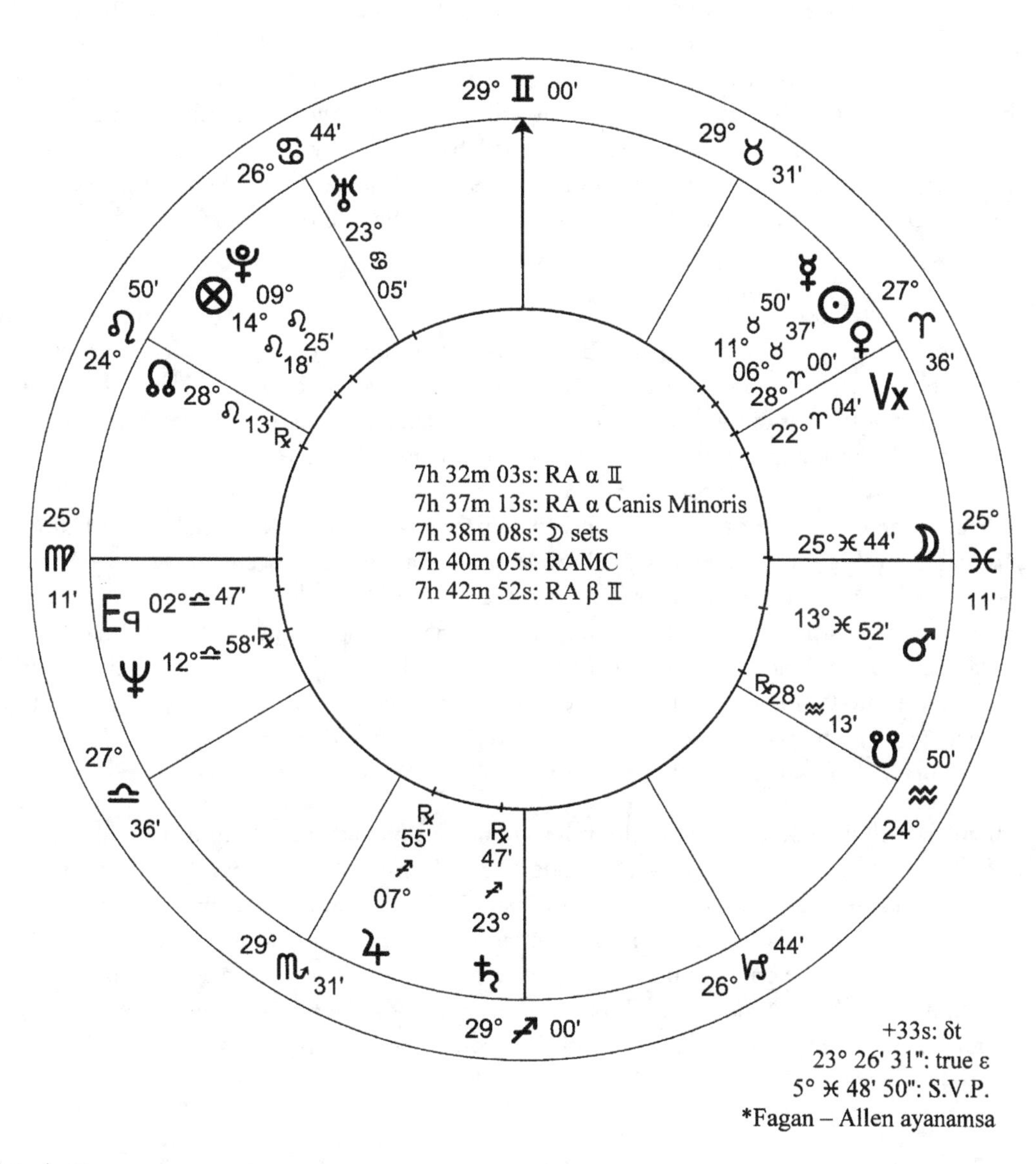

combine with it. The Moon is the strongest planet in the chart by virtue of its angularity. That placement ensures some public notoriety and indicates that the native's personal appetites are inordinately strong for good or ill depending on whatever impinges upon the Moon. The Moon was square Saturn, two degrees from exact and the Moon was also sesquiqua- drate Pluto less than two degrees from exact. The condition of the Moon, which repeats the Sun's relationship with Saturn and Pluto, was monumentally unfortunate because it took a child who was at least odd and possibly primed for failure or difficulty in life and intensified those qualities into morbid fantasies without limit or restraint. Saturn and Pluto were themselves locked into a sesquiquadrate less than a degree from exact which makes its natives intransigent. Both lights therefore plugged into a profoundly difficult, morose and potentially malignant situation which began to manifest in obvious fashion at the onset of puberty. He became markedly withdrawn and was attracted to dead animals that he searched for on his bicycle. He took home whatever road kill he could find and dissected it. Dahmer had Venus in her detriment in Aries less than a degree from the exact semi-square to Mars in Pisces. As a result he was socially awkward and a danger to the people whom he attempted to befriend.

Yet all was not lost because the Moon was semi-square Mercury only a degree from exact. Those planets are a benefit in any combination because they fuel the mind with curiosity and resolve to get answers and understanding, unless, there is simultaneous affliction with malefics to both bodies, that is, on both ends of the Moon-Mercury semi-square. The Moon was already compromised by Saturn and Pluto, but regrettably Mercury was quincunx Neptune slightly more than a degree from exact. Mercury-Neptune consistently requires a stable, successful personality in order to work out well, generally as an intuitive influence. In someone radically less than stable like Dahmer it was suitable symbolism for mental instability. Mercury was also the Ascendant ruler since he had Virgo rising. Pisces, which held the Moon and Mars, is strongly addictive but particularly when bodies contained within it are sorely afflicted, not by a type of aspect but the classical malefic planets. Dahmer was a full blown alcoholic before he was out of high school; and though he was bright enough to get into Ohio State University; he was so drunk on most days that he didn't attend class often enough to keep up with the curriculum and quickly flunked out. He enlisted in the army but was discharged after two years due to alcoholism.

There might still have been hope for him if he had had auspicious stars prominent in his chart but his midheaven was flanked by Pollux, the beta star in Gemini, less than a degree in right ascension east of his meridian and Procyon, the alpha star in Canis Majoris, less than a degree from the midheaven in the west. Pollux has some good qualities but according to the old lore it's like Mars; its natives are said to be cruel, associated with violence and poisons. In a related manner Dahmer dissolved many of his victims in acid. Procyon is even better known as a troublesome and malevolent influence that may end in disaster if other factors provide support. Dahmer was bludgeoned to death in prison.

Dahmer had three planets in the eighth house, the Sun, Venus and Mercury, which is traditionally the house of death, although the vast majority of people with an eighth house emphasis are not murderers or some species of misfit bumbling through life. More to the point, most planets do not flourish in the vicinity of the eighth house no matter what house system is employed because bodies so placed are midway between the strong places: the horizon and the meridian. Dahmer had the Sun quincunx Jupiter a degree and a quarter from exact but it availed him very little because the Sun was in the eighth house, Jupiter was below the horizon and relatively weak in the third house remote from the lower meridian; whereas Saturn was only five degrees from the lower meridian and thus quite strong. He would have felt limitation and pain at home. His parents divorced when he was a teenager which quite likely made the years preceding and following the divorce stressful to him.

In short, this horoscope is spectacularly bad with all of the upside symbolism overwhelmed by the extreme gravity of the bad. Many people have some of the factors that Dahmer had and get through life without horrific results, but this writer has never seen anybody else with all of what Dahmer had.

Adolf Hitler

German dictator Adolf Hitler started the Second World War by invading Poland. Globally, six years of war exacted a toll of 65 million dead, which is the greatest conflagration in recorded history. Hitler was born April 20, 1889 at 6:30 p.m. LMT at Braunau-am-Inn, Austria. His birth data are from the November 1933 edition of the German astrological journal *Zenit*. The same data were found in Hitler's baptismal register discovered by the noted German astrologer Elsbeth Ebertin, according to Ellic Howe, *Astrology: A Recent History* (New York: Walker & Co., 1968), 93.

One's attention is instantly drawn to the loaded seventh house and the two angular bodies in the West: the Sun exalted in Aries that was about to set and Mercury that had recently set. The Sun is most powerful in Leo and Aries, therefore the emphasis of angularity magnified the solar qualities into an overwhelming and domineering presence, possessed of tremendous strength of will and ambition for power. Angular Mercury was symbolic of his extraordinary oratorical skills and strong intellect though he was a high school drop-out. Aries is one of the royal constellations so in effect, he was born to be a leader. Both the Sun and Mercury in Aries love to give orders. The Sun is heavily afflicted however both by planets and stars. The Sun was mundane square Saturn three and a half degrees from exact. That is, if the Sun were placed in the Midheaven Saturn would have risen three and a half degrees before the Sun culminated. That relationship obtained even though he was born near sunset. It symbolizes the poor relationship with his father, made worse by Saturn's detriment in Cancer. The father was a domestic tyrant and a cold, hard character who devalued the son. He died when Hitler was fourteen. The Sun was semi-sextile Neptune only three minutes of arc from exact which is one twentieth of a degree. It bears repeating that so-called minor aspects

Adolph Hitler
April 20, 1889
6:30 p.m. LMT
Braunau-am-Inn, Austria
48°N15' 13°E02'

*Sidereal – Campanus
1h 48m 29s: RA β ♈
13h 54m 13s: β Pers. sets
1h 54m 43s: RAA☉
1h 55m 59s: RAMS
2h 00m 53s: RA α ♈

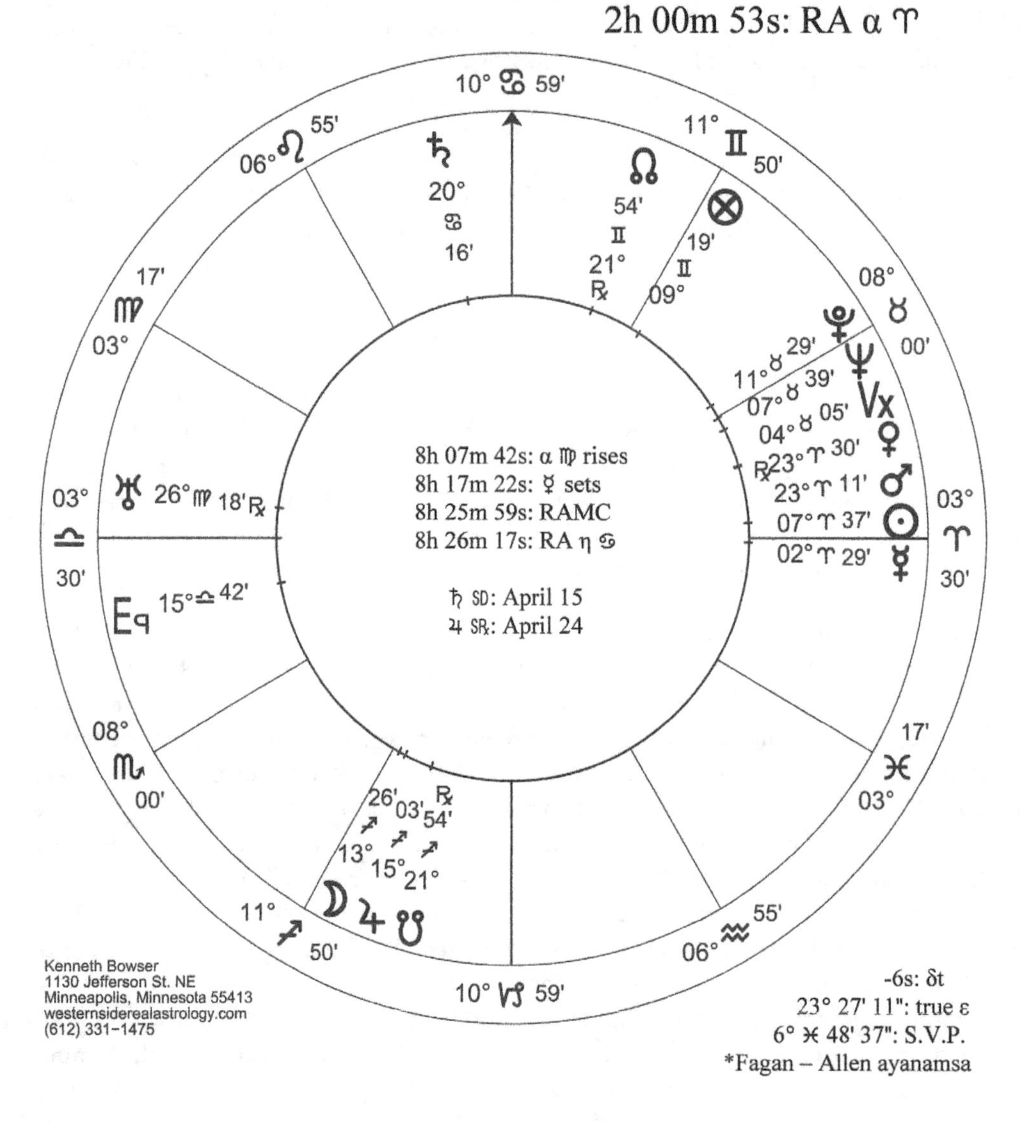

Kenneth Bowser
1130 Jefferson St. NE
Minneapolis, Minnesota 55413
westernsiderealastrology.com
(612) 331-1475

-6s: δt
23° 27' 11": true ε
6° ♓ 48' 37": S.V.P.
*Fagan – Allen ayanamsa

like the semi-sextile are very strong, and thus not secondary influences, if they are close, as in this case. The Neptune contact with the Sun with the other detrimental factors that impinge upon the Sun made him delusional, an extreme ideologue, addicted to drugs and intrigued by the occult. None of that is in the semi-sextile itself; the aspect just connects the two bodies. It all comes from Neptune in a difficult horoscope. An otherwise positive natus symbolizes the benefits that may accrue from a Sun-Neptune contact but that is not reasonable here.

When the stars are examined the situation gets worse. Hitler's Sun was sandwiched between the two principal stars in Aries, the alpha star Hamal and the beta star Sharatan. Both are described very harshly in the ancient lore [See, Vivian Robson, The Fixed Stars and Constellations in Astrology) as connected with "violence, brutishness, cruelty and premeditated crime" for Hamal which is one and a half degrees east of the Sun in right ascension; and as related to "defeat, destruction and war" for Sharatan which was one and a half degrees to the west of Hitler's Sun in right ascension. Worse, Hitler's Sun passed through the lower meridian at his birthplace at local apparent midnight thirty seconds of sidereal time after the beta star in Perseus, called Algol, set there. That is a mundane square which is one eighth of a degree of arc from exact. Algol is a very difficult star, especially if the rest of the horoscope is sorely afflicted. Its symbolism is gruesome. The Chinese called it Tseih She, which is said to refer to piled up corpses.

Right away it's clear from an examination of the Sun with Saturn, Neptune, Hamal, Sharatan and Algol that something is terribly wrong with this person's essential nature. Unless other factors can provide some respite from this symbolism, he may be a monster of stupendous proportions. One tends to hope for extenuating circumstances that may contravene the worst.

The Moon is conjoined to Jupiter in Sagittarius, a good placement for it in one of the royal signs (Aries, Leo and Sagittarius) which further suggests that he was born to lead. Other people attend the Moon-Jupiter people. They are pampered, served and obeyed. But Jupiter and the Moon are spoiled by their conjunction with the south node of the Moon, which is not a positive indicator. It suggests that while he had a good mother and loved her dearly, her influence was not telling in his life. Moon-Jupiter is a very lucky and desirable contact but the south node suggests misuse of power or corruption due to internal failings, possibly a mental illness. The big asteroid Chiron, that orbits the Sun between Saturn and Uranus, is also directly opposite the Moon-Jupiter conjunction. Chiron is an intensifier that marks Hitler as someone who will play a big role in life and exercise extraordinary power.

The Ascendant in Libra, taken alone, is charming, graceful and artistic. Hitler had some artistic skill but he was denied admittance to the Vienna Academy of Fine Arts because of his difficulty in drawing the human figure. The Ascendant ruler, Venus, which relates to one's conception of beauty, is compromised in his horoscope. Venus is associated with Taurus and Libra and is therefore badly placed in the opposite constellations Aries and Scorpio. Hitler's Venus in her detriment, Aries, is conjoined to Mars which is in its own sign, Aries. That produces great enthusiasm for the ladies and no talent for attracting them. He had no girlfriends during his early life and very few male friends, possibly only one. In addition, Saturn which dominates the horoscope from the tenth house, was debilitated in Cancer and square the debilitated Venus and Mars. Cancer, the home of the Moon which is the nursery of the zodiac, cannot tolerate malefic planets which is why Mars is in its fall there and Saturn in its detriment. Therefore the ruler of the Ascendant, Venus, herself debilitated, is configured by the two classical malefics, one of which is also debilitated. It meant that his love and friendship life were likely to be perverse, a source of dismay to him and his lovers. Significantly, six of the eight women Hitler engaged in relationship as an adult committed suicide or made the attempt. Another well known personality with a similar arrangement was Donatien Alphonse François de Sade. The Marquis de Sade had Mars in Aries closely square Saturn in Cancer just like Hitler but de Sade's Venus was conjoined to his Saturn whereas Hitler's Venus was conjoined to his Mars. The difference was that Venus suffers no debility in Cancer which was symbolic of de Sade as the father of three children, although he ruined his marriage through infidelity and bizarre sexual behavior. Venus is debilitated in Aries in Hitler's chart thus he fathered no children. Venus is symbolic of the people who are liked and loved, especially one's children. It is easy to see how Hitler would be attracted to the military, as well as murderers, bullies and other vicious people who delight in slaughter. Such was the composition of the Nazi party. Certainly not everyone with such a badly configured Venus will be so horribly inclined. The general tone of the map is the key as well as the stars that get involved with planets that comprise combinations.

Mars square Saturn is reasonably likely to manifest badly if even one of the bodies is debilitated. At its worst, Mars-Saturn, particularly the conjunction, square and opposition, is brutal, even vicious. Other planet contacts and stars can moderate the effect or cause the native himself to suffer. Mars, the dignified planet in the Venus-Mars-Saturn combination is rendered not merely strong and aggressive by virtue of its placement in Aries but distinctly and deliberately cruel due to its close association with two stars whose malevolent natures are well known. Mars was involved in a mundane square less than one and a half degrees from exact with the upsilon star in the stinger of the Scorpion's tail called Lesath (from Al Las'ah, the sting). Robson says that it makes its natives dangerous and immoral among other things and it is certainly an unwelcome addition to Venus, Saturn and Mars. Finally, Mars was opposite Zubenelgenubi (from Al Zuban al Janubiyyah, the Southern Claw), the alpha star in the southern scale pan of Libra. The old lore is that Zubenelgenubi itself, when prominent, relates to violence, crime and disgrace but when Mars is involved, the effect entails bloodshed. Zubenelgenubi was opposite Hitler's Mars less than a degree from exact in the equatorial system.

The loaded seventh house is the most important house in Hitler's chart and symbolizes his wide public appeal among the Germans though he was Austrian.

Saturn in the tenth house was the ultimate signature of his failure because it was debilitated. Many successful people have Saturn elevated in their horoscopes but much more commonly when it is well placed in Libra or Capricorn, its best venues, and or when Saturn is configured with Jupiter. Saturn was the most elevated body, had no help from good stars or Jupiter and its only contacts were mundane squares to the Sun, Mercury and Pluto and a zodiac square to Mars. Though hard, probably none of that would have brought ruin onto himself, his country and tens of millions of others if Saturn had not lorded over everything from the midheaven in its detriment. Dignities, debilities and elevation count for a lot.

Appendix One

Historical Remarks

The historical context of western sidereal astrology consists of three parts: the Babylonian period, the dormant period and the modern rediscovery and renewal. The first part dates from the third millennium BC, but with very scanty data that is not much supplemented until the end of the second millennium BC. It then emerged in the first millennium BC as a well developed body of lore on a firm astronomical foundation. The end of the first period and the beginning of the dormant period begins with the last currently extant piece of astronomical/astrological data in cuneiform that dates to AD 75. Western sidereal astrology did not go fully into hibernation until the sixth century AD in Egypt. The renewal covers the 1840s to the present day.

There was a great deal of trade in the third millennium BC between the Tigris-Euphrates River Valley civilization in what is modern Iraq and the Indus River Valley civilization in what is modern Pakistan and India. Each side claimed to have taught the other astrology. The matter of priority has not been resolved nor whether each civilization may have independently become aware of the corollary between what happens in the sky and on the ground. The two main schools of thought that embrace the sidereal zodiac remain the Eastern branch, known as Vedic or Indian astrology, and the Western, which is Babylonian. Indian astrology is not treated here because it is very difficult, and perhaps impossible, to document as an ancient discipline, mainly due to the oral transmission of the material. Furthermore, the zodiac is not mentioned and astronomical material is modestly treated in the Rig Veda[9] a primarily second millennium BC work, the most revered in Hinduism, although the nakshatras (small groups of stars) are mentioned in the Atharvaveda. There is little more in the Puranas.[10] The history of early Indian astrology, like early Indian history per se, is an oral tradition; but an oral tradition (unlike a written one) does not constitute an historical record in academia because it instantly elicits the question, "How does one know that the assertions of the tradition with respect to facts, provenance and especially date, are legitimate?" Those things cannot be answered from the claims of an oral tradition itself.

The earliest horoscopes found to date are Babylonian. The earliest records of long-term systematic observations, procedure texts for ephemerides and documentation that lays out the mathematical rationale behind a cinematic model of the sky are also Babylonian.

Except for parts of some early works that address an equatorial orientation which date from 1000 BC—the paths of Ea, Anu and Enlil in the Mul.Apin tablets[11]—the Babylonians were exclusively ecliptic oriented and used the zodiac and the principal stars in it to note celestial longitude. The evidence, to date, for the modern twelve-fold equal division of the zodiac does not appear until mid-first millennium BC. Yet the scholars who have translated the cuneiform texts point out that the Babylonian/Assyrian astrological tradition did not emerge ex nihilo. The best Akkadian scholar of the group, Abraham Sachs Ph.D., speculated that the twelve-fold equal division may very well be two hundred years older than the date of the oldest horoscope for an individual to which a date can be affixed (410 BC).[12] There are other Babylonian texts which are not horoscopes but which give planetary positions in terms of sidereal zodiac signs as early as 445 BC[13] and many others that are older still that reckon bodies with respect to zodiacal stars. Astronomical diaries with many observations date from approximately 750 BC to AD 75.[14]

The last three centuries BC were particularly rich for Babylonian astrology, so much so that the degree to which pure tropical astrology was practiced during the Hellenistic Period, the Roman Imperial Period and beyond is a controversial matter. Vettius Valens, a second century Roman astrologer, did not adhere closely to the vernal equinox. His Anthology of 130 horoscopes has more than twice as many horoscopes as all other Greek papyri on the subject. In most of Valens's collection, only the positions of the Sun, Moon, the horoscopos (Ascendant) and the hour are given. And,

> "In all cases the longitudes of the Sun given by Vettius Valens are greater than the longitudes found by modern computation. The deviations vary between 7° and 2° and show a decreasing trend. The skew line in figure 33 (not shown here) indicates how much the decrease would be owing to precession. It seems to be admissible to assume that the tables upon which these computations were based showed a difference of about + 5° in AD 50 and of about + 3½° in AD 160."[15]

This deviation suggests three things: first, the equinox was defined during this period in terms of the sidereal zodiac and not the reverse; that is, one would say the equinox occurs in the middle of the (sidereal) signs or in eight degrees or five degrees of the (sidereal) signs as several Greeks who achieved astronomical and astrological notoriety such as Eudoxus, Aratus and Geminus, did say; second, the discrepancies in longitude computation are very likely due to the residual effect of a sidereal tradition, because of their decreasing values; and finally, the inability of ancient astrologers to measure the equinox accurately suggests confusion over how to measure it and indeed whether what is to be measured is a sidereal tradition or a seasonal one. Such confusion is entirely reasonable since tropical (seasonal) and sidereal (stellar) reckoning were coincident for the first time in more than 25,000 years at the end of the Age of Aries (AD 221).

The decline of Roman power in the fourth and fifth centuries of the Christian Era, seriously eroded the level of astronomical and technical skill which had never been as high in the Roman West as in Greece, much less at Alexandria (Egypt), the center of the Western intelligentsia in Late Antiquity. The Romans, ever practical and disdainful of theory, did not even develop students capable of producing geometric proofs.[16] The first full translation of Euclid's Elements into Latin (from Arabic via the original Greek) is from the twelfth century of the current era. There is no evidence to date that such a full translation ever existed that predates the twelfth century.[17] One may reasonably surmise that there were very few people alive in Western Christendom after Proclus[18] (who lived in the eastern empire) or perhaps Boethius,[19] who could compute a geometric proof until the twelfth century. There had never been a system of compulsory primary education in the West during Early or Late Antiquity. Even before the descent into civil war and the end of the republic in the first century BC, Roman literacy (men and women combined) is thought to have "not much exceeded ten percent."[20] The degree of numeracy is unknown. Literacy in the West progressively declined from this high water mark during the Roman republic to a much lower figure by the time the last nominal Roman emperor in the West was deposed in AD 476.

With the total collapse of Roman power in the fifth century, the West became a cultural backwater, and slipped into what is fairly termed a "dark age." Education was afforded to fewer people than at any time during the republic or the empire; basic research was apparently nonexistent, large building and engineering projects, except in the eastern (Byzantine) empire, were not undertaken and astronomical observations were all but completely absent in the West, except for timekeeping and calendar purposes, for the remainder of the millennium. Yet even the Roman calendar was two days out of synchronization with the Sun as early as AD 354.[21]

There was a modest and brief surge in the eighth century, at the time of the Carolingian Renaissance in learning and renewed interest in astronomy, but it was in no way comparable to Classical Antiquity. During the Dark Age, the overwhelming majority in every class of society was illiterate and innumerate, with the exceptions of some of the clergy, a few administrators and a few well-born individuals fortunate enough to be tutored. Other exceptions at the modest level of craftsman's literacy were merchants who had to be able make out basic contracts, and foremen who supervised work projects. Astrology fell into this abyss. Ptolemy wrote in Greek but there was hardly anyone in the Latin West who could read Latin, much less Greek during the Dark Ages. Proto-Italian, French, Spanish and Portuguese were not yet in written form. Ptolemy's Almagest (the Syntaxis called al magesti, "the Greatest" by the Arabs from the Greek superlative, μεγιστορς) was not translated from Greek, but more likely Arabic, into Latin until circa 1160.[22] Astrology requires some modest mathematical expertise, literacy, some equipment like a quarterstaff, an astrolabe, an abacus, pen, ink and paper, maybe Theon's Handy Tables and a basic grasp of astronomical ideas that may have been fostered by the most important element: a mentor. Such people were exceedingly rare in the West.

Strange to say, in the face of abject ignorance, scholarship was discouraged by the Catholic Church, the only institution in the West to survive the Dark Age intact. The church taught that the conditions of the natural world should be ignored, to better concentrate on the spiritual aspects of the "next world," that is, the life after death. It is no exaggeration to say that astrology and the academic disciplines fell into desuetude, which was not dispelled to a significant degree in Europe until the minor Greco-Arab renaissance of the twelfth century.

Knowledge of history was modest in the medieval world. There was little information in general circulation about the ancient world until after Gutenberg's work on the forty-two-line bible was completed in 1454—the first book done on a printing press with moveable type. There was a rapid increase from that date in the quantity of scholarly works in circulation, but because there was no system of compulsory elementary education in Europe, literacy remained low and scholarship was pursued by few compared to modern figures. By the middle of the sixteenth century, however, the Reformation, had begun to accelerate literacy due mainly to the work of Martin Luther who maintained that Christians are obliged to read the Bible for themselves. The new literacy posed a problem for astrology because heretofore the art was the nearly exclusive preserve of intellectuals who were not merely literate but educated with a working knowledge of arithmetic, and perhaps some algebra, geometry or even trigonometry as well as astronomy. Many people who could read tables and ephemerides that they didn't have to understand, but only to know how to use, now took up astrology. Some of them were charlatans and too many were a cut or two below the old standards. The new literacy spawned critical evaluation as never before and astrology was found wanting. As a result, even demonstrably capable artists, including the greatest of the English astrologers of the seventeenth century, William Lilly, were sometime objects of derision and attack due to the low standard to which astrology quickly fell, from which it still has not recovered. Astrology and astronomy, which had been partners for more than two thousand years, went their separate ways in the seventeenth century, in particular after astrology was dropped from university curricula.

Renewed Interest of the West in the Near East

After the publication of Newton's Principia in 1686 and 1687 and during the eighteenth century European Enlightenment, Western technical superiority began to accelerate the cultural divide between Europe and the rest of the world, which had begun in earnest during the major renaissance of the fifteenth century. Europeans began to see themselves as the center of mass of cultural sophistication and the worthy inheritors of Western Civilization. It was inevitable that they would show renewed interest in the areas from which the torch of Western Civilization had been passed: Egypt, the Levant, Greece and Rome. Knowledge of the ancient world did not begin to be well sorted out on a large scale until the nineteenth century, but interest in Classical Antiquity in Europe was stirred in the eighteenth century particularly by excavations begun in Italy at Herculaneum in 1709 and Pompei in 1748; and especially by the publication of Edward Gibbon's Decline and Fall of the Roman Empire. The first volume was printed in 1776, immediately sold out and ran to three editions. The sixth and last volume appeared in 1788 and like the preceding volumes, sold fast. Admittedly, Gibbon (1737-1794) wrote a masterpiece, still considered the most beautifully crafted work of its type in English; yet each volume is massive and the entire work an example of prodigious scholarship. Such a work would be an unlikely best-seller today. Its popularity in the eighteenth century is a testament to the widespread enthusiasm in the West, at that time, for information about the ancient Mediterranean world, and the Near and Middle East before and after the Arab conquests in the seventh and eighth centuries of the Christian Era.

Napoleon's invasion of Egypt in 1798 likewise produced in Europe, intense interest in the Middle East. Attached to the French army in Egypt were five hundred French civilians, among whom were artists, engineers and scientists (including three astronomers), who studied the natural history, geography, monuments and art of the country. In 1799 at Rashid (westernized to Rosetta), a city at one of the mouths of the Nile, the French army found a slab of basalt inscribed in three languages, Greek, Demotic and ancient Egyptian hieroglyphs which eventually led to the decipherment of Egyptian hieroglyphs. The British admiral Nelson, later of Trafalgar fame, destroyed Napoleon's fleet in Abukir Bay off Alexandria on August 1, 1798, which created huge problems of supply for the French and sealed the fate of Napoleon's attempt to secure a land route to India. The French were forced out of Egypt in 1801 and the Rosetta Stone fell into British hands. It sits today in the British Museum. But the French, before they left Egypt, compiled a massive survey of the region, which was the first time modern Europeans had seen the architecture, art and lay of the land of ancient Egypt. The work of the five hundred civilian specialists Napoleon had brought with him, the Description de L'Égypte, was published in ten folio volumes and two atlases from 1809 through 1822. The work has 837 engravings and more than 3000 drawings done to a high standard. The path that led to increased Western European engagement with the eastern Mediterranean was widened twenty years after the French left Egypt.

Western Roots

The headwaters of Western culture flow from Rome, Greece and in particular, the Judeo-Christian tradition, Israel, which explains the desire of Westerners to control what they see as home ground. After the fall of Rome, Western European populations had either disengaged from or were fearful of the East, depending on location. Re-engagement between East and West began in earnest with the French excursion into Egypt in 1798, but the sentiment to recover what had been lost was stoked in the minds of Europeans to a much greater degree when Greece erupted into bloody conflict with her Turkish overlords.

Greece has enjoyed pride of place in the West as the fountainhead of individualism, logic, mathematics, debate, classical inquiry, drama, philosophy and democratic government for more than twenty-five centuries. Until recently in the West, a classical education was incomplete without knowledge of the Greek language and history even though Greece was a part of the Ottoman Empire for many centuries. Intermittent war had been underway throughout the fourteenth century between Greeks, Serbs, Bulgars and Turks, until the Ottoman Turks totally subjugated the Greeks in the fifteenth century not long after the fall of Constantinople in 1453. This was particularly galling in the West because of the antagonism between Muslims and Christians. It was considered lamentable in the West that the cradle of Christendom, Israel, was in Muslim hands, hence the Crusades to free the Holy Land from Muslim domination, which ranged from the eleventh century into the thirteenth. When Greece, the cradle of the West, and even older than Christendom, also fell into Muslim hands, this additional shock to Western sensibilities and prejudices once again became an acute irritant, in particular, when the power of the West had distinctly superceded the East in the eighteenth century. The Greeks had been trying to throw off the Turkish yoke with limited success for fifty years when they rose up in a successful revolution (notable for its savagery on both sides) against their Turkish masters in 1821, although Greek independence was not secured until 1829. The war was followed with considerable interest in the West, and there was some commotion in England and France in support of the Greek cause. Echoing the popular sentiment in England, Lord Byron, the greatest poet of his time, lent his personal support in the form of his presence in Greece and grants of money to the Greek cause. Such publicity helped fan the flames of growing European interest in the area.

The major impetus with regard to things specifically Babylonian was the discovery and excavation of the ancient sites in what is now Iraq in the 1840s. Paul Botta, a Frenchman, discovered the ruins of Khorsabad in 1843, a city founded by Sargon II (722-706 BC), king of Assyria. Austen Henry Layard (M.P. for Aylesbury and later prominent in several British governments) worked tirelessly in Mesopotamia for more than a decade excavating monuments and cuneiform (the written form of the Akkadian language) inscriptions. The most impressive of the many objects Layard uncovered are the huge winged bulls that he sent to England in 1846. They reside in the British Museum today. From 1845 through 1852 Layard uncovered and positively identified the sites of Nimrud and the ancient capital of Assyria, Nineveh. In 1845 he found the palace of Shalmaneser III (858-824 BC), son of Assurnasirpal II. Layard found essentially intact the great library of Assurbanapal (669-627 BC) at Nineveh, which was destroyed by the Babylonians in 612 BC under Nabopolasar. That Babylonian victory ended the Assyrian Empire, but the subsequent Babylonian Empire was short-lived as Babylon was herself conquered by the Persians in 539 BC. Layard also excavated Babylon. The science of Assyriology dates from the 1840s with the recovery of large quantities of cuneiform writing due initially, in the main, to the work of Layard. Within thirty years linguists had essentially deciphered cuneiform/Akkadian, the lingua franca of the ancient world before it began to be displaced in mid-first millennium BC by Aramaic, (one of) the language(s) that Jesus spoke. The decipherment of Akkadian/cuneiform continues today but in the details rather than the fundamentals. It is now offered in many American and European university curricula.

The Crimean War (1854-1856) that pitted the English and the French against the Russians, was fought primarily to keep the Russians from exploiting the weakness of the Ottoman Turks and to stop Russian encroachments on Turkish territory. Secondarily the British, in particular, were intent on keeping the Russian navy out of the Mediterranean and bottled up in the Black Sea. In this they succeeded which served to ratchet up the British interest and commitment in the Eastern Mediterranean yet again.

While cuneiform was being sorted out, European interest in the Near and Middle East entered a still more rigorous phase with the construction of the Suez Canal, from the first shovel of dirt turned in 1859 until the opening of the canal in 1869. The Suez Canal was, at the time, the biggest earth-moving project in history. The British opposed it every step of the way and spent years blocking the financing for it and exerting their influence to impede the granting of permission from the Ottoman Turks in Constantinople. The British feared that their control over India, and the India trade, would be threatened by easier European access to the East in general. The Suez Canal shortened the trip to India from England by 5,800 miles. It was built almost entirely with French and Egyptian financing, Egyptian manpower and European steam-driven machines. Ironically, only a year after the canal opened, the French government (the Second Empire) collapsed after the French defeat in the Franco-Prussian War. French ambition and ability to exert serious influence in Middle Eastern affairs evaporated with the demise of the Second Empire.

The great majority of ships passing through the canal were British from the very beginning of its operational life, since England had the largest navy, merchant marine and colonial empire on the planet at the time. By 1875 the khedive (Turkish viceroy) of Egypt, had so badly mismanaged the affairs of the country and run up debts so huge, that he could no longer get credit from European bankers. Boxed into a financial corner of his own making, the khedive's only way out was to sell his shares in the Suez Canal Company, which the British government promptly bought. That purchase gave the British controlling interest in the company but it did not allay their fears that a hostile power could take over or sabotage the canal, which had quickly become vital to British strategic interests. Apprehension over the security of the canal caused the British to occupy Egypt in 1882 when a rebellion there threatened the stability of the khedive's government. The British garrisoned troops in Egypt thereafter and were the force behind the Egyptian government until 1936, although British troops remained in the Canal Zone itself until 1956. It was the British presence in Egypt that attracted many students of the new disciplines of archaeology and Egyptology to the area. Mostly European and American scholars went to Egypt and the neighboring areas under nominal Ottoman control continuously after Britain secured behind-the-scenes control of the Egyptian government.

A lucrative business in antiquities in the Near East expanded so fast after the 1840's that many natives and foreigners alike protested that Egypt and her neighbors were being looted of their treasures under the guise of a paternalistic form of Western imperialism. From the Western perspective, the valid and true point was made that ancient monuments and statuary were being destroyed by the unappreciative native populations, who wanted the stone to build ordinary houses. Stone and timber are in short supply in desert and near desert conditions. As building materials they were all but gone from Mesopotamia even in ancient times, which is why most buildings in that area have not survived: they were made from mud bricks. While Egypt still had quarries, it was very tempting and easier to take stone that had already been cut, dressed and transported from quarries to local sites, than to purchase raw stone. Westerners, seeing the pyramids and lesser structures systematically disassembled for their stone, were aghast and moved to stop such actions by the native populations. The Europeans, especially the British, also took choice items for the greater glory of their own governments, museums and public places.

The Europeans and Americans became self-appointed conservators because they saw themselves as the inheritors of Western Civilization on the current leg of the Egypt-Greece-Rome- Western Europe-America line. The then current residents of the Near and Middle East were not seen in the same light as their ancient ancestors, in large part because the contemporary residents were regarded as heathens, in the eyes of many of the Westerners, who had little knowledge of the local culture or respect for Islam. The cultural divide between East and West and the pronounced technical superiority of the Western powers in the nineteenth century only served to confirm Western prejudices. These sentiments survive in the West to a significant degree today, exacerbated by radical Islam; obviously they are major sources of underlying resentment between Middle Easterners and Westerners. Resentment aside, from the 1840s onward, Egypt and the Levant were continuously plundered, in the name of scholarship and to preserve the legacy of the West, until Arab nationalism stemmed the flow well on into the twentieth century. Still, scholarship was merely a side issue after the completion of the Suez Canal. Control of the region to ensure the security of the canal was the centerpiece of British Near East policy after 1870.

Relevance to Astrology

The texts that were removed from Egypt and Mesopotamia in the first half of the nineteenth century began to be extensively translated in the second half. The seminal work for sidereal astrology was a fifteen page article entitled "Zur Entzifferung Der Astronomischen Tafeln Der Chaldäer" (On Deciphering the Chaldean Astronomical Tables) by Joseph Epping (S.J.),[23] which appeared in the Catholic theological periodical, Stimmen Aus Maria Laach in 1881. The work done by Epping (1835-1894), Johann Strassmaier (S. J. [1846-1920]), and Franz Xaver Kugler (S. J. [1864-1929]) was central to the discovery that all of Babylonian astronomy and astrology was sidereal. That is, the vernal equinox was not used by the Babylonians to reckon celestial longitude. The equinox was used however, to reckon the varying length of daylight, and by extension, the latitude of a place.

Epping was a professor of mathematics and astronomy, well equipped to take on Babylonian astronomical tables. He determined that he was in possession of lunar ephemerides and other observational texts which both solved the chronology of the Seleucid[24] period (began 311 BC) and demonstrated a degree of astronomical sophistication that was heretofore unknown for such an early date. Father Epping published the first book length treatise on the subject in 1889 with his Astronomisches aus Babylon (Astronomical [Materials] From Babylon). He co-authored several important articles with Strassmaier in Zeitschrift für Assyriologie (Journal for Assyriology) between 1890 and 1893, which laid open many Babylonian astronomical tables, Babylonian eclipse canons and lunar observations.

It was later found that since all the fundamentals of Hipparchus's lunar theory can be derived from these early Babylonian sources, extensive borrowing of Babylonian parameters hastened the development of Greek astronomy. Hipparchus also employed the Babylonian sexagesimal (base 6) number system (in common use today—look at your watch). Most important, Hipparchus used the precise values of the Babylonian period relations[25] of the planets and adapted them to use in Greek systems; and his extensive use of Babylonian eclipse records and other observations extended back to 747 BC[26] according to Ptolemy. Period relations are explained in appendix two.

The third great figure in early Assyriology, F. X. Kugler, published Die Babylonische Mondrechnung (Babylonian Lunar Reckoning) in 1900. In this book Kugler showed that the Babylonians used an equal division sidereal zodiac. Additionally, in contrast to what is assumed in Ptolemy's Almagest (Book 4, chapter 2), Kugler showed that Hipparchus got the value of his lunar mean motion (the length of the synodic month[27]) by direct borrowing of period relations and exact parameters that had been long established values in Babylon. In another major work, Kugler published the first part of Sternkunde und Sterndienst in Babel (Starlore and Starwork in Babylon [in two volumes and three supplements]) in 1907, which treated astrology more fully than ever before, although astronomy and astrology were not really separated in antiquity.

By the turn of the nineteenth century Assyriology was providing academic careers throughout Europe and the United States. Many academic journals are even today devoted to it because Akkadian (the language of the Babylonians) is the best link to the ancient Middle East. There are more ancient documents written in it than any other language in that part of the world. The register of cuneiform texts in the British Museum is well beyond 100,000.

Cyril Fagan, the Father of Western Sidereal Astrology

Cyril Fagan (1896-1970), Irish by birth, a career British civil servant and later expatriate to the United States, was one of very few astrologers of the first rank in the twentieth century. He was a voracious reader, fond of study, at home in libraries and archives and doubtless well aware of developments in Assyriology and Egyptology during the nineteenth and twentieth centuries. Fagan's father was a surgeon, but Fagan himself was unable to follow his father in an academic or professional career due to severe deafness, which was the result of scarlet fever he suffered as a child.

Fagan began his study of tropical astrology in 1916 and achieved renown in the 1930s as an astrological writer and scholar. Fagan realized in 1944, after a long career of private scholarship, that astrology had been sidereal in the ancient world until the Greeks arbitrarily created tropical astrology. It is one thing for academics to see that, but quite another for an astrologer to grasp it, especially a tropical astrologer.

The information was available that allowed an independent thinker, steeped in enquiry, especially of an occult type, to see what Assyriologists had seen and dismissed as only modestly remarkable because they weren't students of astrology. Even today there is no onus attached to studying astrology from an academic perspective, as long as one doesn't believe the precepts of the art. To believe them and admit it is anathema in academia, where the occult arts are held in contempt, and sufficient to ruin a career or destroy any chance for promotion for someone without tenure. Academicians were not shouting from the rooftops therefore, that astrology was originally sidereal because they didn't believe in the inherent merit of the art from a tropical or sidereal perspective. Tropical astrologers, except for Fagan, were not reading academic journals that contravened their basic premises, primary among them that Aries is reckoned from the vernal equinox.

Fagan obviously realized that the spring equinox in the Northern Hemisphere had held Taurus, not Aries, at the beginning of recorded history five thousand years ago and that the stars were the original frame of reference in the ancient world. His leap was to see that the sky itself is invested with meaning, not the seasons, which are reversed between Northern and Southern Hemispheres that make a global spring impossible. By this reasoning it is easy to see the great failing of tropical zodiac reckoning: it confounds the seasons with the zodiac. In discarding the seasons that are defined by the Earth, Fagan's frame of reference was transferred from the Earth to the sky, which is the Babylonian position. The logic of this stance is simple yet potent: there is no fixed signpost in the sky that says, "Vernal Equinox here!" Astronomy and astrology are visual. The equinox changes fast with respect to the sky (one degree per 71.6 years). One cannot reckon longitudes from a position unmarked in the sky that changes constantly and quickly, and discover what the period relations of the planets revealed to Babylonian astronomer/astrologers. Period relations are the key to the Babylonian cinematic model of the sky, which in turn produces ephemerides (tables of planetary positions) that provide the positions of the heliacal phenomena,[28] stations and oppositions centuries in advance.

Fagan encountered intense resistance from the Western astrological establishment when its leading figures realized that he was saying that tropical astrology had it all wrong. His first major response was the publication in 1950 of Zodiacs Old and New. Fagan discovered in 1948, with the mathematical assistance of fellow Irishman James Hynes, that the exaltation degrees (see Appendix Three) of Mercury, Mars, Jupiter and Saturn are the heliacal phenomena of those bodies for the parallel of Babylon in the lunar year, i.e. the civil year, 786-785 BC. The positions of the Sun, Moon and Venus are the sidereal positions of those bodies at first Nisan in 786 BC (April 3, Julian), again at Babylon. First Nisan is the new Moon (first appearance of the new crescent Moon) after sunset closest to the equinox. Its date therefore wanders but stays in the vicinity of the equinox. First Nisan, and not the equinox, was the beginning of the civil year in Mesopotamia. There were two reasons for choosing that time of year: the lengths of day and night are equal at the equinoxes, which facilitated intercalation of the Babylonian soli-lunar calendar; and the Tigris and Euphrates rivers, which made life possible in the area, overflowed their banks near the spring equinox[29] in the broad plains of the river valley due to upstream snowmelt.

Much of Mesopotamia is a desert and near-desert climate, receiving 150 millimeters or less of rainfall per year. Two hundred millimeters of annual rainfall is necessary to bring in a barley crop, the staple in the area in ancient times, because it requires less water than wheat[30] (which requires 250 millimeters annually—free standing forests require 300 millimeters). Barley is also the basis of good beer, another Babylonian staple. While 200 millimeters of rain per year brings in a barley crop, for a settled life, the farmer needed to be able to depend on that much rain in three years out of five. Therefore, the practical limit for settled dry farming was actually closer to the 300 millimeter isoheyet (a contour line that defines the limits of areas that receive equal amounts of rain). Without irrigation canals to catch the river flood to supplement the meager rainfall, large portions of Mesopotamia could not be cultivated or immediately returned to desert if the canals were damaged. The spring flood was a life or death matter.

Fagan completed *Symbolism of the Constellations* in 1962 and *Astrological Origins* in 1969, which are expansions on *Zodiacs Old and New*. The work that was most successful though, in spreading information about the sidereal zodiac, was a monthly column in American Astrology Magazine that appeared from 1953 until Fagan's death in January 1970 and for several years afterward, in reprint form. His 2000 words every month for twenty years had a more telling effect than any book could have had and ensured that the sidereal zodiac in the West became a well-known commodity among serious students of astrology.

Because Fagan was a tropical astrologer for almost thirty years, western sidereal astrology is similar in appearance to tropical. It bears no resemblance to Indian astrology except that both Eastern (Indian) and Western (Babylonian) schools use the sidereal zodiac, although the Indian and Babylonian traditions do not agree on the precise location in the zodiac of the starting point. The fiducial, or starting point, adopted by the Indian government diverges from the Babylonian tradition by less than a degree. Many Indians don't agree with their government sponsored fiducial (developed by N.C. Lahiri) either. There are about half a dozen different fiducials in widespread use in India today. A horoscope drawn in the western sidereal fashion looks just like a tropical horoscope except that the celestial longitudes of the signs and the planets are calculated essentially according to the fiducial used in first millennium BC Mesopotamia. There, the resemblance between tropical and sidereal astrology ends.

Appendix Two

The Tropical-Sidereal Debate

The Geocentric World View

Late in the first millennium BC, probably during the lifetime of Hipparchus of Rhodes (mid second century BC), the Greeks introduced an innovation in zodiac reckoning that had heretofore been sidereal in the Near East and Eastern Mediterranean world for many centuries: they began to reckon the positions of planets and stars from the Northern Hemisphere vernal equinox. Until that time the equinox had been described in terms of the degree of the zodiac the Sun traversed when it reached the equinox, variously in the Greek world as 15, 12, 10, 8, 5 and 3 degrees of Aries as precession slowly changed the Sun's position in the zodiac at the time of the equinox. This point however, with regard to the modern units employed, is moot because evidence for the use of degrees in any extant Greek text is wanting before the time of Hypsicles[31] (mid-second century BC) who was a contemporary of Hipparchus. The Greeks used moonbreadths, cubits and fractions of a circle to measure arc before Hypsicles. The use of the 360-degree base six (sexagesimal) notation, is Babylonian.

During Hipparchus' lifetime the Sun rose at the Northern Hemisphere spring equinox with 5 degrees and a fraction of Aries when he was young and 4 degrees and a fraction of Aries when he was old, by sidereal reckoning, the standard of the day. As a careful observer and the foremost astronomer of his era, Hipparchus would have been well aware of these facts. It is unknown if Hipparchus was aware that the Northern Hemisphere vernal equinox is the Southern Hemisphere autumnal equinox, in other words, that the Northern Hemisphere spring is not a global phenomenon. All of Hipparchus' works are lost but one (his sarcastic commentary on the Phaenomena of Aratus).

His achievements are known mainly from Ptolemy's works, primarily the Syntaxis, a treatise on mathematical astronomy, and the *Tetrabiblos*, a treatise on astrology.

One may infer from Ptolemy's works that Hipparchus altered the frame of reference of astronomy and astrology from the reference stars of the Babylonians, who first discerned the zodiac, to make the Northern Hemisphere vernal equinox begin with the zero degree of Aries. This act represents the break with the old tradition; that is, the coincidence of the zero degree of Aries with respect to Babylonian reckoning did not occur in Hipparchus' lifetime. One cannot, however, say with surety based on evidential support that Hipparchus actually invented or adopted the tropical zodiac because his use of it does not appear among his extant works. It is an assumption that he did invent it and not an unreasonable one; but one may be on firmer ground to say that if Hipparchus hypothesized the tropical zodiac, Ptolemy made it gospel. One may reasonably ask why it was invented.

The reason is grounded in the idea of the geocentric universe widely embraced in the Greek world. According to this doctrine the Earth is absolutely still with no motion of any kind: no rotation, revolution, precession, nutation, polar wandering or any of the other Earth motions or galactic motion. Geocentric advocates, like their foremost exponent, Claudius Ptolemy, had long held that the Earth was at the center of the universe and every celestial motion was in relation to it. Naturally enough when Hipparchus discovered long-term differences in the positions of stars observed in different eras in relation to the equinoctial points, it was quite reasonable to assume that the stars had actually moved.

That Hipparchus was not absolutely sure of the facts of relative motion (what was moving in relation to what) is obvious from the title to the work upon which his fame is founded, *On the Displacement of the Solstitial and Equinoctial Points.* If the Earth is motionless the solstitial and equinoctial points cannot be displaced. His positions may have changed over time. Hipparchus probably embraced the scientific method according to which the question, "How do you know?" is never out of bounds. But the supposedly free-thinking Greeks sometimes made life difficult for people whose flights of fancy strayed too far from orthodoxy, mainly because the Greeks let philosophers meddle in matters beyond their purview. For example, Philolaus (480-385 BC) was ridiculed by Aristotle for proposing that the Earth revolves around a central fire; Heraclides Ponticus (387-312 BC) was ridiculed even many centuries later by Simplicius for proposing that the Earth rotates on its axis; and especially Aristarchus (310-230 BC), who proposed that the Earth orbits the Sun (the original heliocentric theory) was threatened by Cleanthes with indictment for impiety because the heliocentric theory was contrary to Platonic thought. An indictment of impiety that led directly to his demise was also brought against Socrates in consequence of his independence of thought. Aristarchus even proposed that the Sun and the stars are fixed and that the Earth moves with respect to those fixed positions. Aristarchus' configuration is remarkably close to the truth, but he was too far ahead of his time. His heliocentric theory was not embraced in the ancient world and did not completely displace the geocentric theory until nearly two millennia after his death.

The pressure against Aristarchus was brought by the arbiters of the then conventional wisdom who "knew better" in the same way that everybody "knew" for millennia that the world was flat. Once presented with compelling evidence that it was actually spherical (first proposed by Pythagoras), they subsequently "knew" that it was motionless and the center of the universe. These ideas dragged on for centuries mainly due to the combined influence of Aristotle and Ptolemy. Martin Luther (1483-1546), like many other intellectuals of his day, savaged Nicholas Copernicus (1473-1543) in the middle of the sixteenth century for advancing the heliocentric theory that places the Sun in the center of the solar system and puts the Earth in motion around it. All of this bogus "knowing" masquerading as knowledge depends on the logical fallacy known as, "an appeal to authority" (argumentum ad verecundiam—[an argument to respect]). In other words, "Such and such is true because everybody says so." Stereotypes that fly in the face of archetypes are usually based on appeals to authority.

Tropical Underpinning

The weight of orthodoxy may not have impressed itself on Hipparchus; perhaps his position on the island of Rhodes was secure and he felt free to speculate; but an argument from silence proves nothing. It is obvious, however, that if the stars are perceived to slowly move over long periods of time, one can only see that in relation to a fixed standard or a much slower changing standard. Without such a standard, era-to-era comparisons would be meaningless. Unless it could be established what was moving and what was fixed in space, the issue of foreground and background would always be confounding.

The need for a fixed standard is one of the twin pillars that supported tropical reckoning; the other pillar rested on the evidence of one's eyes that could not be argued: the spring equinox very nearly coincided with the zero degree of sidereal Aries during Ptolemy's lifetime. That is, one could see the Sun rising due east at dawn on the day of the Northern Hemisphere spring equinox with the earliest part of the constellation Aries in Ptolemy's day, and close to the beginning of Aries for a long time afterward. Refraction and the Sun's glare made any naked eye approximation too difficult to argue for two hundred years after the Age of Pisces began in AD 221 with respect to the *zodia noeta* (equal length signs 30 degrees in extent).

By the fifth century of the Christian Era the curtain had all but completely fallen on Late Antiquity as a sophisticated period in the West. As the Dark Age settled over the West and tropical and sidereal reckoning began to diverge, there was almost beyond question nobody in the West who understood what was happening nor why. The divergence may not even have been noticed since the record of observations in the West during the Dark Age is abysmal. If anybody noticed, understood and wrote about what was happening, such a treatise did not survive or has not yet been discovered. The Arabs and the Indians noted the divergence but they didn't understand it. Dark Age Europeans demonstrated no awareness of astronomical/astrological sophistication except for the minuscule number who had access to and could read Ptolemy's *Almagest* or his *Handy Tables* or Theon's *Handy Tables* that were all written in Greek. Yet this extremely small group also could not have understood why the sky was different than what Ptolemy wrote about it from his own work.

Tromp L'Oeil: How the Tropical Zodiac Appears Fixed But Is Not

It is ironic that Ptolemy's efforts to institutionalize the tropical zodiac, to make it a fixed standard tied to the geodesy of what he asserted was a fixed Earth, made it a permanently changing standard. That is an inevitable fact because the Sun is the center of the solar system which puts the Earth in motion in many long and short term modes. Possibly Hipparchus but definitely Ptolemy got it backwards. The equinox moves very fast in relation to the star field, not the other way around.

For example, the sidereal zodiac is bisected by two first magnitude stars close to the ecliptic, Aldebaran in the center of Taurus and Antares in the center of Scorpio. The tropical position of Antares, the brightest star in Scorpio, was 1° 23' 12.95" greater on January 1, 2001 than it was on January 1, 1901. That may not seem like a large difference, but it is equivalent to 4,992.95 seconds of arc; yet the star didn't move that much with respect to the Earth. The star appeared to move that much with respect to the Earth but what actually happened is that the equinox moved that much with respect to the star. The tropical frame of reference is constantly in motion with respect to the sky because that system is tied to the vernal equinox instead of the sky. Whether or not the equinox moves is no longer a point at issue. Copernicus showed indirectly that it moves in 1543 with the publication of his *De Revolutionibus Orbium Coelestium.* Galileo also showed indirectly that the equinox moves in 1610 with the publication of his *Siderius Nuncius.* With the publication of Isaac Newton's *Principia* in 1686 and 1687 the matter of what is moving in relation to what is fixed was explicitly settled and no longer a point that could be argued, except in astrological circles. Significantly the seventeenth century was also when astrology was being dropped everywhere from university curricula. What had finally been proven was that the geocentric model is without merit. The vernal equinox is not fixed in space as Ptolemy maintained as an absolute incontrovertible fact.

In terms of fixed sidereal reckoning, the proper motion of Antares during the twentieth century—how much it actually moved in 100 years with respect to the Earth—was 2.15 seconds of arc. That bears repeating: Antares moved 2.15 seconds of arc in terms of sidereal reckoning in 100 years versus 4992.95 seconds of arc in terms of tropical reckoning in 100 years. The smaller number is .00043 of the larger one or consider that 4992.95 is more than 2320 times greater than 2.15. The human eye cannot detect an arc of only 2.15 seconds or anything close to it. This is the essential difference between tropical and sidereal reckoning: the tropical zodiac is moving with respect to the stars and the sidereal zodiac is essentially fixed with respect to those same stars. There are 60 seconds per minute of arc and 60 minutes per degree, thus 3600 seconds of arc per degree. At the rate of 2.15 seconds per century, it will take Antares 167,000 years to move one degree from the vantage-point of the Earth. That is 1,670 centuries. The stars are going nowhere fast, but since the advent of writing five millennia ago that invoked the historical era at Sumer in Mesopotamia and pre-dynastic Egypt, the equinoxes have moved seventy degrees with respect to the stars for the same civil date. Half of the Age of Taurus, all of the Age of Aries and most of the Age of Pisces have passed by since then.

Antares is typical of the actual motions of stars as seen from the Earth. Some are faster, some are slower, but as a practical matter they are fixed. The night sky looks today just as it did when Egypt became a federated state in the third millennium BC. Tropical reckoning is fixed with respect to the equinox but the equinox moves with respect to the stars, yet the logic of tropical reckoning that stops at the zero degree of Aries requires the opposite to be true. That is, tropical reckoning requires that the sky moves with respect to a fixed earth; but the appearance is not the reality. The geocentric system is not simply a way of looking at things. It puts the cart before the horse. The solar system is heliocentric. The Sun is at the center of the system and all other bodies in our solar system move around it and not the Earth. The equinoxes and the stars are not simply moving in relation to each other. To maintain as much equates a local and misleading point of view with an overarching one. If Antares were locked up in a glacier and thus, strictly speaking, in motion at a glacial speed, the equinox would streak past it at a speed greater than Mach 3 in comparison. So while it is true that the sidereal zodiac is not absolutely fixed, except to an epoch and a star, it is a fatuous argument to maintain that both sidereal and tropical reckoning are simply in motion because the equinox moves proportionally faster than a bullet against what for all practical purposes is a fixed sky.

How Precession Works

The mechanism of precession cannot be understood from a geocentric point of view. What is actually happening in the Sun-Earth relationship can only be understood when the facts are laid out in the astronomically correct heliocentric system.

Hipparchus is credited with discovering precession of the equinoxes but he couldn't have fully appreciated what he had found for lack of sufficient background information. Precession of the equinoxes is the westward movement of the equinoxes with respect to the stars at the rate of approximately 50.27" per year (in 1975). It is caused by the attraction of the Sun and Moon to the Earth's equatorial bulge. Any non-rigid or semi-rigid rotating body (like the Earth) tends to accumulate material around its equator. Accordingly, the Earth's polar diameter is 27 miles less than its equatorial diameter. The gravitational couples between the Sun and the Earth and the Moon and the Earth are not spread evenly over the planet because of this bulging equator that gets most of the attractive force. The equatorial bulge is especially significant because the Earth's spin axis is not perpendicular to the plane of its orbit, but inclined to it by nearly 23.5° (although that value varies between approximately 22.1° and 24.5° with a period of 41,000 years). The Sun-Moon attraction to the equatorial bulge tends to pull the Earth upright such that its spin axis would be perpendicular to the plane of its orbit if the Earth didn't resist the attractive force through the agency of its rotation. What this resistance feels like can be appreciated by holding a spinning gyroscope in your hand. If you rotate your wrist while holding the spinning gyroscope, you can feel resistance to the change in orientation in space of the gyroscope's spin axis. This is directly analogous to what happens to the Earth.

If a torque (a twisting force) is applied to a rotating body, the body will respond at a right angle to the vector (a line of force) of the applied torque. What that looks like is illustrated by a child's spinning top that wobbles: the instantaneous spin axis of the top will precess. Stated somewhat differently, the effect of gravity on the low point in the spin of a hypothetical top is to pull the low point down to the surface on which the top spins so that the top falls over. The top resists being pulled down to that surface through the agency of its spin but its spin axis moves in a direction that is ninety degrees to the force of the gravitational tug on the low point in its orbit. In the same way on a bigger scale, the primary torques acting on the Earth are the gravitational attractions of the Sun and the Moon. The inertial energy in the Earth's rotation is great enough to resist the gravitational force that would quickly change its orientation in space if it were not spinning. The Earth is affected nonetheless by the gravitational force exerted on its equatorial bulge and responds at a right angle to the applied force, i.e., its spin axis precesses, but very slowly. The image of a child's toy (a wobbling top) has to be slowed down into extreme ultra slow motion. The forces, masses and distances in the three way relationship between the Sun, the Moon and the Earth are so huge that it takes 25,800 years to complete a single wobble cycle. During that time the celestial pole, which is the terrestrial pole extended out into space, will describe a circle with a radius of 23½°. That means that Polaris, currently the pole star, occupies that position only temporarily. Twelve thousand years from now, Vega, the alpha star in the constellation Lyra, will be the pole star. That changes the orientation of the equinox with respect to the ecliptic by thirty degrees every twenty-one and a half centuries which accounts for the astrological ages.

In the total scheme of things all stars that are more than 23½° from the ecliptic poles will successively occupy every second of right ascension, which is a tropical coordinate, in the course of 25,800 years. The declinations of the stars will vary through 47° (2 x 23½) every 12,900 years. That means that the dates and local times when stars rise, culminate and set for most locales on the planet slowly but continuously change over time from the civil dates and local times at which they currently rise, culminate and set. Both the x and the y axes of the equatorial system (the right ascension and declination system) change continuously but only the x axis of the ecliptic system (celestial latitude and celestial longitude) changes because the equinox is in motion along the ecliptic. Only the proper motion of a star in celestial latitude can change that coordinate.

Both features of tropical reckoning that may have seemed secure in Ptolemy's day—a fixed standard of measurement and visual confirmation of the confluence of the Sun, the beginning of Aries and the Northern Hemisphere spring equinox—were quickly demolished. It has taken, however, almost two millennia for that to be understood and then entertained in astrological circles in the

West. The equinox moves fast in relation to the sky and a careful observer would have seen the Sun rising in Pisces at the time of the equinox shortly after the opening of the Piscean Age as the Arabs and the Indians clearly did see it in the latter part of the first millennium AD.

Rising Times

There is a persistent question in the tropical-sidereal debate about the matter of the rising times of the tropical and sidereal signs that has been offered as evidence of the invariability and the possible use of the tropical zodiac by the Babylonians. The rising times of the tropical signs are little changed over several millennia but they do change more substantially over longer periods as the Earth's orbital eccentricity and the obliquity of the ecliptic wax and wane. These change the dates of the solstices, equinoxes, aphelion, perihelion, the lengths of the seasons and the tropical rising times.

The rising times of the sidereal signs change because the rising time of any star that can rise (i.e. that is not circumpolar) is a function of the latitude of the place in question and the declination of the star in question. Since declination is a tropical coordinate and subject to precession, the rising times of stars must change as precession in declination changes. The rising time issue is therefore a circular argument (which is like saying that the rising times change because they change [sic]) except in one special case: at the equinoxes when all bodies rise rightly rather than obliquely and their declinations are not a factor. The rising times of the tropical signs are essentially static (in the short term astronomically speaking) because they have no relation to stars. Therefore, if the sidereal rising times of signs reckoned from the fixed stars change because the orbital characteristics of the Earth make it move in relation to the stars, it is once more merely an appearance that the vernal equinox is fixed. The celestial pole of the Earth precesses. The celestial equator is perpendicular to the pole. They are parts of the same whole (the Earth). When the pole moves, the equator and the equinox move with it. There is no way around that. The argument appears to be valid because the tropical rising times at the equinox change quite slowly, but the sidereal rising times change because the Earth is wobbling on its spin axis and fast in astronomical terms, not because the stars are actually moving above a fixed Earth. The tail does not wag the dog.

The Babylonians were careful to take into account where the beginning of Aries actually was in relation to the equinox. That is abundantly clear from the corrections they applied to the rising times[32] and in particular to the demonstrable fact that the rising times pertain to a sidereal and not a tropical schema.[33] The rising time argument in favor of the constancy of the tropical zodiac cannot trump or somehow obviate that the equinox moves against the field of stars. It is in no way comparable to the overwhelming reality of the total demolition of the geocentric hypothesis by the heliocentric facts. The tropical rising time argument appears to be valid until it is seen as a form of the artistic device known as *trompe l'oeil* (to deceive the eye) in that the equinox appears to be fixed in time but once more, it is an appearance that cannot contravene precession.

Once one grasps what is moving in relation to what is fixed, the slowly changing rising times of the tropical zodiac can easily be seen as a vestige of an antiquated system that is based on the constant effort of astronomers in the ancient world "to save the appearances," i.e., to account for observed phenomena. If a model could do that it was invested with merit whether the model was correct or not. But as every undergraduate knows who has taken his first class in logic, a valid argument is not necessarily true. This is no semantic trick. A valid argument that is not simultaneously true leads to false conclusions. The use of epicycles and deferents employed by Ptolemy was a very impressive achievement for his time because it could describe reality fairly well by the looser standards of the ancient world. Ptolemy's model was flawed, however, and has been totally abandoned because it doesn't describe reality nearly as well as the true facts do. The planets don't move in perfectly circular epicyclic orbits around the Earth. The planets move in elliptical orbits around the Sun. The epicycle/geocentric universe model is valid but it isn't true. The rising time argument also appears to be valid but it isn't true. The rising time issue is due primarily to the obliquity of the ecliptic. Equal arcs of the equator and the ecliptic do not pass through the meridian or the horizon in equal spans of time except at the equinoxes. The attempt is made with the tropical rising time argument to make that exception trump the much bigger issue of precession by ignoring that the equator is connected to the pole.

The Function of the Equinox

The equinox appears throughout Babylonian material but not as a consideration invested with astrological merit (because there are no stars that stay conjoined to the equinox over time), rather as an astronomical one that facilitated the determination of terrestrial latitude (before the latitude/longitude grid came into general use), timekeeping and the intercalation of extra lunar months to keep the calendar synchronized with the solar year. The tropical rising times are merely a device to facilitate some computations. The equinox is a useful point of reference for measuring arc lengths. Yet use of the equinox to note the day when days and nights are of equal duration and as part of the computation to note the ratio between the longest and shortest days has nothing to do with the zodiac.[34] To equate the zodiac with the Northern Hemisphere seasons is to confuse the zodiac with the seasons; they are not the same. The Babylonians never equated the seasons with the zodiac.

The Babylonians generally computed the equinox in astrological work but only approximately. It was rarely observed which was explicitly stated by scribes who recorded astrological material. Most Babylonian horoscopes even show the nearest solstice or equinox but if any astrological influence was attributed to the equinoctial points, it was not recorded[35] thus no argument can be plausibly construed about their use of the equinox beyond what they did say about it. The Babylonians did, however, attribute influence to both the celestial longitude and latitude of bodies, a practice still embraced by Eastern and Western siderealists. The Babylonians took into account the anomaly of the Moon; they determined the length of the sidereal month, they recorded the length of the synodic month correct to the fourth decimal place; they predicted eclipses and heliacal phenomena;

individual stars received special attention; the duration between sunset and moonset, sunrise and moonrise was recorded which helped them construct their cinematic model of the sky. The Babylonians overlooked nothing of importance.

They had nothing to say about the equinox or tropical signs. Yet an argument from silence has been advanced in some circles that attempts to "prove a negative" to impose the tropical zodiac on the Babylonians. That is, the point is sometimes pressed that because the equinox appears frequently in cuneiform records that one cannot dismiss the tropical zodiac as a possibility among the Babylonians. It is always hard to disprove a negative proposition, which can be taken to absurd extremes in order to keep concocted ideas alive. For example, it is impossible to say absolutely, incontrovertibly that the Easter bunny does not exist especially when one sees advertisements and cardboard cut-outs of him every year around the time of the Northern Hemisphere vernal equinox. The Babylonian use of the equinox is just such a cardboard bunny, but there is no evidence that the Babylonians thought the bunny sprang to life, as it were, and was hiding just out of sight. The equinox was a marker that was used to coordinate agricultural activites, geodesy and tell time—as it was for Hesiod[36]—not an astrological idea invested with meaning.

Why the Babylonians Are Celebrated

The Babylonians developed the first mathematical model that could accurately predict future positions of the Sun, Moon and planets,[37] a staggering achievement for the first millennium BC, hailed by historians of science as one of the great technical triumphs of Antiquity. The Greek model was merely explanatory; it was not predictive until Hipparchus in the second century BC adapted Babylonian parameters to the scheme of epicycles and deferents developed by Apollonius of Perga (c. 242 BC-c. 190 BC) that was much used later by Ptolemy. The Greeks benefited enormously from Babylonian knowledge and skill, adopting wholesale Babylonian astronomical and astrological parameters, especially the zodiac, which were the labor of centuries in Mesopotamia, into Greek astronomy and astrology.[38] Hipparchus freely acknowledged his debt to Babylon, according to Ptolemy.

Babylonian priority with respect to the zodiac is their supreme achievement. Ephemerides rank next in importance. All Babylonian astrology, ephemerides, procedure texts and the cinematic model of the sky are in relation to the sidereal zodiac. Babylonian ephemerides are based on many centuries of observations and a brilliant innovation called period relations by modern scholars. Period relations are a combination of sidereal periods and synodic periods. A sidereal period is the time that a planet requires to orbit the Sun as seen from the Earth. A synodic period is the elapsed time between successive conjunctions of a planet with the Sun as seen from the Earth. The sidereal period of Jupiter, for example, is 11.86223 years. The synodic period for Jupiter is 398.88 days. Jupiter's synodic and sidereal periods coincide at intervals of 427 years. That is, 36 revolutions of the planet and 391 synodic periods are both completed in 427 years. That means Jupiter returns to the same positions in the zodiac very closely every 427 years with respect to its synodic phenomena, both in terms of order of appearance and interval in time. A planet's synodic phenomena are its first appearance (visibility), first stationary point, opposition (to the Sun), second stationary point and last appearance (visibility).

Period relations are as effective now as they were three thousand years ago. In 2011 Jupiter turned stationary retrograde on August 30 at 15 Aries 27 and stationary direct on December 25 at 5° 27' Aries. Four hundred twenty-seven years ago in 1584 Jupiter turned stationary retrograde on August 26 at 16° 31' Aries and stationary direct on December 21 at 6 Aries 31. In this particular sequence the difference in positions amounts to four days and 1° 04'. The agreement in some Jupiter period relation sequences differs by a single day and less than a quarter of a degree. There are 155,958 days in 427 years. The agreement between 1584 and 2011 is close enough to allow someone with a record of long-term observations to predict the positions of Jupiter in 2011 by comparing that year to 1584.

Only the Babylonians had the observational data in the ancient world to figure out period relations. Moreover, period relations make no sense in a tropical context unless one uses fractions of the periods in order to make the tropical error due to precession smaller. The problem is most obvious with a large period relation like Jupiter's. In 427 years the difference between tropical and sidereal reckoning is nearly six degrees. That means that tropical reckoning cannot yield accurate long-term positions of bodies, without adopting sidereal parameters, since tropical reckoning gets out of sync with the sky by thirty degrees in twenty-one and a half centuries. The period relations of the other planets with shorter periods display the same type of behavior that is equally close. The epicycle, deferent and equant model used by Ptolemy is far from exact and was found to be wanting in respect of accuracy by the time of Johannes Müller (1436-1476), known to astrologers as Regiomontanus. Furthermore, while the epicycle model can predict retrogradation, it only approximately reflects the movement of the planets because they do not move in epicycles around the Earth. Moreover, their orbits are not circular as Plato insisted that they had to be, rather ellipses. The Babylonians did not impose philosophy on the sky. They did not insist on a geometric model of the sky. But what they had not only worked, it did not compromise astronomical facts. The Babylonians hitched their wagon to a star, so to speak, to something real.

The Evidence for Tropical Reckoning

The most exhaustive compendium of early tropical astrology is the *Catalogus Codicum Astrologorum Graecorum* (Catalog of the Codices of the Greek Astrologers). Known by its acronym, the CCAG is a large work published in twelve volumes between 1898 and 1953. Most of it is written in Greek and Latin. The early history of tropical astrology is unreliable regarding both the quality of the information and their dates which is clearly shown by the scraps, fragments and legends that were gathered together to form the earliest part of tropical astrology. Franz Cumont (1868-1947), the scholar who was the driving force behind the CCAG described the early period as "apocryphal works of a mythical antiquity."[39] He was right to describe it that way because, to date, there is still no evidential support for what is claimed for the early period.

One of the earliest accounts is of a Babylonian priest/astrologer by the name of Berosus who supposedly came to the Greek island of Kos circa 275 BC to dispense astrological wisdom to the Greeks. There is another claim that around the year 150 BC an Egyptian pharaoh, Nechepso (Necho II ?) and his priest/advisor Petosiris, wrote treatises or became known for their astrological acumen but there are no horoscopes or actual works that can be directly attributed to them, if they indeed existed. As with Berosus, there are many references to them but in the absence of hard evidence, one cannot know if their legends are grounded in fact. The legend surrounding Hermes Trismegistus (thrice greatest Hermes—the Egyptian god Thoth [Mercury]) from the same period is enormous. He was another figure who supposedly dispensed wisdom to then contemporaneous Greeks and Egyptians about astrology,[40] but at present it is not known what was dispensed, to whom, when or if any real person or persons is behind the legend of Hermes. Greek astrological works from the first five centuries of the current era are much more complete and sure with respect to date as the CCAG shows. The state of tropical astrology during the Hellenistic Period[41] however, is legendary and unsubstantiated. This condition is underscored by a remarkable fact:

> "It is worth noting that Ptolemy does not cite any planetary observations by Hipparchus, or for that matter, any such observations between the end of the 3rd century and shortly before his own time."[42]

Astrology has always been based on astronomical considerations, even if some of them were not well understood. Unless they were lost, burned or stolen, the dearth of material is amazing. One must wonder, if tropical astrology were well underway during the Hellenistic Period, why there is no record of astronomical work to go with it as there always was among the Babylonians.

In stark contrast to the meager state of tropical astrology during the Hellenistic Period, Babylonian sidereal astrology was at its height during the same period, which is largely unknown in the West. An example of the accuracy of Babylonian positional astronomy during the Hellenistic Period is a table of New Moons that covered the period 104 BC to 101 BC. This table covered the anomalistic month (perigee to perigee) and gave the latitude and longitude of the Moon, the date and time of the first appearance of the crescent Moon and the date and time of the New Moon. For the New Moon of March 23, 104 BC, the text gives 4:11 a.m. LMT in terms of modern reckoning.[43] Modern computation gives 2:46 am LMT. Conjunctions of the Sun and Moon are not visible because the Moon is too close to the Sun to be seen, therefore a Sun-Moon conjunction must of necessity be computed. A time difference of 1 hour and 25 minutes is less than a degree of arc, which is extraordinary accuracy for the era and several orders of magnitude better than any Greek effort extant for the first or second centuries BC. According to Professor emeritus Asger Aaboe of Yale

University who translated it, the text was entirely computed, not observed. Furthermore, there is a large body of hard evidence that sidereal astrology was practiced in Roman controlled Egypt.[44] The Egyptian horoscopes were reckoned from a sidereal ecliptical tradition, whereas earlier Egyptian astrology is mostly reckoned from the equator, not the ecliptic.[45] Horoscopes from the Greek colony, Oxyrhynchus in Egypt, which used mostly Babylonian parameters, are significantly more accurate than then contemporary tropical astrology. The Oxyrhynchus horoscopes are almost uniformly sidereal into the sixth century AD when the record ends. All of these facts strike at the heart of alleged Greek priority in astrology and demonstrate the widespread use of the sidereal zodiac in the ancient world. The astrologers at Oxyrhynchus may also have been the ancestors of the legendary figures from the second and third centuries BC if they existed at all. That is far more likely than that Nechepso, Petosiris and Hermes had any connection with tropical astrology.

Sometimes the claim is made that whereas the Babylonians discovered the zodiac, the Greeks are responsible for modern astrological procedures and rationale as though the Babylonians had been standing still for centuries. Such a sweeping generalization is unwarranted in view of the evidential support from Geminos (Isagoge 2.8-11) in the first century AD, Ptolemy (Tetrabiblos 1.21) in the second century AD and Firmicus Maternus (Mathesis 2.12) in the fourth century AD that the Babylonians are largely responsible for the concept of aspects, the elements and triplicities.[46] These ideas are taken directly, explicitly and in some cases verbatim from cuneiform texts. The concept of the exaltations of the planets is also Babylonian in origin, which is explicitly acknowledged by Julius Firmicus Maternus in his Mathesis[47] (explained more fully in appendix three). Cyril Fagan demonstrated that the specific exaltation degrees cited by Maternus circa AD 334 in a tropical context are the positions of the Sun, Moon and Venus at first Nisan (April 3, 786 BC) and the heliacal phenomena of Mercury, Mars, Jupiter and Saturn during the civil year 786-785 BC in a sidereal context.[48] Fagan considered the exaltation solution his greatest achievement.

Tropical Reckoning Compared to Sidereal

The oldest Greek horoscope from a literary source dates from 72 BC,[49] although its positions correspond very poorly to the date for which it is supposedly computed. In fairness, other early Greek horoscopes from Alexandria, Rome and elsewhere around the Mediterranean, have positions that are only wrong by a few degrees, although they are often wrong by as much as five degrees when degrees are shown. If tropical astrology were well established in the Hellenistic Period, one must wonder why the oldest extant example of a Greek calendrical horoscope is as recent as 62 BC. It is a stone monument, never completed, to a monarch (Antiochus I of Commagene) who ruled a part of what is now Turkey. Otto Neugebauer in 1958 determined the date from the horoscope with some difficulty because the position of one of the planets is incorrect: Jupiter was well into Cancer tropically *and* sidereally, but it was rendered in Leo. In addition, the Sun, Venus and Saturn were omitted.[50] It's hard to know just what Antiochus' Hierothesion actually represents. It is not sidereal and its Jupiter position doesn't make sense if the vernal equinox = 0 Aries standard was in place then.

The earliest known Greek horoscope on papyrus dates from 10 BC.[51] The earliest extant example of sidereal astrology for an individual is precisely *four hundred years* older, i.e., from 410 BC[52] Some have objected that because the 410 BC horoscope doesn't have degrees, only signs, that it could be tropical but the Greeks hadn't adopted degrees from the Babylonians that early. Hipparchus, a second century BC figure, probably converted early Greek units of measure into degrees, according to Goldstein and Bowen,[53] including the work of Timocharis. The authority of Cleostratus who is alleged to have introduced the zodiac into Greece in the sixth century BC has long been discounted for lack of evidence.[54] That the pre-Hellenistic Greeks did use the constellations extensively is not contested; but if there is any credible evidence extant that the 0 Aries = vernal equinox standard was employed in the fifth century BC, there needs to be hard evidential support for it. Certainly the rising time argument cannot be construed as evidence because it requires the inference that the use of an equinox means "tropical" whereas Hesiod and the Babylonian material contravene that assumption; moreover there are no horoscopes or any kind of text advanced to date to support the assertion that tropical zodiac reckoning was in place in the fifth century BC. Thus it is unlikely in the extreme that the 410 BC horoscope could be Greek.

The lives of Hipparchus and Ptolemy were separated by three hundred years. Where then is the tropical astrology from the Hellenistic Period if indeed it had reached a state of development during that period but for which there is almost no evidence? The evidence for tropical astrology does not appear to any significant degree, by any measure, until the Roman Imperial Period, not the Hellenistic period. This is interesting in view of the high state of development of Babylonian planetary and lunar theory, as early as the fifth century BC, their discovery and long-time use of the zodiac, their development and use of accurate ephemerides and hard evidence for the use of astrology many centuries before the Greeks can produce evidence of their use of it.

The Greeks unquestionably came late to astrology, with a massive debt to Babylon, yet the Greeks get most of the credit for modern astrology. Appreciation of the Babylonian place in astrology is only well known among academics, although lack of recognition in the modern astrological community is not the main issue in the tropical-sidereal debate. The most important and fundamental issue to siderealists everywhere is that the Greeks usurped the zodiac from the Babylonians and misapplied it in a tropical context. Whether then contemporary Western astrologers understood the misapplication is not the issue. Few astrologers know this; they assume that Western astrology really begins with the Greeks and that the Northern Hemisphere vernal equinox has always been the standard for reckoning celestial longitude. That is not true. The zodiac was originally reckoned from the stars, not the Northern Hemisphere seasons and for one billion two hundred million Indians, a few thousand Westerners in the United States and Europe presently, and the whole of the ancient world until the Greeks, the stars were the only standard.

In fewer than 400 years, tropical reckoning will be fully 30 degrees removed from the Babylonian marking stars that are the antecedents that define the zodiac still. In 11,000 years the tropical zodiac will be completely upside down with respect to its namesake stars. The difference between tropical and sidereal reckoning is so great even now—almost 25 degrees—that the matter cannot be put off any longer and needs to be re-examined by a new generation.

I wrote down a spirited exchange I had with the renowned twentieth century astrologer Dane Rudhyar in September 1976 at Sunnyvale, California. I asked him why he and Cyril Fagan had not been able to sit down and talk about the tropical-sidereal controversy. His sharp reply surprised me. He said, "What Fagan never understood was that astrology changed as men changed." It was obvious to me at that moment that Rudhyar saw astrology as an anthropomorphic projection and thus subject to revision. The Babylonians, on the other hand, definitely saw astrology as divination by the sky and thus immutable.

It doesn't matter that nobody knows what astrology really is or why it works; but it is evident that one cannot arbitrarily change the most fundamental premise of the art based on an astronomical misconception without consequences. The main consequence is that what the sidereal school has always called Pisces, the tropical school now calls Aries—for the same part of the celestial sphere. The trait characteristics are very different. One cannot reasonably stipulate that two plus two equals four always and in every case, except on alternate Tuesdays (i.e., that they both work), or in like manner, revoke the stars as the standard to make the Northern Hemisphere vernal equinox the new standard because of somebody's decision, mistake or declaration to that effect. Astrology is no more subject to the whim of fashion than the periodic table of elements can be arbitrarily altered. In the same way that the concerted belief, confident assertion and absolute certitude that the world was flat, motionless and the center of the universe could not make it so, no amount of misplaced faith or conviction can supplant the archetypal zodiac reckoned from the sky by a stereotype reckoned from the ground.

Definitions

Equinox: (from Latin means, "equal nights") the days when day and night are equal in length; the day when the Sun reaches the intersection of the celestial equator and the ecliptic, when the Sun's declination is zero. The vernal equinox in the Northern Hemisphere is on or about March 21 when the Sun reaches its ascending node moving from south to north. The autumnal equinox in the Northern Hemisphere is on or about September 23 when the Sun reaches its descending node moving from north to south.

Solstice: (from Latin means, "Sun stands still") the longest and shortest days of the year when the Sun reaches its greatest distance from the equator. The longest day of the year in the Northern Hemisphere, the summer solstice, is on or about June 21 when the Sun reaches its maximum north declination. The shortest day of the year in the Northern Hemisphere is on our about December 22 when the Sun reaches its maximum south declination.

Mesopotamia: (from Greek means "between the rivers") it refers to the Tigris-Euphrates River Valley. The Tigris and Euphrates, the principal rivers in modern Iraq, run approximately parallel for several hundred miles. Their courses approach to within fifty miles in central Iraq before they move apart and come together again in southern Iraq to drain into the Persian Gulf. This central region is called "the waist" by some historians. The area north of the waist was the region called Assyria whose capital was Nineveh. The area south of the waist was called Babylonia after its principal city, Babylon. The two regions often displayed mutual hostility and alternately conquered, controlled and or devastated each other and their neighbors. Astrology was much practiced in both parts of Mesopotamia.

Ecliptic: (from Greek *eclipo*, to leave out, omit, pass by or over) eclipses can only occur when the Moon is on or near the ecliptic; at the time of an eclipse either the Sun or Moon is "left out or omitted." The ecliptic is a plane that passes through the centers of the Sun and the Earth. It represents the Earth's annual path around the Sun, which is the mid-line of the zodiac.

Formal Definition of the Sidereal Zodiac: the zero point of the western sidereal zodiac is the point 45 degrees to the West of Aldebaran (α ♉) for the epoch AD 1950.0 on January 1, 1950.[55] All other zodiacs can be referenced from it and since it is tied to an epoch, this frame of reference is not subject to proper motion. Aldebaran was used by the ancient Babylonians because it is the brightest star closest to the ecliptic and it is directly opposite Antares (α ♏) which divides the sky in half.

Appendix Three

The Origin of the Exaltations

A planet's dignities are the places in the zodiac where the intrinsic nature of the planet manifests in a disitnctly positive manner. As mentioned in chapter one, those places are a planet's natural home which is the source of the concept of rulership. The Sun "rules" or is pre-eminently associated with Leo, the Moon with Cancer, and so on. Muhammad Ali has Mars in its own sign, Aries. He is the greatest prize-fighter of his era. Mohandas Gandhi had the Moon in her own sign, Cancer. He was India's favorite son, gracious, principled, gentle, beloved and an exemplar for his nation and the world.

Better still are the places called "exalted" or the exaltations. The Sun is exalted in Aries where Queen Elizabeth II of England has it; the Moon is exalted in Taurus where President Obama has it. Their stations in life are self-evident.

The places of debility are those positions opposite their dignities, that is, the places opposite their natural homes. Bodies so placed are in their detriment. The Sun is in his detriment in Aquarius; the Moon is in her detriment in Capricorn, for example. The detriments are unfavorable venues where the nature of the body is unlike the nature of the sign of the zodiac.

The places still more difficult are the places opposite their exaltations. Bodies so placed are in their falls. The Sun is in his fall in Libra; the Moon is in her fall in Scorpio, etc. The affect is very real although often downplayed in modern astrology books.

The legitimacy of dignities and debilities, which encompasses the exaltations and falls, has been a source of controversy in Western astrology since the tropical-sidereal debate flared up 60 years ago with the publication of Cyril Fagan's Zodiacs Old and New. The focus of that debate is whether zodiac signs reckoned from the equinoxes and solstices or the stars that constitute the zodiac are the true points of reference of the zodiac. Until 1950 the matter had not been a point at issue in western astrology. The exaltations were discussed by Claudius Ptolemy in the second century AD in his Tetrabiblos, although he did not mention their specific degrees, only the signs. The exaltations were more succinctly laid out in the fourth century AD by Maternus with the specific degrees of the exaltations.

Julius Firmicus Maternus began his Mathesis (from the Greek ìáèçóéò, literally knowledge, in particular mathematics and astrology) in AD 334. He was a Sicilian, a lawyer and a Roman senator. He was considered probably fluent in Greek (as well-educated Romans typically were) by his modern translators. His book, Matheseos Libri VIII (Eight Books of the Mathesis or Theory of Astrology), written in Latin, is the last major work from Late Antiquity on astrology before penalties for practicing astrology were imposed by the Catholic Church with the explicit endorsement of the Roman government. As a result of this prohibition, and later the backwater status of Western Civilization during the Dark Ages, western astrology went into a nearly complete hibernation for the remainder of the millennium. Firmicus's Mathesis reflects the state of western astrological doctrine during the first half of the fourth century of the Christian Era which has remained essentially unmodified to the present day.

Maternus laid out six rules about exaltations and falls of the planets:[56]

> "1. We must know about exaltations and debility—that is, what is meant by the exaltation of each individual planet, in which it is raised up to a maximum of its own natural force and what is its fall, when it suffers loss of that force.
>
> 2. When planets are in their own exaltations we say that they rejoice. Whenever in a chart the majority of the planets is in the exact degree of their exaltation, then they indicate the greatest prosperity. On the other hand, men are overwhelmed by catastrophe whenever the majority of the planets is located in the exact degree of those signs in which they lose their power by debility or fall.
>
> 3. The former are called exaltations, or favorable places in the chart, because they make those who are born with this configuration fortunate and successful. When they are in their debility or fall—that is, in unfavorable places—they make men wretched, poor, of low birth and constantly plagued by bad luck.
>
> 4, The Babylonians called the signs in which the planets are exalted their "houses." But in the doctrine that we use, we maintain that all the planets are more favorable in their exaltations than in their own signs.

5. The Sun is exalted in the nineteenth degree of Aries but is in its fall in the nineteenth degree of Libra. The Moon is exalted in the third degree of Taurus, in its fall in the third degree of Scorpio. Saturn is exalted in the twenty-first degree of Libra, while it is in its fall in the twenty-first degree of Aries. Jupiter is exalted in the fifteenth degree of Cancer, but its fall is the fifteenth degree of Capricorn. Mars is exalted in the twenty-eighth degree of Capricorn, but is in its fall in the twenty-eighth degree of Cancer. Venus is exalted in the twenty- seventh degree of Pisces, in its fall in the twenty-seventh degree of Virgo. Mercury is exalted in the fifteenth degree of Virgo and is in its fall in the fifteenth degree of Pisces.

6. For this reason the Babylonians wished to call those signs in which individual planets are exalted their houses, saying that Libra is the house of Saturn, Cancer of Jupiter, Capricorn of Mars, Aries of the Sun, Taurus of the Moon, Pisces of Venus and Virgo of Mercury."

Maternus did not mention the origin of the specific exaltation degrees, except to note that they came out of a Babylonian tradition. Like Maternus, Ptolemy mentioned the great antiquity of Babylonian astronomical and astrological material. The oldest data available to Ptolemy were eclipse records that date from the reign of the Babylonian king, Nabonassar[57] (begin 747 BC). The origin of the exaltations was almost certainly lost by Ptolemy's day (AD 100-175) or he would very likely have mentioned their provenance.

Cyril Fagan (1896-1970), one of the greatest astrologers of the last century, suspected that the exaltations referred to an actual moment in time during the historical period (begin Aquarius 3000 BC). Since there are no examples of tropical zodiac reckoning extant before the Hellenistic Period (323 BC-31 BC), Fagan was confident that the exaltations refer to sidereal reckoning from a period earlier than the fourth century BC.

An examination of every year during the first three millennia BC that contained both Jupiter in sidereal Cancer and Saturn in sidereal Libra produced one solution. At First Nisan in 786 BC the Moon set in Taurus at Babylon with the Sun in 19 Aries and Venus in 27° Pisces. Nisan was the first Babylonian month of their civil year; the first day of that month was thus New Year's day. It represents the first appearance of the crescent Moon at the New Moon closest to the vernal equinox.

When the Sun's zenith distance was 90 degrees at 6:10:32 p.m. LMT at Babylon on April 3, 786 BC, that is, at the moment of center disk sunset in terms of the rational or computed horizon, the Moon's altitude above the Sun was nearly 11 degrees. That is enough separation for the New Moon to have been seen after sunset according to modern calculation, even when the separation in azimuth[58] between the Sun and the Moon is less than one degree, as it was on April 3, 786 BC. At the moment of center disk sunset the Moon was in 29° 12' Aries in terms of sidereal reckoning. This New Moon was admittedly a young one, only 23.5 hours old, but that is not remarkably young.

New Moons younger than twenty hours old are rare but the record circa 1989 (with the unaided eye) is a New Moon only 14 hours and 51 minutes old.[59] This First Nisan New Moon at Babylon is therefore well within a reasonable range for viewing that does not create a problem regarding its credibility.

The brilliant English scholar and astronomer, J.K. Fotheringham, established a rough rule of thumb based on observations that he made at Athens in 1910 with regard to the appearance of the lunar crescent: he found that if the difference in azimuth between the Sun and Moon at sunset was less than about five degrees that the Moon had to have an altitude of approximately 12 degrees at sunset in order for the Moon to be visible as a thin crescent on that day.[60] This First Nisan New Moon had not quite that much altitude; however, several studies that include thousands of New Moon sightings (by many hundreds of observers) in several countries over the past thirty years have demonstrated that the actual altitude limit for differences in azimuth between the Sun and Moon at sunset as small as this First Nisan New Moon, is 10 degrees,[61] based on factors that Fotheringham did not take into account. Thus this New Moon is within the parameters that allow visibility, and weather permitting, was likely observed.

The end of civil twilight and the beginning of nautical twilight occurs when the Sun is six degrees below the horizon. At this stage of early nightfall, the horizon is still distinct and the new, thin crescent Moon, some planets and bright stars become visible. The Moon at the beginning of nautical twilight on April 3, 786 BC at 6:38:40 p.m. LMT, was at 29° 27' Aries conjoined to Mercury at 29° 22' Aries. The Moon was not on the ecliptic at that moment. She had more than two and a half degrees of north celestial latitude and more than eight and a half degrees of north declination. That means that she would set after her ecliptic degree in the Northern Hemisphere, although only about two minutes later than if she had been on the ecliptic because the ecliptic is nearly perpendicular to the horizon shortly after the equinox.

Center disk moonset was approximately twenty-two and a third minutes later at 7:01 p.m. when the Moon had 29° 38' Aries. That time however relates to the rational horizon, i.e., what an astrologer would compute. What an astrologer would see is a different matter. Horizon phenomena make bodies appear at different times than their calculated positions with respect to the rational horizon—none more so than the Moon. The combined effect of refraction,[62] parallax[63] and the semi-diameter[64] of the Moon would make the Moon's lower limb tangent to the horizon of an observer—i.e., the sensible horizon—when the Moon was fully below the rational horizon by approximately three minutes of time later than when her ecliptic degree set, and possibly later still when air temperature, light scattering, barometric pressure and height of eye of an observer (atop a ziggurat) above the horizon are added to the equation. The hotter the evening the more horizon phenomena are affected. An observer would have seen the Moon still above the horizon at least when 0° Taurus was on the western horizon and she would not have fully set until 1° Taurus was on the western horizon at the latitude of Babylon. Low relative humidity, characteristic of desert and

Sunset (Z. D. = 90 degrees)

Natal Chart
Apr 3 0786 BC, Thu
6:10:32 pm LMT −2:57:40
Babylon, Iraq
32°N33' 044°E25'
Geocentric
Fagan–Allen
Campanus
Mean Node

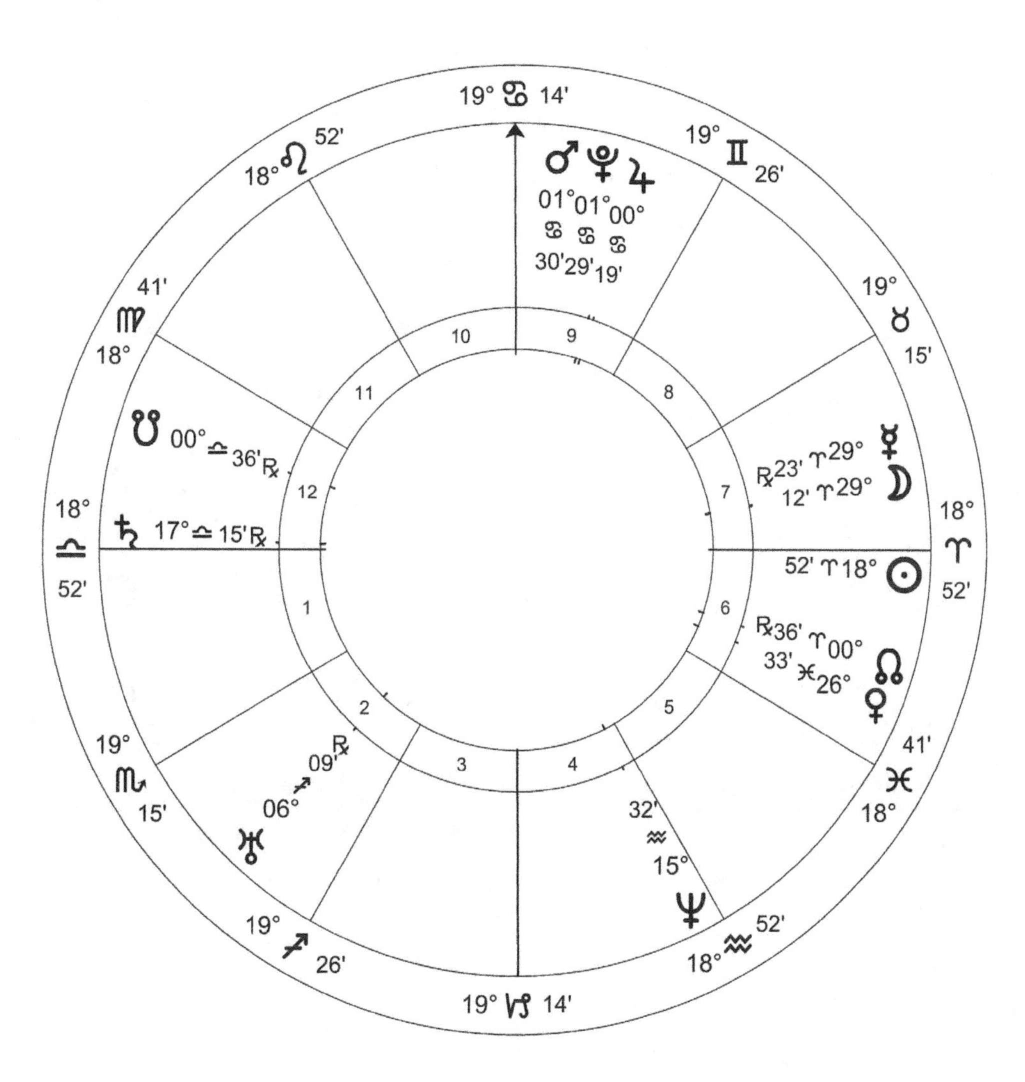

Nautical Twilight
Natal Chart
Apr 3 0786 BC, Thu
6:38:40 pm LMT −2:57:40
Babylon, Iraq
32°N33' 044°E25'
Geocentric
Fagan−Allen
Campanus
Mean Node

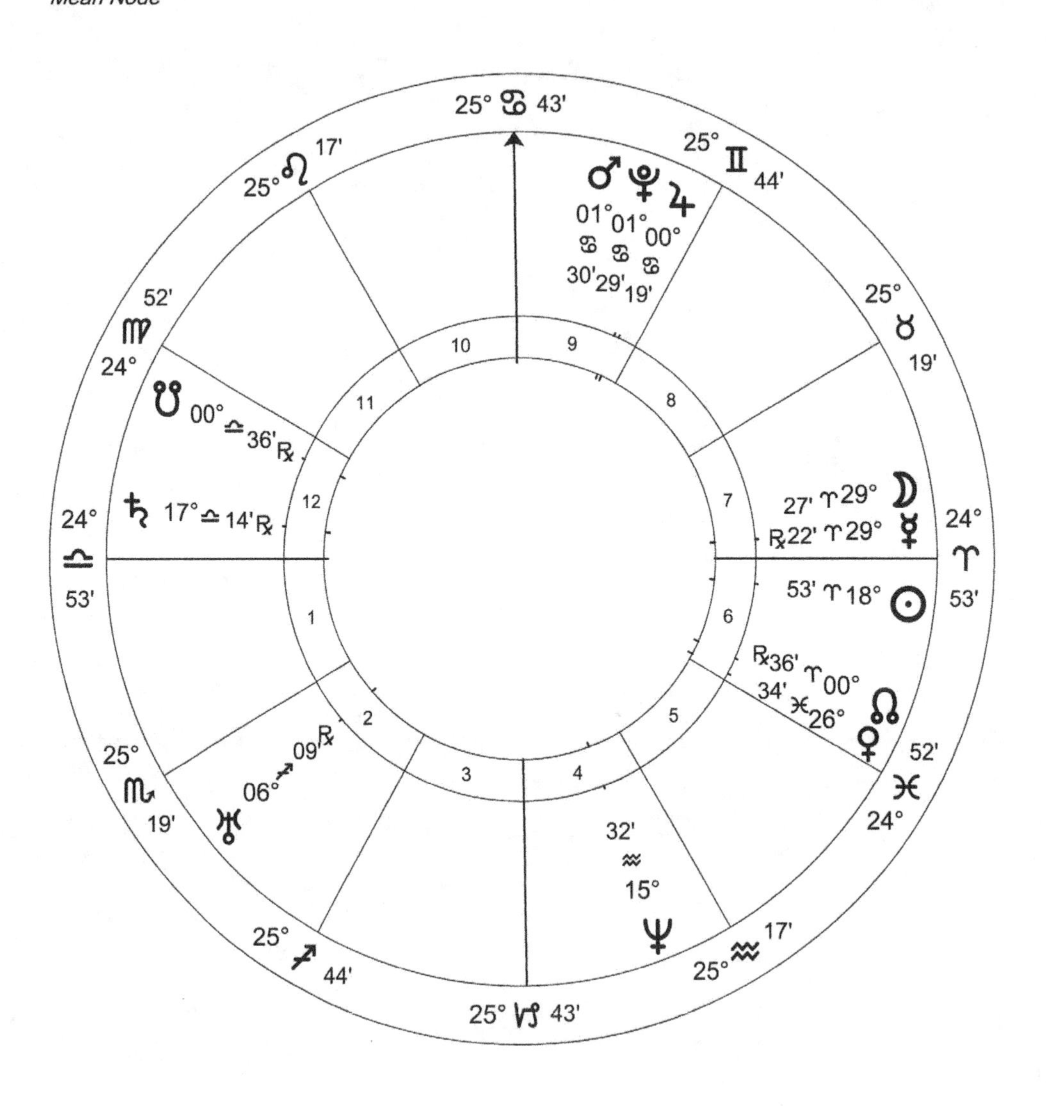

near desert conditions, and the height of eye of an observer above ground level would have heavily influenced a still later moonset.

It is only in the last several centuries that astrologers have all but completely abandoned the sky for tables and lately, computer programs. In the ancient world astrology was very much a visual affair. It didn't matter that the Moon's ecliptic longitude was 29° Aries at First Nisan because she was seen against the backdrop of stars in Taurus due to her celestial latitude and declination, refraction, parallax and semi-diameter. That the Moon set with 0 or 1 degrees or still later in Taurus to the naked eye is close enough to 3° Taurus, except for the most punctilious pedagogue, to constitute an acceptable fit for the exaltation solution considering the great antiquity of the date; i.e. twenty-eight centuries ago. The secular acceleration of the moon[65] is not a factor because the value between April 3, 786 BC and the present day is only a little more than a minute of arc, i.e. celestial longitude.

At the beginning of nautical twilight the Sun's sidereal longitude was 18° 54' Aries and Venus was at 26° 35' Pisces, which both round up to the positions Maternus quoted in his Mathesis. The significance of this particular New Year's day probably relates to the conjunction of the Moon with Mercury. Mercury set less than three minutes before the Moon and almost with the same azimuth as the Moon. They would have appeared together on a sea or desert horizon. Small wonder that this New Year's Day commemorated the installation of a temple to the Babylonian god Nabu (Mercury). But since the exaltation of Mercury is Virgo, other phenomena besides the New Moon that rang in this year must relate to the exaltations of the other planets.

The Babylonians were very concerned with horizon phenomena especially heliacal phenomena. Heliacal phenomena refer to the first appearance of a body after a period of invisibility and its last appearance before a period of invisibility. They only occur at sunrise and sunset, hence the term "heliacal"from the Greek *helios* for the Sun.

Fagan realized that heliacal phenomena were associated with the other exaltations from fragments of Babylonian tables in the British Museum (B.M. 55466, 55486 and 55826)[66] from the second century BC. The relevant passage reads, "The hiding places of the Moon are Sugi (Perseus) and Zappu (the Pleiades)." The Pleiades are in the earliest part of Taurus and most of Perseus is the constellation north of Taurus. Perseus is a paranatellonton[67] of Taurus; i.e, the stars of both constellations rise at the same time with different azimuths. Since the hiding places of all bodies are constantly changing, the text from the British Museum tablets suggested that there was something very special about the exaltation degrees of one particular time because they were repeated as part of doctrine from an earlier period.

Fagan produced stunning fits when he showed that Jupiter set heliacally on June 22, 786 BC in 15° 15' Cancer. In addition, Mercury set heliacally (Mercury sets heliacally in the east and rises in the West before its superior conjunction) in the east on September 14, 786 BC in 16° 21' Virgo; however, because Mercury had north declination, it would have risen when 15° 57' Virgo was on the Ascendant at Babylon and somewhat earlier than that if horizon phenomena were taken into account. In other words, an observer expecting Mercury's heliacal rising would have observed it rise on the sensible horizon with 15 Virgo. Furthermore, Saturn set heliacally on September 23, 786 BC in 21° 10' Libra. Finally, Mars rose heliacally probably on or about January 31, 785 BC in 28° 18' Capricorn. The elongation between the Sun and Mars changes slowly near conjunction. The issue of Mars's brightness and its elongation taken together determine the necessary separation between the two bodies for them to become visible. The dates for these heliacal phenomena have to be considered somewhat approximate because atmospheric conditions may alter the *arcus visionis* (arc of vision), i.e., the elongation from the Sun necessary for a body to become visible. The actual date of the heliacal phenomena may be a day earlier or later for Mercury and a couple days earlier, but not likely later, than the assumed date for Mars. Mars is brighter at dawn than at sunset, thus its arcus visionis is less for its morning appearance. Obviously the heliacal positions for Jupiter and Saturn are not affected significantly if they are wrong by a day or two because their daily motions are not great enough to take them out of their exaltation degrees. They all relate to specific dates, for the latitude of the ruins of Babylon (32N33) in a sidereal format. The difference between tropical and sidereal reckoning for the year 786 BC was 13° 54'; therefore, it is impossible for these degrees to represent a solution in terms of tropical zodiac reckoning.

Fagan's exaltation solution aroused a great deal of commotion in the tropical—sidereal controversy. Some have objected to it but it has never been refuted. The precision of the solution has aroused suspicion in some circles because later Babylonian astrological material often did not use degrees until the fourth century BC, only signs. Some skeptics doubt that the twelve-fold equal division scheme of the zodiac had become finalized in Babylonia and Assyria as early as the eighth century BC. However, Professor Abraham Sachs, a renowned authority in ancient Near Eastern astronomical/astrological material, pointed out that there are Babylonian astronomical ephemerides from the middle of the seventh century and complete eclipse tables from the eighth century.[68] A modern critic asserted that Babylonia may have been too much subject to sandstorms for its horizon phenomena to be considered reliable. Yet authorities with astronomical credentials who have made observations in the area[69] noted that Babylonian skies were "very clear." Very clear skies are associated with low relative humidity. It is the reason that modern observers have noted a big difference between Ptolemy's arcus visionis values at Alexandria, that is situated on the shores of the Mediterranean Sea—and is consistently hazy—and locations with better seeing conditions at similar inland latitudes.

The closeness of the exaltation fits and the astounding, indeed astronomical, odds against a random solution, constitutes a compelling argument not easily dismissed except by the most biased antagonists or those who will not accept that the Sun will rise tomorrow until it does. It definitely silences those who suspect that these positions could have been post-calculated from a much later date. Orbital parameters for the Moon, were not known with sufficient accuracy until late in the nineteenth century that could reproduce these positions. (See, Ernest W. Brown. *An Introductory*

Treatise On The Lunar Theory, Cambridge University Press, 1896; repr., New York: Dover Press, 1960.). The Greeks and the Romans were not sufficiently advanced to accurately undertake such a task, i.e., accurately post-calculating a much earlier date. Only the Indians might have been able to do it during their Golden Age (the Gupta period: A.D. 320 BC to AD 711) yet the errors[70] in the calculation of the Kali Yuga Era (February 18, 3102 BC)—which is all but surely post-calculated—suggest that even they were not up to the task.

Despite objections to the Babylonian exaltation degrees, there are no tropical positions that satisfy the degree requirements for years when Jupiter was in tropical Cancer while Saturn was simultaneously in tropical Libra. Yet there they are: the explicit degrees in Maternus's Mathesis more than eleven centuries after the date that produces the solution but only in terms of the sidereal zodiac. There may be another solution earlier in the Holocene Period (the last 12,000 years), but Fagan's is the only solution in either tropical or sidereal reckoning since Egypt became a federated state early in the third millennium BC that ushered in the historical era. Everything before then—at least at the moment—is archaeology. It is irrelevant that Maternus didn't realize that the exaltation degrees were sidereal in origin, but rather that the tradition survived intact to his day. It is entirely relevant, however, that the exaltations—indeed, all the dignities and debilities—are entirely meaningless today in a tropical context. Maternus would have seen dignities and debilities operate in his own day because tropical and sidereal reckoning were nearly coincident during his lifetime. Now, more than twenty-three degrees of precession have accrued since Maternus' time and nearly 25 degrees since the beginning of the Age of Pisces (A D 221). Tropical positions are that far removed from their original sidereal venues. In other words, 19 degrees of sidereal Aries does not translate into 19 degrees of tropical Aries.

Examples of the power of the exaltation degrees are compelling. Consider that when George Washington was inaugurated president of the United States on April 30, 1789 sometime between 12:45 pm and 1:15 pm local apparent time at Federal Hall in New York, the Sun was at 18 Aries 56 and 18° 57' Aries in terms of sidereal reckoning. The Sun was at 18° 54' Aries at First Nisan. Maternus said that the tradition is that the Sun is exalted at 19° Aries. Even though the United States was a tiny nation of four million in 1789, in no way the equal of the great European powers of the day, implicit in the office of the U.S. presidency is the most powerful executive position on the planet. Washington's first inauguration is really the chart of the presidency itself.

Sometimes just having a number of dignified planets and having a planet in the exaltation degree of another will produce an extraordinary life. Consider that the late and much loved pope John Paul II (1978-2005) had the Moon exalted in 9° Taurus and the Sun in the Moon's exaltation degree, 3° Taurus. The Moon bears directly on the public at large. He was not called "the people's pope" for nothing. Furthermore John Paul's Jupiter was exalted in 17° Cancer near its exaltation degree and his Neptune was in Jupiter's exaltation degree, 15° Cancer. A Jupiter-Neptune conjunction can easily be seen as the right symbolism for someone well-placed in an ecclesiastical hierarchy, but such a conjunction in and near Jupiter's exaltation degree suggests the highest rung of the ladder.

A similar condition obtains with Queen Elizabeth II, the reigning monarch of the United Kingdom. She has the Sun exalted in a royal sign, Aries, the Moon in its own dignity, Cancer, and Jupiter in the exaltation degree of Mars, 28, that is also conjoined to her exalted Mars in 27° Capricorn. Obviously she enjoys an extraordinary station in life. She has the Moon conjoined to Neptune, symbolic of an inherited position, and that her power is symbolic. True power resides in Parliament. Yet there is no other person more celebrated, reverred, loved and respected in the entire country, a nation of more than sixty million people.

The most successful monarchs generally have horoscopes heavy laden with dignities. Vespassian, the Roman general who returned Rome to stability after the excesses of the deranged emperor Nero, had Jupiter exalted in 14° Cancer opposite Mars exalted in 12° Capricorn, both square Saturn exalted in 13° Libra. Vespassian captured the throne after three emperors had been quickly deposed and killed in a single year following the death of Nero. Vespassian ruled for ten years and initiated huge building projects, chief among them, the Colisseum that still stands mostly intact today, more than nineteen centuries after it was raised. Jupiter-Saturn is pre-eminently a constructive and foundation-laying combination. With both Jupiter and Saturn exalted Vespassian was able to bring his ideas into concrete manifestation, which is literally true. The Colisseum is mostly a concrete structure. The symbolism that facilitated the building projects is Jupiter opposite Mars. That combination is good for athletes and soldiers because it makes its natives successful in competition and combat. Usually Jupiter-Mars is also very successful at making money and even better at spending lavishly. Vespassian imposed heavy taxes on the rich. Exalted Jupiter configured with exalted Mars are suggestive of someone who doesn't merely desire to raise money or become successful, but one who has the power to compel others to acquiesce to his demands. Behind that power ultimately was intimidation. Exalted Mars square exalted Saturn suggests someone who can exercise overwhelming power, i.e., someone who will back up his policies by force, and thus is feared because he has done it in the past. Yet a Mars-Saturn combination with both bodies exalted points to the correct use of force directed toward a result hard to achieve but necessary. Vespassian put Rome "back on track," as it were.

Another superb example is "the Sun King" Louis XIV, king of France, so called because he outshone every other monarch in the seventeenth century and became eponymous with an entire period of cultivation and refinement. Louis had Mercury exalted in Virgo, the Sun in its own sign, the royal Leo, the Moon in her own sign, Cancer and Saturn in his own sign, Capricorn. Unless the angles hold the malefics, in particular Neptune, those with this many dignities either rise to high positions in life or are born to them as was Louis.

The opposite conditions obtain when debilitated bodies dominate the horoscope. Grave robber, necrophiliac, murderer and cannibal, Edward Gein illustrates the effect. He had Mars in its fall in

Cancer sextile Venus in her fall in Virgo and as well as trine the Moon in her fall in Scorpio.

A lesser degree of debilitation can produce similar effects if the debilitated bodies configure other malefic bodies. Serial killer Ted Bundy had the Moon in her fall in Scorpio conjoined to Mars in Scorpio. Mars operates well in Scorpio but its proximity to the fallen Moon exacerbated the Moon's debilitation; it made him inclined to nurse early life wounds and grievances and finally to take them to extremes. Furthermore, Mars was trine Pluto almost exact to the minute and therefore also trine the fallen Moon which made him still more strongly inclined toward violence. Saturn in its detriment in Cancer loosely conjoined to Pluto and trine Mars further aggravated the situation and was also symbolic of the orientation of his madness: it was directed against women.

Often when planets are simply in exaltation degrees, regardless of any horoscope they are part of, extraordinary conditions obtain that may be long remembered. When the Roman emperor, Marcus Aurelius died on March 17, AD 180, Mars and Saturn were conjoined in the exaltation degree of Jupiter: 15° Cancer. Marcus Aurelius, known as the "philosopher emperor" and for his charity and leniency, was the last of the so-called "good" emperors. His demise instantly began Rome's long descent into decline. The conjunction of the two classical malefics, Mars and Saturn, both debilitated (Mars in his fall and Saturn in his detriment) in the exaltation degree of the most fortunate planet, Jupiter, was symbolic of deep lamentation at the loss of a great man in a position of power and a turning point for the worse in the fortunes of the Roman Empire. Of course there were other effects but every planet combination has implications in the general and the particular. Some of the particulars are more noteworthy than others, as in this instance.

Debilitated planets that configure each other are especially bad although the nearby presence of Venus or Jupiter can do a lot to facilitate repair. When that help is not there, serious problems may result. Lee Harvey Oswald had Saturn in his fall in Aries opposite the Sun in his fall in Libra. Oswald assassinated President John Kennedy in 1963. Oswald's Pluto was square the Sun-Saturn opposition which made him an outcast, a loner, a misfit and unable to deal with his problems. Mercury closely square Mars produced a level of mental instability sufficient to act out his unhappiness and difficulty in life. Arguably that would not have happened if he had had the Sun exalted in Aries opposite Saturn exalted in Libra. Saturn relates to self-control, judgment and one's sense of purpose in life. When the native shows lack of same he betrays a debilitated Saturn. If Saturn is elevated over the Sun as in Oswald's case the problems around limits and restraint are compounded.

A debilitated body configured with a helpful planet can work out well however if the rest of the horoscope is a good one. Bill Gates, who founded Microsoft, has the Sun in his fall in Libra but the Sun is square Uranus which is a very lucky, innovative and independent planet. It made him able to recognize early the possibilities inherent in the business he founded and an immensely wealthy man as a result (with Jupiter conjoined to Pluto in the second house). Gates has three dignities: Mercury exalted in Virgo, Saturn exalted in Libra and Venus in her own sign, Libra. Since he has sidereal Gemini rising, it is an enormous benefit to have the Ascendant ruler exalted and in an angular house (the fourth). With exalted Mercury conjoined to Mars (which acts much better than the square) he is brilliant. The Sun conjoined to Neptune and both square Uranus, is nothing less than visionary and philanthropic considering the extremely positive tone of the horoscope in general. Saturn and Venus both dignified in Libra are trine the Midheaven which might have limited his success were Saturn not exalted. Gates also has three children. Saturn-Venus combinations are notorious for damaging one's hopes with regard to love and children but Gates has both a stable marriage and healthy children, because both Saturn and Venus are dignified. Martin Luther, who also had the Saturn-Venus conjunction in Libra, eventually married and fathered five children. These facts are consistent with what Maternus wrote to expect from dignified bodies.

Endnotes

[1]G. J. Toomer, *Dictionary of Scientific Biography*, s.v. "Hipparchus" (New York: Charles Scribner's Sons, 1978): 15, supplement 1, p. 218.

[2]W. M. Smart, *Textbook on Spherical Astronomy*, fourth edition (Cambridge: Cambridge University Press, 1960), 226. Smart wrote on page 226 about the annual increase in the longitudes of the stars observed by Hipparchus which were the same for every star: "There are two possible explanations: either all the stars examined had real and identical motions in longitude—an improbable hypothesis—or the fundamental reference point, the vernal equinox Aries from which longitudes are measured along the ecliptic, could no longer be regarded as a fixed point on the ecliptic. Now Aries is defined to be one of the two points of intersection of the ecliptic and the equator on the celestial sphere; the observations showed no changes in the latitudes of the stars and therefore it was legitimate to conclude that the ecliptic was a fixed plane. According to the second hypothesis (which was adopted by Hipparchus [parentheses are Smart's]), it was necessary to assume that the equator had moved and, in consequence, the vernal equinox moved in such a way that the longitudes of the stars increased uniformly by an amount in accordance with the observations."

[3]A. E. Roy, "The Origin of the Constellations," *Vistas In Astronomy* 27, (1984): 183.

[4]A geocentric world view assumes that an immobile Earth is at the center of the universe and that the Sun, Moon and planets revolve around the Earth. This is the view of Claudius Ptolemy, whose name is most closely associated with the tropical zodiac. A heliocentric world view assumes that the Sun is at the center of the universe and that the Earth and all other bodies orbit the Sun. There was tremendous opposition to the Copernican model, which is heliocentric, because it dispensed with some of the mainstays of the Ptolemaic system (Sun versus Earth at the center of things and epicycles) but more to the point, it contravened Holy Writ (Joshua 10:12-14) which aroused the attention of the Inquisition (Inquisito Haereticae Pravitatis Sanctum Officium). The Inquisition was a very old instrument of the Catholic Church designed to detect and punish heresy and enforce Catholic orthodoxy. It gained much strength in the thirteenth century and was turned loose during the Counter Reformation on scholars and intellectuals whose views did not conform to Catholic dogma. Giordano Bruno 1548-1600) and Lucillo Vanini (1585-1619), two of the better known victims, were burned at the stake for what were in effect "thought crimes." Galileo only escaped by recanting the heliocentric position he had held for decades.

[5]Michael Elliot, *Time*, "Eighty Days that Changed the World," 2003, 36.

[6]C. J. Cohen, E. C. Hubbard and Claus Oesterwinter, "Elements Of The Outer Planets For One Million Years," Astronomical Papers Prepared for The Use of The American Ephemeris And Nautical Almanac, vol. XXII, part 1 (Washington: United States Government Printing Office, 1973), 31-33.

[7]Guido Bonatti, "The One Hundred Forty-Six Considerations of the Famous Astrologer Guido Bonatus," trans. Henry Coley, ed. *William Lilly in Anima Astrologiae* (London: William Lilly, 1676); quoted in *The Astrologer's Guide* (London: George Redway, 1886; reprint, Washington D.C.: American Federation of Astrologers, 1970) 55-56.

[8]Vivian E. Robson, *The Fixed Stars and Constellations in Astrology*, second edition (New York: Samuel Weiser, 1972), 124.

[9]Asko Parpola, *Deciphering the Indus Script* (Cambridge: Cambridge University Press, 1994), 201.

[10]The Puranas are mostly first millennium B.C. religious works and a primary source of Hindu mythology.

[11]Hermann Hunger and David Pingree, "Mul.Apin, An Astronomical Compendium in Cuneiform," *Archiv für Orientforschung*, beiheft 24, 1989, 12.

[12]Abraham Sachs, "Naissance De L'Astrologie Horoscopique En Babylonie," *Archaeologia* 15, March-April 1967, 13-17.

[13]Abraham Sachs, "Babylonian Horoscopes," *Journal of Cuneiform Studies* 6, 1952, 52.

[14]B. L. van der Waerden, "The Date of Invention of Babylonian Planetary Theory," Archive for History of Exact Sciences 5, 1968, 72-77.

[15]Otto Neugebauer and H. B. van Hoesen, *Greek Horoscopes* (Philadelphia: American Philosophical Society, 1959), 179-180.

[16]William Harris Stahl, Richard Johnson and E. L. Burge, *Martianus Capella and the Seven Liberal Arts* (New York: Columbia University Press, 1971), 3.

[17]Marshall Clagett, "The Medieval Latin Translations from the Arabic of the Elements of Euclid, with Special Emphasis on the Versions of Adelard of Bath," *Isis*, 44, 1953, 18.

[18]Proclus (410-485 A.D.) was born in Byzantium and taught at Athens. He was the greatest of the later Neoplatonists and wrote a commentary on the first book of Euclid's Elements.

[19]Boethius (480-524 A.D.) was a Roman scholar, theologian and statesman who either translated or elaborated upon at least some of Euclid's Elements, but Boethius's work (Geometria) is almost completely lost.

[20]William V. Harris, *Ancient Literacy* (Cambridge: Harvard University Press, 1989), 329.

[21]Michele Renee Salzman, *On Roman Time* (Berkeley: University of California Press, 1990), 183. Compare Roman calendar codex of 354 A.D. with the true summer solstice.

[22]Paul L. Butzer, *Science in Western and Eastern Civilization in Carolingian Times* (Basel: Birkhäuser Verlag, 1993), 445.

[23]S.J. for Society of Jesus is the Jesuit order founded in 1540 by Ignatius of Loyola.

[24]Seleucus was one of the generals of Alexander the Great who divided Alexander's empire after his death in 323 B.C. at Babylon.

[25]A period relation is that relationship whereby a regular and fixed number of synodic periods of a planet corresponds to a regular and fixed number of revolutions of the planet. A synodic period is the time elapsed between successive conjunctions of a planet with the Sun as seen from the Earth. Only sidereal reckoning

yields the correct value of period relations. The period relations model initially requires very old observations, which is attested only at Babylon.

[26]The first regnal year of Nabonassar, king of Babylonia, 747-734 B.C.

[27]The average length of time from New Moon to the next New Moon: 29.53059 days. The Babylonians had it right to the fourth decimal place.

[28]Heliacal phenomena are the dates when planets or stars disappear or reappear before or after a period of invisibility that may last weeks or months. Stations are those places where a planet appears to be stopped in the sky just before it is about to turn retrograde or direct. Oppositions are alignments when planets are closest to the Earth with the Earth interposed between the Sun and the planet all in a straight line through their centers.

[29]J. Norman Lockyer, *The Dawn of Astronomy* (London: Cassell & Co., 1894), 85.

[30]J. N. Postgate, *Early Mesopotamia* (London: Routledge, 1994), 13.

[31]Bernard R. Goldstein and Alan C. Bowen, "The Introduction of Dated Observations and Precise Measurement in Greek Astronomy," *Archive for History Of Exact Sciences* 43 (October 1991), 103.

[32]Otto Neugebauer, "The Rising Times In Babylonian Astronomy," *Journal of Cuneiform Studies*, vol.7, no. 3 (1953), pp. 100-103.

[33]Francesca Rochberg, "A Babylonian Rising-Times Scheme in Non-Tabular Astronomical Texts," *Studies in the History of the Exact Sciences in Honour of David Pingree* (Leiden: Brill, 2004), 56-94. System A (vernal equinox = 10 Aries) and System B (vernal equinox = 8 Aries) are the only references attested.

[34]Otto Neugebauer, *The History of Ancient Mathematical Astronomy*, vol. 1 (Berlin: Springer-Verlag, 1975), 369.

[35]Francesca Rochberg, *Babylonian Horoscopes* (Philadelphia: American Philosophical Society, 1998), 43.

[36]Hesiod, Theogony, *Works and Days*, trans. M. L. West (Oxford: Oxford University Press, 1988), 48. See his statement, "When the Pleiades, born of Atlas rise before the sun, begin the reaping; the plowing when they set." Hesiod spoke often of the dog star (Sirius), Arcturus, Orion, the Hyades and other stars. Neither astrological signs nor the zodiac are mentioned in his Works and Days. Hesiod used the equinoxes and the solstices like the Babylonians did, as a marker but not as a point of reference invested with astrological merit. This matter is fundamental and not a point of pedantry because the mention of the equinox has often been taken uncritically as a sure sign of a tropical zodiac corollary in ancient works, but there is no evidence for such an assumption. There is a wide gulf between the mere mention of the words, "solstice" and "equinox" and their astrological application as tropical zodiac parameters. The tropical zodiac is relatively new and does not appear in Greek works until very late in the Hellenistic Period.

[37]Asger Aaboe, "Babylonian Mathematics, Astrology and Astronomy," *The Cambridge Ancient History*, vol. III, part 2, second edition (Cambridge: Cambridge University Press, 1991), 290.

[38]See, John K. Fotheringham, "The Indebtedness of Greek to Chaldaean Astronomy," *The Observatory*, vol. li, no. 653, 1928, 301-315. In particular, on page 302 Fotheringham writes: "So far as I can see the Greeks took and used Chaldaean science but gave nothing to the Chaldaeans whose lunar theory was complete before Greeks brought their mathematical skill to bear upon it."

[39]Franz Cumont, *Astrology And Religion Among The Greeks And Romans* (New York: G. P. Putnam's Sons, 1912), 76.

[40]G. R. S. Mead, *Thrice-Greatest Hermes* (London: Theosophical Publishing Society, 1906; repr., Detroit: Hermes Press, 1978), 1:101.

[41]The Hellenistic Period is the period of greatest expansion of Greek culture from the ascension of Alexander the Great to the throne of Macedon in 336 BC. to the beginning of the Roman Imperial Period in 31 BC.

[42]Goldstein and Bowen, *Dated Observations*, 99.

[43]Asger Aaboe, "Scientific Astronomy in Antiquity," *The Place of Astronomy in the Ancient World*, F. R. Hodson ed. (London: Oxford University Press, 1974), 30.

[44]Alexander Jones, *Astronomical Papyri From Oxyrhychus* (Philadelphia: American Philosophical Society, 1999), 49.

[45]Otto Neugebauer and Richard Parker, *Egyptian Astronomical Texts* (London: Lund Humphries, 1969), vol. III, Decans, Planets, Constellations and Zodiacs, 203. Note also their statement, "All our source material confirms the conclusion that the Egyptian zodiacs belong to the Hellenistic-Roman period and that the corresponding astrological concepts are of Hellenistic, hence, in part, ultimately Babylonian origin." Ibid.

[46]Francesca Rochberg-Halton, "New Evidence for the History of Astrology," *Journal of Near Eastern Studies* 43 (1984): 123-127.

[47]Julius Firmicus Maternus, Ancient Astrology Theory and Practice, *The Mathesis of Firmicus Maternus*, Jean Rhys Bram, trans. (Park Ridge, New Jersey: Noyes Press, 1975), 34.

[48]Cyril Fagan, *Zodiacs Old and New* (Los Angeles: Llewellyn, 1950), 19.

[49]Neugebauer and van Hoesen, *Greek Horoscopes*, 76.

[50]Theresa Goell, Nemrud Dagi, *The Hierothesion of Antiochus of Commagene*, Donald Sanders, ed. (Winona Lake, Indiana: Eisenbrauns, 1996), 89.

[51]Alexander Jones, "The Place of Astronomy in Roman Egypt," Apeiron, *The Sciences in Greco-Roman Society*, vol. 27, no. 4 (1994): 31.

[52]Sachs, "Babylonian Horoscopes," 52.

[53]Goldstein and Bowen, Dated Observations, 104-105.

[54]D. R. Dicks, "Solstices, Equinoxes & the Presocratics," *The Journal of Hellenic Studies* 86 (1966): 26-27.

[55]Robert Powell and Peter Treadgold, *The Sidereal Zodiac* (Tempe, Arizona: American Federation of Astrologers, 1979), 31.

[56]Julius Firmicus Maternus, Ancient Astrology Theory And Practice, 34.

[57]G. J. Toomer, trans. and annot., *Ptolemy's Almagest*, (New York: Springer-Verlag, 1984), 9.

[58]Azimuth: the horizontal direction of a point on the horizon or the celestial sphere measured from the north point on the horizon east or west through 180 degrees.

[59]Dennis di Cicco, "Breaking the New Moon Record," *Sky and Telescope*, September 1989, 323.

[60]J. K. Fotheringham, "On the Smallest Visible Phase of the Moon," *Monthly Notices of the Royal Astronomical Society*, vol. LXX, (1910): 531.

[61]Bradley E. Schaefer, "Lunar Crescent Visibility," *Quarterly Journal of the Royal Astronomical Society* 37, No. 4 (1996): 765.

[62]Refraction: the bending of light as it passes from one medium to another (from air to water, for example)

at some angle other than a right angle. The effect of astronomical refraction is to make a body appear higher in the sky than its true position. The effect is greatest for bodies on the horizon.

[63]Parallax: the difference between the apparent position of a body as seen from a point of reference on the surface of the earth compared to a position computed with respect to the center of the earth as the point of reference. The effect of parallax is to make bodies appear lower in the sky than their tabular position in an ephemeris. The effect is greatest for bodies on the horizon. In this case (First Nisan 786 BC) because the Moon was near apogee, its parallax value is almost the opposite of its refraction value: that is, they differ by two minutes of arc, and thus as a practical matter, cancel each other.

[64]Semi-diameter: the apparent diameters of the Sun and the Moon on the horizon are so large that their angular distance has to be taken into account when measuring their upper and lower limb positions. The position of the Moon is given for its center. Half its semi-diameter (the radius of the body) is added to the lower limb value to give its true position.

[65]The secular acceleration of the Moon is an acceleration of the Moon's motion in its orbit measured in mean solar time which makes that motion independent of the rotation of the Earth. It is measured in seconds per century.

[66]Cyril Fagan, *Zodiacs Old And New*, 19.

[67]Paranatellonton: from the Greek, to rise or appear beside or near. Often abbreviated to "paran," in astrology, it refers to planets or stars that appear on the horizon at or near the same time, as well as to planets that rise and culminate or culminate and set at or near the same time.

[68]Abraham Sachs, "Naissance De L'Astrologie Horoscopique En Babylonie," 16.

[69]Carl Schoch, "The Arcus Visionus of the Planets in the Babylonian Observations," *Monthly Notices of the Royal Astronomical Society*, vol LXXXIV, (1924): 734.

[70]B. L. van der Waerden, "The Conjunction of 3102 B.C.," *Centaurus* 24 (1980): 117-131. Note that in the most recent of the great cycles which are one of the hallmarks of ancient Indian reckoning, the so-called super conjunction that invoked the Kali Yuga Era (midnight February 17-18, 3102 BC at Varanasi), all the planets were supposedly in sidereal Aries. This date however, places Saturn in Aquarius forty-one degrees to the west of Jupiter in Aries. It is therefore all but totally sure that the Kali Yuga Era was post-calculated in error using inaccurate parameters for Saturn because nobody who took note of the planets in the ancient world would have missed the Jupiter-Saturn conjunction in December 3105 BC. Configurations between Jupiter and Saturn were the most important combinations in the ancient world after those that involve the Sun and the Moon.

Note on LAT

Regarding the notation "LAT" (Local Apparent Time) for the birth times in the horoscopes of Luther and Newton, LAT was the standard throughout the world until the first appearance of LMT (Local Mean Time) as a civil standard in 1780 at Geneva, Switzerland. LMT was not adopted anywhere else until London, England in 1792. LMT subsequently but slowly replaced LAT throughout the world such that when the standard time zone system was adopted in 1884, most of the world was on LMT by then.

It is important to observe LAT, which is the same as sundial time, in the construction of horoscopes during the era when it was in use. If the equation of time is large, disregarding LAT and misapplying LMT to a horoscope for an era before LMT came into use, can make a big difference in the angles of the horoscope.

Sundial time was a more accurate standard than a mechanical clock standard until, at the very earliest, the late sixteenth century because of the error in a mechanical movement before gear cutting machinery became available, and in particular due to the absence of minute hands on early clocks. Minute hands did not become a commonplace feature of mechanical clocks until the seventeenth century.

The equation of time (E of T) is the difference between the Right Ascension of the Apparent Sun (commonly noted by its acronym, RAAS or RAA!) and the Right Ascension of the Mean Sun (commonly noted by its acronym, RAMS).

The rules for converting from apparent to mean time that I placed in the center of those two horoscopes are necessary for someone to know how to arrive at a mean time equivalent of a time rendered in terms of apparent time. If they are eliminated the horoscope will be wrong for someone who assumes no difference between LMT and LAT or simply puzzling to someone who would otherwise not know how the angles were determined. Anyone interested in the matter can refer to my article, "Local Apparent Time" that appeared in the June/July 2000 issue of *The Mountain Astrologer*.

Here are the complete rules:

If the RAMS is greater than the RAAS, the E of T is +.

If the RAAS is greater than the RAMS, the E of T is –.

If the birth time was reckoned in apparent time and the E of T is +, subtract the E of T from the apparent time to get the mean time equivalent.

If the birth time was reckoned in apparent time and the E of T is –, add the E of T to get the mean time equivalent.

If the birth time was reckoned in mean time and the E of T is +, add the E of T to get the apparent time equivalent.

If the birth time was reckoned in mean time and the E of T is –, subtract the E of T to get the apparent time equivalent.

Printed in the USA
CPSIA information can be obtained
at www.ICGtesting.com
CBHW082321280724
12325CB00014B/544